Modern Shakespeare Offshoots

Modern Shakespeare Offshoots

by Ruby Cohn

Princeton University Press, Princeton, New Jersey

Published by Princeton University Press, Princeton, New Jersey
In the United Kingdom: Princeton University Press,
Guildford, Surrey

Library of Congress Cataloging in Publication Data will be found on the last printed page of this book
This book has been composed in Linotype Baskerville
Printed in the United States of America
by Princeton University Press, Princeton, New Jersey

To Don Doub for the beginning
and Jerry Sherwood for the completion

Foreword

It is easy to predict a conclusion to this book: Shakespeare offshoots are not Shakespeare. Or, a little less tersely, no modern Shakespeare offshoot has improved upon the original. Maybe so, but more interesting—and even enthralling—to me has been the investigation of which moderns rewrote Shakespeare. Why and how?

After five years of research, I have still not answered the first question with any claim to completeness. Starting with the modern offshoots I knew, I reached out in hit-or-miss ways. I combed the "Shakespeare" entries of bibliographies and library catalogues, even traveling to the Birmingham Shakespeare Library when I was (mistakenly) informed that that fine collection had a winnowed list of "Shakespeare alterations." More helpful than catalogues was the encyclopedic drama knowledge of Martin Esslin, the first person I thank for invaluable guidance. Since my expertise in the arts is limited, I confined my research to *dramatic* offshoots; not operas, musicals, movies, or burlesques; still less, plays about Shakespeare's life or actors in Shakespeare's plays. And dramatic offshoots have remained the groundwork of my exploration, though I have foraged in other genres.

Before beginning to write, I decided to limit this book to those plays I could read or hear in the original languages, since linguistic intimacy is for me a necessity; I examined plays written in English, French, German. Early in my investigation I decided to compare the offshoots with their Shakespearean sources. Then I became interested in tracing the effect of Shakespeare on certain modern playwrights—Shaw, Brecht, Beckett. Later, I learned of the Triple Action Theatre, an English fringe group whose repertory was built around Shakespeare offshoots. Thus evolved the patterns for my separate chapters: offshoots of three Shakespeare tragedies and a comedy, productions of a theater company committed to Shakespeare offshoots, and three major playwrights whose creations show the impact of Shakespeare. But my discussions are not so neat as this summary, for modern Shakespeare offshoots are as various—even chaotic—as the modern theater that harbors them.

My outline was set and my offshoots well garnered when I met Dolores Gros Louis, who had written her doctoral dissertation on "my" subject. She generously gave me her bibliography, and I am grateful for it, as for her advice to ignore it, continuing my less complete and narrower way. My study focuses on Shakespeare offshoots intended for—and usually performed in—a serious theater. Not only Broadway, the West End, the Boulevards, subsidized theaters, but theaters that are staffed by trained and/or committed workers. Through the knowledgeable enthusiasm of Ted Shank I have learned of Shakespeare offshoots in the New or Alternative Theater.

In reading, writing, and theater-going with my attention fixed on Shakespeare offshoots, I have been helped by many people. My fumbled footnotes were retrieved by Ree Adams, Roger Bensky, Eric Bentley, Nello Carlini, Dorrit Cohn, Dolora Cunningham, Bernard Dukore, Jim Eigo, Gil Elvgren, Fred Gardner, Anthony Graham-White, Margery Grene, John Hayden, Denise Helmer, Gilbert Helmer, Bob Hopkins, Russell King, Manfred Kusch, Maurice Lebel, Nora McGuinness, Carl Menges, Walter Meserve, Len Pronko, Brian Richards, Eve Richards, Al Rossi, Robi Sarlos, Charles Shattuck, Alan Stambusky, Valerie Tumins, Leo Weinstein, Ulrich Weisstein, Jack Zipes, whom I thank more warmly than can be indicated in this alphabetical listing. For translations from the French, I most particularly thank Jan Hokenson, and for helping me with translations from the German, Everard D'Harnancourt. I am grateful to the editors of *Modern Drama* and *The Educational Théatre*

Journal, who allowed me to revise and reprint the sections on "Beckett and Shakespeare" and "The Triple Action Theatre," respectively. Above all I thank Bill Coco, Dan Gerould, Robert Kellogg, and Walter Sokel for reading (and improving) parts of the manuscript, but for the whole I alone am perhaps too obstreperously responsible.

Shakespeare has never had a wider audience than now. His plays are performed on amateur and professional stages throughout the world; films, tapes, and records have clipped his works to their dimensions, and a single television broadcast gives him a larger audience than any of his plays acquired during his lifetime. This wide viewing is complemented by in-depth reading of specialists; Shakespeare scholars have verified the texts of his plays; they have enlightened us about contemporary language, references, and theater practice. Shakespeare commentators—amateur and professional—have interpreted the plays for us. Paradoxically, some of our contemporaries cherish Shakespeare for his relevance to us, whereas other contemporaries remold him into relevance for us.

Though Shakespeare's plays have been a quarry for three centuries of exploiters, our time has seen a marked increase in Shakespeare offshoots. Some writers have updated his stories, others his themes, still others his language. His dramas have been literal points of departure, and I propose to examine such departures. Because I am interested in a gamut of alterations, I deliberately chose the inclusive word "offshoots." My main concern, however, is *theater* offshoots. Not merely modern production ideas—*Hamlet* in modern dress, an all-male *As You Like It,* a Napoleonic *Coriolanus,* an Edwardian *Merchant*—but verbal departures from Shakespeare's texts, intended for performance in the theater. For purposes of comparison, I also consider fictional offshoots of *Hamlet* and essays sparked by *King Lear.*

Ignoring the many Shakespeare analogues, I examine works in which his characters play other roles. Though dramatic texts are the substance of my text, I do not hesitate to summarize production details. My analysis focuses on drama, but I stray into fiction, essay, and theater. In these several genres, dependence on Shakespeare implies a particularly modern awareness of art and artifice. Almost all art builds on previous art, but much modern art builds *with* previous art.

And an addendum on the mechanics of reading: 1) Page numbers of quotations from offshoots are enclosed in parentheses in the text. 2) Quotations from non-English offshoots are asterisked and translated below the pages on which they appear.

Contents

Modern Shakespeare Offshoots

Chapter 1

A Mishmash of Adaptations and Transformations

Rewriting of Shakespeare is known by an array of names—abridgments, adaptations, additions, alterations, ameliorations, amplifications, augmentations, conversions, distortions, emendations, interpolations, metamorphoses, modifications, mutilations, revisions, transformations, versions. In contrast, I use a looser and more neutral word, "offshoot," but I should like to indicate how far the shoots grow from the Shakespearean stem. (And that stem itself is problematical, since eighteen Shakespeare plays exist in Quarto versions of varying quality, as well as in the more carefully edited First Folio of 1623.)

Almost every professional production modifies a Shakespeare text, usually by cutting lines and/or emending words. So widespread is this practice that William Bridges-Adams, who produced many *un*cut Shakespeare plays at Stratford, was nicknamed Unabridges-Adams. I classify offshoots that are close to a Shakespearean text by the process that molds them: *reduction/emendation.* No examples are cited because reduction/emendations are properly considered as theater history rather than literary alteration.[1]

Adaptation, probably the most overused term for a Shakespeare offshoot, will constitute the second group. Christopher Spencer supplies a definition: "The typical adaptation includes substantial cuts of scenes, speeches, and speech assignments; much alteration of language; and at least one and usually several important (or scene-length) additions."[2] *Additions* are crucial in distinguishing reduction/emendation from adaptation, but my definition is wider than Spencer's, including plays that are relatively faithful to Shakespeare's story, however far they depart from his text. Spencer drew a line between Colley Cibber's *Richard III,* which is based on Shakespeare's text, and John Dryden's *All for Love,* which provides a new text for the old story of Antony and Cleopatra. I would classify both as adaptations.

Invention will be the basis for the third grouping, *transformation.* This "brightest heaven of invention" is studded with stars of varying brilliance. Shakespearean characters are often simplified or trundled through new events, with the Shakespearean ending scrapped. In transformations Shakespearean characters move through a partly or wholly non-Shakespearean plot, sometimes with introduction of non-Shakespearean characters.

This first chapter examines a mishmash of adaptations and transformations, including significant (and some insignificant) offshoots that do not fall into another rubric. History and Roman plays preponderate, probably because they are most easily convertible into contemporary commentaries. The plays are treated in an order of increasing distance from the Shakespearean source, but different offshoots of the same Shakespearean play are considered in sequence.

A. Adaptation.

The impetus to adaptation, as to reduction/emendation, is often a specific production. Orson Welles' *Five Kings* of 1938 is an extreme example of reduction, compressing Shakespeare's eight history plays into two parts for performance. The ambitious project never reached Broadway, for which it was intended, and the script was never published. In contrast, the Hall-Barton *Wars of the Roses,* an adaptation of the same eight plays, has received wide acclaim both on the stage and in print.[3]

Peter Hall (b. 1930) then director of England's Royal Shakespeare Company, wished to celebrate the Bard's centennial year, 1964, by playing a full week of history plays, from *Richard II* to *Richard III*. Since eight plays had to be performed in seven days, he decided to compress the three *Henry VI* plays into two. He enlisted the aid of director John Barton (b. 1928), a friend from their Cambridge University days, who had a flair for composing pastiche Elizabethan blank verse. It is because of Barton's additions that *The Wars of the Roses* is classified as an adaptation.

Hall and Barton justify their "directorial interference" by three considerations: 1) The *Henry VI* plays are early and inferior examples of Shakespeare's drama, 2) The plays may not be entirely by Shakespeare (so that, the directors imply, a twentieth-century collaborator is as legitimate as a sixteenth), 3) The three *Henry VI* plays have never attracted sizable audiences, but, revised into two, *Henry VI* and *Edward IV*, and capped by *Richard III*, their stageworthiness might be enhanced.

The three plays of *The Wars of the Roses* abridge some 12,000 lines of Shakespeare to 7,500, of which about 6,000 are Shakespeare's. The rest were written by John Barton and edited by Peter Hall. Each of the three new plays is more centrally focused: *Henry VI* on the relationship between Henry and old Gloucester; *Edward IV* on the York-Warwick plot; *Richard III* on the hateful monarch's machinations. Designer John Bury helped unify the plays visually, through a relatively bare stage on which were moved two walls of varying textures that could suggest various boundaries. Action was centered on such large significant properties as a throne, a bed, an altar, a council-table.

Rewriting is most extensive in *Henry VI*. In the final scene the Cardinal of Winchester dies; Queen Margaret, cradling Suffolk's bloody head, cries for revenge, and inept Henry closes the play with the new lines:

> Come, wife, let's in and learn to govern better:
> For yet may England curse my wretched reign.

The very title *Edward IV* signals Henry's failure, since Edward of York is crowned while Lancastrian Henry lives. More pointedly than in Shakespeare, the French wars of the first play give way to the civil wars of the second—the Jack Cade rebellion and the rivalry of the nobles. And this emphasizes the change from ceremonial death to butchery; the heroic deaths of Talbot father and son degenerate to young Clifford's killing a child (Rutland), a nameless son slaying his father, and a nameless father his son. Over the end of *Edward IV*, as over the end of Shakespeare's *Henry VI*, Part 3, hovers the crooked shadow of Richard of Gloucester. Both plays end with a scene celebrating Edward's victory, but Barton invents lines for him:

> And for the last, my thanks to you, dear Gloucester,
> Our partner and our second in these wars,
> And now our chiefest minister in peace. (154)

When the court exits with a flourish, "*Gloucester remains.*"

At the opening of the third Royal Shakespeare Company play peace is threatened by Gloucester's desire to be crowned Richard III. Of the three Hall-Barton adaptations *Richard III* is closest to Shakespeare, Barton's main task being the abridgment that has been usual from the time of Colley Cibber's 1700 version. Barton's cutting tends to be linear rather than scenic, and what suffers is the Satanic humor of Richard's role-playing. Linear cutting also compresses Shakespeare's Act V, Scenes 4 and 5 into a swift scene that diminishes Richmond's prowess on the battlefield. The very end—and the end of *The Wars of the Roses*—returns to Shakespeare, for a shortened version of Richmond's final ceremonial speech.

The new structural clarity of *The Wars of the Roses* resembles Shakespeare's mature style, but Barton's new lines conform to Shakespeare's early verse style—restricted in vocabulary and thin in imagery. The continuity of *The Wars of the Roses* is stressed by inserted adverbs of time and place.

Moreover, in Barbara Hodgdon's words: "Other links, such as tense changes which focus both language and action in the present; lines which point to comings and goings, and to future meetings; and transitional introductions and 'wrap-up' lines clarify the general movement of the plays for their audience."[4] These unifiers, along with excising minor characters and lines that do not further the plot, yield a swiftly moving series of actions. The wars drive more directly to the final establishment of order, for the Hall-Barton *Wars of the Roses* presents the Elizabethan world picture as adumbrated by such scholars as E.M.W. Tillyard. Shakespeare's form and content teeter on the disturbance of order, and though Richmond (later Henry VII) triumphs in both versions, that triumph seems more tentative in Shakespeare because of the ubiquity of the preceding disorders.

Peter Hall decided to adapt the Shakespearean plays when he felt he had "only deeply understood Shakespeare's philosophy of order in the last few years. . . . As a student I never felt there was much life in this theory—perhaps because I learnt it as a mechanical set of rules. But as I worked year in and year out on Shakespeare I began to see it not as a relic of medievalism but as a piece of workable human pragmatism, humanitarian in its philosophy and modern and liberal in its application." (x) As he matured, Peter Hall claimed Shakespeare as his contemporary.

The most obvious reason for adapting Shakespeare is to modernize him, even when the language remains Elizabethan, as in the Hall-Barton *Wars of the Roses*. Modernization of the language can be accomplished more easily in translation than in the original English, and the history of translation—faithful and unfaithful—is rather different in French and German.[5]

Classicism reigned in seventeenth-century France, and this was the wrong climate for Shakespeare appreciation. French taste pervaded cultured Europe well into (and sometimes beyond) the eighteenth century. But dissident voices arose in Germany. The influential critics, Johann Gottfried von Herder and Gotthold Ephraim Lessing, praised Shakespeare despite his "irregularities." Between 1763 and 1766 the poet Christoph Martin Wieland translated (and sometimes adapted) twenty-two Shakespeare plays into German prose. The actor-manager Friedrich Ludwig Schröder staged his own adaptations. Johann Wolfgang Goethe, sometimes called the Shakespeare of Germany, praised the Bard as early as his Strasbourg student days and late in life as the Sage of Weimar. Of primary and lasting importance was the project of A. W. Schlegel, who translated sixteen Shakespeare plays between 1797 and 1801, then *Richard III* in 1810, with observance of the Bard's prose-verse divisions. Ludwig Tieck, who translated *The Tempest* while still a student, supervised translation of the remaining nineteen plays (including *Macbeth* and *King Lear*) by his daughter Dorothea and her husband, Wolf Graf Baudissin. This uneven collection gradually acquired the status of a German classic, though it did not inhibit other translations.

The French have no translation of comparable authority. Voltaire boasted of introducing Shakespeare to France, but he later turned against him, engaging in a literary duel with the Bard's defender, Mrs. Elizabeth Montagu. When Pierre Le Tourneur published his prose translation with an enthusiastic preface on the Bard (1776), Voltaire thundered in a famous letter to the Académie Française:

> Figurez-vous, messieurs, Louis XIV dans sa galérie de Versailles, entouré de sa cour brillante; un *Gilles* couvert de lambeaux perce la foule des héros, des grands hommes, et des beautés qui composent cette cour: il leur propose de quitter Corneille, Racine et Molière, pour un saltimbanque qui a des saillies heureuses, et qui fait des contorsions. Comment croyez-vous que cette offre serait reçue?[6]*

* Imagine, gentlemen, Louis XIV in his great hall at Versailles, surrounded by his brilliant court; a ragged *commedia* player cuts through the crowd of heroes, great men, and beauties of this court;

However Louis XIV would have reacted, Shakespeare found French defenders at the end of the eighteenth century, and the Bard stumbled onto the French stage in several adaptations, transformations, pantomimes, tableaux, and musical comedies. With the 1810 publication of Mme. de Stael's *De l'Allemagne*, the Voltaireans were defeated (though she was not uncritical of the Bard). In 1814 A. W. Schlegel's lectures on dramatic literature were published in Paris, laying a theoretical basis for embryonic French Romanticism. Revision of Le Tourneur's translation began in 1821, but in 1822 Penley's English company, playing *Hamlet* and *Othello*, were hissed off the Paris stage.

"Shakespeare" became a battle cry of the French Romantics, with the poets Alfred de Musset and Alfred de Vigny offering translations, with Alexandre Dumas père and Ludovic Vitet dramatizing history, after Shakespeare. The nineteenth century provided eight different translations of Shakespeare's complete works, the most esteemed being that of François-Victor Hugo, whose father wrote of its genesis (years after he himself had invoked Shakespeare to justify a union of the sublime and the grotesque):

> Tout à coup le fils éleva la voix et interrogea le père:
> —Que penses-tu de cet exil [de la France]?
> —Qu'il sera long.
> —Comment comptes-tu le remplir?
> Le père répondit:
> —Je regarderai l'Océan.
> Il y eut un silence. Le père reprit:
> —Et toi?
> —Moi, dit le fils, je traduirai Shakespeare.[7]*

---

he proposes that they leave Corneille, Racine, and Molière for a showman who has flashes of wit and makes wry faces. How do you suppose that offer would be received?

* Suddenly the son raised his voice and asked the father:
—What do you think of this exile [from France]?
—That it will be long.
—How do you expect to fill the time?

François-Victor Hugo produced a scholarly version in prose, but the theater relied on the transformations of Jean-François Ducis. Knowing no English, Ducis nevertheless composed a verse *Hamlet* with a happy ending (first version 1769, but revised for some thirty years thereafter), *King Lear* with a happy ending (1783), several different versions of *Macbeth* that obeyed the unity of place while ennobling the hero at the expense of his wife, a *Jean-sans-Terre,* a *Romeo and Juliet* with two different endings, an *Othello* with two different endings and the offending handkerchief transformed into a diamond bracelet.[8]

Dumas' *Hamlet* displaced that of Ducis in 1847, and by the twentieth century Dumas too was laid to rest, for Shakespeare was translated by poets such as Pierre-Jean Jouve, Jules Supervielle, Yves Bonnefoy; playwrights such as Maurice Maeterlinck, Jean Cocteau, Marcel Pagnol, André Obey, Jean Anouilh, André Gide, and Jean Vauthier; or even directors such as Gaston Baty and Roger Planchon. With differences in approach and quality, these men tried to be faithful to Shakespeare, and such fidelity is not my concern. Instead, I begin my foray into foreign adaptations with the French *Coriolan* of a lesser figure, René-Louis Piachaud (1896-1941).

The fourth longest of Shakespeare's plays, *Coriolanus* has attracted audiences mainly in times of political unrest. The earliest recorded performance—1681—is of Nahum Tate's adaptation, and James Thomson's version served John Philip Kemble and Mrs. Siddons for their triumph at the turn of the nineteenth century. Though most stars of the English and American stage played some form of *Coriolanus,* it did not achieve the popularity of other Shakespeare tragedies, and it was less favored in France and Ger-

---

The father replied:

—I'll look at the ocean.

There was a silence. The father continued:

—And you?

—I, said the son, I'll translate Shakespeare.

many, whose dramatic literature sports other versions of the Coriolanus story. After World War I, however, *Coriolanus* took on a new timeliness.[9] T. S. Eliot's "Coriolan" poems of 1931 and 1932 imply a plague on both "a press of people" and "a tired head among these heads," but playwrights were more partisan.[10]

Of all Shakespeare offshoots the *Coriolan* of René-Louis Piachaud is the only one that led to bloodshed—in the Paris riots of February, 1934. The Swiss journalist, poet, critic, theater amateur had already penned versions of *A Midsummer Night's Dream, Othello,* and *The Merry Wives of Windsor*—all "traduite et adaptée" into modern French prose. His adaptation of *Coriolanus* does not seem to be Fascist-inspired, as is sometimes charged. It was apparently undertaken in 1929 at the suggestion of French actor Léon Bernard, who later played Menenius.[11] The director Aurélien Lugné-Poe recommended Piachaud's version to the Minister of Education, who in turn recommended it to the reading committee of the state-subsidized Comédie Française, who accepted it unanimously. Nevertheless nervous about possible repercussions in a politically divided France, the Minister of Education submitted the text to Shakespeare experts, who found that Piachaud "avait suivi scrupuleusement le texte de Shakespeare et que certaines expressions, loin de dépasser la pensée du génial dramaturge anglais, se trouvaient plutôt adoucies par notre langue."[12]* The head of the Comédie, Émile Fabre, directed the play, which opened on December 9, 1933.

Early in 1934 several French government officials resigned because they were discredited in a Watergate type of scandal. The new Premier Daladier dismissed other officials, among them Fabre, appointing in his place a former director of the Sûreté Générale. After the February riots

* had scrupulously followed Shakespeare's text and that certain expressions, far from going beyond the thought of the brilliant English dramatist, were instead softened by our language.

and the resignation of Premier Daladier, performances of *Coriolan* were suspended until March 11. Neither Piachaud's published text nor the Comédie Française promptbook quite explains the violent audience reactions, especially on February 4, but the production has to be visualized against the rising support for law and order at any price. (Piachaud's translation was revived in 1956, without incident.)

The Folio text divides *Coriolanus* into acts but not into scenes; however, most printed versions follow the Globe Edition division into twenty-nine scenes. Piachaud's published text contains twenty-three scenes, omitting Shakespeare's I, 2, 4, and 7; IV, 3; and portions of Acts IV and V.[13] The printed text places intermissions after Shakespeare's II, 1 and III, 3, but the Comédie production apparently had only one intermission.

Piachaud's summary of his three acts suggests his admiration for a hero: "Coriolan jusqu'à son triomphe romain; Coriolan, l'Un, dans son duel avec le Nombre, jusqu'au banissement du héros; Coriolan le Vengeur, fléchi par sa mère Volumnie, et la mort du héros."* Of the translation he writes: "On s'est attaché à rendre le double rythme du modèle, le réalisme quotidien de sa prose, le lyrisme sublime et familier des mouvements qu'il a traités en vers."† (11) But the verse of Shakespeare's *Coriolanus* is rarely lyrical, much less sublime, and Piachaud's version, being prose throughout, does not offer the double rhythm he claims. By 1934 Greek myth, biblical legend, and Shakespearean verse had been dramatized into modern colloquial French by Jean Cocteau and André Obey. Piachaud follows their example, varying the tone neither with speaker nor

* Coriolanus up to his Roman triumph; Coriolanus, the One, in his duel with the Many, up to the hero's banishment; Coriolanus the Avenger, yielding to his mother Volumnia, and the hero's death.

† There was an effort to render the double rhythm of the model, the everyday realism of his prose, the sublime and well-known lyricism of the movements that he treated in verse.

with event. He eliminates some of Shakespeare's images, though he faithfully translates the details of Menenius' famous parable of the belly. Occasionally, Piachaud adds a sentence or a scenic direction, and these additions lead me to classify his version as an adaptation rather than a reduction/emendation.

In his Translator's Note Piachaud attests to Shakepeare's "sereine impartialité qui est le propre de son génie." (11) Piachaud dissolves that impartiality by vulgarizing the Plebeians and ennobling Coriolanus. Several of the hero's most acidulous speeches are cut or shortened (and further reduced in the Comédie promptbook). Stage tableaux tend to set Coriolanus off in solitary splendor, as at his first entrance. The Folio reads: "*Enter Caius Marcius.*" Piachaud adds: "*La Plèbe a un mouvement de recul: il y a dans les uns de la haine rentrée; dans les autres, ceux qui aiment à être matés, une sorte d'épanouissement naïf à sentir sur eux l'autorité d'un chef.*"*(21) Few audiences could detect the second Plebeian sentiment through which we can read Piachaud's anti-Plebeian sentiment. And in staging, Émile Fabre emphasized the opposition of hero and Plebs: "En opposant ainsi les tableaux populaires dont j'ai volontairement exagéré le mouvement, on obtient, me semble-t-il, plus de grandeur dans les scènes calmes à deux ou trois personnages."[15]† Fabre threw some two hundred extras into his crowd scenes, but the battles were apparently perfunctory.

After the victorious return of Coriolanus from Corioli, the Tribunes plot his downfall, and the intermission comes on a suspenseful curtain-line of Brutus: "Et, le moment venu d'agir, on aura du coeur à l'ouvrage."‡(56) The mo-

* *The Plebeian crowd makes a backward movement: in some there is repressed hatred; in others, those who like to be mastered, a naive exhilaration at the sensation of a leader's authority over them.*

† In thus opposing the crowd scenes whose movement I have deliberately exaggerated, it seems to me one obtains more grandeur in the calm scenes of two or three characters.

‡ And, when the moment comes to act, we'll have our heart in our work.

ment soon comes to act, and the action militates against Coriolanus. At the end of Piachaud's Scene XI (Shakespeare's II, 3) he invents dialogue to prove the demagogic hypocrisy of the Tribunes:

> Brutus: Les tribuns n'ont rien fait!
> Sicinius: Les tribuns n'ont rien vu!
> Brutus: Les tribuns n'ont rien su!
>
> (*Ils sortent dans un mouvement de fièvre et de gaîté violente.*)* (73)

By the end of Piachaud's second act Coriolanus at last rages against the offending Plebs, and the Comédie Française audiences cheered.

Shakespeare's Plebs banish Coriolanus, who leaves them with these words:

> Despising,
> For you, the city, thus I turn my back.
> There is a world elsewhere.[16] (III, iii)

Piachaud precedes this sentence with: "Romains dégénérés, vos pires ennemis, c'est vous-mêmes." (98) He translates Shakespeare's first sentence, but it is crossed out in the Comédie promptbook, and the next sentence is changed to: "Adieu! Rome n'est pas le monde." Piachaud's Plebs cry more vindictively than in Shakespeare: "A bas le traître, à bas Coriolan!"

Since Piachaud's third and final act elides Shakespearean scenes and cuts lines, the heroism of Coriolanus continues to dominate even his treason. But events are faithful to Shakespeare: Menenius sues in vain for mercy, and Coriolanus yields to his mother's entreaties. However, when the

* Brutus: The Tribunes did nothing!
Sicinius: The Tribunes saw nothing!
Brutus: The Tribunes knew nothing!
(*They exit in feverish movement and violent mirth.*)

Roman ladies bring the good news to Rome, the Shakespearean cry is: "Welcome, ladies, / Welcome!" (V, v, 6) In Piachaud it is followed by: "Vive Coriolan!"

Toward the end of Shakespeare's tragedy, Aufidius taunts Coriolanus as "thou boy of tears," and the hero reacts with boasts climaxed by the powerful eagle-image:

> Boy? False hound!
> If you have writ your annals true, 'tis there
> That, like an eagle in a dovecote, I
> Fluttered your Volscians in Corioles.
> Alone I did it. Boy? (V, vi)

Piachaud drops the eagle and begins the speech with a reminiscence of Julius Caesar surrounded by conspirators: "Ha! Volsques, vous aussi!"

Coriolanus calls to Aufidius: "Comme un petit garçon. . . . Canaille!" Then to the conspirators: "Il est écrit pourtant dans vos annales, si vos annales sont sincères, qu'un jour, ici, dans Corioles, tous! Je vous ai vus, tous, vous sauver devant moi: alors, comme à présent, j'étais seul."* (141) Direct as the new wording is, it loses the sting of Shakespeare's repeated "Boy." And the repetition of *tous* prepares for the final lone stand of Coriolanus-hero against the many —*tous*.

At the last Piachaud translates the eulogy by Aufidius:

> Ma colère, ma haine avec lui sont tombées. Relevez-le. Trois chefs le porteront avec moi. Tambours, battez une marche funèbre. Le fer en bas, toutes les lances. Bien qu'il ait fait ici plus d'une veuve, bien que beaucoup de mères pleurent encore les enfants qu'il leur a pris, ses funérailles seront dignes de sa gloire. Et c'est

* It is, however, written in your annals, if your annals are sincere, that one day, here, in Corioli, all! I saw you, all, flee before me: then, as now, I was alone.

> à nous, soldats, d'honorer sa mémoire. Aidez-moi. (*Marche funèbre. Aufidius et trois chefs emportent Coriolan sur un bouclier.*)* (143)

However, the Comédie promptbook omits: "Bien qu'il ait fait . . . leur a pris." The final tribute cleanses Coriolanus of war-slaughter and retains only his "noble memory."

Piachaud's adaptation was produced by the state-subsidized Comédie Française, opening on December 9, 1933. That year marked the beginning of exile for Bertolt Brecht (1898-1956), widely acclaimed as the greatest modern German playwright. After the burning of the Berlin Reichstag, Brecht left Germany for what proved to be an exile of fifteen years. He spent spring and summer, 1933, in Paris, where he collaborated with Kurt Weill on a ballet, *Die sieben Todsünden der Kleinbürger*. As late as September of that year, he again visited Paris, but preoccupied as he was with finding a home in Denmark, he probably knew nothing about the Piachaud *Coriolan*. Brecht's opposing view of Shakespeare's tragedy was not penned until after World War II.

Back in Berlin, he worked at the play in 1951 and 1952, but the adaptation was unfinished when he died in 1956. Still missing is his Act I, Scene 3, which was to combine Shakespeare's scenes 4 to 10, and which he wanted to work out in rehearsal. With these scenes in their Shakespearean form, Brecht's *Coriolan* is about a thousand lines shorter than the original.[17] He reduces and paraphrases, but he also adds and alters, so that his adaptation strays further from Shakespeare than Piachaud's.

Brecht used the Dorothea Tieck translation as his basic

* My anger, my hatred have fallen with him. Lift him up. Three chiefs will join me in carrying him. Drums, beat a funeral march. All lances, tips down. Though he widowed more than one woman here, though many mothers still weep for the children that he took from them, his funeral shall be worthy of his glory. And it is up to us, soldiers, to honor his memory. Assist me. (*Funeral march. Aufidius and three chiefs carry Coriolanus out on a shield.*)

text, but Ralph Mannheim has summarized what Brecht did to it: "Many of the Tieck lines and phrases have been taken over unchanged or still remain recognizable, some passages have been paraphrased and condensed; others have been entirely rewritten, sometimes for dramaturgical reasons, sometimes to bring them closer to the English."[18] Brecht was not concerned about fidelity to Shakespeare, much less to Tieck, and yet he does preserve most of their prose-verse rhythms.

Brecht noted his own purpose in adapting *Coriolanus*: "So scheint es uns am besten, aus dem verletzten Stolz des Coriolan eine nicht allzu shakespeareferne anderer bedeutende Haltung zu machen, nämlich den Glauben des Coriolan an seine Unersetzlichkeit."[19]* Shakespeare's tragedy of pride thus becomes Brecht's tragedy of illusion. Brecht's Coriolanus is destroyed because he labors under the illusion that he is indispensable. That illusion is strengthened by his triumph at Corioli. After he is banished from Rome, however, the Plebeians grow powerful, realizing that their enemies are not the Volscians but Patricians everywhere. Encouraged by their Tribunes, they take up arms and successfully defend a democratic Rome. Warrior Coriolanus thereby becomes obsolete.

Brecht's adaptation uses most of the Shakespearean events, but he places them in another historical perspective. Structurally, however, he remains surprisingly close to Shakespeare, preserving the five-act form (though the acts are differently divided) and several scenes in each act. Moreover, Brecht and Piachaud take diametrically opposing attitudes toward Coriolanus: Piachaud cuts many scathing remarks of Coriolanus, whereas Brecht cuts the many references to his nobility.

Our first view of Brecht's Coriolanus reveals an aggressor. Piachaud had the crowd recognize in him a master, but

* So it seems best to us to convert the wounded pride of Coriolanus into another important character trait, which is not too far from Shakespeare—namely Coriolanus's belief in his own indispensability.

Brecht has him enter with armed men, while the crowd's attention is diverted by the belly parable of Menenius. Brecht adds lines to arouse sympathy for the plight of the Plebeians, who are neither fickle nor cowardly. Brecht invents a nameless Plebeian with a child, who appears in two scenes to suggest that the working class is building for the future. When they examine Coriolanus for the Consulship, the Plebeians are concerned with the present more than the past; Brecht invents a shipful of Volscian corn that Coriolanus refuses to distribute after his victory. The Plebs turn against the warrior because he denies them food, and they do so without actually electing him Consul.

In contrast to Piachaud, who decreases playing time in which Coriolanus appears as a traitor to Rome, Brecht increases it. But Brecht is concerned less with his treason than with the growing independence of the Plebs. Brecht makes his main changes in Acts IV and V. He rewrites the mirror scene between the two commoners, to show the halcyon days of peace; Brecht has Coriolanus and Aufidius delight in their specialty, which is war. When the two military technicians attack Rome, Brecht invents a smoke signal to announce the city's capitulation. It is never seen.

In Brecht's Act V, Scene 1 the Tribunes are onstage throughout, encouraging Roman resistance by distributing arms to the people. But most striking is Brecht's change of the climactic scene of the play—Coriolanus yielding to the plea of his mother, Volumnia. More pointedly than in Shakespeare, mother and wife threaten to commit suicide if Rome is defeated, but then Brecht's Volumnia goes on to describe the new Rome, united and determined to resist both the Volscians and the Patricians. This blurs the motivation of Coriolanus in acceding to her plea, but Aufidius condemns him, as in Shakespeare. Coriolanus reacts to Aufidius by boasting, and the Volscians fall upon Coriolanus with cries of pain for those he has killed. Unlike Shakespeare, however, Brecht sends no Second Lord to try to stop the killing: "*Die Offiziere des Aufidius fallen über*

Coriolan her und durchbohren ihn." (vi, 2496) No one stands on the hero's corpse, but no one sings his praises.

Brecht adds a final scene that punctuates his view of the dispensability of a military technician in a people's republic. The scene was undoubtedly suggested by Plutarch, who notes that the family of Coriolanus was permitted to wear mourning for ten months. Brecht reverses Plutarch; when the Senate learns of the death of Coriolanus, Menenius makes a motion for special commemoration of the hero. But before long-winded Menenius finishes his motion, Tribune Brutus moves that the Senate proceed with current business. Then the family's petition to wear public mourning is denied, to conclude the play.

It was probably the pressure of other work that prevented Brecht from producing his *Coriolanus*. Seven years after his death, in 1963, Manfred Wekwerth and Joachim Tenschert directed his adaptation for the Berliner Ensemble—with modifications.[20]

Since Brecht did not adapt Shakespeare's battle-scenes, leaving them to be worked out in rehearsal, these scenes were the starting-point of the two directors. "Wir rückten die sonst gestrichenen Schlachtszenen in den Mittelpunkt der Inszenierung. Wir zeigen sie als das Werk grosser Spezialisten des Kriegs (Coriolan, Aufidius). Auch deren Verhalten im Frieden ist nur von hier aus erklärbar: Sie kämpfen auch im Frieden gegen alles, was sich dem Wunsch nach Kämpfen entgegenstellt. (335) Die Bühne ist der Kriegsschauplatz, auf dem der Held seine Talente zu beweisen hat im Krieg, und—beinahe zum Verhängnis einer ganzen Stadt—auch da, wo Friede herrscht."*(336)

The Berliner Ensemble has often used its revolving stage

* At the center of our production we placed the battle-scenes, which are usually cut. We show them as the work of great specialists of war (Coriolanus, Aufidius). Even their behavior in peacetime derives from their battle skill; even in peacetime they fight against everything that opposes the wish to fight. The stage is the theater of war, in which the hero has to display his talents for war, even in peacetime, almost destroying a whole city.

for impressive theatricalization of crowd movements, and this was true of the battle for Corioli, fought with bloody precision. In contrast, the battle for Rome showed the Plebeians' determination to stand fast and defend their city. In Wekwerth's words: "Und es ist auch das Unzeremonielle der Volksbewaffnung am Ende des Stücks, das die grosse Erschütterung der guten Sitten bringt, die gefährlicher ist als ihr militärischer Nutzen."[21]* In the first battle the hero triumphed by the brave efficiency with which he led his men, by his skill in individual combat with Aufidius, and by the force of a ceremonial military tradition. In the second battle, ceremony and individual combat were obsolete, and Coriolanus could not pierce a defense in depth.

The staging of the siege of Corioli impressed almost all viewers, and Kenneth Tynan has described it vividly:

> Corioli is conquered in three great flourishes of action, wordless except for deafening rhythmical chants of "*Cai-us Mar-cius*!" and "*Au-fi-di-us*!" yelled by the black-clad armies into the resonant concavity of their shields.
>
> First the gates are stormed, with attack by siege-ladders, counterattack by vast nets of heavy rope, renewed attack by shield-plated phalanx. Next: battle in the open, with waves of soldiers clashing in the stylised manner of Chinese opera, knees akimbo and swords maniacally brandished. As they part, the mortally wounded slowly spin and fall. Finally: the generals meet in single combat, covered in blood yet *grinning* as they face each other, like two young Samurai delighting in their expertise.[22]

Stemming from these central battle-scenes, the Berliner Ensemble production restored certain Shakespearean notes

* More dangerous than the military results is the lack of ceremony in the arming of the people at the end of the play—which shatters good old traditions.

to Brecht's adaptation—the strong Coriolanus-Aufidius rivalry and the dependence of Coriolanus upon his self-consciously Patrician mother. To stress the latter, Wekwerth and Tenschert borrowed a scene from Shakespeare's *Antony and Cleopatra*, where the heroine arms the hero for battle. During the course of the action, the Berliner Ensemble Tribunes are *gradually* educated in opposition to the war. Not only they but all the Plebeians are individualized, each man having a name and often a profession, though little was added to Brecht's dialogue. The Berliner Ensemble play moves more swiftly than Brecht's, since several scenes are run together, which Wekwerth and Tenschert justify mistakenly: "Der Verzicht der Folio-Edition von 1623 auf Akteinteilung kam unserer Konzeption sehr entgegen. Er ermöglichte u.a. in balladesker Erzählweise die Veränderungen, die schnellen Wechsel der Situationen und Vorgänge zu zeigen, das Thema von Sieg und Niederlage, vom Aufstieg und Fall der Helden entsprechend zu erzählen."* (334) And finally, the two directors change the end of Brecht's last scene. The Roman Senate receives the news of the assassination of Coriolanus, and business goes on as usual. There is no request to wear mourning and no refusal.

Wekwerth and Tenschert received wide acclaim for their adaptation of Shakespeare *and* Brecht whereas a 1962 Frankfurt production of Brecht's text has faded into oblivion. The Berliner Ensemble version traveled to several Western countries, including England, and in 1971 the Berliner Ensemble directors were invited to direct *Coriolanus* for the London Old Vic. However, there appears to have been a misunderstanding about whether the *Coriolanus* was to be that of Shakespeare or Brecht.[23] The promptbook was changed several times during rehearsals, and the leading actor, Christopher Plummer, resigned, to be replaced by

* The lack of act division in the 1623 Folio supported our conception, enabling us to show (among other things) the swift change of situations and events in balladlike narration, and accordingly to narrate the theme of victory and defeat, of the rise and fall of the hero.

Anthony Hopkins. Newspapers reported "British Resistance" to the directors, which the cast denied in a letter to *The Times*. After the opening, reviewers complained of treason to Shakespeare, as they do after any unusual production. But Wekwerth and Tenschert acted like many directors whose native language is English; they abridged, rearranged, and interpreted through staging; they did not introduce additions into Shakespeare's text.[24]

Nevertheless, their interpretation was undoubtedly influenced by Brecht's adaptation; a paragraph in the Old Vic program is a direct translation of directorial notes for the Berliner Ensemble production—on the centrality of the battle-scenes. But the Old Vic program does not indicate the main textual changes (through abridgment and rearrangement) that ennoble the people's Tribunes so that they behave with consistent and unselfish loyalty to their class. Rather than opposing Shakespeare's scheming pair to an intransigent warrior, the Wekwerth-Tenschert production pits the people's legitimate representatives against their oppressor, Coriolanus, who is his mother's spoiled son. After their Coriolanus yields to Volumnia's plea for Rome, he speaks the "O mother, mother! / what have you done? . . ." lines as a soliloquy. And after his assassination, the final tribute of Aufidius is truncated to: "My rage is gone, / And I am struck with sorrow." The Wekwerth-Tenschert production ends with Aufidius' non-Shakespearean demand for Coriolanus' sword, which he raises aloft in his own triumphant march.

The secretary of playwright John Osborne (b. 1929) has written me that his 1973 adaptation of *Coriolanus* "was not a reaction against the Brecht version but a reaction to the Shakespeare version." However, Osborne did see the Berliner Ensemble production, and he may have read hostile accounts of the 1971 Old Vic production before writing *A Place Calling Itself Rome*.[25] Like Piachaud, Osborne aggrandizes the hero and, like Piachaud, he emends Shakespeare's verse into modern colloquial prose. Osborne condenses Shakespeare's twenty-nine scenes (in the Globe Edition) to twenty-five. Most radical are his intrascene cuts, but the play is an adaptation mainly because of the addition of a non-Shakespearean opening scene.

John Osborne began his theater career as an actor, but he has done little acting since the production of his first successful play, *Look Back in Anger* in 1956. During the course of some twenty subsequent plays for stage, radio, film, and television, Osborne has written three adaptations—of Lope de Vega's *La Fianza Satisfecha* (*A Bond Honored*), Ibsen's *Hedda Gabler,* and Shakespeare's *Coriolanus.* Only the last was published before performance.

A Place Calling Itself Rome opens in the bedroom of Caius Marcius, where he lies uneasily beside his wife Virgilia. "*He cries out, half waking.*" What he cries out reveals an obsession with Aufidius as opponent. He gets out of bed and "*writes in an unsure hand*" a confessional diary that exposes a typical Osborne protagonist—able, neurotic, self-absorbed. Shakespeare presents a tragic hero without inner conflict, but Osborne introduces one who bares his soul in the opening scene. In the rest of the play, however, Osborne limits our view of Coriolanus to the external man, even abridging Shakespeare's two brief soliloquies of Act IV, scene 4.

Osborne's second scene is Shakespeare's first, but Osborne gives us a modern mob: "*a cross-section* MOB *of* STUDENTS, FIXERS, PUSHERS, POLICEMEN, UNIDENTIFIABLE PUBLIC, *obvious* TRADE UNIONISTS, JOURNALISTS *and the odd* NEWS CAMERA TEAM, SOUND MEN, *etc., shrills of police horses, linked arms on all sides; screaming girls, banners of the nineteenth-century sort, banners of the modern kind. . . .*" (13) This mob does not take kindly to Menenius, stifling with a pun his effort to narrate the parable of the belly:

> Menenius: I appeal to you!
> Voice: Oh, no you don't. (17)

But Menenius is not only long-winded; he is also persistently reasonable and good-humored. After a series of patriotic generalizations, "*He stands down to an ovation—more or less—from the mob.*" (19) He tries to turn this into a welcome for Caius Marcius, who enters with invective derived from Shakespeare: "Thanks. So what goes on here, with these rabbling, purblind doomsters. Still scratching at their opinions like armpits!" (19) The rest of the scene is an abbreviated version of Shakespeare, with the Tribune Sicinius converted into "*a pale-skinned coloured woman.*" Abridged and modernized are the following two scenes, introducing Aufidius, then the women of Coriolanus' family. The battle for Corioli contains "*Flak jackets, berets, helmets, rifles, shields, home-made bombs and bottles hurling, the sound of gunfire and sniping.*" (26-7) Though Osborne apparently intends to subsume all battles in this battle, the main impression is that of World War I, where modern weapons were in use but individual exploits could still be achieved. More neatly than in Shakespeare, Osborne's Coriolanus moves from a tough eloquence that inspires the Roman soldiers to a successful pistol duel with Aufidius.

Victorious, Coriolanus stands for a Senate seat, and as in Shakespeare the Tribunes manipulate the Plebeians to turn against him. Urged by his mother, Coriolanus goes back to the Plebs, and as in Shakespeare loses his temper at the word "traitor:" "Call me traitor, you dead droppings of old cant. You lie. You lie in your green teeth!" (57) When Coriolanus is banished, he retorts: "Banish me? *I* banish *you*! Stay here in your slum. And strike. Communicate. Get shaken with rumours; fads; modishness; greed; fashion; your clannishness; your lives in depth. May you, but you won't, one minute of that depth, know desolation. May your enemies barter and exchange you coolly in their own better market-places . . . I have seen the *future* . . . here . . . and it doesn't work! *I* turn my back. There is a world *elsewhere*!" (57-8) This is a typical example of how Osborne simplifies Shakespeare's imagery and converts the rhythm to telegraphese.

Events follow Shakespeare: Coriolanus joins Aufidius, who waits for him to fall: "When, Caius, Rome is yours, you will never have been so poor, for I think then you might belong to *me*." (69) When Rome is besieged, Menenius pleads in vain, but Volumnia is successful. Where Osborne differs from Shakespeare, however, is in the few minutes before the death of Coriolanus. For the second time, the Roman hero is called a traitor; Coriolanus answers Aufidius not with boasts and vituperations, but with generalized accusations: "You have no system, no abstract ideas. You are everything by starts, and nothing long. You are a wild lot. You hate any law that imposes on your understanding or any kind of restraint at all. You are all fierceness and levity. If you have any feelings, when they aren't excited by novelty or opposition, they grow cold and stagnant. If your blood's not heated by passion, then it turns to poison." (76-7) Coriolanus charges Aufidius with lacking theory and principle upon which to base his actions. But the speech is puzzling because Coriolanus himself is even more remiss in ideology. And there is no indication that Osborne means us to notice the self-blindness of Coriolanus, since he is killed almost immediately afterward. Aufidius offers a not unmixed eulogy, marred by non-Shakespearean abstractions: "Even so, he was like some of us, unable to forgive wrongs when they seemed to darken death or night, to defy power, which seems omnipotent . . . neither to change, nor falter, nor repent even this . . . this to him was to be good, great and joyous, beautiful and from this alone, yes, life, joy, empire and victory." (77) His body is borne aloft, and finally "*All that remains on the stage is the lone figure of a piper playing a lament*." This lament is surely meant to confirm sympathy for a hero whom his murderer has just linked with good, beauty, and especially joy, though the qualities have not been evident in the play itself. Such abstractions are a confusing and nondramatic lapse in Osborne, whose main gift has always been his vigorous dialogue of specific images.

Osborne's title indicates the intention of his adaptation. Not *Rome* but *A Place Calling Itself Rome* in spite of its political cleavages. Osborne presents the Patricians as honest men with civic traditions, whereas his Plebeians are an unruly mob who are an easy prey for demagogues. This view resembles Piachaud's, and in both adaptations Coriolanus rises tall and scornful against the masses and in spite of his faults. Neither adapter was able to fit the language to the hero; both competently emended his invectives, but Piachaud could not accommodate such lofty images as the eagle, and Osborne wafted off into abstraction.

Tempting to modern playwrights and directors, Coriolanus was long thought to have grown on solid historical ground, but the nineteenth-century German historian Theodor Mommsen took that ground away from the Roman warrior.[26] By the twentieth century, the several modern adaptors of *Coriolanus* were interested in reading their own history into his story.

The adaptations of *Coriolanus* and *The Wars of the Roses* follow Shakespearean events rather than history. The next few adaptations to be discussed graft non-Shakespearean events onto the Shakespearean frame, and a line of demarcation between adaptation and transformation is harder to draw. Where the basic Shakespearean plot is preserved, the plays are classified as adaptations. Transformation occurs where the main story strays from Shakespeare.

Two little-known offshoots of *Timon of Athens* are adaptations, though the dialogue is non-Shakespearean. For his least-performed tragic hero, Shakespeare conflates Plutarch's bitter misanthrope with Lucian's lavish spendthrift. Though French Émile Fabre (1869-1955) and Austrian Theodor Tagger (1891-1958) may have gone to Shakespeare's sources for their tragedies, they probably found his play readier to hand. Both rewriters trace Timon's transition from prodigality to misanthropy, without Shakespearean phrasal echoes.

Émile Fabre was head of the Comédie Française from 1915 to 1934, and he directed the stormy *Coriolanus* that occasioned his dismissal from the state-subsidized theater. Earlier, in 1907, he adapted *Timon* for direction by Firmin Gémier (who had created the part of Alfred Jarry's Ubu, and who was to play a celebrated Shylock).[27] Fabre's Timon moves from riches to rags, to riches again, to final rags, but this is subordinated to his involvement in the politics of Athens. Timon spends huge sums in preparation for war against Lacadaemonia. After he loses father, wife, son, and wealth, he still opposes surrender. Timon's aristocratic friends reject his requests for war loans, rather than the personal loans of Shakespeare. Disillusioned, Timon joins Alcibiades in the siege of Melos, which makes him rich again. Placing his trust in the common people, he betrays his former friends, aristocrats all, to the enemy. But when the democrats are in power, they unjustly condemn the generals who lost the war. Timon realizes: "Ainsi, une aristocratie esclave de ses intérêts, une démocratie esclave de ses passions, voilà Athènes." (28) Inviting the Athenians to hang themselves on his fig-tree, Timon flees the civilization of his city. But he refuses to flee from the conquering Lacadaemonian army. At the last Timon prepares to hang himself while Lacadaemonian women dance on Athenian ruins.

What is curious in this exceedingly verbose play, geared to *grand spectacle,* is Fabre's injection of a theme from Shakespeare's *Coriolanus*: neither Patricians nor Plebeians are concerned with justice, and each class has a selfish view of the city's best governance. In Fabre's 1907 play these opposing views take the form of lengthy academic debate; in spite of Timon's war losses, in spite of lip service to the miseries of defeat, Fabre lacks experiential conviction.

Theodor Tagger's *Timon: Tragödie* (written under the pseudonym Ferdinand Bruckner) is a sparer play.[28] Like

French Fabre, Austrian-born Tagger wrote and directed. His early poems and plays are marked by Expressionist self-indulgence. In 1923 he became director of Berlin's Renaissance Theater, where he produced fairly traditional plays. At the same time, as Ferdinand Bruckner, he achieved some success as a playwright, particularly in his creation of multiple settings. *Timon* was written in 1932, before Tagger fled from Nazism, spending 1933-1951 in the United States, where a number of his plays were performed. After his Expressionist beginnings, most of his plays are drawn from history or from other plays, though *Timon* is his only Shakespeare adaptation.

Tagger's Timon is a cultured and peace-loving man in a period of big-business speculation that thrives on war. Perhaps influenced by Shakespeare's scenes with Painter and Poet, Tagger creates an art-lover who spends most of his money on the building of an Odeon. In contrast to Fabre's warmongering Timon, Tagger's is a resolute pacifist, refusing his friend Alcibiades money for new weapons. Tagger changes the names of Shakespearean characters, but he retains Timon's three false friends and his true servant; however, he drops Apemantus and incidental characters.

After Timon loses his money, each of his friends refuses a loan. His impoverishment is swift and graphic; the first friend refuses to make a loan toward the building of the art center, but by the time Timon comes to the third friend, he is hungry and ragged. He realizes that the arts are a luxury, and that he is "ein überflüssiger Mensch."

Going out into the wilderness with his faithful servant, Timon inveighs against man and god: "Denn um mich kümmern sie sich längst nicht mehr. . . . Was können sie mir noch tun."* (89) Since Olympus suddenly becomes visible in one of Tagger's double settings, the gods do seem to care about Timon, and the rest of the play belies his implication that he can suffer no further misfortune. Zeus is persuaded

* For they've stopped caring about me long ago. . . . What more can they do to me?

to restore him to riches. On earth Timon's shovel strikes gold; master and servant return to Athens.

In the last act Timon rejects the plea of his former friends to use his wealth to intercede with Macedonian Alexander on behalf of Athens. Alone with his faithful servant, Timon engages in an imaginary continuation of Plato's *Symposium* while the Macedonian armies destroy Athens, street by street. Unheeding of the danger, Timon recalls his youthful decision to forsake the life of the senses for that of the mind, and he invites laughter at that decision. His faithful servant suggests that the two men die holding one another's hands, but Timon closes the play on a question: "Halten wir uns an den Händen?" (139) Presumably he cannot grasp such fellowship.

Tagger's intellectual, like Fabre's seeker of power, is incapable of a meaningful human gesture. They both die with Athens collapsing around them. But the implied reasons are quite different: Fabre shows the failure of a just man to accommodate clashing interests in his country; Tagger shows the failure of a "superfluous man" to accommodate himself to *realpolitik*. The flat modern prose of each hero lacks the ring of distinction. In spite of Fabre's spectacular mass scenes and Tagger's occasionally moving minor characters, the two plays tend to make an abstraction of Shakespeare's puzzling but passionate hero.

The *Timon* plays depart from Shakespeare in language, characters, and world of the play, but they follow Shakespeare's structure, main events, and ending. They represent a limit-line of adaptation, and the two plays of Friedrich Dürrenmatt (b. 1921) illustrate a different form of limit, through change of tone.

After nearly two decades of writing original plays, the Swiss author Dürrenmatt adapted Strindberg and Shakespeare. His *König Johann* (1968)[29] departs from Schlegel's translation, and his *Titus Andronicus* (1970)[30] from that of Dorothea Tieck. In choosing *King John* Dürrenmatt cites politics as the main impetus: " 'König Johann' ist ein politisches Stück, das ist es bei Shakespeare und das ist es bei mir. Es zeigt die Maschinerie der Politik, das Zustandekommen ihrer Abkommen und ihrer Unglücksfälle, doch ist es ein Spiel unter den Mördern, nicht unter den Opfern."* (101) The latter sentence indicates that his play will contain no class conflict, as in the *Coriolanus* adaptation of Brecht, who influenced Dürrenmatt's *Frank V* and *Die Physiker*. Dürrenmatt claims to dramatize the power play of murderers who belong to the same class.

Does such power play constitute political drama, as he says? The root meaning of "political" links it to the state, rather than to passing personalities who may occupy offices in the state, and Dürrenmatt's play focuses on such personalities. Despite his claim, Dürrenmatt's *König Johann* is less political than that of Hartmut Lange (b. 1937), an East German playwright who moved to West Berlin in 1965, the year of his adaptation of *King John*.[31] Remaining closer to Shakespeare-Schlegel, Lange's adaptation provides a pointed contrast with that of Dürrenmatt.

Lange follows Shakespeare in structure—sixteen scenes, though the divisions are not identical. He sharpens the conflict between King John and his baronial enemies. Most important politically is the subservience of Lange's King John to his role as king. He may lose battles and land; he may antagonize lords and cardinals; but he never forgets the symbolic importance of his kingship, and he therefore has himself crowned on four different strategic occasions. Lange gives John non-Shakespearean lines that show his awareness of the stranglehold of his office. Moreover, Lange's invented soldiers, speaking prose, obscurely understand that progress lies in the movement away from feudalism and toward a strong centralized monarchy. Lange's John dies like Shakespeare's, after receiving the Bastard's

* *King John* is a political play, both for Shakespeare and for me. It shows the machinery of politics, the progression of its alliances and its accidents. However, it is a game among killers and not among victims.

bad news, but first he momentarily and self-indulgently neglects his office, eating cherries. Lange's King John dies, but his Prince Henry will be king of a stronger if smaller kingdom.

Straying further than Lange from Shakespeare, Dürrenmatt uses the Bard's source in an earlier anonymous play, from which he borrows the love of the Bastard for John's niece, Blanch of Spain. Shakespeare's John is a pragmatic king who is opposed by a perfidious Philip of France, a cowardly duke of Austria, a scheming Cardinal Pandulph, and his own barons. Loyal and brave throughout is Philip Faulconbridge, a bastard of King Richard Coeur de Lion. In the stage history of the play (and its several early adaptations) strong actors have preferred the Bastard's role to that of John.

Dürrenmatt claims to change Shakespeare's Bastard: "Der Bastard ist bei Shakespeare ein Ideologe. . . . Mein Bastard ist weder Ideologe noch Moralist, für ihn sind die Könige die Machthaber und die Völker die Opfer dieser Machthaber. Was er von den Königen verlangt, ist allein, dass sie vernünftig regieren, er versucht Johann vernünftig zu machen."* (101) Whether or not Shakespeare draws an ideological Bastard, Dürrenmatt does insist on his reason. Energetic and unconventional as in Shakespeare, the Bastard directs his unconventional energies toward convincing the king that reasonable behavior can be profitable; he does not mention that it is also humane.[32] Dürrenmatt not only portrays the Bastard as a modern man of reason, but he also translates reason into peace-loving pragmatism. Thus the Bastard is John's wise counselor rather than, as in Lange and Shakespeare, his bravest warrrior; it is he who proposes a truce at Angers through the double marriage of King John to the duchess of Angoulême and

* Shakespeare's Bastard is an ideologist. . . . My Bastard is neither an ideologist nor a moralist. For him, kings are powers, and common people are the victims of these powers. What he requires of kings is only that they rule reasonably; he tries to make John reasonable.

the Dauphin Lewis to Blanch of Spain, even though he is in love with the latter. It is the Bastard who convinces John not to kill the child Prince Arthur precisely because he is expected to. (Unlike the John of Shakespeare and Lange, Dürrenmatt's never gives the order for Arthur's death, which happens in the same accidental way.) It is the Bastard who advises John to submit to the Church, after he is deserted by his barons. Finally, it is the Bastard who informs John that he has been poisoned by Pembroke. So it is the Bastard who receives John's dying curse:

> Du hast mich mit Vernunft vergiftet! . . .
> Die Welt verbessernd, machtest du sie nur
> Verdammter. Kehr zurück zu deinen Schweinen,
> Zurück in deinen Bauernmist.* (93)

After advising the king throughout the play, the Bastard will accept the curse-advice of the dying king. But through the Bastard's guidance, John has become more sympathetic than in Shakespeare; he is shrewder than Lange's hero, proposing the Magna Charta, but he does not understand his historic role. Nor do John's enemies, caricatured by Dürrenmatt: the duke of Austria is not only a coward but also a *gourmand*, Philip is outrageously perfidious, Lewis ridiculously weak, and Pandulph brazenly hypocritical. Elinor and Constance as power-hungry termagants are present in Shakespeare, though their fierce exchange is traditionally omitted on the English stage; Dürrenmatt has Elinor taunt Constance so that she stabs herself. The third-ranking woman, Blanch of Spain, is developed by Dürrenmatt into a sadistic nymphomaniac; not only does she sleep with every man in sight—"Kurz, mit ganz England, Madame, das ist viel."—but she orders that the Bastard be whipped to punish him for his political pragmatism in obtaining peace

* You've poisoned me with reason! . . . Improving the world, you've merely damned it worse. Go back to your pigs, back to your farm manure.

through her marriage to the Dauphin. In other changes Dürrenmatt eliminates Shakespeare's Hubert, and Pembroke becomes John's enemy rather than his retainer.

Like Lange, Dürrenmatt tidies Shakespeare's sprawling play by providing motivations for every deed, but Dürrenmatt's deeds turn out ironically: good intentions go invariably awry. The ultimate motivator is usually the Bastard with his penchant for bettering the world through reason, and he is also the cause of motivation in others whose penchant is less pure. Thus, John's submission to the Church is the Bastard's idea for supplying the lord-abandoned king with a new ally, but that ally will arrange for his death. Cardinal Pandulph convinces Pembroke to poison John, and the French to applaud the deed, because John's young son can be more easily manipulated than can the grown man. More than Shakespeare, the Swiss dramatist stresses the *calculations* of political personalities. In contrast to Lange, it is not the office that governs the man, but the man who manipulates the office. Dürrenmatt shares neither Shakespeare's desire for order in England nor Lange's belief in monarchy as progress over feudalism. The final hell in England is paved with the Bastard's excellent and reasonable intentions.

Dürrenmatt tightens plot and motivation; he imbues the bloody chronicle with a comic tone through word-play, modern slang, and loose meter. When he retains Schlegel's lines, he often adds syllables, and when he writes his own verse, it sounds like prose. He excises patriotic speeches and injects grotesque images. In Act V especially, Dürrenmatt stages incongruous scenes: John and Pandulph literally share the same bed; each in his washtub, King Philip and Dauphin Lewis receive Cardinal Pandulph.

Without overlong quotation, the respective endings epitomize the difference between Shakespeare's chronicle play and Dürrenmatt's cynical play. Shakespeare's Bastard kneels to Prince Henry and delivers his well-known bravura lines:

This England never did, nor never shall,
Lie at the proud foot of a conqueror
But when it first did help to wound itself.
Now these her princes are come home again,
Come the three corners of the world in arms,
And we shall shock them. Nought shall make us rue
If England to itself do rest but true.

Dürrenmatt's Pembroke offers the Bastard an earldom, but he declines, in order to return to the country, as predicted in the curse of dying John:

Auf deinen Adel, deine Ehren pfeifend,
Mit jeder Kuhmagd schlafend, die ich schnappe,
Mit jeder Wirtshausköchin, deren Hintern
Mir diese Welt voll Finsternis erleuchtet,
Zeug ich Bastarde, wie ich selber einer,
Und senke in das Volk die Kraft des Löwen!
Nur so ist diesem England noch zu helfen.*

But the play's last words are spoken by Pembroke, who discounts such "Narren" as the Bastard.

Remaining fairly faithful to the events of Shakespeare's play, Dürrenmatt cloaks them in his typically modern cynicism. As a town murders by democracy in *The Visit*, as a nuclear physicist is "protected" by an insane psychiatrist in *The Physicists*, moral intention fails grotesquely in this adaptation of *King John*.

Even more grotesque is that failure in Dürrenmatt's second Shakespeare adaptation, *Titus Andronicus*, which he subtitles "Eine Komödie nach Shakespeare." The genre designation is all-important, especially since Dürrenmatt is again fairly faithful to Shakespeare's events. In Dürren-

* Not giving a damn about your titles and honors, sleeping with every farmgirl I catch, I'll produce bastards like myself with every kitchenmaid whose behind lightens this dark world for me; and I sink in the common people the strength of the lion. Only so can this England still be helped.

matt's original "comedies," corpses are strewn as liberally as in Shakespeare's tragedies. In Shakespearean tragedy the hero falls in spite of his good intentions, but Dürrenmatt ridicules the process of falling, and that tonal shift converts potential tragedy into grotesque comedy.

The events of Shakespeare's *Titus* are bloody and extreme: a prisoner is butchered, a father slays his son, Titus' daughter is kidnapped and raped, her husband is slain, Titus' two sons are beheaded though he chops off his hand to save them, the queen bears an illegitimate son, his father kills the midwife, an innocent clown is hanged, the queen and her sons disguise themselves as Revenge, Rape, and Murder, Titus slays those sons and serves them to their mother in a Thyestean feast, Titus kills his daughter Lavinia and the queen Tamora, he is stabbed by Emperor Saturninus who is in turn stabbed by Lucius, the one remaining son of Titus. Finally, Lucius and his uncle attempt to rebuild Rome, after sentencing Aaron to be buried and starved to death. Though the sixteenth-century audience evidently had a taste for such dishes, other centuries have not welcomed *Titus* in the theater. A 1923 performance at Stratford dissolved in audience laughter. Not until 1955, when Peter Brook directed Laurence Olivier as a grief-burdened veteran rather than an avenging maniac, was the play taken seriously.

Dürrenmatt, however, does not take *Titus* seriously. Reducing Shakespeare's fourteen scenes to nine, he retains all the violent deaths, speeding their succession in what has been called cabaret-style.[33] And he adds a few deaths, for good measure. Titus' brother, Marcus Andronicus, a kind of *raisonneur* in Shakespeare, becomes a sycophant of Emperor Saturninus, and is killed by that emperor. An invented Executioner justifies any cruelty, so long as "sagt der Kaiser." Most important is Dürrenmatt's invention of Alarich, ruler of the Goths, to whom Lucius Andronicus turns after his two brothers are executed in Rome. As

Lucius tries to persuade Alarich to learn modern warfare methods, the latter condemns to death successively a Hun, a Slav, a Turk. Alarich is persuaded, and their meeting closes on Alarich's "ewig treuen Bruderkuss." At the end of Dürrenmatt's comedy, after Lucius stabs Saturninus, Alarich stabs Lucius. No Andronicus is left to rebuild Rome, and Alarich orders all Romans destroyed, closing the comedy on the absurdity of destiny:

> Was soll Gerechtigkeit, was soll da Rache?
> Nur Namen sind's für eine üble Mache.
> Der Weltenball, er rollt dahin im Leeren
> Und stirbt so sinnlos, wie wir alle sterben:
> Was war, was ist, was sein wird, muss verderben.*

If Dürrenmatt's *Titus* is a comedy, it is not so by virtue of a happy ending, since all roads lead to ruin, as in *König Johann.* Both adaptations are black comedies, or, in the term usually applied to Dürrenmatt, grotesque comedies, in that the laughter is mixed with horror. Though Dürrenmatt introduces puns, rhymes, and repetitions to arouse laughter, most of the comedy resides in scenes of horror. Not only does the tightened structure stress the poetic injustice already present in Shakespeare, but Dürrenmatt also invents a crowd of crippled veterans who surround Titus, their cynical wit reinforcing their clumsy gestures, both warped by war. In the opening scenes almost the whole cast steps over Titus as a kind of obstacle in their way to the Capitol. After he chops off his hand, he thanks each one who steps over him on the way from the Capitol, but when he receives a basket containing the heads of his two sons, he declares: "Denn Torheit ist, sein Vaterland zu lieben." (41) When Lavinia writes the names of her ravishers in the sand, Titus reacts in rhyme: "Die Hand ist fort / Das Herz verdorrt /

* What's the use of justice and vengeance? They are mere names for a bad production. The earthball rolls around in the void, dying as senselessly as all of us die. Whatever was, is, or will be must rot away.

Es stinkt die Welt wie ein Abort."* (43) Titus gathers his crippled veterans about him: "Den Unsinn / Der Welt kann nur der Wahnsinn noch bezwingen."† (44) "Der Wahnsinn" takes the form of successive stabbings that resemble a comic routine.

Commenting on his adaptation of *Titus*, briefer and freer than his *König Johann*, Dürrenmatt wrote: "Mich lockte die poetische Thematik, in der sich meiner Meinung nach später sowohl der *König Lear* als auch *Hamlet* bewegt."‡ (jacket) This may be tongue-in-cheek provocation, since Dürrenmatt's rhythm, language, and pointless cruelties give his play a cabaret cynicism that does not describe Shakespeare's tragedies, whose seriousness is intensified through their comedy. On the other hand, Dürrenmatt may be reading Shakespeare through the spectacles of Jan Kott, as a playwright of the grotesque. Kott writes: "The downfall of the tragic hero is a confirmation and recognition of the absolute; whereas the downfall of the grotesque actor means mockery of the absolute and its desecration."[34] The absolute can manifest itself in civic order, and Kott uses Dürrenmatt's original plays to illustrate the grotesque he finds in Shakespeare.

Since the publication of Kott's book in English, Shakespeare scholars have laboriously and correctly pointed to the restoration of order at the end of his tragedies, and few have credited Kott with perceiving how precariously that order was based, and with demonstrating how theatrical that precariousness could be. But Dürrenmatt, often dubbed a playwright of the grotesque, felt that he had to write grotesque elements into Shakespeare, in very large letters.

Another German adaptation—of *Measure for Measure*—also introduces grotesque notes into serious scenes, but po-

* My hand is off, my heart dried up; the world stinks like a latrine.

† Only madness can still overcome the world's folly.

‡ I was attracted by the poetic context in which I believe Shakespeare later developed *King Lear* and *Hamlet*.

litical cynicism does not seem to be the motivating drive.[35] The adaptation evidently began as a translation which director Peter Zadek requested in 1967 from playwright Martin Sperr (b. 1944). Three versions were offered, each shorter than the last. With conventional set and costumes in mind, Zadek started rehearsals; he wished sharp realism in each scene of this prose translation. However, stylization gave a more striking result, according to the assistant director, Burkhard Mauer. A fter rehearsing scenes in both styles, and carrying on lively discussions, Zadek decided to abandon previous work on the play, setting each scene only after actual experiment on the rehearsal stage. (This was in 1967, before various theater collectives adopted the process as their basic methodology.) Mauer describes that process as a ritual, and he closes his program note with a clarion call for a new kind of theater: "Das Ergebnis unserer Arbeit liegt jetzt vor Ihnen. Statt Literaturtheater ist es Volkstheater geworden."* Whether or not the result was people's theater, the text is more literary than many subsequent experiments of collective theater.

The simplicity of stage setting contrasts with the rather pretentious program description: "*Mass für Mass* von William Shakespeare in der Übersetzung und Bearbeitung von Martin Sperr unter Mitarbeit von Peter Zadek und Burkhard Mauer als Ausgangspunkt einer Inszenierung des aktuellen Stückgehaltes auf freier Bühne von Peter Zadek."† However, the stage was not quite so free as claimed, since it was framed by high-powered light bulbs. Chairs were the only stage furniture, and the fifteen actors wore dungarees; as the action progressed, both men and women removed their shirts, the latter keeping on their

* The result of our work now lies before you. Instead of a theater of literature, we have people's theater.

†*Measure for Measure* by William Shakespeare in the translation and adaptation of Martin Sperr, with the cooperation of Peter Zadek and Burkhard Mauer, as point of departure for a production of the contemporary content of the play on the free stage of Peter Zadek.

brassieres. Several scenes began with a circle of actors, from which one entered the center to recite his lines, until the recitation developed into a scene.

In the program text the division is not into scenes but into twenty-five *Bilder.* Basically, the text follows Shakespeare's plot, though the name of Mistress Overdone is changed to Frau Meier, Barrabas to Charli; a non-Shakespearean Schaum is introduced, and the actor Georg Martin Bode appears briefly under his own name. Pompi is blind but attentively watches the action.

In spite of simplification of setting, condensation of plot, and determined physicalization, it is possible to feel some concern for the plight of Claudio until the key brother-sister scene, in which Isabella virtually rapes her brother. When the duke suggests the bed-trick, it is made ridiculous through repetition by Mariana and Isabella. While Angelo and Escalus discuss the absent duke, a scream is heard, and we are told that the other actors have lynched the duke, after which Frau Meier puts on his concealing overcoat, to be accepted as his replacement. When Angelo is accused, he asks for death, and the pseudo-duke sentences him, then orders the deaths of Georg Martin Bode and of Elbow. He/she closes the play with a travesty of Shakespeare's lines.

> Dear Isabel,
> I have a motion much imports your good,
> Whereto if you'll a willing ear incline,
> What's mine is yours, and what is yours is mine.
> So, bring us to our palace, where we'll show
> What's yet behind, that's meet you all should know.

> Liebe, schöne Isabella, ich hab eine Bitte, die sehr gut für dich ist: Wenn du es gerne und nicht ungern hörst, dann wird, was mein ist, dein und was dein ist, mein. Bringt uns zu unserem Palast. Sonst ist nichts mehr

> zu sagen und was jetzt kommt, könnt ihr euch denken.* (13)

Shakespeare's problematical play about chastity closes in frivolous titillation.

One might think that this is mere burlesque of Shakespeare's *Measure for Measure,* but apparently the playwright, directors, and performers took it seriously. Reviewers heralded it as a "make-love-not-war Shakespeare." The text has been published only in the theater program, and Martin Sperr has found his own voice as playwright of evil in his native Bavaria. This version is unlikely to be revived, but it is an early example of group adaptation of Shakespeare, with features that would be incorporated into Alternative Theater idiom: minimal set and costumes, arduous physicalization and reduced verbalization, self-conscious imitation of ritual, direct address to the audience, and various states of undress. But the adapted text follows Shakespeare more closely than would be usual in the Alternative Theater—except for the burlesque tone.

Radical change of tone seems to be both intention and achievement of the Zadek-Sperr *Measure for Measure,* as of the two Dürrenmatt adaptations. The Swiss playwright claims politics as his purpose, but Lange more pointedly introduces a modern (Marxist) political viewpoint into his adaptation. The adaptations of Plutarchian tragedies, *Coriolanus* and *Timon,* emphasize a particular attitude toward the hero, often dissolving or resolving Shakespeare's ambiguities, and in the adaptations of Piachaud and Brecht these attitudes are political. Similarly, the condensing and ordering tendency of the Hall-Barton *Wars of the Roses* confers clear purpose on the history plays. This miscellaneous group of adaptations clarifies Shakespeare as to plot,

* Dear, fair Isabel, I have a request which is very good for you. If you hear it willingly and not unwillingly, then what's mine becomes yours, and yours mine. Bring us to our palace. Otherwise, there's no more to be said, and what comes now, you can imagine.

hero, attitude, or politics. Without exception, this group traces Shakespearean events but colors them with modern tints. When the language is Shakespearean (Hall-Barton), the philosophy of order is modern, *pace* Tillyard. When the language is Romantic (Schlegel-Tieck residue), the historical or cynical interpretation is modern. And sometimes the language runs unabashedly to colloquial prose (Piachaud, Osborne, Sperr), implying the modernity of the Shakespearean conception.

The modern colloquial prose of two other adaptations makes such implication more explicit. André Obey (b. 1892) based most of his plays on myth and legend, clothing them in brisk modern French. Working closely with Jacques Copeau and his Compagnie des Quinze, Obey was overvalued during the 1930s. His *Noé*, a sentimental play about the biblical patriarch, influenced Thornton Wilder's *Skin of Our Teeth* and impressed the usually astute critic Francis Fergusson, so that he analyzes it among the masterpieces of his *Idea of a Theater*.

After *Noé* came *Le Viol de Lucrèce* (1931),[36] as Obey intended: "Le premier de ces spectacles 'sentirait le moyen âge et le mystère,' tandis que le second 'aurait le parfum de Shakespeare et de la scène élizabéthaine.' "* (10) In publishing the play some seventeen years after first performance, Obey apparently wished wide diffusion for "le parfum de Shakespeare." He visualized his drama as an oratorio, adding to the Shakespearean cast servants of the household and, pre-eminently, a *Récitant* and *Récitante* to describe, respectively, the emotions of Tarquin and Lucrece. Instead of moving, as Shakespeare does, from Tarquin's inner turmoil to that of Lucrece, Obey has them engage in conflict through the two Narrators "comme des coryphées, mais allégés du choeur, donc plus libres, plus actifs, allant jusqu'à prendre part au drame, à doubler cer-

* The first of these plays "would have the scent of the Middle Ages and mysteries," whereas the second "would have the perfume of Shakespeare and the Elizabethan stage."

tains personnages et même à se substituer à eux."* (122) Actually, however, the Narrators are masked majestic figures in raised chairs, chanting in repetitious prose that strives for dignity.

In Act I, Scene 1, soldiers describe the competitive boasts of the Roman generals about the fidelity of their wives, with Lucrece winning easily. In Scene 2 the *Récitante* describes faithful Lucrece at home, and the *Récitant* describes Tarquin's approach to her home. The act ends when Lucrece welcomes Tarquin to the home of her husband, Collatin—closing on the suspense of the well-made play. In Act II the two Narrators describe Tarquin's guilty approach to the bed of Lucrece—a condensed modernization of Shakespeare's account. When Tarquin reaches her bed, the two principals speak, and the act closes upon Tarquin's threat to malign Lucrece if she does not accede to his lust. In Act III Lucrece, after a puzzling "Mon âme s'est trahie," decides on suicide and then sends for her husband—another climactic curtain. In Act IV she confesses the rape to Collatin, who speaks like a proper bourgeois husband of 1931, questioning his wife: "Jusqu'au bout?" After her confession, Lucrece drops dead, without a hint of the Shakespearean dagger. And Collatin's fellow-warrior Brutus converts her into a symbol: "Il y a une femme, comme celle-ci, noble et pure comme celle-ci, que Tarquin violente chaque jour! Et c'est notre mère a tous! C'est Rome."† (193) All leave, on vengeance bound, while the two Narrators close the drama with phrases of pity for Lucrece.

Obey was not the first French dramatist to approach mythic material in modern colloquial prose. Cocteau precedes him, and he is followed by Giraudoux, Sartre, Anouilh, but he is the only one to use such prose for the

* Like the leaders of the Chorus [in Greek tragedy], but relieved of the Chorus itself, and therefore freer, more active, actually taking part in the drama, to support certain characters and even substitute for them.

† There is a woman like this one, noble and pure like this one, whom Tarquin violates every day! And she is the mother of us all! She is Rome.

Ovidian elaborations of Shakespeare's complaint poem. In spite of the evocative staging, the colloquial diction robs the characters of stature.

Venus and Adonis, Shakespeare's first narrative poem, would seem to offer more fertile terrain for modernization Inherently dramatic, the erotic poem undoubtedly appealed to a sense of lascivious comedy in the aristocratic Elizabethan reader for whom it was intended. Both Shakespeare and Obey evoke laughter at the jaded goddess of love unable to awaken an erotic response in the young hunter Adonis. But Shakespeare moves from comedy into Venus's growing worry about Adonis, when he fails to return from hunting. Venus addresses herself to Death, first blaming her for stealing young Adonis—"thus chides she Death"—then asking pardon in the hope that he may be spared. When Venus finds the mangled body of Adonis, she interprets the mangler, the boar, as one who also loved Adonis—"the loving swine / Sheathed unaware the tusk in his soft groin." Shakespeare suggests a grotesque transformation of Venus into boar, before she curses the day of Adonis's death. After the body of Adonis melts away, flowers grow from his blood, and Venus cradles these to her bosom before returning to heaven.

Obey shifts quite suddenly from a comic to a serious Venus, who tries to persuade Death not to take young Adonis. In vain. Servants and minor characters soon bring the news of Adonis's death to Venus, who does not stir from the garden. They describe the wafting away of his body, and they bring her his bloody handkerchief, from which flowers grow. Adonis is compared to these flowers as the curtain falls, Venus still very much on earth.

Of slight literary quality (though *Le Viol de Lucrèce* was ambitiously produced), the two Obey adaptations are examples of a rarity, a change from narrative to dramatic genre. The reverse process, drama to narrative—is more frequent among Shakespeare offshoots, and it usually entails enough changes to classify it as transformation.

B. Transformation.

Transformation moves Shakespearean characters through non-Shakepearean stories, and perhaps the simplest transformations trace Shakespearean characters in a pre-Shakespearean past or a post-Shakespearean future. Examples of the first are found in the chapters on *Macbeth* and *King Lear* offshoots, but the second may be briefly examined in two slight plays of the 1920s.

Written in 1924, *The Lady of Belmont* by St. John Ervine (1882-1971) seeks to rehabilitate Shylock in accordance with modern liberal sentiment against anti-semitism.[37] The biography of St. John Ervine attests to his long association with the theater in Dublin and London, occasionally working with men of Jewish origin, to one of whom, Lawrence Langner, he dedicates the play.

The Lady of Belmont takes place ten years after Shakespeare's play ends. Portia's husband Bassanio is embarking on an affair with Shylock's daughter Jessica. Arriving from Venice to see his grandsons, Shylock faints at the door of Portia's Belmont estate, where he is treated kindly by his erstwhile opponent. In contrast, Jessica refuses to receive her father in her own house, and Bassanio orders the Jew out of Belmont, increasing the discord between husband and wife.

Shylock bribes Gobbo to lead him to Lorenzo's house, where he inadvertently interrupts a Jessica-Bassanio rendezvous. When Portia and Lorenzo arrive, Shylock swears that he was alone with his grandchildren, but Portia perceives her husband sneaking out. Shylock takes Jessica's family to Venice, thereby also removing her from the temptations of Belmont. Before they leave, Portia muses: "Suddenly I thought to myself, 'Shylock's got his pound of flesh! . . . Nerissa with her drunken, faithless husband, Lorenzo deceived by Jessica, and I married to a husband I despise!' " (93) At the end of the play Portia, the titular Lady of Belmont, and Shylock engage in a debate on anti-semitism, Portia explaining its reasons and Shylock presenting its injustices, but concluding: "We cannot go back, madam—we must go on and mingle with the world and lose ourselves in other men. . . . We must all forgive, because we have so much to be forgiven." (95) "So much," including Shakespeare transformations.

Comparably slight is the fictional transformation of James Branch Cabell (1879-1958) *The Line of Love*.[38] An American Southerner with an elegant style, Cabell was an obscure novelist until his *Jurgen* was condemned for obscenity in 1919. This notoriety and the support of influential H. L. Mencken gave him good sales in the 1920s, before he fell back into obscurity in spite of—or perhaps because of?—prolific production.

The Line of Love is composed of ten episodes (the subtitle is "Dizain des Mariages") of which the third derives from Shakespeare, "The Episode Called Love-Letters of Falstaff." Set in 1414 at the Boar's Head Tavern, the episode shows an aged Falstaff still given to epicurean delights, not the least of which is a pseudo-Shakespearean loquaciousness. A lady comes to visit him: "We have summoned up no very fearful spectre, I think, . . . at most, no worse than a pallid, gentle spirit that speaks—to me, at least—of a boy and a girl who loved each other and were very happy a great while ago." (73) In London to see her son off to the wars, the lady wants to return Falstaff's old love letters, lest they fall into the hands of her grandchildren. After she leaves, Falstaff reads the lies he wrote, muses on the respectable husband he might have been, and closes the anecdote predictably: "A cup of sack to purge the brain! . . . And I will go sup with Doll Tearsheet." (83) The incident, like others in Cabell's collection (first published in 1905, revised 1921), illustrates that golden lads and lasses must, like chimney-sweepers, come to dust, and before that they must become grotesque old men and women.

Cabell's incident could be wrapped around any old man, but he undoubtedly chose Falstaff in a desire to imitate

Shakespeare's comic prose. Though H. L. Mencken in his introduction affirms that Cabell "knows where a red noun should go, and where a peacock-blue verb, and where an adjective as darkly purple as a grape," the colors pale in the shadow of Shakespeare. The Bard himself could not sustain the quality of Falstaff's prose in *The Merry Wives of Windsor,* and Cabell is hardly second-best Shakespeare.

H. L. Mencken may serve as a bridge to the next trivial transformation of Shakespeare, *The Avon Flows* by George Jean Nathan (1882-1958).[39] Mencken championed Cabell, and he occasionally collaborated with Nathan, who was the most powerful American theater critic of the 1920s. His *Avon Flows* dates from 1937, "being an editorial variation constituting a comedy of modern marriage." That "editorial variation" presents a three-act play, in which each of the acts derives from a different Shakespeare play—Act I *Romeo and Juliet,* Act II *Othello,* and Act III *The Taming of the Shrew.* Restricting himself to selected Shakespeare lines, Nathan ends Act I upon Friar Laurence's marriage of Romeo and Juliet. Keeping their Act I names, the star-crossed lovers are transformed into Othello and Desdemona in Nathan's Act II, with Tybalt becoming Iago; this act ends after a jealous Romeo strikes his wife and kicks Tybalt, as in Act IV of *Othello.* Nathan reassigns lines, so that Romeo utters Desdemona's protestations of fidelity. In Nathan's Act III Romeo regains mastery of his household by taming his Jule; the play closes: "Come, Jule, we'll to bed!" Though Nathan's intention may have been merely burlesque, he predicts collage technique, which was introduced as a novelty in the 1960s.

The Avon Flows is only in part an offshoot of *Romeo and Juliet,* and the paucity of *Romeo and Juliet* offshoots was one of the surprises of my research. There are many analogues, but the characters themselves make so brief an appearance in Max Frisch's *Chinese Wall* that it does not deserve discussion. Their modern avatars appear in *Romanoff and Juliet* by Peter Ustinov (b. 1921),[40] replete with balcony and warring families. Ustinov's transformation changes time to the present, place to the imaginary, tragedy to comedy. Ustinov summarizes the plot on his title page: "A comedy of Russian-American relations during the Cold War in and around their embassies in a tiny neutral state in Europe. A young Russian and an American girl fall in love and so create great embarrassment for their diplomat fathers, with at least some moderating of the feud." That feud is further moderated through the lovers' marriage, arranged by the nameless general-president of the smallest country in Europe. The lovers escape from their embassies by descending from their respective balconies on bedsheet-ropes. They then take the place of statues in a church ceremony, and they are married by proxy. Like Restoration adapters of Shakespeare, Ustinov provides a foil-couple in an American capitalist (Juliet's fiancé) and a Russian sloop captain (Romanoff's intended). The Cold War thaws into the improbable warmth of a double wedding.

Shakespeare transformations tend to be slighter than adaptations, but this is not always so. One of the most ambitious transformations is *Die Krönung Richards III* by Hans Henny Jahnn (1894-1959), which preserves some Shakespearean events but invents others.[41] Virtually unknown outside his native Germany, and not well-known in that country, Jahnn was a remarkably versatile autodidact. His literary beginnings coincide with those of Expressionism, and he displays that movement's emotional self-indulgence, formal freedom, and sexual daring, as well as a fascination with several arts. While writing fiction and poetry as well as dramas that were difficult to stage, he learned to restore baroque organs, and he participated in architectural projects. A pacifist, he left Germany during World War I and in 1933. After World Wars I and II, he returned to Germany, pursuing his several crafts until his suicide.

Though he later wrote a *Medea,* his only Shakespeare offshoot was *Die Krönung Richards III,* revised from verse to prose in 1921. Inordinately long, it was produced in shortened versions in Leipzig, 1922, and Berlin, 1926. It is a strange play for a pacifist, since it outdoes Shakespeare in cruelty and bloodshed.

Jahnn's major change in the Shakespearean facts is to have Richard III (who is crowned offstage between Acts I and II) marry his sister-in-law, Queen Elizabeth, after the death of his wife Anne, thus securing firmer hold on the throne. Jahnn's lesser characters—Hastings, Stanley, Catesby, Tyrrel, Gurney—play approximations of their Shakespearean roles, but Queen Elizabeth is steeped in evil. Her hobby is taking adolescent boys as lovers, casting them off when she tires of them. As the play opens, she woos a new lover, Euryalus, then orders her ex-lover, Paris, to be castrated. With the help of a sinister Dr. Pulter, she plans to drink the blood of her new lover after disposing of him. But Euryalus already has a lover, the page Hassan, who hides under the queen's bed while she woos. Gloucester, the future Richard III, breaks into her room, routs out Hassan, and plunges his sword into the two teen-age boys as they cling to one another. The Act I curtain falls as a new couple recognize their common evil:

> Elizabeth: Ihr seid grauenhaft, nicht menschlich; wissend, doch ohne Ziel.
> Richard: Auch Ihr, Frau Königin.* (304)

Act II dramatizes facets of King Richard's *grauenhaft* nature: he urges his pregnant wife to declare her princely sons illegitimate, and when she refuses he plots her murder; he arranges for the off-stage execution of Rivers, Vaughan, and Gray; he pushes his compassionate (and invented) fool out of the window to his death; he reports to his Council that someone has poisoned the queen, and he has the cook tortured; he orders the boy princes imprisoned in the Tower,

* Elizabeth: You are horrible, not human: knowledgeable but purposeless.
Richard: You too, o Queen.

and he implies an order for their murder; he conspires against Lords Hastings and Buckingham. Thus Jahnn combines Shakespeare with an invented Richard who speaks of himself as a "Werkzeug ohne Sinn."

Act III deals in some detail with Richard's betrayal of Buckingham. The queen attempts resistance to Richard, manoeuvring her page and doctor to kill one another. In the Tower the boy princes meet castrated Paris, who dies trying to save them from Gurney and Tyrrell. The boys cling to one another and enter a single coffin, whose lid Tyrrell orders closed. Richard III enters almost immediately and stabs his obedient murderers. Alone, he praises God and plays solitaire through the night. Messengers enter with news of the queen's death and of Buckingham's capture. Richard predicts that at some point he will offer his kingdom for a horse, though what he will most want is a quiet grave. At the play's end Richard tells a German stranger that kings will be powerless in the future: "Die Heiligtümer über Königsleiber wird man zerstören. . . ."* (440) Alone he closes the play: "Weh mir, ein neuer Tag ist da, und ich bin einsam in dem Licht."†

This early Jahnn play announces several themes that were to become obsessive with him: human animality, mysterious destiny, the innocent love of adolescent boys, the evils of heterosexual passion, the cruelties of social organization. Though Jahnn gave less turgid expression to these obsessions in later dramas, he never learned to discipline his dramatic form, but his creations nevertheless achieve elemental power.

A last transformation—in a comic mode—achieves greater power, but before turning to Alfred Jarry's *Ubu Roi*, an exceptional offshoot, I would like to review the entire miscellany. Modern Shakespeare offshoots are initiated by writers or directors who can prove to be hacks or craftsmen. Their intention is modernization, from the Hall-

* The shrines built around kings will be destroyed.

† Woe is me; here is a new day, and I am lonely in the light.

Barton condensation to Ustinov's pacification of the Cold War. But some modernizations reflect a nineteenth-century attitude toward fictional characters as people with complete biographies—Ervine's Shylock or Cabell's Falstaff. The two *Timon* plays and the two Obey plays reveal more than Shakespeare does of the characters' pasts, families, and destinies. However, most modern offshoots are more firmly planted in the twentieth century: the *Coriolanus* versions reflect political cleavages in modern Europe; Lange's *König Johann* springs from a Marxist reading of history; and the two Dürrenmatt adaptations convey their author's political cynicism that borders on nihilism; the collective *Mass für Mass* is a travesty not only on Shakespeare, but on the very possibility of ethical measure. Jahnn's *Richard III* predicts modern preoccupation with immanent, myth-rooted evil.

The appearance of Jarry's *Ubu Roi* in Paris in 1896 is striking in light of the fact that Shakespeare's words, themes, and characters have been modernized less often in French than in English and German. It is even possible to view France as a Shakespearean century behind England and Germany. In the eighteenth century many Shakespeare adaptations were played in Germany and especially England, but, except for a few radical alterations, he was not played at all in France. In the nineteenth century, English actor-managers gradually returned to Shakespeare's text, and German actors gradually turned to the faithful Schlegel-Tieck translations. Paris, on the other hand, slowly admitted faithful translations on its stages, culminating in 1899 in the Morand-Schwob *Hamlet*, starring Sarah Bernhardt. The first complete Shakespeare translation on the Paris stage is usually said to be the Vedel-Loti *Lear* of 1904, directed by André Antoine, the pioneer of realism. But it was not quite complete, since the tragedy closes on Lear's death. Still, the English-German nineteenth-century movement toward fidelity did reach the French stage in the twentieth century. But Jarry closed the nineteenth century in irreverent infidelity.

As performed on the night of December 19, 1896, a notorious night in theater history, *Ubu Roi* was recognized as a burlesque of Shakespeare, among many other things. In my own terms, however, I cannot quite justify its inclusion in this book since *Ubu* does not "contain Shakespeare's own characters" *in propria persona.* Nevertheless, I think it meaningful to discuss *Ubu* as a masterwork nourished by Elizabethan staging (through Lugné-Poe's direction) and Shakespearean reminders.

Ubu Roi was at least eight years in the making, and that making poses a problem for the scholar who is interested in who wrote what.[42] When fifteen-year-old Alfred Jarry (1873-1907) arrived at the Lycée de Rennes in 1888, there existed a series of lampoon sketches about the fat, unpopular physics teacher, M. Hébert. These sketches may have originated with a single student, Charles Morin, or they may have been a collective accumulation. In one episode, M. Hébert, abbreviated to Père Heb or P.H., dueled with the king of Poland. Jarry and Henri Morin, younger brother of Charles, dramatized that incident for performance by puppets in what they called a Théâtre de Phynances. From existing evidence it is impossible to say how Jarry added to these sketches, though he had already composed several farces on his own. Possibly Jarry would have agreed with a statement found in Henri Morin's letter, written fourteen years after Jarry's death: "Depuis l'origine jusqu'aux *Polonais,* le P.H. subit de nombreuses transformations, mais il est et reste un géant malfaisant."[43]* That maleficent giant might have died in Rennes if eighteen-year-old Jarry had not taken him to Paris, there to continue his studies and to continue the adventures of Père Heb, whom he renamed Père Ubu. In 1893 Jarry began to publish bits and pieces of what was to become *Ubu Cocu,* or *Ubu of the Second Cycle,* which included Mère Ubu and Conscience as separate characters who may have been suggested by *Macbeth.*

* From the beginning up until *Les Polonais,* P.H. underwent numerous transformations, but he is and remains a maleficent giant.

In 1896 Jarry urged production of his *Ubu Roi* and/or *Ubu Cocu* on Aurélien Lugné-Poe, the young director of the experimental Théâtre de l'Oeuvre. But first Jarry published *Ubu Roi* as a book, with the following dedication: "Adonc le Père Ubu hoscha la poire, dont fut depuis nommé par les Anglois Shakespeare, et avez de lui sous ce nom maintes belles tragoedies par escript."[44] (30) The pun on "hoscha la poire" (shook-his-pear) testifies to Jarry's knowledge of English, which he had studied before coming to Rennes. The dedication (to Marcel Schwob, who was to translate *Hamlet* for Sarah Bernhardt) testifies to Jarry's whimsical linking of Shakespeare and Ubu, whose portrait he drew with a pear-shaped head.

The book *Ubu Roi* was favorably received by the Paris Symbolists of the 1890s, but the performance of *Ubu Roi* made Jarry famous. At the well-attended dress rehearsal on December 9, 1896, the audience grew unruly only at the third of the five acts, but on opening (and closing) night, December 10, there was a near-riot. Jarry, face painted red, white, and black, introduced his play, but he was evidently inaudible to most of the audience. Then the Comédie Française actor Firmin Gemier (who imitated Jarry's speech in playing Ubu) stepped forward to utter the play's opening word loud and clear: "Merdre." Pandemonium stopped him from continuing while the spectators vociferously attacked or defended the still unplayed play. The scandal carried over into the reviews, some five vigorously supporting *Ubu* and about a dozen vigorously denouncing it. Catulle Mendès, a playwright now forgotten, was prescient in defense:

> Quelqu'un, parmi le tohu-bohu des huées a crié: "vous ne comprendriez pas davantage Shakespeare!" Il a eu raison. Entendons-nous bien: je ne dis pas du tout que M. Jarry soit Shakespeare, et tout ce qu'il a d'Aristophane est devenu un bas guignol et une saleté de funambulasquerie foraine; mais, croyez-le, malgré les

> niaiseries de l'action et les médiocrités de la forme, un type nous est apparu, créé par l'imagination extravagante et brutale d'un homme presque enfant, Le Père Ubu existe.[45]*

(Perhaps the educative effect of *Ubu* contributed to Mendès' duel in 1899, defending Bernhardt's right to play Hamlet!)

In the existence of Père Ubu the plot counts little, yet a summary reveals Shakespearean echoes, mainly from *Macbeth.* In Act I Ubu, ex-king of Aragon and now captain of the Polish dragoons, is incited by his wife to assassinate Polish King Wenceslas and substitute himself on the throne. Unlike Banquo, Ubu's fellow-warrior Bordure agrees to help the usurper to the dukedom of Lithuania. Though Wenceslas decorates Ubu, as Duncan does Macbeth, the conspiracy progresses. In Act II Queen Rosemonde tells the king about premonitory dreams, and she urges him to call off the review of his troops. However, like Shakespeare's Julius Caesar, the king ignores her warning and goes out to his death. The signal is Ubu's "Merdre"; when the conspirators hear it, they surround and kill their monarch. Queen Rosemonde and her son Bougrelas take shelter in a mountain cavern where the ghosts of their ancestors appear to them, and the most ancient spirit gives Bougrelas a sword with which to kill the usurper. On the Polish throne Ubu reveals his insatiable lust for "phynances." In Act III Ubu's reign begins: he executes nobles, judges, and financiers in order to obtain their wealth. He breaks his promise to Bordure, imprisoning him in a dungeon rather than installing him in a dukedom. But Bordure appears in Moscow and

* Someone shouted, in the hurly-burly of the catcalls: "You wouldn't understand Shakespeare any better!" He was right. Let us understand each other: I am in no way saying that Mr. Jarry is Shakespeare; and everything that he has taken from Aristophanes has become a low Punch-and-Judy show and grotesque filth for a fair. But, believe me, in spite of the silliness of the action and the mediocrity of the form, a new type has emerged, created by the extravagant and brutal imagination of a man who is almost a child. Père Ubu exists.

obtains from the Czar an army. Though Ubu refuses to finance his own troops, they arm for war with some momentum, as in Shakespeare's history plays. Ubu carries his "sabre à merdre . . . et le croc à finances." Leaving Mère Ubu to govern the country, he sets out with ferocity: "Torsion du nez et des dents, extraction de la langue et enfoncement du petit bout de bois dans les oneilles [*sic*]."* (88) The act closes upon Mère Ubu's resolution to kill Bougrelas and steal the national treasure.

By the beginning of Act IV she seeks the treasure in the royal crypt of Warsaw Cathedral, but Bougrelas and his men put her to flight. In the meantime Ubu's army is routed in the Ukraine, though he personally tears apart several of his enemies, including Bordure. He and two companions seek shelter in a Lithuanian cavern, where the companions kill a bear, then desert Ubu. In his sleep Ubu summarizes his adventures and his undiminished ferocity: "Décervelez, tudez, coupez les oneilles, arrachez la finance et buvez jusqu'à la mort, c'est la vie des Salopins, c'est le bonheur du Maître des Finances."† (112)

Act V opens with the arrival of Mère Ubu, coincidentally taking refuge in the same cavern as her husband. In the darkness she pretends to be an angel in order to sing her own praises and obtain forgiveness for stealing the national treasure. Discovering her true identity, Ubu is ready to tear her apart when he is interrupted by the arrival of Bougrelas and his men. Aided by sudden reinforcements—"Vive le Père Ubu, notre grand financier!"—and the corpse of the bear, Ubu escapes, after soiling his trousers in fear. No longer covetous of a crown, the Ubs (as Jarry calls them) board a ship for France and ultimately Spain. The sea is

* Torsion of the nose and teeth, extraction of the tongue and thrust of the little twig into the earres.

† Disbrain, killup, chop earres, snatch cash and drink until death; that's the life of the Salopins, that's the happiness of the Master of Finance.

somewhat rough as they round the Cape of Elsinore. They then pass by Germany, but finally no country can rival Poland in beauty: "S'il n'y avait pas de Pologne, il n'y aurait pas de Polonais!" (131) Ubu closes the play subtitled *Les Polonais*.

In *The Banquet Years*, a vivid account of the French avant-garde at the turn of the century, Roger Shattuck suggests the Shakespearean shadings of *Ubu Roi*:

> The motto inscribed on the dedication page of *Ubu Roi* begins thus in fraudulent archaic French: "*Adonc le Père Ubu hoscha la poire, dont fut depuis nommé par les Anglois Shakespeare. . . .*" *Hoscha la poire* translates loosely into "shook (his) pear (head)"—namely Shakespeare. It comes as no surprise, then, that Ubu enacts a schoolboy travesty of King Lear's fate, and instead of losing a kingdom usurps one. Like Macbeth, Ubu is tempted to his first crime by his wife, who fires his ambitions. The assassination parodies Brutus's plot against Julius Caesar, including the queen's dream of evil foreboding. Most obviously, Ubu derives from Falstaff, whose benignly corrupt personality could never be confined to one play or action.[46]

To these parallels may be added the closet-scene from *Hamlet* and the cavern-scene from *Ubu*, in which both mother-obsessed sons are haunted by ancestral ghosts. The family tree of ghosts may correspond to Macbeth's vision of Banquo's descendants. And the many battles (which Jarry wanted played with a one-man army) burlesque those of Shakespeare's history plays.

The basic plot of *Ubu Roi* is loosely structured on that of *Macbeth*: a usurper kills a king and then is deposed by the king's son. When Mère Ubu tries to spur her husband's desire for the Polish crown, he replies in a parody of Macbeth's objection to the Witches: "Le roi Venceslas est encore bien vivant; et même en admettant qu'il meure, n'a-t-il pas des légions d'enfants?"* (34) As Mère Ubu arouses his ambition, she praises him in words that recall those of Lady Macbeth: "Ah! bien, Père Ubu, te voilà devenu un véritable homme."† (36) But it is Bordure who wants to imitate Macbeth's bloody deed: "Moi, je suis d'avis de lui ficher un grand coup d'épée qui le fendra de la tête à la ceinture."[47]‡ (48)

The personality of the usurper is much more significant than these few verbal echoes or the plot structure. As Shattuck notes, Ubu resembles Falstaff in physique, cowardice, and appetite. However, Jarry's Ubu is strained through Macbeth and a child's vision; he is neither benign nor corrupt, but ruthless and direct. Ubu combines Falstaff's gusto for food and Macbeth's lust for power. Above all, however, Ubu wants money. *Phynances* and *Merdre* link Jarry's Ubu plays, as Freud was also to link them.

A monster of anarchic self-indulgence, Ubu towers over his several backgrounds. His evil is amoral and unsubtle, with none of Macbeth's preoccupations about guilt or decorum. He cowers when faced by strong opponents but tears the weak ones apart. He relishes inventive tortures as he devours all forms of wealth, and he relishes the neologisms that have entered the French language with all their vulgar power of suggestion—*gidouille, bouzine, sagouin, bouffre,* and the thirty-three times repeated *merdre.* Instead of dying in a duel, Ubu runs away from his opponents. *Ubu Roi* changes Shakespeare's tragic ending to rollicking comedy, in keeping with the whole spirited farce.

Ubu is anti-Shakespearean in temper, since it revolutionizes esthetics and ethics. The serious staging of tragedy is

* King Wenceslas is still very much alive; and even if he were to die, has he not legions of children?

† Ah! good, Père Ubu, now you've become a true man.

‡ I'm of a mind to clout him with a good sword-blow that will split him from head to waist.

mocked by Jarry's scene directions: heroes move like marionettes, geographic leaps are announced by signs, horses are made of cardboard, warring armies are played by a single soldier. A French tradition of resonant rhetoric is ridiculed by colloquialisms, fake archaisms, and childish excremental neologisms. *Ubu* has been interpreted as a reaction against realism,[48] and it is certainly that. But realism in the French theater is the legitimate offspring of the well-made play, which in turn is the descendant of both classical tragedy and bourgeois *drame*. The whole family is marked by coherent action, clearly designated setting, suspenseful time of play, and adoration of a single figure or two. It is against this family and its values that *Ubu* jeers, since all traditional values are grist for Ubu's "*merdre*." With extraordinary prescience, Jarry theatricalizes a monster whose frank desire for "Phynances" erupts into a delirium of destruction.

Artless on its surface, *Ubu Roi* challenges ethics and esthetics because its protagonist is innocent of both. Ubu behaves with the selfish candor of a child, reveling in excrement and demolition, without risking his skin. Some of Ubu's early admirers were men of nuance and sensitivity—Mallarmé, Valéry, Symons, Yeats—and yet they understood that this creature of boundless and vulgar appetite appealed to the child in most of us, merrily and murderously fulfilling lusts that are restrained by adults during our actual childhood.

From the first, there were many who refused to recognize this uncharming myth of childhood. Not until fourteen years after Jarry's death did Charles Chassé give the authorship of *Ubu* to the Morin brothers, while insisting on its worthlessness. That book concludes:

> Quel est le véritable auteur de cette ouvrette? La question en soi est peu importante et les frères M*** en conviennent avec moi. L'important est de savoir si,

maintenant que l'outre est vide de tout le vent qui la gonflait, elle pourra, néanmoins, parvenir à rester debout.[49]*

Precisely. The Ubu-goatskin has remained standing, round and tall, a superb example of modern myth.

Whatever the origin of Ubu, Jarry must be credited with the marvelously impudent harmony of the parts of *Ubu Roi*. Jarry himself was probably obsessed with the figure because he sensed its mythic dimension. In the program note to the first performance Jarry wrote that the neologism "Cornegidouille" summarizes Ubu's tripartite power, based on "appétits inférieurs"—physics, "phynance," and "merdre." Jarry affirms: "Monsieur Ubu est un être ignoble, ce pourquoi il nous ressemble (par en bas) à tous."† (23) Ubu originated as a schoolboy caricature, and Jarry's genius was never to allow the fully grown work to violate the *merdre*-centered, money-centered, phrasemongering titan. Ubu resembles us all "par en bas" in all senses of *bas*. We recognize ourselves in him; we shrink from ourselves in him even as we warm to him.

Roland Barthes, reviewing the *Ubu* production of the French National Popular Theater (1958), wrote: "Molière a fustigé les médecins, Lesage les financiers, et Jarry nos ministres, tout cela est de la même veine: on sourit, cela ne fait de mal à personne."[50]‡ But I think that we smile *and* we hurt. We warm to the monster even as we see his monstrosity in ourselves.

It is nearly a century since Ubu exploded into theater, and in that interval Jarry himself came to resemble his cre-

* Who is the true author of this little work? The question in itself is scarcely important and the M. brothers agree with me. The important thing is to know whether, now that the goatskin is empty of all its wind, it can still manage to stand upright.

† Mister Ubu is an ignoble being, which is why he resembles us all (from below).

‡ Molière slapped the doctors, Lesage the bankers, and Jarry our government officials; all that is part of the same vein: we smile, it hurts no one.

ation, political figures came to resemble his creation, Artaud's experimental theater bore Jarry's name, and, particularly since World War II, daily life has acquired the texture of an excremental farce. *Ubu* has proved almost as prophetic as Shakespeare.

Chapter 2

Macbeth: Poor Players That Strut and Fret

In contrast to the Shakespeare hopscotch of the last chapter, each of the next four chapters focuses on offshoots of a single play. This *Macbeth* section examines the offshoots chronologically because they accumulate into a discontinuous history of modern theater styles, with the notable exception of the dominant style, realism.

Macbeth has long been susceptible of adaptation. Even John Milton thought of writing a *Macbeth,* but the first actual adaptation was published in 1674 and played over a decade earlier. Its author is William Davenant, who, according to John Aubrey, "seemed contented enough to be thought [Shakespeare's] son."[1] Theatrically, however, Davenant was not a loyal son to his putative father, since he altered *Macbeth* to the taste of his time. Purifying the tragic mood, Davenant dropped the comic porter; providing foils for the Macbeths, he expanded the parts of the Macduffs. Davenant clarified images, smoothed pentameters, replaced metaphors with similes, and robbed the dialogue of its Shakespearean density. Typical are his revisions of Macbeth's reaction to the death of his wife:

> She should have Di'd hereafter, I brought
> Her here, to see my Victimes, and not to Die.
> To Morrow, and to Morrow, and to Morrow,
> Creeps in a stealing pace from Day to Day,
> To the last Minute of Recorded Time:
> And all our Yesterdays have lighted Fools
> To their Eternal night: Out, out short Candle,
> Life's but a Walking Shaddow, a poor Player
> That Struts and Frets his Hour upon the Stage,
> And then is Heard no more. It is a Tale

> Told by an Ideot, full of Sound and Fury
> Signifying Nothing.[2] (102)

This first *Macbeth* adaptation simplifies the conflict between ambition and rectitude, the Macbeth couple representing the former and the Macduffs the latter. But the two members of the Macbeth couple are not equally ambitious; at least they do not simultaneously translate their ambition into deeds. Any production of *Macbeth* has to proportion the hero's ambition against that of his wife, and Davenant presents an evil Lady Macbeth who blames her husband for her own misdeeds:

> You were a Man.
> And by the Charter of your Sex you shou'd
> Have govern'd me, there was more crime in you
> When you obey'd my Councels, then I contracted
> By my giving it. (92-93)

Unliberated in today's sense, she blames the Witches a moment later: "Curse on your Messengers of Hell. Their Breath / Infected first my Breast." In her guilt she sees a ghost, invisible to Macbeth. But he alone sees the witches, whose role is enlarged, foreshadowing many subsequent productions of *Macbeth* and its offshoots. Davenant's *Macbeth*—clear, tidy, and moral—was long preferred to Shakespeare's original. Today we laugh at it, but our century's *Macbeth* offshoots reflect our taste, as his reflected that of the Restoration.

In 1744 actor-manager David Garrick announced that he would revive *Macbeth* as written by Shakespeare. However, Garrick's *Macbeth* did not fully restore the Folio text; the Porter and young Macduff remain absent, and the Witches are all too present. In performance, Garrick subsequently alternated between Shakespeare and Davenant, with the same underlying conception of his Macbeth, who displayed common humanity and uncommon courage, both faltering at the murder of Duncan. Outnumbered by his enemies, Garrick's Macbeth dies heroically onstage, mouthing a blank verse passage that recalls the last soliloquy of Marlowe's Faustus:

> 'Tis done! the scene of life will quickly close.
> Ambition's vain, delusive dreams are fled,
> And now I wake to darkness, guilt and horror.
> I cannot bear it! let me shake it off—
> 'Two' not be; my soul is clogg'd with blood—
> I cannot rise! I dare not ask for mercy—
> It is too late, hell drags me down. I sink,
> I sink—Oh!—my soul is lost forever! (15)

This interpolated finale arouses sympathy for a basically noble Macbeth who is misled by conniving women—wife and Weird Sisters. But such lines belie Garrick's claim of producing Macbeth as written by Shakespeare, to which a rival actor, Richard Quin, responded: "What does he mean? Don't I play *Macbeth* as written by Shakespeare?"[3] Quin didn't even know he was acting in Davenant's popular adaptation.

In the twentieth century actors would know the answer to Quin's question, but directors nevertheless stage *Macbeth* not as written by Shakespeare. The Bard's shortest tragedy has been remolded for diverse reasons. Unlike *Hamlet,* in which individuals and nations see *im*pressions of themselves, *Macbeth* productions tend to be *ex*pressions of a particular enthusiasm.

These expressions form a discontinuous history of modern theater, and that history begins on December 10, 1896, with the first performance of *Ubu Roi,* whose slight debt to Shakespeare has been described in Chapter 1. In the audience that night was a young Irishman who understood little French, but who understood *Ubu* better than many of Jarry's countrymen. W. B. Yeats' account, not published until 1922, has often been quoted:

> I go to the first performance of Alfred Jarry's *Ubu Roi*, at the Théâtre de L'Oeuvre, with the Rhymer who had been so attractive to the girl in the bicycling costume. The audience shake their fists at one another, and the Rhymer whispers to me, "There are often duels after these performances", and he explains to me what is happening on the stage. The players are supposed to be dolls, toys, marionettes, and now they are all hopping like wooden frogs, and I can see for myself that the chief personage, who is some kind of King, carries for sceptre a brush of the kind that we use to clean a [water] closet. Feeling bound to support the most spirited party, we have shouted for the play, but that night at the Hôtel Corneille I am very sad, for comedy, objectivity, has displayed its growing power once more. I say: "After Stéphane Mallarmé, after Paul Verlaine, after Gustave Moreau, after Puvis de Chavannes, after our own verse, after all our subtle colour and nervous rhythm, after the faint mixed tints of Conder, what more is possible? After us the Savage God."[4]

Yeats was only a little premature in mourning the death of subtle color and nervous rhythm. He himself used them in his verse plays, and Gordon Bottomley (1874-1948), much influenced by Yeats, tried to use them in *his* verse plays based on *Macbeth* and *King Lear*. Both these plays, *Gruach* and *King Lear's Wife* are transformations in that they dramatize Shakespeare's characters in their pre-Shakespearean years.

As St. John Ervine extrapolates *The Merchant of Venice* forward, Bottomley extrapolates *Macbeth* backward into the past of Shakespeare's characters. In *Gruach* Macbeth meets Gruach, the future Lady Macbeth.[5] A descendant of an older line than King Duncan's, she is betrothed to a royal Scot. The night before her wedding, the king's envoy Macbeth loses his way, finds himself at her lonely castle, and the young pair experience a dark attraction for one another. Walking in her sleep, Gruach comes to Macbeth during the night, then wakens to urge him to flee with her, even though this means his betraying hospitality by stealing the bride-to-be.

Though Bottomley's *Gruach* was published in 1921, it lingers over the faded blank verse of nineteenth-century romanticism, and it shares the nineteenth-century attitude to Shakespeare's characters as real people with complete biographies. The two are poorly blended. Bottomley strives for credible psychology in painting Gruach as a Hedda Gabler, but her sleepwalking is unmotivated and untinged by guilt. Bottomley strives for delicate blank verse, but his diction is neither Elizabethan nor modern. An example is Gruach's effort to inspire Macbeth:

> You can be great if you are so great-hearted.
> You are my redeemer, you shall have my faith;
> Service, and I can serve you with men's truth;
> Devotion, and I could wreck myself, my world,
> To reach its end, your good. (47)

The dramatic efforts of the English Romantic poets were marred by the heritage of Shakespeare, and this is true, too, of Gordon Bottomley, a latter-day Romantic, even though Sybil Thorndike played Gruach in the first London performance. Bottomley's *Gruach* is exceptional among twentieth-century *Macbeth* transformations, in its combination of outworn phrasing, realistic psychology, and atmospheric effect.

It was time, by the 1920s, for drama to live up to the theater advances of Craig, Copeau, Stanislavsky, Meyerhold. In France the very Lugné-Poe whom Jarry persuaded to stage *Ubu* managed to keep the experimental Théâtre de l'Œuvre going (with interruptions) until 1929, playing a largely non-French repertory, including Shakespeare translations. In 1922 he revived *Ubu* to an icy reception, but it was not yet the respectable classic that Jarry had predicted, with official honors bestowed on its creator:

> Nous deviendrons aussi des hommes graves et gros et des Ubus et après avoir publié des livres qui seront très classiques, nous serons tous probablement maires de petites villes où les pompiers nous offriront des vases de Sèvres, quand nous serons académiens, et à nos enfants leurs moustaches dans un coussin de velours; et il viendra de nouveaux jeunes gens qui nous trouveront bien arriérés et composeront pour nous abominer des ballades; et il n'y a pas de raison pour que ça finisse.[6]*

Since there is no reason for it to end, each successive generation continues to show its contempt for its respected predecessors.

Over three decades apart, Alfred Jarry and E. E. Cummings (1894-1962) showed contempt for the same respectable predecessor, realistic staging—each in his own way. *Him* (1927) is almost as oblique a *Macbeth* offshoot as *Ubu*, but it does contain the Shakespearean Weird Sisters.[7] Possibly (though not probably) Cummings knew *Ubu*, since he drove an ambulance in France during World War I. Ironically, he was imprisoned by the French, but nevertheless spent 1921-1923 and holidays thereafter in the heady expatriate air of Paris. In America Cummings published an autobiographical novel and idiosyncratic poetry.

Him was his first venture into drama, preceded in 1926

* We too will become grave portly men and Ubus; after publishing books that will be classics, we will all probably be mayors of towns in which firemen will present us with Sèvres vases when we enter the Academy, and will present our children with their moustaches in a velvet pillow. And a new generation will find us very much dated and will compose ballads to show their contempt for us, and there is no reason for it to end.

by a brief stint of theater reviewing for *The Dial.* As reviewer, Cummings inveighed against American theater realism, calling instead for the theatricality of such native popular forms as burlesque, minstrel show, vaudeville, and especially circus. At the same time, Cummings apparently knew that Expressionism was in the air on both sides of the Atlantic. He tried to merge that newest dramatic style, a residue of *Macbeth,* and an amalgam of American popular theater.

Robert Maurer has aptly summarized the ingredients of *him*: "First, a large portion of burlesque, a little Dada, and a soupçon of Surrealism. Second, a story which was not a story, two characters without real names, one character who played nine parts, a great deal of theorizing about love and art, much genuine passion, and an ending that might be regarded as tragic."[8] Though the ending does not seem to me tragic, and though the Surrealistic associations are rationally explicable (induced by an anesthetic), this summary of variety suggests why *him* was misunderstood when staged by the Provincetown Players in 1928.

Even today, nearly half a century later, events are not quite pellucid. In 1950 the intrepid Eric Bentley was the first to state the play's central situation: "*Him* is about a young American couple [Him and Me] and their quest for reality. The action is seen through the eyes of Me who is lying under an anesthetic awaiting the birth of a child."[9] The quest structure links the play to Expressionism, but unlike most Expressionist plays, which view the action through the eyes of the questing protagonist, *him* lacks that fixed focus. Cummings' text is not as clear as Bentley's summary. The play nevertheless meets Expressionist criteria as delineated by such scholars as Walter Sokel: subjectivity, distortion of plot and language, staging of metaphor, dreamlike irrationality rather than Surrealist rendition of actual dreams. Sokel writes: "What strikes one first about Expressionist plays is an extremism of theme, language, stagecraft, mixed with . . . features of realistic or classical drama."[10] All the extremisms are extreme in *him*; realistic features are absent; but *Macbeth* supplies a classical residue.

In the first of Cummings' three acts the scenes alternate between Him-Me conversations and the pronouncements of the Weird Sisters, whose name and prophetic role derive from *Macbeth*. Cummings' Act II stages a play by its hero, Him (or his avatar O. Him) in nine scenes, a phantasmagoria of modern American life. Act III returns to the alternating scenes of Act I, with the addition of a *Walpurgisnacht* in the Paris market and a Vanity Fair in an American circus, featuring nine freaks.

The Weird Sisters are present in five scenes, and unlike spectacular witches of English stage tradition, they are tame and domestic. With backs to the audience and masked faces to the backdrop on which is painted Me under an anesthetic, they knit in rocking-chairs. Though named after Shakespeare's supernatural figures, they are classical in occupation, since the spinning Fates determined the length of each human life, and they were sometimes thought to be present at each human birth. Cummings' Weirds combine classical and Shakespearean involvement with birth, death, and prophecy. Like the Fates, Cummings' Weirds express pleasure at wholesale death. Like Shakespeare's prophetic hags, they foresee the hero's future; they read Him's palm in traditionally gnomic phrases but modern idiom. Their pronouncements culminate in statements of relevance to Him as playwright: "You suffer from noble-blood-poisoning. Time is the autobiography of space. Give a woman everything and she has nothing. Life is a matter of being born. Treat a man like dirt and he will produce flowers. Art is a question of being alive." (16) Unlike their ancestors in *Macbeth*, the Weirds do not spur the hero's ambition; they don't have to; he has already dedicated himself to art.

Much of *him* is played against a backdrop of Me under an anesthetic during the birth of her baby. The utterances of the three Misses Weird (Stop, Look, and Listen) are climaxed by their hostility to birth. In the penultimate scene of the play the three Weird Sisters begin as an audience for circus freaks, but they end as metaphoric freaks, in opposing life. To the ninth circus freak, Me's newborn baby, the Weird Sisters react disgustedly: "It's all done with mirrors!" (111) An invisible mirror has been hanging on the invisible wall of Cummings' stage room (invisibility mocking the realist stage convention), which has been a delivery-room for births that parallel that of the baby—the new and separate self-awareness of Him and Me.

Cummings' Weirds, like those of *Macbeth,* are steeped in evil, and yet they speak truth. The Weirds tell Him obliquely that art feeds on life, that the creative artist must lead a creative life: "Art is a question of being alive." In her own way this is also what Me tells Him throughout the play: that Him's surface brilliance is trivial, for true significance lies in deep feeling. Though it is hard to impose sequence and coherence on Him's scenes with Me, her attitude is consistent. An anti-Lady Macbeth, Me rejects the ambition of Him's art; she is involved in birth and not murder. She wants Him to accept the personal; hence her name *Me* in contrast to her lover's preoccupation with externals, suggested by his name *Him.*

Shakespeare's Macbeth is conquered by Macduff, who fulfills the Witches' prophecy because he is not of woman born (naturally). Him is challenged by a baby, naturally born of Me. Cummings parodies Shakespeare's Weird Sisters, but his main plot performs a serious inversion on the pattern of *Macbeth,* above all on the function of Macbeth's mate. Rather than dying by her own hand, Me reveals Him's inadequacy, for he cannot believe what is true—stage reality in opposition to conventional realism.

Him transformed aspects of *Macbeth* to become a milestone in American non-realistic theater. Less than a decade later, an adaptation of *Macbeth* became a milestone in the social aspect of American theater. In 1936 John Houseman, first head of the American Works Progress Administration Negro Theatre, asked twenty-one-year-old Orson Welles to stage an Elizabethan drama. In spite of his youth, Welles had lived with Shakespeare for years. As a child he attended professional productions and staged his own. At the progressive Todd School he played Marc Antony, the Soothsayer, and Cassius in his own production of *Julius Caesar* (at the age of thirteen). At Todd, too, he first telescoped Shakespeare's eight history plays. After graduation from Todd, Welles went to Europe and at sixteen played a season at Dublin's Gate Theatre, including the roles of the Ghost and Fortinbras in *Hamlet*. He left the Gate Theatre when he could not persuade the management to let him play Othello. Spurned on Broadway, he returned to the Todd School, and with headmaster Roger Hill he published illustrated acting editions of *Julius Caesar, Twelfth Night*, and *The Merchant of Venice*.[11] At nineteen he was admitted to the Broadway company of Katharine Cornell, where Houseman noticed his "overwhelming and unforgettable Tybalt."

After Houseman gave Welles the major role in Archibald MacLeish's *Panic*, the thirty-three-year-old director listened in fascination as the twenty-year-old actor planned exuberantly for *'Tis Pity She's a Whore*, "of such energy and violence as New York had never seen."[12] Actual production never began, but Welles imbued *Macbeth* with its energy and violence.

When Houseman asked Welles to direct a classic with a Negro cast, "Orson said yes immediately, then called me at two in the morning to announce that [his wife] Virginia had just had an inspiration: our first production would be *Macbeth*, laid in the island of Haiti in the early nineteenth century, with the witches as Voodoo priestesses!"[13] Welles later told Bosley Crowther of *The New York Times*:

> We were very anxious to do one of Shakespeare's dramas in the Negro Theatre . . . and *Macbeth* seemed, in all respects, the most adaptable. The stormy career of Christophe, who became "The Negro King of Haiti"

> and ended by killing himself when his cruelty led to a revolt, forms a striking parallel to the history of Macbeth. The costumes and settings of the production are therefore in the period of Haiti's grimmest turbulence. Place names have been altered with particular care to retain the rhythm of Shakespeare's lines. Malcolm and Donalbain don't flee to England but to "the Coast". . . . The witch element in the play falls beautifully into the supernatural atmosphere of Haitian voodooism. We've taken full advantage of that. Instead of using just three witches, as most productions of *Macbeth* conventionally do, we have an entire chorus of singers and dancers. And Hecate, who is seldom presented, is the leading spirit in their midst—a sort of sinister Father Divine—a man witch who leads the others.[14]

Welles was wrong in thinking that a full chorus of witches was original, but he was right in realizing the spectacular impact of the Black Voodoo *Macbeth.*

Harlem's Lafayette Theater was to house the large all-Negro company made up of "an amazing mishmash of amateurs and professionals, church members and radicals, sophisticates and wild ones, adherents of Father Divine and bushmen from Darkest Africa"—137 strong.[15] The miracle in 1936 was that Welles was able to find Black professionals for the major roles. Tall, light Jack Carter, fresh from success as Crown in *Porgy,* was Macbeth; the experienced actress Edna Thomas was a maternal Lady Macbeth, and RADA graduate Eric Burroughs played that virtually invented character of Hecate, replete with twelve-foot bull-whip. Canada Lee, fresh from the prize-fighting ring, played Banquo. In addition to witches and ghosts, the company boasted a troup of African drummers coached by Asadate Dafora Horton, later minister of culture of the Republic of Sierra Leone.

Most of Welles's changes involved the Witches and especially Hecate. The Voodoo *Macbeth* opens with Chief Witch Hecate on stage, and he speaks each of the three act-endings by which Welles punctuated the tragedy: "Peace! The charm's wound up!"[16] After the prophecies to Banquo and Macbeth, Hecate asserts his authority over the other Witches, reciting the spurious lines of the Folio's Act III, Scene 5. Hecate rhythmically underlines Macbeth's panic in "Is this a dagger which I see before me . . . ?" Though the Witches are not visible just before Macbeth's murder of Duncan, their Voodoo chants are audible. After Duncan's murder and the court's dispersal, Hecate and the Witches dominate the stage, insistently evil. Voodoo drumming and chanting precede Banquo's murder, and Hecate is the Third Murderer. Banquo's Ghost materializes as a giant death mask, after which Macbeth hears Voodoo music and sees Hecate beckoning. It is Hecate who convinces Macbeth to murder the Macduff family, to whom is added a newborn babe: "Seize on Macduff, give to the edge o' the sword / His Wife, his babes, and all the unfortunate souls / That trace him in his line." (But mother and son meet death by shooting, not the sword.) The Witches are mocking witnesses of Lady Macbeth's sleepwalking. Hecate instructs Macduff in the mechanics of moving Birnam Wood to Dunsinane. The final duel between Macbeth and Macduff takes place high on a backstage battlement, beginning with guns and ending with swords, Macduff running Macbeth through onstage.

> MACBETH falls dead. The derisive cackle of the witches is heard. MACBETH has fallen so his body is hidden behind the battlements at the top of the tower. MACDUFF kneels behind this during the laughter and rises to silence it, holding in his hand MACBETH's bloody head. MACDUFF throws the head into the mass of waving leaves below. . . . At this the army drops the branches and jungle collapses; revealing a stage full of people. MALCOLM is on the throne, crowned. All bow before him—All but HECATE and

> the Three Witches who stand above the body of LADY MACBETH. THEY have caught MACBETH's head and they hold it high, triumphantly.
>
> Hecate closes the tragedy: "Peace! The charm's wound up!" So reads the script, and so it was played most nights. Just before moving downtown to white New York, however, Eric Burroughs as Hecate strode to the front of stage, held Macbeth's head high, and shouted the well-known line of Father Divine: "Peace! It's wonderful!"[17] He brought the house down with tumultuous recognition.

Opening in Harlem on April 14, 1936, the Voodoo *Macbeth* ran for ten weeks without an empty seat, as opposed to the single performance of *Ubu,* or twenty-seven of *him.* The reviews were favorable if somewhat condescending. Then the Voodoo *Macbeth* moved downtown to the Adelphi Theatre with continued acclaim, and the production toured WPA theaters throughout the country.

Replaced by Negro administrators, Houseman and Welles left the Works Progress Administration to found the Mercury Theatre, which produced a modern dress, anti-fascist *Julius Caesar* and, with Theatre Guild backing, a short-lived out-of-New-York tryout of *Five Kings.* The latter was Welles' anthology of Shakespeare's York-Lancaster sequence, the five kings being Richard II, Henry IV, Henry V, Henry VI, and Richard III. Intended for performance on two successive nights, the Shakespearean material was (precariously) joined by excerpts from *Holinshed's Chronicles.* Welles was to direct and to play Falstaff.

To finance the colossal project, Welles signed a Hollywood contract which resulted in *Citizen Kane.* It is to film rather than the stage that Welles committed his subsequent Shakespeare offshoots—*Macbeth, Othello,* and *Falstaff* or *Chimes at Midnight.*[18]

Houseman summarizes a sad aftermath to the Voodoo *Macbeth*:

> Negro playwriting was not appreciably encouraged by our efforts, and Negro actors (with a few notable exceptions) were held, for another twenty years, within the galling bounds of stereotyped roles. The theatre technicians . . . (being excluded from every professional theatre union in America except as cleaners or janitors) went back into other trades. No Negro company came into existence for thirty years after the dissolution of the Federal Theatre and no Negro audience clamored for a continuation of the entertainment they had apparently enjoyed under the auspices of the WPA.[19]

Forty years later Black Theater is one of the liveliest aspects of theater in America. A new age reflects a new Black artistic consciousness, and in 1973 an American Black group returned *Macbeth* to Harlem, as street theater with a Haitian setting, under the title *Mr. Duvalier.* In October, 1973 the Caribbean-American Theatre in New York City played a *Black Macbeth* directed by Sullivan H. Walker. Though Banquo's heirs may reign in Britain, *Macbeth* has been popular in countries of African culture, where Zulu and Nigerian adaptations emphasize Macbeth's scorn for a native tribal civilization. Each of these productions was individually conceived, but the totality testifies to the ethnic attraction of *Macbeth.*

Unable to see or gather information about these productions (Their directors do not answer letters.), I turn to Europe to continue the discontinuous history of modern Western theater, traceable through *Macbeth* offshoots. *Ubu* and *him* were radical and oblique transformations of Shakespeare's tragedy, and the Voodoo *Macbeth* an adaptation steeped in racial consciousness. On the European continent, class consciousness rather than race consciousness colored Bert Brecht's treatment of *Macbeth,* whose first version dates from 1927, the year *him* was written.

In the 1920s, as Brecht was finding his dramaturgical

stance, bourgeois German theater was concerned with how to perform the classics, among them Shakespeare. At the age of twenty-five, as Dramaturg of the Munich Kammerspiel, Brecht briefly considered adapting *Macbeth,* but instead collaborated with Lion Feuchtwanger on an adaptation of Marlowe's *Edward II.* In effect, Brecht was saying that one should perform the classics by not performing them, for a virtually unknown Marlowe (in Germany) was not a classic. He explains his choice: "Wir wollten eine Aufführung ermöglichen, die mit der Shakespeare tradition der deutschen Bühnen brechen sollte, jenem gipsig monumentalen Stil, der den Spiessbürgern so teuer ist."* (GW XVII, 951)

In 1927 Radio Berlin commissioned a *Macbeth* from Brecht, and he collaborated with the station director, Alfred Braun. Broadcast on October 14, 1927, the script has been lost. All that survives are Brecht's Introduction, two manuscript pages in the Brecht Archives, and a description in a book by a hostile critic, Erich Schumacher. But this is sufficient to indicate that Brecht's radio *Macbeth* was one of his first efforts at epic dramaturgy.

Brecht's Introduction is typical of his ambivalent attitude toward Shakespeare; for about half the piece he appears to denigrate the Bard but then terminates with measured praise. He begins provocatively: "Einige meiner Freunde haben mir offenherzig und rückhaltlos versichert, dass sie sich für das Stück 'Macbeth' auf keinen Fall interessieren würden."† (GW XV, 115) He does not name these friends but agrees that *Macbeth* is logically and psychologically flawed. Moreover, the most important part of the play "die den Macbeth in blutige, aber aussichtslose Unterneh-

* We wanted a production that would break with the Shakespeare tradition of the German theater—that plaster monument style cherished by the bourgeoisie.

† Some of my friends have frankly and openly assured me that they were not at all interested in the play *Macbeth*.

mungen verwickelt,"* cannot be represented in today's theater for reasons impossible for him to go into. Brecht then turns from criticizing Shakespeare to criticizing the contemporary German theater, which he feels cannot represent life accurately; Shakespeare's theater could, because epic elements could be performed.

Brecht's radio *Macbeth* evidently tried to combine Shakespeare's material with a revaluation of its ideas through epic dramaturgy. Most important is Brecht's first use of a narrator who not only summarizes background information about the sequence of scenes but evidently assigns each scene an interpretive title, as in Brecht's later epic plays. The action itself opens not on the Witches but on the battlefield. In Schumacher's description: "Aus dem Lärm einer modernen Schlacht lösten sich die Stimmen des 'Felgeistlichen,' des 'Pacifisten,' eines 'Etappenhelden,' des 'schneidigen Offiziers,' des 'Landesverräters,' des 'Unhelden,' eines 'Okkultisten' und eines 'Sterbenden.' Den Text mussten verunstaltete Stellen aus den Schlachtenszenen der Königsdramen von Sh. liefern."[20]† Possibly the next scene was a conversation between Macbeth and Banquo, as found in the Brecht Archives manuscript.[21] Macbeth predicts the royal inheritance for Banquo's progeny, and Banquo predicts Macbeth's rise to the throne. Neither of them mentions the Witches.

As the action progresses, scene fades into scene in montage effect. Schumacher says that this is especially noticeable at the banquet honoring King Duncan, which is not shown by Shakespeare. The last few scenes are much shortened and joined by music. Schumacher denounces Brecht's "fanatische und ehrfurchtslose Absicht, das Dichtwerk in

* which involves Macbeth in bloody but hopeless undertakings.

† From the sound of a modern battle emerge the voices of the Chaplain, the Pacifist, a Rear-Echelon Hero, the Reckless Officer, the Traitor, the Non-Hero, a Fortune-Teller, and a Dying Man. Distorted passages from the battle-scenes of Shakespeare's history plays were forced into the text.

den Dienst kleinlicher und zersetzender Parteipropaganda zu stellen."[22]* Brecht evidently focused on Macbeth's *social* evil rather than his *personal* ambition, and he dramatized this through such epic devices as narrator, estranging music, independent scenes.

Over a decade later, when Brecht in exile had written several epic dramas, he returned briefly to *Macbeth*. While living in Sweden in 1939, his wife Helene Weigel taught acting technique, and Brecht wrote for her several rehearsal scenes to encourage actor estrangement from traditionally heroic roles. (I prefer to translate Brecht's *Verfremdung* by "estrangement," rather than the more usual "alienation," with its Existentialist resonances.) In scenes for *Romeo and Juliet* and *Hamlet*, the heroes are portrayed as selfish examples of their ruling class, but the hero does not appear at all in the *Macbeth* scene. It focuses instead on the Porter who, in German as in English stage tradition, is usually played as a drunken lout.

Brecht, however, takes him seriously, explaining his estrangement:

> Die folgenden Übertragungen der Mordszene aus "Macbeth" . . . in einen prosaisches Milieu sollen der Verfremdung der klassischen Szenen dienen. Diese Szenen werden auf unsern Theatern längst nicht mehr auf die Vorgänge hin gespielt, sondern nur auf die Temperamentsausbrüche hin, welche die Vorgänge ermöglichen. Die Übertragungen stellen das Interesse an den Vorgängen wieder her und schaffen beim Schauspieler ausserdem ein frisches Interesse an der Stilisierung und der Verssprache der Originale, als etwas Besonderem, Hinzukommendem.† (GW VII, 3003)

* fanatic and irreverent intention of placing creativity in the service of petty and destructive propaganda of the [Communist] Party.

† The following transpositions of the murder scene of *Macbeth* . . . into a prosaic milieu should serve the estrangement of classic scenes. In our theaters these scenes have for a long time underemphasized

The scene's title, "Murder in the Porter's house," links servant to master—Macbeth—who is not mentioned by name. The Mistress is giving the Master for his birthday a valuable statue of a Chinese God of Good Luck. As the Porter's Wife complains of the inequitable distribution of wealth, she drops the statue and breaks it. Terrified, the Porter and his Wife seize a Beggar and rush him into a back room of their house, along with the broken statue. They will pretend innocence and blame the Beggar, their social inferior.

As the Porter worries about being discharged, the bell rings, and the palace servants come for the statue. When one of them reports that it is broken, the Porter's Wife exclaims: "Was? Kaputt? In meinem Haus?" As Macbeth will rationalize his killing of the grooms, the Porter rationalizes his rage at the Beggar. When the Beggar is accused, the palace servant affirms: "Den wird die Polizei schnell aufgegriffen haben." (3007) That will be the titular murder at the Porter's house—an innocent Beggar falsely accused.

Brecht designated this rehearsal scene as a parallel scene, and the parallels are obvious with II, 2 of Shakespeare's *Macbeth*: Duncan's murder becomes a broken statue; the knocking at the gate is the ringing of a bell; above all, the guilty blame the innocent, for Macbeth and the Porter conceal their guilt by pretending righteous rage. As the Macbeths desire the kingship, their servants desire security within the feudal system. Even though Macbeth and Lady Macbeth do not appear, Brecht's scene compels a critical attitude toward them.

English stage tradition regards *Macbeth* as an unlucky play, and some misfortune seems to have carried over to its offshoots. The mythical farce *Ubu* had to wait a half-century for appreciation in the theater, and the Expressionist *him* had to wait about a quarter-century. In spite of suc-

the actions and instead emphasized emotional outbursts which these actions bring about. The transformations refocus the interest on actions and also arouse the actor's fresh interest in the stylization and verse-speaking of the original, as something special and accessory.

cess at the time, the WPA Negro *Macbeth* opened no doors for Blacks in the theater. Brecht's epic radio *Macbeth* is not extant. But fortune smiled upon *MacBird!* by Barbara Garson (b. 1937), a play written almost by accident.[23]

The Foreword states: "*MacBird!* originated in August, 1965, as a slip of the tongue when Barbara Garson, speaking in an anti-war rally in Berkeley, California, quite accidentally referred to the [then] First Lady of the United States as Lady MacBird [instead of Ladybird] Johnson. Since it was just a few weeks after the Watts insurrection and the Berkeley troop-train demonstrations, the opening lines of a play suggested themselves immediately: 'When shall we three meet again / In riot, strike, or stopping train?' " (ix) It is not clear why the Watts insurrection and Berkeley troop-train demonstrations should have suggested *Macbeth*'s Three Witches to a young radical, and the Witches have an ambiguous role in her play, alternately tempting MacBird to power and opposing his power by their revolutionary activity.

The play, expanded through several versions, was immediately successful both in print and off Broadway in New York. The book jacket quotes extravagant praise by such intelligent critics as Dwight MacDonald, Robert Lowell, and Robert Brustein. Richard Gilman has cogently analyzed play and praise,[24] but *MacBird!* merits examination as a social oddity.

As Shakespeare's Macbeth murders King Duncan, Garson's MacBird murders President John Ken O'Dunc—a murder preceded by Witches' prophecies and wife's exhortations. Garson's Act I closes with the murder. In Act II the two remaining Ken O'Dunc brothers flee. Against their forces MacBird consolidates his power with the help of his loyal wife (and daughters). The faithful retainers of the Ken O'Dunc brothers are the Wayne of Morse and Lord Stevenson, the Egg of Head, who dies in mid-campaign.

The Three Witches are particularized as Beatnik, Black Muslim, and old-time Revolutionary; they prophesy that

MacBird will reign till Washington burns. At MacBird's banquet they put on a minstrel-show, which is a variant on Hamlet's play within the play, and that show grows into a fire that devours Washington: "Burn, baby, burn." The final battle takes place on the Democratic Convention floor; like MacDuff, Robert Ken O'Dunc is victorious.

The genre of *MacBird!*, burlesque, is at least as old as Aristophanes, and like the comedies of Aristophanes this burlesque is meant to serve a political purpose. But Garson ridicules political figures with small regard for political fact. Springing from sonic similarity between the names Macbeth and MacBird, Garson's play adheres to Shakespeare's plot, so that her mock-Macbeth murders a mock-Duncan, though she did not believe Johnson responsible for the assassination of John Kennedy, though Robert Kennedy did not succeed Johnson in the White House, and though Edward Kennedy has declined to be a candidate for the presidency. But facts need have nothing to do with fun.

The mocking intention of *MacBird!* is at once evident in the Prologue's combination of business suit, plumed hat, and toy sword. Parodying the Prologue of *Henry V*, Garson's modern avatar asks: "Can costume kings who sweep across this stage / With antique garb and flashing swords of old / Be likened to our sober-suited leaders, / Who plot in prose their laceless, graceless deeds?" (1) The question is of course rhetorical. And misleading, for the sober suits are gaily embellished, and rhyme or pastiche displaces prose. But the deeds *are* laceless and graceless, often comic in their rough-and-ready clumsiness, especially as rendered in the New York production.

In the first exchange between Jack and Bobbie Ken O'Dunc *Julius Caesar* supplies the portrait of MacBird: "He has a fat, yet hungry look." (5) And *Richard II* a vision of American power: "And for this land, this crownèd continent, / This earth of majesty, this seat of Mars, / This forceful breed of men, this mighty world, / I see a . . . *New Frontier* beyond her seas." (6)

It is mainly *Hamlet* that is twisted to satirize political ambition. The experienced Revolutionary Witch advises her two younger colleagues in a parody of Polonius: "Be thou militant but by no means adventurist. . . . Neither a burrower from within nor a leader be. . . . And this above all—to thine own class be true." (8) When MacBird appoints the Earl of Warren to investigate John Ken O'Dunc's assassination, he exclaims like Hamlet: "Oh, cursèd spite / That ever I was born to set things right." (48) When MacBird assures him that that is not his function, the Earl retracts to: "Oh, whine and pout, /That ever I was born to bury doubt." (48) The Revolutionary Witch spurs Robert to vengeance with the words of *Hamlet*'s Ghost: "I could a tale unfold whose lightest word / Would harrow up thy soul, freeze thy young blood. . . ." Robert replies with a blend of *Hamlet* and T. S. Eliot's *Prufrock*: "I'm no prince Hamlet, nor was meant to be. . . . Yea, I have heard / That guilty creatures, sitting at a play / Have by the very cunning of the scene / . . . revealed their malefactions." (83) At the play's climax Robert aims his spear at MacBird, "*but before he can hurl it, MacBird clutches his heart*" and expires with Horatio's words: "Thus cracks a noble heart!" (107)

More inspired than most of the lines was the colorful staging—the golden baseballs of John Ken O'Dunc's sceptre, Lady Macbeth's curlers and cold cream, the Airwick spray in her sleepwalking scene, MacBird's battle dress of football-player's padding and baseball-catcher's mask. But in spite of such all-American props, the production was weighed down by its words.

In Joan Littlewood's London production satiric point was sharpened by deleting the ambiguous Witches. Littlewood focused on the conflict between a crooked clownish MacBird and a crooked sanctimonious Robert Ken O'Dunc. The racial overtones resonated differently when John Ken O'Dunc in blackface appeared after his murder, as a Schweikian minstrel figure in MacBird's entourage. Thus, MacBird's crime was always visible, and Shakespeare's plot was not quite so irrelevant to the Johnson administration, straddling the racial issue as it did. Joan Littlewood used Barbara Garson's script as modern adapters use that of Shakespeare, but Garson's defenders howled louder than those of the Bard. Barbara Garson is no prophet, and it is not her fault that her adaptation was hailed as a prophecy, theatrical and political.

The success of Garson's *MacBird!* depends upon some familiarity with well-known lines of Shakespeare. So, in a different way, do the collages of the American-born British director, Charles Marowitz (b. 1934). Evidently knowing nothing of Nathan's 1939 collage, *The Avon Flows*, Marowitz thought he invented a technique that estranges the play by omitting and repeating Shakespearean lines, assigning them to different characters, and thus emerging with different scenes. His first collage was *Hamlet* in 1966; *Macbeth* came in 1969.[25] *A Macbeth Freely Adapted from Shakespeare's Tragedy* reorders the story into a transformation that is difficult to follow on stage.

Marowitz explains his collage as the product of Macbeth's own hallucinatory vision—a hallucination achieved by the witchcraft of his wife and the Weird Sisters: "What we see on stage is only a reflection of what Macbeth sees, and so all questions of reality have to be referred back to the psychotic protagonist through whose distorted vision we view the play." (15) As one might guess with a psychotic protagonist, the Witches play a major role, and they play in a Voodoo style reminiscent of Orson Welles' 1936 production. Witches are present at the beginning, end, and many intermediate points of Marowitz' collage. They crown Macbeth in a mock-ceremony, mourn at Duncan's funeral, dine at Macbeth's banquet, and shadow Lady Macbeth in her sleepwalking scene, the only scene in which she is unattended by her demon. Several times during the course of the play they dance around an effigy of Macbeth, toward which Lady Macbeth gestures with hostility. When Birnam Wood comes to Dunsinane, it is in the form of Witches' broomsticks, which finally beat Macbeth to death. At the end of the play Lady Macbeth cuts the head off Macbeth's effigy, and the stage clears except for the Witches, who conversationally recite Shakespeare's opening lines.

In his Introduction Charles Marowitz writes: "The first section of the play—from the imaginary murder of Duncan and Banquo to the meeting with Lady Macbeth—is viewed here as a prophetic vision of everything that will befall Macbeth. A true prophetic vision contains, as does this opening collage, all the high-points of a man's life circumscribed by the spirit which will eventually destroy him. . . . If collage-playing has any essential corollaries, they are speed and definition." (12) Marowitz's production achieved speed, but definition remained problematical.

The play opens on Lady Macbeth standing before an effigy of Macbeth. After the Witches enter, they give Lady Macbeth a smoking poker, which she plunges into the eyes of the effigy. Shortly afterward, Macbeth stabs Duncan, and Lady Macbeth stabs Banquo. (There is no way of knowing that these are imaginary murders.) Macbeth is joined by two more Macbeths who at times act like his conscience, but after his coronation and Banquo's second murder, they remove the body. Malcolm, Macduff, and Duncan turn on Macbeth, and Lady Macbeth intones the "Come you spirits, unsex me" speech.

Shortly before the play's midpoint, Macbeth murders Duncan, with considerable help from his wife: "LADY MACBETH appears, takes hold of MACBETH's hands [each containing a dagger] and drives the daggers into DUNCAN's heart." (62) Again Macbeth is crowned, this time on a child's highchair-throne. Again Banquo is killed. At the banquet the Ghost of Banquo empties his blood into a goblet and offers it to Macbeth, who upsets the banquet table, causing everyone to exit in pandemonium. Then Macbeth questions the Witches, who raise up dead Duncan, then dead Banquo, then a second Macbeth wearing the mask of the first Macbeth. Soon afterward Macbeth stabs Lady

Macduff and her child, who have earlier been burlesqued by the Witches. Prefiguring Polanski's nude Lady Macbeth, Marowitz has Lady Macbeth sleepwalk in a "transparent nightdress." Her funeral follows immediately upon that scene, and it is a Priest who speaks the "Tomorrow and tomorrow and tomorrow" speech. From the body of Lady Macbeth the First Witch takes the crown, to place it on her own head.

There is a quick cut to Macbeth on his throne, Malcolm and Macduff opposing him from two distant platforms. In the final battle against a background of brooms, the whole cast is present, including Duncan, Banquo, Lady Macbeth, and the two alter egos of Macbeth. Lady Macbeth is clasped tightly in Macbeth's arms as he cries out: "I have lived long enough," and describes what he "must not look to have." (102) He repeats lines that he has spoken after Duncan's murder, and she tries to comfort him. "Bucked," he delivers in broken rhythms the "Bring forth men-children only" speech. He then turns to kiss her, but she resists him: "The queen, my lord, is dead." (103) After the Witches carry off her body, an army of broomsticks closes in on Macbeth, and, as already described, the play ends on the Witches' conversation.

In entitling his collage *A Macbeth,* Marowitz implies that this is only one possible version of the tragedy. It is a version in which the Witches are omnipotent and almost omnipresent; they can drive men mad or use them as pawns in their hands. In the Marowitz production those hands hold crowns, daggers, broomsticks, and they seem to hold a volume of popularized Freud. There are no political implications to the actions, and Marowitz has written: "Personally I am bored silly by all that 'bleeding country,' 'See us crowned at Scone' bunkum in the play, and find the testing-scene between Malcolm and Macduff one of Shakespeare's more laboured naiveties." (14)

In contrast, most *Macbeth* offshoots insist upon politics. Robert Brustein wrote of *MacBird!*: "It is a work in which all political leaders are seen as calculating, power hungry and bloody, and nobody comes off well."[26] His words are more applicable to two *Macbeths* of 1972, one in French by Eugène Ionesco and one in German by Heiner Müller.

After some two decades of original playwriting, in which he became famous as a playwright of the Absurd, Eugène Ionesco (b. 1910) adapted *Macbeth* to *Macbett*, normal French pronunciation for the Scottish name.[27] Roughly, very roughly, he follows Shakespeare's story, so that his play may be called an adaptation. But into that story he tries to inject elements of Ubuesque farce.

Though Ionesco follows Shakespeare's story-line, he complicates the plot. *Macbett* opens on two of Archduke Duncan's generals, not in war but in peacetime. Candor and Glamiss enumerate Duncan's misdeeds, and they arouse one another to rebellion. Two other Duncan generals, Macbett and Banco, are incorruptible; theirs not to reason why, theirs but to win or die in Duncan's cause. In a swift civil war, where Duncan shows himself a comic coward, where Macbett and Banco speak almost identical soliloquies, they win.

After the victory, Macbett and Banco separately meet two Witches, who make the Shakespearean predictions. In precisely the same words each general protests that he is not ambitious. Before Macbett's amazed eyes, the First Witch turns into a beautiful Lady Duncan, who tempts Macbett to kill her husband. The Second Witch, transformed into a beautiful handmaiden, declares: "Omnia vincit amor." (61)

With peace restored, Duncan makes the mistake of rewarding Macbett but not Banco. When Macbett and Banco meet again, they repeat the angry words used by Generals Candor and Glamiss, who rebelled against Duncan. Then, crying: "Assassin!" Macbett, Banco, and the false Lady Duncan assassinate Duncan. Macbett learns of the Witches' prediction that Banco's heirs will inherit the archduchy, and he kills Banco. The false Lady Duncan and her attendant, their work accomplished, revert to Witches' form and disappear. At his coronation banquet Macbett sees the ghosts of Banco and Duncan, and then the true Lady Duncan, who announces that Duncan's son, Macol, is coming to avenge his father. Macbett replies with the Witches' predictions that he cannot be harmed by any man of woman born, that he will be defeated only when the forest turns into a regiment. Macol, leading an army that carries real or cardboard branches, proves to be the adopted son of Duncan but the natural son of Banco and a gazelle bewitched into a woman—thus fulfilling two prophecies when he ascends the ducal throne by stabbing Macbett in the back.

Acclaimed by those who previously acclaimed Macbett, and who acclaimed Duncan before him, Macol delivers the words of Shakespeare's Malcolm to Macduff (in Gilbert Signaux's translation). To close the play, Ionesco's Macol adds: "De cet archiduché, commençons d'abord par faire un royaume—et je suis roi. Un empire, je suis empereur. Supra-altesse, supra-sire, supra-majesté, empereur de tous les empereurs.

> *Il disparaît dans la brume.*
> *La brume se dissipe. Le chasseur de papillons traverse le plateau.*"* (104)

Power is a butterfly by which man after man is tempted. The play ends substantially where it began, with a power-greedy monarch on the throne. But whereas Duncan occupied his throne by heredity, and Macbett seized it with pious platitudes, Macol twists Shakespeare's words to candid tyranny.

* Let's begin by making a kingdom of this archduchy—and I am king. An empire, and I am emperor. Super-highness, super-majesty, emperor of all the emperors.
He disappears into the mist.
The mist dissolves. The butterfly-catcher crosses the stage.

Ionesco subtitled his *Chaises* "une farce tragique." *Macbett* carries no genre designation, but the play itself mentions genre. When Banco first sees the Witches, he asks: "Que veut dire cette farce?" (44) When Macbett insists that he is not ambitious, the First Witch exclaims: "Quelle farce que tu te joues à toi-même." (53) When Macbett at his coronation is confronted by a portrait of Duncan, he askes: "Qui a eu l'idée de cette farce sinistre?" (89) Ionesco's play implies that the power drive converts life into a sinister farce.

Ionesco's early plays, as Serge Doubrovsky pointed out in a seminal essay, convey metaphysical absurdity through comic circularity and proliferation.[28] *Macbett* also winds back to its beginning, a power-grasping ruler. Though the play lacks the proliferational frenzy of Ionesco's earlier plays, he suggests political absurdity through metamorphosis, verbal repetition, and such doubles as Candor and Glamiss, Macbett and Banco, two witches. In a duologue of repetitions Candor and Glamiss envy Duncan's power. In a duologue of repetitions Macbett and Banco support Duncan's power. In repeated duologues two witches tempt Macbett and Banco through prophecy. Duncan cannot tell Macbett from Banco, and when they oppose him, they use the very words earlier used by Candor and Glamiss. As in earlier Ionesco plays, Doubrovsky's summary holds true: "Instead of men using language to think, we have language thinking for men."[29]

Objects also contribute to the absurdity of the stage world. After the first battle, Duncan orders mass executions of the rebels. Lady Duncan washes her hands, scents them with *eau de cologne*, and supervises the tea service to those who watch guillotines chop off head after rebel head. Her insouciant cruelty is as farcically outrageous as that of Mère Ubu. At the end of the play, just before Macol utters Shakespeare's lines: "*Guillotines nombreuses dans le fond, comme au premier tableau.*" (103) This is the most menacing invasion by objects, but Macbett's coronation is undercut by the servants' enumeration of its splendors—wine, beer, gin, beef, venison, pastis, vodka, eggs, crêpes, melons, cake, wine, mustard, frankfurters, sauerkraut, beer, wine, gin.

The sudden arrival of Macol dooms Macbett, but there is no possibility of a heroic end for farce. Macol enters to fanfares, but he and Macbett hurl insults at each other in Ubuesque fashion; they battle with vulgar names. When Macol reveals that he is the son of Banco and a gazelle, he names himself Banco II, and he foresees his heirs in visible heads of comic-book characters and Ionesco himself. When he informs Macbett that the regiment has turned into a forest, the response is "Merde!" That is Macbett's dying word, an echo of irrepressible Ubu's explosive opener.

Ionesco was conscious of the echo, for he said in an interview that his *Macbett* "leans more . . . toward Jarry's 'Ubu Roi' [than toward Shakespeare's 'Macbeth']. In any case, there is none of Shakespeare's compassion." And he concluded the interview: " 'Macbett' is a comedy nonetheless. I hope that people will laugh."[30] Ionesco wrote a farcical plague on all politico-military ambition in his *Macbett*; his combination of swords, guns, and guillotines implies that this sinister farce can be played any place at any time.

In 1972, too, the East German playwright Heiner Müller (b. 1929) completed a *Macbeth "nach Shakespeare"* that was unlocalized, but the times are quite clearly feudal.[31] His exceptionally cruel Macbeth flouts the German tradition of a noble Macbeth. Schiller's translation, for example, omits the onstage murder of Lady Macduff and her child; at the end Macduff shows Macbeth's crown instead of his severed head. Heiner Müller *adds* stage cruelties to Shakespeare, and he phrases his play with crisp concision that betrays both Shakespeare and the natural sinuosity of the German language.

When Müller's *Macbeth* opened in Basel, Switzerland, journalists labeled it Theater of Cruelty.[32] An East German writer, Wolfgang Harich, attacked the play as pornographic, sadistic, and historically pessimistic, whereupon East German director Hansgünther Heyme tried to soften some of the cruelties in his production, but they are inescapably in Müller's text. Of his intention, Müller said in an interview: "*Macbeth* war das Shakespeare-Stück, das ich am wenigsten mochte. Vorher hatte ich *Wie es euch gefällt* übersetzt, so wörtlich wie möglich. Bei *Macbeth* wollte ich nun den Shakespeare verändern, von Zeile zu Zeile."* Müller has worked over the lines, but he has also altered some of the scenes, compressing Shakespeare's twenty-eight into twenty-three, of which three are original. Müller's Character List reads like Shakespeare's, except for the addition of peasants, who give his adaptation a Brechtian resonance: common people have nothing to gain and everything to lose, when lords battle.

Like Brecht in his lost radio play, Müller begins on the battlefield. Twenty Shakespearean lines describe the conflict and Macbeth's role in it; Müller compresses them to ten. The rest of Shakespeare's scene of reported action seems almost leisurely by comparison with Müller's, whose verse lines are sometimes shorter than pentameters.

As in Shakespeare, the Witches prophesy, and Ross arrives to announce Macbeth's new title. As in Shakespeare, Duncan announces that Malcolm will be his successor. Lady Macbeth inflames Macbeth's ambition, but Müller's scene ends when Lady Macbeth asks to see a peasant who has been flayed for not paying his rent. Before the bloody corpse, she covers her eyes as Macbeth laughs. Yet Lady Macbeth cruelly spurs her husband's wavering ambition: "Es juckt ihn und er fürchtet sich zu kratzen. / Es könnte Blut ihm untern Nagel kommen."† (39)

The "Is this a dagger" soliloquy is shorter, swifter, more cynical. Macbeth calls the Witches his sisters, and sometimes sounds like Dürrenmatt's barbaric Alarich. Duncan's

* *Macbeth* was the Shakespeare play I liked least. Earlier I had translated *As You Like It* as faithfully as possible. In *Macbeth* I wanted to alter Shakespeare, line by line.

† He itches but fears to scratch. Blood might appear under his nail.

murder occurs much as in Shakespeare, and after the knocking at the gate the Porter admits Lenox and Macduff. Müller's Porter has fought in Scotland's wars, losing a leg and "aus Liebe zur Symmetrie" the opposite arm. Both noblemen taunt and strike the Porter for pleasure. When Duncan's murder is discovered, Macduff cuts the tongue off a servant who cries out: "Es lebe der König. . . . Der oder der." After Malcolm and Donalbain go their separate ways, Müller shows the peasant skeleton with its rotting flesh. The peasant's wife mourns him, but Ross and Macduff do not even notice the grisly remains.

At the banquet Müller adds lines between Macbeth and Lady Macbeth, indicating that he is impotent: "Meine Braut heisst Schottland." (43) Before killing Banquo, the First Murderer robs and kills the Third Murderer. After cutting Banquo's throat, the murderers cut off his genitals, which they bring back to Macbeth. He tells them to take that toy to their children, whose lives will answer for their secrecy.

Into Macbeth's second meeting with the Witches Müller inserts a grotesque but spectacular scene. Drunk, on hands and knees, looking for his crown, Macbeth implores the Witches to tell him the future: "*Die Hexen reiten auf ihm, reissen ihm die Haare aus und die Kleider in Fetzen, furzen ihm ins Gesicht usw. Schliesslich lassen sie ihn liegen, halb nackt, werfen einander kreischend die Krone zu; bis eine von ihnen sie aufsetzt, Kampf um die Krone mit Klauen und Zähnen.*"* (45)

Macbeth not only orders but witnesses the murder of Lady Macduff and her son. A lord is delivered to the sadistic fantasy of Macbeth's soldiers. As the lord's widow-to-be watches, the men peel off the lord's skin while Macbeth recites from Ovid the passage about the flaying of Marsyas.

* The Witches ride on him, tear his hair out and his clothes into rags, fart in his face, etc. Finally they leave him lying half naked as they shriek while throwing his crown to one another, until one of them puts it on; then they fight for the crown with claws and teeth.

Lenox and Ross look on, the latter remarking lightly: "Marsyas war ein Bauer." To which Macbeth retorts that times change.

In Lady Macbeth's sleepwalking scene the Doctor begins by noting her words, but he tears up his notes when he realizes that knowledge of an impending war against England might be dangerous for him. Müller invents a scene in which Lenox and Ross separately lead their men, the former to aid Malcolm, the latter Macbeth. Lenox challenges Ross's men to choose between Scottish gunpowder and English beer. The men acclaim the beer, and both armies leave for Birnam Wood. In the next scene soldiers of each side in turn wish to hang a confused peasant, who finally hangs himself to escape them both.

After Lady Macbeth's death, Müller changes the rhythm of Macbeth's most celebrated speech, so that it appears less meditative and more nervous:

> Ja.—Morgen und morgen und morgen. Das kriecht
> Mit diesem kleinen Schritt von Tag zu Tag
> Zur letzten Silbe. Der Rest ist aus der Zeit.
> All unsre Gestern, von Blinden am Seil geführt
> In staubiges Nichts. Weisst du was andres, Seyton.
> Aus, kurze Flamme. Leben ein Schatten der umgeht
> Ein armer Spieler, der sich spreizt und sperrt
> Auf seiner Bühne seine Stunde lang und
> Nicht mehr gehört wird nachdem. Ein Märchen, erzählt
> Von einem Irren, voll mit Lärm und Wut
> Bedeutend nichts. (47)

When Macduff's men attack a Macbeth whom everyone has deserted, the tyrant asks whether the soldiers are of woman born, and Macduff answers that no one woman's womb could have given birth to so many. Macbeth prophesies that his death will not improve the world, but Macduff's men plunge their weapons into Macbeth.

Macduff warns young Malcolm to learn by this example

of his predecessor, and the new king laughs as he puts Macbeth's head on his spear. At a signal from Lenox and Ross, soldiers kill Macduff, and Malcolm begins to cry, wishing he had stayed in England. The soldiers set the crown on Malcolm's head, and the Witches close the play: "Heil Malcolm Heil König von Schottland Heil."

It is clear that the slaughter has only begun. Macbeth has been villain and victim; Macduff has been villain and victim. Malcolm wears the crown as the curtain falls, and he is not likely to favor Ross or Lenox in a new confederacy of dubious durability. One can understand why an East German critic would find the play historically pessimistic. But Müller defended his optimism: "Ausserdem gibt es in 'Macbeth' ein geschichtsoptimistisches Moment: die Hexen. Jede Revolution braucht ein destruktives Element, und das sind in meinem Stück die Hexen; weil sie ausnahmslos alle Mächtigen zerstören. Wichtig ist auch: der Macbeth ist eine grosse Figur, kein Schurke. Was ich bei Brecht—wenn man ihn mit Shakespeare vergleicht—im Moment ein bischen langweilig finde, ist, dass er Figuren kleinmacht."* Brecht's radio *Macbeth* is lost, so that we cannot know whether he diminished that hero. Instead, it is Ionesco, one of Brecht's most hostile critics, who most blatantly diminishes Macbeth. With small and large protagonists, the *Macbeth*s of Ionesco and Müller make similar statements about power politics. Both adaptations lean on Shakespeare's plot, but Ionesco uses colloquial French to show the mundane repetitiveness of power politics inevitably resulting in war, whereas Müller creates a crackling German idiom to portray feudal heroes whose life is war.

Though spanning half a century—1921 to 1972—these

* Besides there is in *Macbeth* an optimistic historical factor: the Witches. Every revolution needs a destructive element, and in my play this is the Witches because they destroy all the mighty, without exception. It is also important that Macbeth is a large figure, not a mere scoundrel. What I at present find somewhat boring in Brecht, compared to Shakespeare, is that he diminishes figures.

several *Macbeth* adaptations and transformations are posited on the same kind of theater, in which actors memorize a text, wear costumes, move on sets, and perform before audiences that expect to be entertained. The next transformations of *Macbeth,* in contrast, belong to what is called the New or Alternative Theater, in which texts are less important than thematic physicalization, audience entertainment than actor exploration.

The patron saint of this New or Alternative Theater is Antonin Artaud (1896-1948), actor, poet, playwright, prophet, and theoretician of what he called the Theater of Cruelty. Franco Tonelli has summarized the esthetic of this theater: myth is the dynamic impetus to action; dialogue is lyrical rather than logical; events unfold in an eternal present.[33] Space rather than time is the vital dimension of Artaud's theory of theater. Feeling that most dramatic literature of the West did not lend itself to genuine theatricalization, he inveighed against masterpieces. Nevertheless, Artaud himself flirted with masterpieces, notably Shakespeare.[34] In 1929 he asked director Gaston Baty for a role in his *Macbeth* (which, however, was not produced until 1942!). In 1934 Artaud gave a two-hour reading of *Richard II,* to help raise money for his Theater of Cruelty. Always in financial need, he finally did manage to produce *The Cenci,* based on texts of Stendhal and Shelley. After its failure in May, 1935, Artaud wanted to perform *Macbeth,* but he was unable to find funds. Probably he would have de-emphasized language and psychology, in favor of large movements through space. And this has been the approach of New Theater groups that admire Artaud.

Like most avant-gardes, New or Alternative Theater leads a precarious existence, and survival is a feat. Several such groups have been drawn to *Macbeth,* but I report only on those productions I have discussed with their directors, for unfortunately I was unable to see any of them: The Performance Group *Makbeth,* Group N's *Autopsy of Macbeth,* and in another chapter The Triple Action Theatre *Macbeth.*

The Performance Group, or TPG, was founded by Richard Schechner (b. 1934) in 1967, and *Makbeth* was their second production.[35] Like Euripides' *Bacchae,* which was the point of departure for their first production, the work was chosen because it seemed malleable into environmental theater, about which Schechner has published a book.[36] Paramount is the interaction of actor (as a kind of shaman) and audience within an environment specially constructed for each production.

The environment of *Makbeth* was a maze. In the words of Brooks McNamara, who designed it: "Like the performance itself, the maze was seen as an attempt to create a new organization of the Macbeth legend, previous performances of *Macbeth,* and the performance which was to take place." (254) The performance space was divided into many cubes at different levels; on vertical mirrors were pasted pictures of earlier *Macbeth* productions and handwritten words from Shakespeare's text. Spectators had to make their way through the maze and see themselves reflected through facets of *Macbeth,* before seating themselves on one of the several carpeted platforms.

The action was played throughout the space, sometimes with two scenes going simultaneously, so that no spectator could see all the actions. Nevertheless, the spatial center seemed to be a large table (25 x 12 feet), on or around which many scenes were played. This was appropriate since, in Schechner's words: "Totemistic cannibal feasting is the major image of *Makbeth.*" (276) An early scene involved a banquet at Dunsinane, to honor Duncan's arrival (offstage in Shakespeare); as Schechner describes it: "[Duncan] is the meal's main course. Awaiting him, the Makbeths and their friends devour each other. The three Dark Powers stand to one side, intervening only to serve one person to another. Throughout the meal they sing Shakespeare's lines to the tune of 'Happy Days Are Here Again.'" (140) This is typical of the way TPG changed *Macbeth* into *Makbeth*.

The Performance Group story follows Shakespeare's, but there are two main differences: 1) Duncan has four sons—the Thane of Cawdor, Malcolm, Macduff, and Banquo, all but the last seeking his throne; 2) The Witches are called Dark Powers (played by TPG's leading actors, two men and one woman) who revel in the violence of the bloodthirsty nobles. During performance "The Dark Powers are servants, lower-class people, soldiers; they are also gargoyles hanging over the action, eyes and ears spying, hands casting spells." (315) Ubiquitous, the Dark Powers see the Shakespearean tragic events as a farce.

As in most Alternative Theater productions, the action of *Makbeth* is played straight through without a break, lasting some seventy minutes. As in some *Macbeth* adaptations of the old theater, the first scene is a battle in which the noblemen perform their bloody deeds. Makbeth gains Duncan's gratitude in a war against his rebellious son, the Thane of Cawdor. Afterward, the Dark Powers receive Makbeth in a pit, the audience looking down as they hear the prophecies. Slowly, tension builds toward the murder of Duncan, which occurs at about the middle of the performance. Though Makbeth's whole body becomes a knife to perform the crime, he barely beats Duncan's sons (Macduff and Malcolm) to the deed.

When Makbeth becomes King, Macduff and Malcolm conspire against him. At the end Macduff slays Makbeth—his body becoming a knife—but he is himself wounded, and is thus an easy victim for Malcolm, who orders the murderers to slay him, in the same words that Makbeth used to the murderers of Banquo. Malcolm, as self-seeking as Makbeth, is triumphant at the last. Or nearly the last, for the performance closes on the Dark Powers (designated by their real names), wondering where next to exercise their nefarious talents:

Joan: And to conclude, the victory fell on us. Receive what cheer you may.

Richard: We are reckless what we do to spite the world. There's nothing in mortality, all is but toys.

Jason: I'll devil porter it no further. I had thought to let in some of all professions that go the primrose way to the everlasting bonfire. But this place is too cold for hell.

Richard: What will you do now? How will you live?

Jason: As birds do.

Joan: What, with worms and flies?

Jason: With what I can get. So, I pray you, remember the porter.

The lines—a collage of Shakespeare's Ross, Macbeth, Porter, Lady Macduff, and young Macduff—imply that the Witches are at once responsible for events and bored by them. As in the adaptations of Ionesco and Müller, the Performance Group Makbeth is superseded by a cooler tyrant, victorious mainly through his own machinations.

In accordance with their conception of Shakespearean events, TPG collaged the text, though less drastically than Marowitz had done. Most of the lines were retained, though the celebrated "Tomorrow and tomorrow and tomorrow" speech was omitted. All verse was deliberately spoken as prose, and the words often converted to pure sound. Paul Epstein composed incidental music for the performance and also invented a kind of scoring for the words:

> In much of the music of *Makbeth* the selection of text, on the basis of phonetic content as well as meaning, was a major part of the compositional task. "Text setting" came to mean literally that, placing pieces of text in relation to one another and to a context of scenic action. Duncan's funeral procession reverses itself to become Makbeth's coronation march. The transition is

> made musically as the funeral chants are replaced by miniature fanfares, the themes of the text fragments changing from purification and sleep to duty, honor, and the crown. (170)

The crown, made of heavy brass, is the only prop. All the actors touch it at some point: Duncan, Makbeth, and Malcolm have special relationships to it. Duncan bends over and bows under its weight. When Makbeth wears it, he continually feels and adjusts it. Malcolm grasps at it hungrily without putting it on; at one point, he sinks his teeth into it, breaking them. In Schechner's words: "The crown of *Makbeth* is both a rhythm and an ikon. By keeping one's eye on what happens to the crown, a spectator can understand the action of the play." (316)

For the most part audiences were mere spectators in the environment, but occasionally Schechner achieved unusual participation:

> On several occasions I met with audiences before the show and told them they could move during the performance. "If you are noisy or block the performers' movements, you can bust this thing up. If you take off your shoes so that you are absolutely silent and move from carpeted area to carpeted area, you can intensify your own and our experience. Try to understand the action and go with it. Think of yourselves as witnesses, or people in the street. Something happens—you go to see what. But you can't interfere or change what's happening." The audience were beautifully cooperative and some impressive things occurred. During the banquet scene the empty table swiftly filled with people who became guests at Dunsinane. The murder of Banquo under a platform was witnessed by a few. During the prophecy scene in the trench where Makbeth learns of Macduff and Birnam Wood, 50 spectators stood or crouched, as around a bear-pit, while Mak-

> beth talked to the Dark Powers who dangled upside down from pipes. Duncan's funeral cortege and Makbeth's coronation parade were augmented by people lining the ramp and joining in the procession. The soldiers advancing through Birnam Wood found allies. In many ways the performance found focus as crowds condensed and dispersed; as a few people showed up here and there; as many silently and swiftly tip-toed stocking-footed through this open but secretive castle. The audience became the soldiers, the guests, the witnesses, the crowds—the powerless but present and compliant public.[37]

The Performance Group *Makbeth* suffered at the box office, and Schechner attributes this in part to rehearsals in an environment different from that of the performance. This is often necessary with the slenderly financed resources of the Alternative Theater. Most of the performers have to work at other jobs than acting. Yet enthusiasm continues among its members, so that the phenomenon of such groups has spread throughout the world, with heavy concentration in Europe and America.

Springing from different experience, the Paris-based Group N developed a quite different *Macbeth.* The founder and sustaining presence of the group is Peruvian Emilio Galli, who was Professor of Theater before leaving his country for political reasons. He then taught theater in Venezuela, where his students performed a *Henry IV* in which Falstaff is a caricature dictator. Local authorities related the performance to contemporary events in Venezuela, and Galli fled after a week in prison. In Paris he hopes to investigate the psychopolitics of theater through using the actor's body as his instrument, with special attention to respiration.

In 1970 he formed Group N to work on an *Autopsie de Macbeth.*[38] His program note states: "AUTOPSIE DE MACBETH fait ressortir une fois encore les méthodes de terreur, de persécutions et de crimes, des coups d'état militaires, des dictatures ou des juntes 'révolutionnaires,' comme on a encore l'habitude de les dénommer."* Having decided to autopsy *Macbeth,* Group N focused its exploration on the craft of acting, thus demystifying the theater star, the *monstre sacré* of French tradition.

Autopsie de Macbeth was developed by Galli and a group of seven actors over a period of six months. The group worked four hours a day wherever they could find space, improvising upon ideas suggested by Galli. He gradually selected certain physical improvisations and combined them with about fifty short speeches from Shakespeare's *Macbeth.* The group translated these speeches into French, dissected them, and rearranged them, with different actors sometimes speaking simultaneously and sometimes in Spanish, German, or English. Each actor took several roles, and the main roles could shift from actor to actor, without transition.

In actual performance on a bare stage the actors in leotards go through warming-up exercises before the audience. Just before the action starts, the actors who will most often play Macbeth and Lady Macbeth put on Renaissance tunics and torn lace dresses. Although roles shift, the principal Macbeth is played by a frail-looking boy, and the principal Lady Macbeth by an attractive woman with a rather masculine voice, who also plays the main Witch. All seven actors—five men and two women—are in whiteface with heavily made-up eyes and mouths.

The short speeches from Shakespeare are interspersed with nonverbal sounds—shrieks, clicks, gurgles, moans, gutturals, and labials. Actors also make percussive sounds by slapping chests or thighs, stamping on the floor. Occasionally, these are representational, as when they suggest horses galloping, but more often they contribute to the mood of

* *Autopsy of Macbeth* brings out once again the methods of terror, persecution, and crime, the military *coups*, dictatorships, or "revolutionary" juntas, as they are still habitually called.

the moment, as when sharp angular gestures blend with body percussion to announce the presence of the Witches. Such use of sound illustrates Galli's feeling that traditional language is inadequate in the theater.

In spite of the paucity of text and high degree of physicalization, the main theme was evidently clear—the interdependent sexuality and fascism of the Macbeths. When Duncan's arrival is announced, Lady Macbeth performs a wild dance, bouncing up and down from a squatting position; while the other actors make farting sounds, she smiles demurely. When Duncan arrives, she welcomes him by forming a circle with her thumbs and fingers, then forcing the suggested open vagina over the extended forearm of the king. Anticipating the murder of Duncan, she is sexually aroused and approaches her husband, who has an erection suggested by another performer extending her stiffened arm between Macbeth's legs. Macbeth, unnerved at the thought of murdering the king, loses potency; the arm slowly sags toward the floor and disappears. During the murder of Duncan, three performers thrust their knife-hands in and out of the king's body.

At the end of the *Autopsie de Macbeth* the whole cast turns toward the audience and assaults them with the cry: "Complices!" many times repeated. Galli has explained the rationale of this ending: "L'anecdote dans mon spectacle est très schématisée. Le public ne peut que rester froid. Je ne veux pas qu'il puisse s'identifier aux personnages de la pièce, de même que les comédiens ne s'identifient pas à leurs rôles. Il ne peut donc pas participer, 's'engager,' et ne s'engageant pas, il devient complice. On peut être complice actif ou passif. Le spectateur est passif. Ce qui m'intéresse, c'est qu'il puisse réfléchir sur les problèmes et s'il réfléchit, il prend position et ajuste sa conduite, son attitude et se libère de lui-même."[39]*

* In my show the story is very schematic. The public can only remain detached. I don't want them to identify with the characters, any more than the actors identify with their roles. Therefore the

This passage, with its insistence upon the "cool" spectator, suggests a debt to Brecht. Another statement by Galli reveals that he has also meditated on Artaudian cruelty: "J'ai fait une autopsie de Macbeth, car c'est l'étude d'une maladie au niveau viscéral. J'ai voulu montrer les viscères du personnage, tous les éléments de castration, de frustration permanente dont il souffre dans les mains de sa femme, toute la dévastation qui est faite sur la famille McDuff."* (*sic*)[40]

With the same basic conception, Galli returned to *Macbeth* in December, 1973, using a group reduced to four—one actor, three actresses. The new title is *Supermaclady Ltd.*, and again an actress alternates between Lady Macbeth and the Witch. But Macbeth, dressed in black tights on a motorcycle, is successively Mac, Prime Minister, then President of the Republic. Again, some fifty lines of text are used in three languages, but most of the performance consists of highly physical, almost acrobatic activities, with accent on the erotic.

Though Galli and Schechner have reduced and distorted Shakespeare's words, they are highly verbal in publicizing their intention, which is to obliterate the heroic resonance of Macbeth and to stress his manipulation by wife or Witches.

Macbeth may well be the most popular classic of the New Theater, as Shakespeare's version has been most popular in the old theater. The reasons are apparent: simplicity of plot, paucity of characters, clean thematic line, suggestive theater imagery. The New or Alternative Thea-

---

public cannot participate or commit itself, and it thus becomes an accomplice—either active or passive. The spectator is passive. What interests me is that he be able to reflect on the problems, and if he reflects, that he take a stand to which he fits his conduct and attitude, freeing him from himself.

* I performed an autopsy on Macbeth, for it is the study of a sickness at the visceral level. I wanted to show the viscera of the character, all the elements of castration, of permanent frustration from which he suffers at his wife's hands, all the devastation perpetrated on the Macduff family.

ter derives from literal cruelties *and* Artaud's Theater of Cruelty; it thrives on *Macbeth*'s continuous battles, several conspiracies, and Witches' prophecies. The old theater blood of the illusionist stage has been augmented or replaced by the real exertions of New Theater actors.

Old Theater and New, most *Macbeth* offshoots remain relatively close to Shakespearean detail: Welles, Brecht, and Müller highlight special aspects of the text; Garson, Marowitz, Ionesco, Schechner, and Galli slant, select, and reinterpret the Shakespearean events; Bottomley invents a preplay incident; only *Ubu* and *him* depart radically from Shakespeare.

In this preponderantly masculine tragedy, almost all offshoots expand the roles of Lady Macbeth and the Witches. Modern adapters do not follow directors Kommisarjevsky and Guthrie in eliminating the supernatural; rather, they support Gordon Craig, who in 1910 wrote that Shakespeare's spirits "are integral, not extraneous parts of the drama."[41] In *Macbeth* "we have never yet felt these spirits working through the woman at the man." They were perhaps felt during World War II when Sybil Thorndike played Lady Macbeth *and* the First Witch. By 1972 Ionesco merges the First Witch and Lady Macbeth into a single character as well as a single actress.

Almost all modern offshoots are hostile to Lady Macbeth, recalling the old limerick:

> There once was a king named Macbeth;
> A better king never drew breath;
> The faults of his life
> Were all due to his wife
> The notorious Lady Macbeth.

Nowhere in modern offshoots do we find the poignancy of Lady Macbeth's guilt in Shakespeare's sleepwalking scene. Perhaps today's Lady Macbeth needs Women's Liberation added to the Shakespearean original.

Macbeth's Witches can be irritating, combining as they do puerile prattle with smug mysticism. But three centuries of popular staging approve Shakespeare's stagecraft in creating them. Not until the second half of the twentieth century was Lady Macbeth dissolved into the Witches, and not until the second half of the twentieth century were the Witches played sympathetically—Garson, Müller, and Schechner. The Marowitz *Macbeth* casts Witches and bitchy wife as demonic possessors of Macbeth, cooperating in his downfall. In Galli's physical transformations of *Macbeth* the same actresses alternate in playing Lady Macbeth and a Witch, both working toward Macbeth's emasculation into fascism. Though Garson's text casts the Witches in an ambiguous role, opposing MacBird but also tempting him, the New York production tried to underline their radical triumph. And that view might have influenced The Performance Group vision of the Dark Powers, common people who mock the bloodthirsty feudal rulers. Modern Witches remain spectacular, but there has been a change of spectacle.

For all the new movement of bitch and witch, however, Macbeth himself rests at the uneasy center of most *Macbeth* offshoots. Though many "straight" Shakespeare productions have portrayed him as a blunt, unimaginative soldier, most modern offshoots grant his obsessive introspection, but the rationale differs: sex-aroused in Ionesco and Galli; demonic in Welles and Marowitz; merely fearful in Garson, Müller, and Schechner. As none of the offshoots render the poignancy of Lady Macbeth's conscience, so none of them risk the full imaginative horror of "Is this a dagger which I see before me" or "Tomorrow and tomorrow and tomorrow."

This last justly celebrated Shakespeare passage climaxes the tragedy's reiterated concern with time. While the short drama moves swiftly, its characters—above all Macbeth—are acutely aware of playing out their lives in time.[42] Banquo asks the Witches to look into the seeds of time. Before he murders, Macbeth can philosophize that "Time and the hour runs through the roughest day." Lady Macbeth lives in the expectancy of hereafter, feeling "now / The future in the instant." The Macbeths' course determined, they must "beguile the time" and "mock the time with fairest show," the Elizabethan locution implying the transitory nature of the world. In feigning grief at Duncan's death, Macbeth uses time imagery: "Had I but died an hour before this chance, / I had lived a blessed time." Feigned grief but true wish for the innocence that can never again be his.

After Duncan's murder, Macbeth speaks with Banquo of "tomorrow," the word he has already associated with dead Duncan. But to Banquo's potential murderers, Macbeth stresses "tonight." He resolves to question the Weird Sisters "tomorrow," and after he sees the prophetic visions, he cries out: "Let this pernicious hour / Stand aye accursèd in the calendar!" Even as he prepares for battle, Macbeth declares that he has lived long enough. His "Tomorrow and tomorrow and tomorrow" speech is the reaction to news of Lady Macbeth's death. The very words "time" and "tomorrow" are tainted by associations with death. As Tom Driver has written: ". . . the theme of time is woven into that of evil. . . . Macbeth, who starts out to 'mock the time with fairest show' comes in the end to face the prospect of living 'to be the show and gaze o' th' time.' "[13] It is against this background of time's defilement that Malcolm's brief sentence rings so clearly: "The time is free." By slaying Macbeth, Malcolm frees the time.

Many conventional productions of *Macbeth* fail to theatricalize Shakespeare's virtual translation of time into consciousness, but such failure is even more prevalent among *Macbeth* offshoots. In the New Theater stage space becomes palpable, and this has often meant devaluation of time. New Theater productions sometimes seem interminable, but they rarely *dramatize* duration. Yet time-consciousness is vital to Macbeth's self-knowledge, and this consciousness is lacking in *Macbeth* offshoots. Macbeth often looks the same before and after the febrile traffic of the stage. Quips have often been made about playing *Hamlet* without the prince, and perhaps they should be made about playing *Macbeth* without the time.

Whatever their inadequacies, these versions of *Macbeth* accumulate into a history of modern theater. *Ubu* is the most important but also the most oblique derivation, exploding heroic nostalgia, middle-class decorum, and the tidiness of a well-made play in a well-made world. *Ubu* holds nothing sacred as it embraces incongruities—slapstick and assassination, mysticism and marionettes, archaisms and neologisms, painting and music, Shakespeare and shit. In Yeats' brilliant prophecy: "After all our subtle colour and nervous rhythm . . . what more is possible? After us the Savage God." The prophecy was slowly fulfilled in the theater, through Artaud's theory, Grotowski's practice, and the well-publicized anarchy of the 1960s.

Of the various twentieth-century *Macbeth* offshoots, Bottomley's *Gruach* is the only throwback to nineteenth-century theater idiom. Less than a decade later, in 1928, audiences and reviewers were confused by E. E. Cummings' *him,* an Expressionist phantasmagoria reaching out from its intimate center to embrace popular forms such as jazz, circus, medicine-men, and burlesque. In 1927, Brecht's epic radio adaptation of *Macbeth* was dismissed as political, Marxist, and Bolshevik. And twelve years later, Brecht's rehearsal scene was unregenerately all those. Social significance merged with the occult in the very fact of a Negro production of the 1936 Voodoo *Macbeth,* where a Haitian setting provided the rationale. Though the 1965 *MacBird!* hits at contemporary political figures in its burlesque of *Macbeth,* its weapons are traditional. On the other hand, Charles Marowitz in 1969 stated that his collage was a new approach. Only superficially political, the 1972 *Macbeth*s of Eugène Ionesco and Heiner Müller may easily be pigeonholed into Theater of the Absurd and Theater of Cruelty, respectively, but they do not fit into any rigorous definition of the modes. Though Ionesco's play exhibits the circularity, metamorphosis, and proliferation that designate absurdity on his stage, the metaphysical implications are lacking. Though Müller's *Macbeth* exhibits cruelties that are as prevalent in our time as in Shakespeare's, Artaud's mythic Cruelty is lacking. In the work of Alternative Theater groups, words are drastically curtailed and sometimes distorted, so that impact comes through the senses as much as the mind. Theater and drama strain to part, most strongly in *Macbeth.*

Chapter 3

Whole *Hamlets* of Tragical Speeches

> Yet English Seneca read by candlelight yields many good sentences as "Blood is a beggar," and so forth, and if you entreat him fair in a frosty morning, he will afford you whole Hamlets, I should say handfuls of tragical speeches. *Thomas Nashe,* 1589, about the pre-Shakespearean *Hamlet*

Macbeth and *Hamlet* have often been contrasted, and their offshoots, too, form different patterns. More words—tragical, mock-tragical, or merely serious—have been written about Hamlet than about any other character of stage or literature. More than any other play, *Hamlet* has provoked closet criticism, though actors have consistently relished some form of the drama as a performance vehicle. More than any other work, *Hamlet* has infiltrated imaginative writing—fiction, drama, and an occasional poem. More than any other character, and in sharp contrast to Macbeth, Hamlet has inspired self-identification, as the following quotations attest:

> We feel not only the virtues, but the weaknesses of Hamlet as our own. Henry Mackenzie, *The Mirror,* 1780

> It is *we* who are Hamlet. William Hazlitt, *Characters of Shakespeare's Plays,* 1817

> Hamlet's heart was full of such Misery as mine is when he said to Ophelia: "Go to a Nunnery, go, go!" John Keats, *Letters,* 1820

> I have a smack of Hamlet myself, if I may say so. S. T. Coleridge, *Table Talk,* 1827

> We feel and see our own selves in him [Hamlet]. G. G. Gervinus, *Shakespeare Commentaries,* 1849

> We all sympathize with Hamlet, and that is understandable, because almost every one of us recognize in the prince our own characteristics. . . . Ivan Turgenev, *Hamlet and Don Quixote,* 1860

> This struggle between Will and Fate belongs not alone to the history of Hamlet,—it belongs to the history of us all. François-Victor Hugo, Introduction to his Translation, 1873

> Hamlet fascinates us . . . because we see in him ourselves; we are all actual or potential Hamlets. E. K. Chambers, Introduction to *Hamlet,* 1894

> We of later days have read our sensitive bewilderments into a character which his creator designed more simply. Desmond MacCarthy, *Drama,* 1940

> [Hamlet's] circumstances are ours, to the extent that every man, in some measure, is born to privilege and anxiety, committed where he has never been consulted, hemmed in on all sides by an overbearing situation, and called upon to perform what must seem an ungrateful task. Harry Levin, *The Question of Hamlet,* 1959

Self-identification with Hamlet is recorded most profoundly in fiction, and such fiction offers a fascinating contrast with dramatic offshoots.

A. Fiction: Digging into *Hamlet*

Examination of *Hamlet*'s fictional offshoots begins with two eighteenth-century novels because they strike me as modern in sensibility (and because I cannot resist them). *Tristram Shandy* by Laurence Sterne (1713-1768), first published in 1760, contains two characters with well-known Shakespearean names, Uncle Toby and Yorick.[1] The first of these characters is almost an antithesis of Olivia's Uncle Toby from *Twelfth Night*—generous rather than greedy, ingenuous rather than scheming, addicted to his Hobby Horse rather than to cakes and ale. It is not impossible that Sterne, with his irrepressible sense of irony, chose the name for a character who is the obverse of Shakespeare's.

In contrast, Sterne's Parson Yorick is of explicitly Shakespearean lineage:

> . . . the family was originally of *Danish* extraction, and had been transplanted into *England* as early as in the reign of *Horwendilus,* King of *Denmark,* in whose court, it seems, an ancestor of this Mr. *Yorick,* and from whom he was lineally descended, held a considerable post to the day of his death. Of what nature this considerable post was this record saith not;—it only adds That, for near two centuries, it had been totally abolished as altogether unnecessary, not only in that court, but in every other court of the Christian World.
>
> It has often come into my head, that this post could be no other than that of the king's chief jester;—and that *Hamlet's Yorick,* in our *Shakespeare,* many of whose plays, you know, are founded upon authenticated facts,—was certainly the very man. (24)

Sterne ironically grounds his fictional character in a fiction that he claims as fact. Shakespeare's "fellow of infinite jest" breeds Sterne's parson who "loved a jest in his heart." But Shakespeare's Yorick is dead in *Hamlet*, and very early in *Tristram Shandy* Sterne's Yorick dies. On his gravestone, "serving both for his epitaph and elegy," are inscribed Hamlet's words: "Alas, poor YORICK!"

Sterne kills Parson Yorick early in *Tristram Shandy,* but he resurrects the parson to figure in later incidents of the novel. It is not Shakespeare's Yorick but his descendant who is dear to Sterne's Tristram, and yet that descendant is patterned on the Shakespearean original. Like the court jester of Prince Hamlet's childhood, Sterne's Parson Yorick is a man of infinite jest who can set a table or a town in a roar. And since both jesters are dead at the time of the main action, we view their jests against a graveyard background.

Like Hamlet, Tristram appreciates the jester, but Parson Yorick's quips are unappreciated by his coevals, Squire Shandy and Uncle Toby, who often vie for attention. Not for them, his enemies, nor the reader would Parson Yorick ever "take pains to set a story right." He is a creature of paradox: death combined with jest, narrative combined with digression, chronological time perforated by memory, piety peppered with ribaldry ("I think the procreation of children as beneficial to the world, said *Yorick,* as the finding out of the longitude.") (588) So it is entirely fitting that the Yorick who dies early in *Tristram Shandy* should close Sterne's long novel with a jest: "A *COCK* and a *BULL,* said Yorick—And one of the best of its kind I ever heard." Yorick's words embrace the Shandy bull, the novel *Tristram Shandy,* and the ambiguous virility of all fiction.

Created as a fictional character in *Tristram Shandy,* Parson Yorick became Sterne's signature for his own sermons, also published in 1760. In *Tristram Shandy* Parson Yorick remarks disapprovingly of one of his sermons: "I was delivered of it at the wrong end of me—it came from my head instead of my heart." (317) In 1767 Sterne published a book in which Parson Yorick is a creature of heart rather than head—*A Sentimental Journey.*[2] Almost every Sterne critic has described the difference between Parson Yorick, a jester's descendant of *Tristram Shandy,* and Parson Yorick, a sentimental philanderer of *A Sentimental Journey*, but the first to do so was Laurence Sterne, as his very title indicates.

Though the journeying pastor travels far from his jesting ancestor, the two converge at one point in the novel. Suddenly aware that he lacks a passport in France, the sentimental Parson Yorick presents himself to the Count de B, whom he knows to be a lover of Shakespeare.

> —*Et, Monsieur, est il Yorick*? cried the Count.—*Je le suis,* said I.—*Vous?—Moi—moi qui ai l'honneur de vous parler, Monsieur le Compte.—Mon Dieu*! said he, embracing me—*Vous etes Yorick.*

Within two hours, which Parson Yorick spends reading *Much Ado About Nothing*, the count returns with a passport for the king's jester:

> —Had it been for any one but the king's jester, added the Count, I could not have got it these two hours.—*Pardonnez moi,* Mons. le Count, said I, I am not the king's jester.—But you are Yorick?—Yes.—*Et vous plaisantez*?—I answered, Indeed I did jest—but was not paid for it—'twas entirely at my own expense. (233)

In the novel itself, however, Yorick does not jest, and yet it is he who acquires a passport as king's jester.

Yorick figures in these two Sterne novels, and the writer also signed himself Hamlet.[3] His fiction and non-fiction abound in quotations from that tragedy, and he was not alone to appreciate it in eighteenth-century England. However, Sterne's fictional incident would have been improbable in fact, since Shakespeare was virtually unknown in eighteenth-century France.

It was nineteenth-century personalities who most frequently identified with Hamlet, more often in Germany than in England or France. Perhaps such identification should be laid at the door of the writer sometimes called Germany's Shakespeare, Johann Wolfgang Goethe (1749-

1832), who expressed admiration for the Bard early and late in his long life, and who also directed versions of his plays.[4]

In *Dichtung und Wahrheit* Goethe recalls the steps of his early acquaintance with Shakespeare: reading excerpts in Dodd's anthology, reading Wieland's prose translations (published in 1766), discussing Shakespeare with the critic Herder and the playwright Lenz in Strasbourg. Back home in Frankfurt, Goethe penned a eulogy, *Zum Shakespears Tag.* The Bard influenced his plays *Götz* and *Egmont,* and the novel *Wilhelm Meisters Lehrjahre* pivots on *Hamlet.* When Goethe was theater director at Weimar, he produced *King John, Julius Caesar, Othello, King Lear,* and *Romeo and Juliet* in more or sometimes less faithful versions. In 1813, at the age of sixty-four, Goethe began his most extended examination of the Bard, *Shakespeare und Kein Ende.* The three divisions of that essay are: I. Shakespeare primarily as poet, II. Shakespeare compared with ancients and moderns, and III. Shakespeare as theater poet. In substance, Part III repeats the claim of Part I, that Shakespeare was not primarily a playwright but a poet: "So gehört Shakespeare notwendig in die Geschichte der Poesie; in der Geschichte des Theaters tritt er nur zufällig auf."* In an 1825 conversation with Eckermann Goethe pronounced a similar judgment: "An die Bühne hat er nie gedacht, sie war seinem grossen Geiste viel zu eng, ja selbst die ganze sichtbare Welt war ihm zu enge."[5]† This opinion had been voiced often enough in England, but not by someone who had directed Shakespeare's plays in the theater.

In none of Goethe's works does Shakespeare—and specifically *Hamlet*—play a more significant role than in *Wilhelm Meisters Lehrjahre,* begun when Goethe was in his

* So Shakespeare necessarily belongs to the history of poetry; he enters the history of theater only by chance.

† He never thought about the stage, which was much too narrow for his great spirit; indeed the whole visible world was too narrow for him.

twenties. Though Cervantes is the prototype of an author who weaves fiction into the texture of his own fiction, and Sterne pays tribute to his Spanish predecessor (his Yorick's last sentence quotes Sancho Panza "with something of a Cervantic tone"), their protagonists are not absorbed in a *single* fictional character, as is Wilhelm Meister.

Wilhelm Meister haunted Goethe almost as long as Faust did. Shortly after moving to Weimar at twenty-six, Goethe conceived Wilhelm. For some eight years he worked on a novel that he called *Wilhelm Meisters Theatralische Sendung*, but he never completed it.[6] The title is accurate in pointing to theater as Wilhelm Meister's main preoccupation. As a child, he is enthralled with puppets. As an adolescent, he writes and acts in Biblical plays. Under the name Geselle (Journeyman), he plays the hero of his own drama, *Belsazar*. Goethe's fiction breaks off when Wilhelm consents to act in the professional company of the actor-manager Serlo. But in spite of Goethe's title, Wilhelm Meister does not engage in anything so sustained as a theatrical mission, since his desire for a National German Theater (in a disunified nation) is mentioned only occasionally, and his theatrical adventures come about by chance.

Though the word *Sendung* (mission) no longer appears in the title of Goethe's finished novel, *Wilhelm Meisters Lehrjahre*, that hero is more aware of a theatrical mission. Eight years separate Goethe's last work on the *Sendung* from his first work on the *Lehrjahre*. Only in 1793, at forty-four—after Goethe had completed most of his own dramatic work, after he had made a crucial trip to Italy, after he had become director of the Weimar Theater—did he begin to rework the novel. In 1795 he published the first two (of eight) books, then sent the others to Schiller as they were completed, for comments and suggestions. After *Wilhelm Meisters Lehrjahre* was finally published in 1796, Goethe piloted Wilhelm Meister through several further episodes, published as *Wilhelm Meisters Wanderjahre* in 1829, three years before his death.

Goethe's portrait of Hamlet became famous through the fame of *Wilhelm Meisters Lehrjahre,* but that portrait is substantially present in the unfinished *Wilhelm Meisters Theatralische Sendung* (whose manuscript was discovered only in 1910). In both books a nobleman, Jarno, introduces the hero to Shakespeare's plays in the Wieland prose translation. Wilhelm reacts with enthusiasm in both books, and both Wilhelms are drawn to *Hamlet* above Shakespeare's other plays. The early Wilhelm Meister wants to enact the Prince, and he identifies with Hamlet more closely than in the revised novel:

> Wir haben schon im vorigen Buche gesehn, dass [Wilhelm] die Rolle des Prinzen studiert, und es ist natürlich, dass er mit den stärksten Stellen, den Selbstgesprächen und jenen Auftritten angefangen, wo Kraft der Seele, Erhebung, Lebhaftigkeit Spielraum haben und ein freies, edles Gemüt in gefühlvollem Ausdrucke sich zeigen kann. Auch die Last der tiefen Schwermut war er geneigt auf sich zu nehmen, und die Übung der Rolle verschlang sich vergestalt in sein einsames Leben, dass endlich *er und Hamlet eine Person zu werden anfingen.** (209-210; my italics)

The narrator of the earlier version describes Meister's view of the idealistic prince before his father's death, but Wilhelm himself compares Hamlet's tender soul to a precious vase and his vengeful duty to a growing oak. Goethe's early version breaks off before Wilhelm's *Hamlet* production is past the planning stage. In the *Sendung* the hero re-

* In earlier books we saw that Wilhelm studied the part of the Prince, and it is natural that he began with the highpoints, the soliloquies, and those scenes in which strength of spirit, exaltation, vivacity have full scope, and in which a noble soul can be shown in emotional expression. He was also inclined to take upon himself the burden of deep melancholy, and the rehearsal of the part was inextricably blended with his own lonely life so that finally he and Hamlet began to be one person.

acts emotionally to Hamlet, identifying with him, but in the *Lehrjahre* the production of *Hamlet* becomes an important event in Goethe's plot. A fiction is incorporated into fiction.

Wilhelm Meisters Lehrjahre is a long novel, at once a narration of picaresque adventures, a description of passionate feelings, a reflection of bourgeois, theatrical, and aristocratic circles in provincial Germany of the mid-eighteenth century.[7] Most centrally, it is an account of the hero's education to responsibility. Though the novel moves slowly, it does move, and its power is cumulative. Goethe uses such stock fictional devices as journeys, chance meetings, secret societies, quoted letters, literary insertions, and yet the novel vividly evokes several social strata, even while it focuses on its hero. Its modernity, like that of *Don Quixote* and *Tristram Shandy*, rests on the intricate interweaving of two levels of fiction, enhancing the felt life of the primary level.

Wilhelm Meisters Lehrjahre is divided into eight books, but it falls into three parts: the first five books (incorporating and extending the material of the *Sendung*) treat Wilhelm's theater activities; the sixth is the journal of a woman whom Wilhelm never meets, and its subject is a religion that renounces the world; the last two books return to Wilhelm as he moves in aristocratic circles. By the end of Goethe's novel, Wilhelm can literalize his name *Meister*, for his apprenticeship is at an end.

Goethe's long novel opens: "Das Schauspiel dauerte sehr lange." In that *Schauspiel* a breeches role is played by Mariane, Wilhelm's first love. During their affair he describes his childhood enthusiasm for puppet-plays. He does not tell Mariane what he later comes to suspect—that this bourgeois is attracted to her because she is an actress.

On a business trip Wilhelm befriends a traveling actor, but back at home he falls ill when he suspects that Mariane is unfaithful to him. Once his health is regained, he leaves on another business trip. (Like Willy Loman, Wilhelm is engaged in a business whose particulars we never learn.)

This time he meets the actor as part of a traveling troupe that he informally joins. Notable among its members are an uninhibited actress Philine, a temperamental actor Laertes, a homeless waif Mignon, and a half-crazed harper without a name. While the group performs at a count's castle, Wilhelm is introduced to Shakespeare by Jarno, a young aristocrat. At the castle, Wilhelm is strongly attracted to a countess.

After the group leaves the castle, it is attacked by highwaymen, and disperses. Wilhelm, Philine, Laertes, Mignon, and the harper remain together. After the death of Wilhelm's father, he enters a professional theater under the management of Serlo. With that director and his sister Aurelie, Wilhelm discusses theater and literature. Under Wilhelm's tutelage, the newly constituted company successfully performs a modified version of *Hamlet,* with Wilhelm in the title role. Shortly afterward, Aurelie dies after playing Countess Orsina in Lessing's *Emilia Galotti.*

Aurelie's doctor gives Wilhelm the book that forms Goethe's Book VI. After Aurelie's death, Wilhelm seeks out Lothario, her aristocratic lover, to confront him with the child Felix, whom he assumes to be theirs. But the gay Lothario is not the boy's father. Felix proves to be Wilhelm's son by Mariane, now dead and not unfaithful.

Lothario introduces Wilhelm into an aristocratic Society of the Tower, headed by an Abbé who officially declares the end of Wilhelm Meister's apprenticeship. However, Goethe's novel continues for another few chapters during which Wilhelm contracts an engagement with a rich bourgeoise, Therese, and extricates Lothario from another amatory adventure. Finally, Lothario is engaged to Therese, and Wilhelm to Natalie, who is the sister of Lothario, of the countess at the castle, and of a scapegrace Friedrich who was infatuated with Philine. Mignon proves to be the harper's daughter, and these romantic figures die romantic deaths—Mignon of excessive emotion and the harper by suicide. The book closes on the promise of a double marriage, and on Wilhelm's answer to Friedrich's quip that he is like Saul, who went out to seek his father's asses and found a kingdom: "Ich kenne den Wert eines Königreichs nicht . . . aber ich weiss, dass ich ein Glück erlangt habe, das ich nicht verdiene und das ich mit nichts in der Welt vertauschen möchte."*

It is Wilhelm himself, and not the narrator, who confronts Shakespeare's tragedy in Goethe's revised novel. *Hamlet* is the meeting-point of the two main lines of Wilhelm's education: it is a book given him by the aristocrat Jarno, who will lead him to the Society of the Tower, and it is a tragedy in which Wilhelm plays the lead, only to realize that he will never be an actor. *Hamlet* spans both theater and aristocracy, and its impact on Wilhelm demands detailed examination.

When Jarno hears Wilhelm hold forth on Racine, he asks whether the young bourgeois has ever seen a Shakespeare play. The answer is negative, and it is expressed in words that epitomize much eighteenth-century criticism of dramas that "über alle Wahrscheinlichkeit, allen Wohlstand hinauszuschreiten scheinen."† (180) Jarno sends Wilhelm a book, which we later learn is the Wieland prose translation in which Goethe himself first read *Hamlet*.

While the theater troupe behaves obstreperously at the count's castle, Wilhelm loses himself in Shakespeare. Intensely moved, he gives vent to egocentric emotions, and egocentricity is perhaps the most consistent trait of his apprenticeship. But it is to his emotion that Jarno responds, asking about Wilhelm's background as opposed to that of his theater companions. Wilhelm defends his colleagues. But devoted as he is to them, he has a post-Shakespeare image of himself as Prince Hal in Eastcheap, and he therefore begins to pay attention to the way he dresses, toward

* I know not the worth of a kingdom . . . but I know I have attained a happiness which I have not deserved, and which I would not change with anything in life.

† appear to set probability and dignity alike at defiance.

the time when he will reveal his princely identity. After leaving the count's castle, the theater company declares itself a republic, electing Wilhelm as its director. The would-be prince becomes a kind of president, who, like Hamlet, gives acting instructions to the players.

Having decided to perform *Hamlet*, with Wilhelm in the title role, the players listen to Wilhelm's comments on the play. More or less on the play, since Wilhelm imagines the Prince before his father's murder: "Angenehm von Gestalt, gesittet von Natur, gefällig von Herzen aus, sollte er das Muster der Jugend sein und die Freude der Welt werden."* (217-218) For these cheerfully grasping Bohemians, Wilhelm draws an idealized model. (The idealization is not entirely intentional on Goethe's part, depending on Wieland's changes of Shakespeare's play.)[8] Wilhelm's Hamlet has lived virtuously and loved Ophelia truly. "Er besass mehr Frölichkeit der Laune als des Herzens, war ein guter Gesellschafter, nachgiebig, bescheiden, besorgt, und konnte eine Beleidigung vergeben und vergessen; aber niemals konnte er sich mit dem vereinigen der die Grenzen des Rechten, des Guten, des Anständigen überschritt."† (242)

The theater group travels somewhat aimlessly. Wilhelm and Laertes practice fencing for their fatal duel in *Hamlet*. Playing at theater, they are attacked by actual armed men. Both duelists defend their companions, but the robbers make off with the actors' possessions. Wounded, and deserted by all but Philine and Mignon, Wilhelm is tended by a doctor in the entourage of a beautiful noblewoman whom the narrator calls the Amazon. It is Wilhelm's first glimpse of Natalie, who will be his wife.

When Wilhelm's wounds are healed, he seeks out the actor-manager Serlo, in the hope that he will employ the players for whose losses he feels responsible. Serlo has a

* Pleasing in form, polished by nature, courteous from the heart, he was meant to be the pattern of youth and the joy of the world.

† He possessed more mirth of humour than of heart; he was a good companion, pliant, courteous, discreet, and able to forget and forgive an injury; yet never able to unite himself with those who overstept the limits of the right, the good, and the becoming.

low opinion of traveling actors, but he welcomes Wilhelm and his passion for *Hamlet.* Wilhelm repeats his earlier portrait of the Prince, overcomes Serlo's objections to his view, and expands on the Prince's plight. The young bourgeois imagines the effect on Hamlet of his king-father's murder and his queen-mother's marriage; he then delivers an impression of Hamlet, which Arthur Eastman in his *Short History of Shakespearean Criticism* calls "the summary, the climax, and probably the most famous of all the remarks ever made about a Shakespearean character."[9]

> Die Zeit ist aus dem Gelenke; wehe mir, dass ich geboren ward, sie wieder einzurichten.
>
> In diesen Worten, dünkt mich, liegt der Schlüssel zu Hamlets ganzen Betragen, und mir ist deutlich, dass Shakespeare habe schildern wollen: eine grosse Tat auf eine Seele gelegt, die der Tat nicht gewachsen ist. Und in diesem Sinne find' ich das Stück durchgängig gearbeitet. Hier wird ein Eichbaum in ein köstliches Gefäss gepflanzt, das nur liebliche Blumen in seinen Schoss hätte aufnehmen sollen; die Wurzeln dehnen sich aus, das Gefäss wird zernichtet.
>
> Ein schönes, reines, edles, höchst moralisches Wesen, ohne die sinnliche Stärke, die den Helden macht, geht unter einer Last zugrunde, die es weder tragen noch abwerfen kann; jede Pflicht ist ihm heiling, diese zu schwer. Das Unmögliche wird von ihm gefordert, nicht das Unmögliche an sich, sondern das, was ihm unmöglich ist. Wie er sich wendet, dreht, ängstigt, vor- und zurücktritt, immer erinnert wird, sich immer erinnert und zuletzt fast seinen Zweck aus dem Sinne verliert, ohne doch jemals wieder froh zu werden!* (246)

* The time is out of joint: O cursed spite,
That ever I was born to set it right!

In these words, I imagine, will be found the key to Hamlet's whole procedure. To me it is clear that Shakespeare meant, in the present case, to represent the effects of a great action laid upon a soul unfit for the performance of it. In this view the whole piece seems to me to be

Though it is evident that Wilhelm ignores much of Shakespeare's play and much of the Prince's character, he empathizes with the hero, and he does so in images. However, an oak tree with its associations of age and strength is not the aptest metaphor for the necessity of the Prince's revenge.

Wilhelm's famous portrait is punctuated by the entrance of musicians, and Aurelie leads him into another room to ask about Ophelia, but Wilhelm's description accords better with Goethe's Gretchen than with the daughter of Polonius. Wilhelm's sympathy for Ophelia inspires Aurelie to tell him the story of her own unhappy love. However, she wallows in grief rather than revealing facts, and it is the actress Philine who summarizes the situation for Wilhelm: Aurelie has been abandoned by Lothario, her aristocratic lover. With verve, Philine outlines a drama in which several can play: "Sie läuft ihrem Ungetreuen, du ihr, ich dir, und der Bruder mir nach."* (248)

Wilhelm thinks about Hamlet, even as he becomes initiated into the professionalism of Serlo's company. Serlo objects that the play loses interest after the third act, but Wilhelm defends it. However, Serlo retorts to the defense in words that have often been flung at Shakespeare supporters: "Dann scheinen Sie mir wieder zu Ehren Ihres Dichters, wie andere zu Ehren der Vorsehung ihm Endzweck und Plane unterzuschieben, an die er nicht gedacht hat."† (254)

---

composed. There is an oak-tree planted in a costly jar, which should have borne only pleasant flowers in its bosom; the roots expand, the jar is shivered.

A lovely, pure, noble and most moral nature, without the strength of nerve which forms a hero, sinks beneath a burden which it cannot bear and must not cast away. All duties are holy for him; the present is too hard. Impossibilities have been required of him; not in themselves impossibilities, but such for him. He winds, and turns, and torments himself; he advances and recoils; is ever put in mind, ever puts himself in mind; at last does all but lose his purpose from his thoughts; yet still without recovering his peace of mind.

* She pursues her faithless swain, thou her, I thee, her brother me.

† It appears to me that, for the honour of your poet, as others for the honour of Providence, you ascribe to him an object and a plan, which he himself had never thought of.

As the climax of Wilhelm's passion for the theater, he signs a formal contract with Serlo, who is willing to produce *Hamlet,* but he wants a shorter play with a happy ending (as actor-manager Friedrich Ludwig Schröder played it in eighteenth-century Germany). Intransigent about the tragic ending, Wilhelm is surprisingly agreeable to cutting the text. He has divided the plot into internal (and indispensable) relationships and external (and therefore dispensable) relationships. Among the latter he lists Hamlet's Wittenberg past, the Fortinbras plot, Laertes in France, Hamlet's English adventure. He cheerfully replaces these with a plot of his own: Hamlet's Horatio becomes the son of the Danish regent of Norway, sent to Denmark to outfit the navy. As in Shakespeare, Horatio sees the Ghost and befriends Hamlet; but then he urges the Prince to accompany him to Norway, so as to return with an invading army. In the meantime the suspicious King and Queen set Rosencrantz, Guildenstern, and Laertes to spy on Hamlet, whom they send to Norway with the fatal letter. But the ship cannot leave, because of unfavorable winds. In conclusion

> Hamlet kehrt nochmals zurück; seine Wanderung über den Kirchhof kann vielleicht glücklich motiviert werden; sein Zusammentreffen mit Laertes in Opheliens Grabe ist ein grosser unentbehrlicher Moment. Hierauf mag der König bedenken, dass es besser sei, Hamlet auf der Stelle loszuwerden; das Fest der Abreise, der scheinbaren Versöhnung mit Laertes wird nun feierlich begangen, wobei man Ritterspiele hält und auch Hamlet und Laertes fechten. Ohne die vier Leichen kann ich das Stück nicht schliessen; es darf niemand übrigbleiben. Hamlet gibt, da nun das Wahlrecht des Volks wieder eintritt, seine Stimme sterbend dem Horatio.* (298)

* Hamlet returns: for his wandering through the churchyard perhaps some lucky motive may be thought of; his meeting with Laertes in Ophelia's grave is a grand moment, which we must not part with. After

Serlo is delighted with the Meister version, but casting is a problem, particularly since Wilhelm objects to combining Rosencrantz and Guildenstern into a single role. By impressing every able body, they manage to fill all parts except the Ghost. As they brood about this difficulty, Wilhelm receives a mysterious note:

> Du bist, o sonderbarer Jüngling, wir wissen es, in grosser Verlegenheit. Du findest kaum Menschen zu deinem Hamlet, geschweige Geister. Dein Eifer verdient ein Wunder; Wunder können wir nicht tun, aber etwas Wunderbares soll geschehen. Hast du Vertrauen, so soll zur rechten Stunde der Geist erscheinen! Habe Mut und bleibe gefasst! Es bedarf keiner Antwort, dein Entschluss wird uns bekannt werden.* (304)

Wilhelm shows faith, but then rehearsals occupy him so that he forgets about the Ghost. During the rehearsal period Serlo speaks enthusiastically of his role as Polonius, but Aurelie thinks she is not right for the young and innocent Ophelia. Wilhelm, trying to reassure her, mentions his own difficulty in playing a fat blond prince, since he is presumably lean and dark—a spiritual rather than physical brother of Hamlet.

For rehearsals, the actors are joined by two men who are a blend of what would today be called costumers, stage

---

this, the King resolves that it is better to get quit of Hamlet on the spot: the festival of his departure, the pretended reconcilement with Laertes, are now solemnized; on which occasion knightly sports are held, and Laertes fights with Hamlet. Without the four corpses I cannot end the piece; not one of them can possibly be left. The right of popular election now again comes in force, and Hamlet gives his dying voice for Horatio.

* Strange youth! we know thou art in great perplexity. For thy Hamlet thou canst hardly find men enough, not to speak of Ghosts. Thy zeal deserves a miracle: miracles we cannot work; but somewhat marvellous shall happen. If thou have faith, the Ghost shall arise at the proper hour! Be of courage and keep firm! This needs no answer: thy determination will be known to us.

managers, and special-effects people. They coach Wilhelm and Laertes for their duel, more expertly than the two young actors had practiced fencing so many adventures ago. Wilhelm blocks the opening scene and the closet scene. Serlo again urges that the Prince be left alive at the play's end, but Wilhelm is unbending, and the narrator concludes the matter: "Wir lassen uns hierauf nicht weiter ein, sondern legen vielleicht künftig die neue Bearbeitung Hamlets selbst denjenigen Teile unsrer Leser vor, der sich etwa dafür interessieren könnte."* (313)

However, he does no such thing. Instead, he gives us a marvelously authentic feeling of all that remains to be done between a dress rehearsal and a performance, even while offstage life goes on. Wilhelm, pressed by Aurelie, denies that he is having an affair with Philine, but he finds Philine's slippers in his room. The curtain is up, and the house is full. Wilhelm listens to the Danish soldiers. After Horatio describes the Ghost, the figure—although no one had been cast for the part—miraculously appears on cue: ". . .die edle grosse Gestalt, der leise, unhörbare Tritt, die leichte Bewegung in der schwer scheinenden Rüstung machten einen so starken Eindruck auf ihn, dass er wie versteinert dastand und nur mit halber Stimme: Ihr Engel und himmlischen Geister, beschützt uns! ausrufen konnte."† (321) As Partridge describes Garrick's fright in *Tom Jones,* Goethe's narrator describes that of Wilhelm.

When the Ghost declares: "Ich bin der Geist deines Vaters," Wilhelm seems to hear the voice of his own father, recently deceased. Spellbound, he listens to the Ghost's tale until the figure disappears.

The rest of the *Hamlet* performance is not described, but

* We shall not enter farther on those points at present; but perhaps at some future time we may admit this altered Hamlet itself to such of our readers as feel any interest in the subject.

† . . . the tall noble figure, the low inaudible tread, the light movement in the heavy-looking armour, made such an impression on him, that he stood as if transformed to stone, and could utter only in a half-voice his: "Angels and ministers of grace defend us!"

applause is loud, and the cashbox heavy. At the opening-night party, the actors go over the details of the performance, as actors always go over an opening. But, exceptionally, these actors ponder the identity of the Ghost, who has disappeared as mysteriously as he arrived. When Wilhelm falls into bed after the night's merrymaking, he thinks he hears a ghost in his room, but he sinks instead under a passionate body. Awakening late, he finds that the unknown woman has gone, but in his room is the Ghost's veil with a note attached: "Zum ersten- und letztenmal! Flieh! Jüngling flieh!" (328)

Wilhelm shows the veil to the others, and there is general agreement that the Ghost will not return, so that his role is quickly given to someone else, newly available. But Wilhelm does not heed the Ghost's command. He remains with Serlo's group, and as the days go by he becomes disenchanted with them. He notices careless craftsmanship, and the actors speak of putting on a light opera, thus mocking his high aims for theater. In the meantime they produce Lessing's *Emilia Galotti*, with Wilhelm ill at ease as the Prince, and Serlo able as Marinelli. On opening night, Aurelie plays the abandoned Countess Orsina with such passion that she receives an ovation. However, Serlo finds her acting exaggerated and berates her in her dressing-room. She runs out into the cold rainy night and catches a fatal fever. Glad to die, she has her doctor bring her a book that she peruses during her last hours of consciousness. After giving her friend Wilhelm a letter, she sinks into death. Wilhelm is so moved that he finds it impossible to continue in theater. Wilhelm Meister leaves the theater, not knowing that the departure is permanent.

When he arrives at the home of Aurelie's lover, Lothario, he again meets the nobleman Jarno, who greets him warmly. As Wilhelm becomes involved with the lives of the members of the Society of the Tower, he realizes that theater is not for him. He writes to his bourgeois friend Werner: "Ich verlasse das Theater und verbinde mich mit Männern, deren Umgang mich in jedem Sinne zu einer reinen und sichern Tätigkeit führen muss." (491) But there is one scene left for him to play, and it springs directly from *Hamlet*.

Wilhelm formally enters the Society of the Tower in a deconsecrated chapel where four figures in succession appear before him—a man who speaks of his grandfather's art collection, a clergyman who says that one learns through error, an officer who advises him to know whom to trust. Last appears the Ghost from *Hamlet*, in full armor, who speaks: "Ich bin der Geist deines Vaters . . . und scheide getrost, da meine Wünsche für dich, mehr als ich sie selbst begriff, erfüllt sind. Steile Gegenden lassen sich nur durch Umweg erklimmen, auf der Eben führen gerade Wege von einem Ort zum andern. Lebe wohl, und gedenke mein, wenn du geniessest, was ich dir vorbereitet habe."* (495) Present and past merge in Wilhelm's mind—when the Abbé enters and presents Wilhelm with the letter announcing the end of his apprenticeship. Its phrasing reproves Wilhelm's prior imitation of the heavily burdened Prince, who wastes his life in words rather than deeds: "Das echten Künstlers Lehre schliesst den Sinn auf; denn wo die Worte fehlen, spricht die Tat. Der echte Schüler lernt aus dem Bekannten das Unbekannte entwickeln, und nähert sich dem Meister."† (496) Mastership is achieved by imitating deeds rather than words—an anti-Hamlet. And thus Hamlet has served Wilhelm as a stepping-stone toward becoming a man of action.

After Wilhelm is reunited with his son Felix, after Mignon and the harpist are dead, Jarno informs Wilhelm

* I am thy father's spirit . . . and I depart in comfort, since my wishes for thee are accomplished, in a higher sense than I myself contemplated. Steep regions cannot be surmounted save by winding paths; on the plain, straight roads conduct from place to place. Farewell, and think of me, when thou enjoyest what I have provided for thee.

† The instruction which the true artist gives us, opens the mind; for where words fail him, deeds speak. The true scholar learns from the known to unfold the unknown, and approaches more and more to being a master.

of how the Society of the Tower mysteriously selects its members, educating them through their own errors. One of Wilhelm's errors was theater, in which he could never achieve mastery because he could play only himself. As a deedless young man, he could excel in the role of Shakespeare's Prince, but to achieve his own goals, he had to follow the injunction of the Ghost and flee. Wilhelm asks Jarno about the identity of the Ghost, and the nobleman replies that it is either the Abbé or his twin brother. Finally, then, the Ghost retains some of his mystery, but he has acted *in loco patris,* guiding Wilhelm away from theater toward responsibility in the world at large. The role of Hamlet helped Wilhelm achieve self-definition. Shakespeare's tragedy of *Hamlet* has served Goethe in achieving a comic ending, with its promise of a double marriage.

Skillfully, Goethe binds his rambling plot with *Hamlet.* Not five per cent of his novel is taken up with Shakespeare's play, but from the first mention it is crucial. Wilhelm feels the Prince's woes even before he thinks of enacting him. Hot-headed Laertes plays hot-headed Laertes. Aurelie, believing herself rejected, plays a rejected Ophelia, and she too dies a virtual suicide. Philine shows no comprehension of the Gertrude she plays, and Serlo approaches Polonius with cool professionalism. The relations of actors to roles are various and complex. And the Ghost literally comes from another world, that of aristocratic responsibility, to direct Wilhelm's destiny, which the young bourgeois nevertheless works out for himself.

Wilhelm's destiny is pointedly contrasted with that of Hamlet. Wilhelm's portrait of the Prince as passive and idealistic intellectual is the self-portrait he is incapable of drawing. Nor does he come to know himself through the Shakespearean lens. Rather, *Hamlet* is the error through which Wilhelm has to graduate to maturity. Instead of obeying the Ghost's injunction to flee the world of theater, he lingers on without a plan. Back in the theater company after having breathed the Tower's busy air, Wilhelm realizes that the theater is not for him. He returns to the Tower and is confronted by the Ghost, who speaks the Shakespearean line: "Ich bin der Geist deines Valters." It is to his father's spirit that Wilhelm returns, graduating from his artistic (and untalented) apprenticeship to self-imposed duty. With his father's fidelity to serious business, and as the father of Felix, Wilhelm enters the aristocracy that is opened to him through the Society of the Tower and his engagement to Natalie. By the end of the novel Wilhelm has outgrown his indecisive Hamletic self, though he still bears the Christian name of Hamlet's playwright.

The question arises: Does Goethe share his Wilhelm's view of Hamlet? For over a century after the publication of *Wilhelm Meister* it was assumed that he did. Even Friedrich Schlegel, who was sensitive to the book's ironies, finds no discrepancy between the creative criticism of Goethe and Wilhelm: "Die in diesen und dem ersten Buche des nächsten Bandes zerstreute Ansicht des Hamlet ist nicht so wohl Kritik als hohe Poesie. Und was kann wohl anders entstehn als ein Gedicht, wenn ein Dichter als solcher ein Werk der Dichtkunst anschaut und darstellt? . . . [Der Dichter] wird das Werk ergänzen, verjüngern, neu gestalten."[10*] Not only does Schlegel give no indication that Goethe himself delivers no view of *Hamlet,* but he praises Wilhelm's reaction as poetic. The influential German scholar, Friedrich Gundolf, seems to be the first (in 1911) to suggest a discrepancy between the criticism of Goethe and that of his fiction.[11]

The question influences any view of Goethe's novel. Does Wilhelm have to outgrow his Hamlet-portrait as he does his Hamlet-role? Or is his education to be contrasted with a basically sound interpretation of the Prince? Is one of the novel's multiple ironies an implicit critique of what is

* The view of Hamlet scattered through this and the first book of the next volume is not so much criticism as poetry. And what indeed but a poem can result if a poet as such views and describes a great poetic work? . . . The poet will complete the work, rejuvenate it, form it anew.

"probably the most famous of all the remarks ever made about a Shakespearean character?"

I think that Goethe shares Wilhelm's view of Hamlet. Dennis W. Mueller has shown how heavily that view rests on Wieland's prose version of Shakespeare's tragedy, which cuts the get-thee-to-a-nunnery scene, the graveyard scene, and Hamlet's wit turned on Rosencrantz, Guildenstern, and Polonius.[12] U. Henry Gerlach has drawn a detailed comparison of Wilhelm's analysis with Goethe's non-fictionalized remarks about *Hamlet*, and he finds them similar, especially with respect to destiny.[13] To this may be added the fact that Goethe made no changes in Wilhelm's opinions about *Hamlet* between the *Sendung* and the *Lehrjahre*, though he increased his ironic distance from his protagonist. And late in his life, Goethe remarked to Eckermann: "Man kann über Shakespeare gar nicht reden, es ist alles unzulänglich. Ich habe in meinem Wilhelm Meister an ihm herumgetupft; allein, das will nicht viel heissen."[14]* Not *er* [Wilhelm] speaks about Shakespeare, but *ich*. The logical assumption is that Goethe infused Wilhelm with his own Hamlet-interpretation.

Moreover, the logic of the novel seems to demand such an assumption. Unless Wilhelm's Hamlet-portrait is taken as true, one loses the central contrast between Hamlet whose character is fixed (by Goethe) and Wilhelm who plays and then outgrows him. Hamlet fails in a duty that is impossible for him to fulfill—avenging his father. But Wilhelm succeeds in a duty that is possible for him to fulfill—educating himself to be a responsible father.

Goethe was already a respected writer when the *Lehrjahre* was published, and the Meister-Goethe Hamlet was read as his own. That Hamlet-portrait played a part wherever Romanticism burgeoned. In England Thomas Carlyle wrote in 1828: "*Meister* is the mature product of the first

* One can't talk about Shakespeare at all; whatever one says is inadequate. In my Wilhelm Meister I dabbled at it, but that doesn't mean much.

genius of our times." But while working on his translation in 1824, his feelings fell short of such unstinted admiration, and he wrote to his future wife:

> When I read of players and libidinous actresses and their sorry pasteboard apparatus for beautifying and enlivening the "moral world," I render it into grammatical English—with a feeling mild and charitable as that of a starving hyena. . . . *N'importe*! . . . Goethe is the greatest genius that has lived for a century, and the greatest ass that has lived for three. I could sometimes fall down and worship him; at other times I could kick him out of the room.[15]

Carlyle was deaf to the irony of Goethe, who also thought that the theater is a "pasteboard apparatus for beautifying and enlivening the moral world," but Goethe made vigorous fiction of that apparatus, and he was the first to beautify and enliven a Shakespearean character so that his hero could empathize with him.

"Ich habe Hamlet ein langes Leben hindurch zum unsterblichen Freunde gehabt. Überall ist er um mich gewesen und hat sich dabei allmählich von den schönen Fesseln der Shakespeareschen Dichtung ganz befreit."[16]* At least a dozen Romantic writers might have penned these lines—Novalis, Heine, or, changing the language, Stendhal, Musset, Vigny, Coleridge, Keats, Pushkin, Mickiewicz, Melville, Lowell.

In actual fact, Gerhart Hauptmann (1862-1948) wrote these sentences in the preface to his play *Hamlet in Wittenberg* (1935).[17] But the evidence points to only minimal accuracy. In his memoirs Hauptmann tells of playing with a paper-doll Hamlet when he was eight years old. As adolescent and adult, he saw various Shakespeare plays in the the-

* Throughout a long life, I have had Hamlet as an undying friend. He was everywhere with me and therefore gradually freed himself from the lovely shackles of Shakespeare.

ater, *Hamlet* among them. At twenty-two, in Rome to study sculpture, he was impressed by the actor Salvini's Hamlet. A year later Hauptmann came to Berlin to study acting, with the intention of playing Hamlet, but he was soon swept up in the avant-garde of the time, Naturalism. His first play, *Vor Sonnenaufgang* (1889), was the opening salvo of German Naturalist drama; it was dedicated to Bjarne P. Holmsen "dem consequentesten Realisten, Verfasser von 'Papa Hamlet' . . . in freudiger Anerkennung der durch sein Buch empfangenen entscheidenden Anregung."* In 1899 Hauptmann turned from Naturalism to a romantic fantasy-farce *Schluck und Jau,* based on the induction to Shakespeare's *Taming of the Shrew.* In 1912 he received the Nobel Prize and began an adaptation of Shakespeare's *Tempest,* which he did not complete. In 1915, during World War I, he wrote praise of Shakespeare for the German Shakespeare Society: "Wenn er in England geboren und begraben ist, so ist Deutschland das Land, wo er wahrhaft lebt!"† In 1920 Hauptmann drew upon *Hamlet* for the title of his Memoirs, *Die abgekürzte Chronik meines Lebens.* In 1927 he combined the three English texts of *Hamlet,* the German *Bestrafte Brudermord,* and Shakespeare's predecessors Saxo and Belleforest, to compose what he called an *Ur-Hamlet.* In 1935 he wrote a play about the pre-Shakespearean Prince, *Hamlet in Wittenberg.* Concurrently, he worked on a novel that was published a year later, *Im Wirbel der Berufung,* in which *Hamlet* figures importantly.[18]

The last work is patterned on and against *Wilhelm Meisters Lehrjahre* and should be discussed in its proximity. Separated by one hundred forty years, the two novels focus on young heroes engaged in theater activity that is climaxed by a production of *Hamlet.* In each novel, divided into eight books, a sensitive bourgeois bears a name too large for

* the most consistent realist, author of "Papa Hamlet," in grateful acknowledgment of the decisive inspiration aroused by his book.

† Even if he was born and buried in England, Germany is the country in which he truly lives.

his achievements—Wilhelm Meister and Erasmus Gotter. Though both novels are third-person narratives, events resemble those in the lives of their respective authors. In both books, love stories are interwoven with theatrical adventures, against a cultivated and aristocratic background. Enraptured with *Hamlet,* both heroes adapt it (using different translations), and both enact the Prince, but both heroes are haunted by the Ghost as well as the Prince. In both novels the hero's *Hamlet* experience results in his withdrawal from the theater. But through the agency of theater, and especially of *Hamlet,* both heroes develop and mature so that they face their respective futures resolutely, with newly acquired self-awareness.

Hauptmann must have been conscious of some of these similarities, though his hero specifically opposes Wilhelm Meister on several points—the erotic experience of Ophelia, the importance of Wittenberg in Hamlet's background, the unplayability of Hamlet's tragedy as written. In Hauptmann's novel as a whole, the major difference with Goethe arises from a similarity. Both authors draw upon their own lives for their fiction, but the difference lies in the artistic use of their lives. Goethe was able to achieve ironic distance from his characters; the most obvious example is Werther, for Goethe did not commit suicide after an unhappy love affair, but wrote *Die Leiden des Jungen Werthers.* And his entrance into an aristocratic milieu was made, not as in Meister's case, through marriage, but through his own gifts. With less ironic distance, Hauptmann transferred from his life to his novel a conflict over two women who loved him.[19] However, this protagonist returns to his wife, whereas Hauptmann did not, so that the novel may be seen as sublimation.

Hauptmann's strength as a Naturalist lay in his meticulous observation of people and the conditions in which they lived. He filled innumerable notebooks with details, which he later incorporated into drama and fiction. Though *Im Wirbel der Berufung* is not a Naturalistic novel, many characters are based on real people. *Im Wirbel der Berufung,* published in 1936, takes place in 1885, when twenty-three-year-old Hauptmann was first married. Hauptmann's twenty-three-year-old hero has a wife and two children, but, alone on a holiday, he is asked to supervise a production of *Hamlet.* Erasmus Gotter is attracted and attractive to two women who alternate in the role of Ophelia, and it is they who correspond to the rival women in Hauptmann's own life.

Im Wirbel resembles the *Lehrjahre* in its interweaving of Shakespeare's fiction with fictionalized autobiography, but Hauptmann was more heavy-handed than Goethe both in his fidelity to fact and in his insistence on the relevance of *Hamlet* to that fact. Unlike Goethe, whose successive titles *Sendung* and *Lehrjahre* point to a change of intention in revision, Hauptmann's successive titles seem to reflect difficulty in deciding on his central emphasis: *Katharsis, Hamlet Prinz von Dänemark, Hamlets Geist, Die Eheferien des Erasmus Gotter,* and finally *Im Wirbel der Berufung* (In the Turmoil of the Calling). Hauptmann evidently wished to include all these aspects in his novel, two of which refer directly to *Hamlet.*

Goethe's Meister unconsciously identifies with Shakespeare's Prince as he studies the role, but we are made very conscious of Gotter's identification. Several of his companions remark on the resemblance of the young Germanist to the Danish Prince—his actor friend Jethro, the two rival Ophelias, and, most insistently, the Royal Librarian Dr. Ollentag. Gotter himself admits to having Hamlet's (unnamed) weaknesses but few of his virtues. And the narrator writes at one point: "Erasmus fühlte, wie er mit diese Worten fast in der Hamlet-Gestalt aufgegangen war und diese mit ihm ein und das gleiche würde."* (252)

However, though both protagonists identify with Hamlet, it is with different Hamlets. Wilhelm's is a sensitive

* Erasmus felt how, with these words, he almost dissolved into the Hamlet-figure, which became his very self.

idealist who is destroyed by the necessity for action. Erasmus' reacts against Wilhelm's, which had become the traditional German *Hamletbild.* Erasmus Gotter, a Germanist with his doctor's degree at the age of twenty-three, modifies Shakespeare's text (in the A. W. Schlegel translation) and rationalizes the modification as the true original text. Instead of Laertes, says Erasmus, it is Hamlet who leads a mutinous army in Act IV, Scene 5. Hamlet then accedes to his mother's protest of Claudius' innocence, and he disperses his followers. Knowing that he has lost the initiative, Hamlet thinks of suicide, so that Erasmus shifts the "To be or not to be" soliloquy from III, 1 to V, 2. Thus, Hamlet's actual death is tinged by his readiness to die, and Hamlet is linked to Erasmus who "hatte diese Frage in den Wirren seines Inneren mehr als einmal in allem Ernst vorgelegt."* (108)

Goethe's Wilhelm expresses a consistent if inadequate view of Hamlet. The pre-play idealist grows into the incapable intellectual. Erasmus first sees the play as a power-contest between Hamlet and Claudius, but this view changes through his personal experience. It is because Erasmus is on a vacation from his wife that he has an affair with the actress Irina Bell and thereupon ascribes that affair to Hamlet and Ophelia. Similarly, Erasmus transposes Princess Ditta's magnetism to Ophelia, and he exaggerates the importance of the Hamlet-Ophelia scene of Shakespeare's tragedy. Hauptmann is not clear as to whether Erasmus infuses his illicit eroticism into the performance text or only into the rehearsal passion.

This uncertainty hovers also over what comes to be *Hamlet*'s main meaning for Erasmus Gotter, designated by the rejected title *Hamlets Geist.* After Erasmus has begun rehearsals, he is convinced by Rector Trautvetter (who plays the Ghost) that in *Hamlet* the traditional cult of heroes is transformed into a cult of the dead. Rector Trautvetter

* had more than once seriously posed this question, in his inner turmoil.

links the Ghost with Dark Powers still active in today's world, which manifest themselves in human drives to lust and murder. Hamlet has tried to escape these forces in Wittenberg, but on his return to Elsinore he is haunted by Furies, like Orestes.

Not only does Erasmus introduce a demonic element into his production of *Hamlet,* but he himself is assailed by Furies. He lives in the home of the royal gardener's widow, whose name is *Gertrud* Herbst, and whose husband is dead (by suicide); his ghost is rumored to haunt the dwelling. After the dress rehearsal of *Hamlet,* Frau Herbst anxiously asks Erasmus whether he believes in vengeful Furies, and the young Germanist assures her that they are an anachronism. Then, while everyone is celebrating the *Hamlet* rehearsal at a royal party, young Walter Herbst dies. Erasmus Gotter is so stricken that he has to be immediately transported to a sanitarium in Switzerland.

His physical illness leads to a spiritual *catharsis,* the first of Hauptmann's titles for his novel. In Erasmus Gotter's letter to the Royal Librarian Dr. Ollentag, the ex-director declares that they were wrong to produce *Hamlet*:

> Je weiter ich mich von dem Spuk im Sommertheater entferne, je mehr will mir scheinen, dass die Rachenrasereien des ermordeten Dänenkönigs noch immer nicht gesättigt sind. Es war gefährlich, ihn aufzurufen, mit unserem Totenspiel lebendig zu machen und uns in das Bereich seines Grimmes hinein zu wagen: wenig fehlte, so hätte selbst ich, der harmlose Spielleiter, wie die Hauptpersonen des Dramas, meinen Fürwitz mit dem Leben gebüst.* (276-277)

* The farther I go from the mystery in the summer theater, the more it seems to me that the vengeful raving of the murdered Danish king is still not appeased. It was dangerous to call him up, to vivify him through our death-play, and to venture into range of his fury. I myself, a harmless theater director, nearly had to atone for my curiosity with my life, like the main characters of the play.

Erasmus Gotter's letter continues with passing mention of the fate of the other characters, and then he invites the Librarian to his estate, to which he hopes to return in good health, ending Hauptmann's novel.

What distinguishes the Hamlet-portrait of Wilhelm Meister is so intense an absorption in the Prince that his experience can grip us after two centuries. We hear Wilhelm analyze the pre-tragedy Hamlet, and we feel his empathy for the melancholy idealist. We accompany Wilhelm on the stage, and we feel his awe at the intervention of the mysterious Ghost.

Hauptmann creates a hero who is obsessed with Shakespeare's Prince, but the obsession is too baldly described by a narrator who intrudes the *Hamlet* material in too systematic and repetitious a way. On the other hand, the narrator proposes three alternative Hamlets—the actor Mario Syrowatky, the gardener's son Walter Herbst, and Princess Ditta, who loathes her hypocritical court milieu. Even Shakespeare is Hamlet, according to Erasmus, who writes a prologue in which the Bard gives Hamlet's advice to his own actors, assembled at the start of the play.

Hauptmann also relates his other characters to Shakespeare's play. The Gardener's Wife is named Gertrud, and she feels guilty toward her dead husband, whose Ghost haunts his house. Rector Trautvetter, who plays the Ghost, adumbrates the cult of the dead. Erasmus Gotter's friend Jethro plays Horatio, but he proves to be a false friend, who does not take Erasmus' tuberculosis seriously, and himself dies of that disease. After the success of the dress rehearsal of *Hamlet* (we never see the performance), Dr. Ollentag calls Erasmus "Hamnet" to show that he is truly Shakespeare's son.

Though the fictional protagonists of both Goethe and Hauptmann achieve a successful production of *Hamlet*, the success is differently integrated into the novels. For Wilhelm Meister *Hamlet* is at first an obstacle and then a stepping-stone in his graduation from theater to a life of serious responsibility as a father and an aristocrat. For Erasmus Gotter *Hamlet* is a trap from which he must escape to achieve a catharsis that will presumably enable him to return to his family and his profession. But Goethe makes us believe in Wilhelm's evolution through his experience of death, his introduction into the Society of the Tower, his assumption of fatherhood, and his betrothal to Natalie. In Erasmus Gotter's letter to Dr. Ollentag, the protagonist asserts that he feels as though he has just passed through puberty, but we have to take his word that puberty is behind him, as we have to take his many statements as truth, and surrounding him, the narrator's statements as truth. With few exceptions, each dogmatic statement demands to be taken at face value; no one in *Im Wirbel der Berufung* seems capable of ironic distance, least of all its author.

Lack of irony is especially surprising in a novel written in 1936, after the fictional achievements of Joyce, Woolf, Mann, Kafka. But Hauptmann seems to hammer autobiographical facts into fiction, using *Hamlet* as an anvil. The botanist Goethe, impressed with organic forms, implies that *Hamlet* grows organically in Wilhelm Meister's experience. Erasmus Gotter, in contrast, sees ubiquitous ghosts, fits them into *Hamlet,* and the narrator fits *Hamlet* determinedly to his story. Though Goethe wrote no dramas except *Faust II* after *Wilhelm Meisters Lehrjahre, Hamlet* functions dramatically in his plot, whereas Hauptmann, celebrated as a playwright, stretches and distorts *Hamlet* to accommodate his own autobiographical plot. Perhaps he himself made the best critique of his relationship to Shakespeare, on December 12, 1943, less than three years before his death: "Bei allem schuldigen Respekt: zu viel und zu ausschliesslich Shakespeare kann eine Hemmung bedeuten, und die habe ich empfunden."[20]*

In the century and a half between Goethe's novel and Hauptmann's, Hamlet was naturalized as a German, even

* With all due respect: too great and exclusive [preoccupation with] Shakespeare can inhibit one, as I have discovered.

The Representative German. The melancholy intellectual appealed to the Romantics to such an extent that an aged and anti-Romantic Goethe described the phenomenon: "Hamlet und seine Monologe blieben Gespenster, die durch alle jungen Gemüter ihren Spuk trieben. Die Hauptstellen wusste ein jeder auswendig und rezitierte sie gern, und jedermann glaubte, er dürfe ebenso melancholisch sein als der Prinz von Dänemark, ob er gleich keinen Geist gesehen und keinen königlichen Vater zu rächen hatte."[21]* The Romantic generation extracted Hamlet from his play, in order to make of him a mythic poet who felt that the time was out of joint in its indifference toward sensitivity. Especially appealing to the Romantics were Hamlet's loneliness, his madness, and his *Weltschmerz.*

The post-Romantic generation, known as Junge Deutschland, accepted this portrait of a sensitive, meditative Hamlet but reacted against it. They felt that oppression and tyranny ruled Germany because, like Hamlet, Germans were lost in melancholy self-pity; they were therefore incapable of necessary revolutionary action. In mid-century (1844) Karl Gutzkow wrote a *Hamlet in Wittenberg* that shows how a revolutionary student Hamlet, speaking with the vocabulary of Junge Deutschland, is turned by Mephistopheles into an ineffectual dreamer. Heinrich Heine wrote that when German youth looked into a mirror, it saw the dreamer Hamlet, and yet there might be surprises in store. But it is the nine-stanza political poem of Ferdinand Freiligrath, written in 1844, that had repercussions lasting a century in Germany's intellectual life, with its ringing opening: "Deutschland ist Hamlet!" This Hamlet has spent too much time at the university, with Hegel and Schopenhauer, and he is therefore incapable of revolutionary action. He can

* Hamlet and his soliloquies remained spirits that haunted all these young souls. Everybody knew the important speeches by heart, reciting them willingly, and everybody believed he had to be just as melancholy as the Prince of Denmark, although he had seen no ghost and did not have to avenge a kingly father.

only make trivial gestures, such as stabbing Polonius-Kotzebue. In the concluding lines, the poet recognizes himself in Hamlet.

It was partly to this poem that the critic Gervinus replied in his influential Shakespeare study of 1849. Gervinus agreed with the adverse view of Hamlet taken by Young Germany, but he maintained that that was also Shakespeare's view. Shakespeare was a moral writer whose esthetics are ethical; thus his tragedies criticized egotism, his comedies vanity, and only in the middle genre, drama, was there an ethical ideal of self-reliance. It was perhaps with this in mind that H. H. Furness dedicated the Variorum *Hamlet* "To the German Shakespeare Society of Weimar Representative of a People whose Recent History has proved ONCE FOR ALL that Germany is NOT Hamlet."[22] He didn't convince Nietzsche, whose view of *Hamlet* in *The Birth of Tragedy* is a throwback to Romanticism.

In the nineteenth century, German enthusiasm for Shakespeare trickled across the Rhine through Mme. de Stael's *De l'Allemagne*, published in 1810, with a summary of the Goethe-Meister view of a sensitive dreamer adrift in a hostile world. But native appreciation had already begun in respectful statements by Diderot, Mercier, Sedaine. Early in the nineteenth century Chateaubriand praised Shakespeare's individual scenes while lamenting his dramatic structure. By 1825 Stendhal was pitting Shakespeare against Racine as a source of vigor, and by 1827 an English theater company won Parisian applause (in a *Hamlet* butchered by stars and censors, with the Prince alternately played by Kemble and Macready to Harriet Smithson's Ophelia). Many French Romantics flew the Shakespearean banner. Alfred de Vigny's adaptation of *Othello* assaulted the Bastille of Classicism, the Comédie Française, a year before Hugo's *Hernani* toppled it. In various ways, Vigny, Hugo, Musset, Berlioz, Doré, Delacroix, and even Baudelaire identified with the melancholy Prince. Delacroix did a series of lithographs of Hamlet, and the most celebrated stage Hamlet, Rouvière, studied those prints for his role. By the time another English troupe visited Paris in 1844 (with Macready as Hamlet) the Prince was familiar to sophisticated Parisians. Hamlet had been reflected in such descendants as Musset's Lorenzacchio, Vigny's Chatterton, and, more obliquely, the swashbuckling but soliloquizing heroes of Dumas and Hugo. Hugo himself, as an exiled elder statesman of the 1860s, wrote a book-length tribute to the Bard, in which he quotes Wilhelm Meister but also resembles the Young Germany activists in likening the youth of his own nation to Hamlet, charged with a mission too great for them.

The prose translation of *Hamlet* by Hugo's son, François-Victor Hugo, is still one of the most scholarly and faithful. On the Paris stage, however, Ducis' adaptation with a happy ending was played until the Dumas version replaced it (first played in 1847 but revised to kill Hamlet only in 1886). Not until 1896 did Paris see a stage Fortinbras. On the other hand, some form of *Hamlet* was seen on the Paris stage in the second half of the nineteenth century, and critics did not follow the Anglo-German drift of relegating Shakespeare in general and *Hamlet* in particular to the study. But even after the Romantic revolution of taste, the French felt *Hamlet* to be too theatrical, as compared with the French classics. For that very reason, perhaps, Hamlet appealed to successive generations of Romantics: those of the 1830s hailed his *panache*; by the 1850s, through the Delacroix prints, his pensiveness was imitated. By 1886, when Jules Laforgue coined the word *Hamletism*, the phenomenon had been part of French culture for nearly half a century. Nineteenth-century French Hamletism took several forms: creating Hamletic characters such as Musset's Lorenzacchio and Vigny's Chatterton; imitating Hamlet in life like Villiers de l'Isle Adam; celebrating Hamlet in the theater through performances of Talma, Rouvière, Mounet-Sully, and Bernhardt; appreciating Hamlet through the visual artists, notably Delacroix and Manet; and finally elevation of Hamlet by the Symbolists to a kind of artist-saint.

Jules Laforgue (1860-1887) frequented the Symbolists only in the last two years of his short life, and by then he had absorbed Hamlet and reflected that absorption in his writing. Dead at twenty-seven of tuberculosis, after publishing two volumes of poetry and miscellaneous pieces in periodicals, Jules Laforgue presents a marked contrast with the two celebrated and long-lived German Hamlet-lovers Goethe and Hauptmann. Today it is difficult to think of Laforgue as Hauptmann's contemporary, also excited by Naturalism, living in Berlin at the same time.

Laforgue was born in Montevideo, Uruguay, of French parents, but at the age of six he came to Southern France, where he felt himself a foreigner—a feeling that was to remain with him always and everywhere. He attended a Paris lycée and began to write poetry at that time. When he was twenty, his father died, leaving him head of a large family. Friends obtained for him a lucrative and leisurely post as reader to the francophile empress of Germany. From a student-room he was suddenly transported to a German palace, where he lived between the ages of twenty-one and twenty-five. When he decided to marry an Englishwoman, Leah Lee, he had to resign his post, for the empress permitted no married employees. He left for Paris, poverty, illness, and death.

Published material does not reveal when Laforgue first became acquainted with Shakespeare or *Hamlet,* but by the time he was nineteen, Laforgue dedicated his poem "Excuse Macabre" to the Danish Prince. Several subsequent poems contain references to *Hamlet*; thirteen poems are preceded by epigraphs from *Hamlet,* all but one in English. Personal letters testify to his involvement with the Prince.

While working on his long short story, *Hamlet,* Laforgue made a pilgrimage to Elsinore for New Year, 1886, about which he published a brief sketch, "A Propos de Hamlet."[23] Though the Elsinore beach is deserted, the first-person narrator whistles the Siegfried theme of Wagner's *Ring*, and the Prince appears, "notre maître à tous." Hamlet asks the narrator about Henry Irving's performance and about his legend, and the narrator finds the former too serious, the latter maintained by Paul Bourget, Arthur Rimbaud, and himself "en gaîté, Altesse, à la Yorick." An inquiry about Ophelia elicits a reply about the inscrutability of women, which culminates in a twenty-line poem: "Cueillons sans espoirs et sans drames; / La chair vieillit après les roses."* Hamlet reacts by shouting: "Aux armes, citoyens! Il n'y a plus de Raison!" Infected with this madness, the narrator dances the *Critérium de la Certitude humaine*, which causes him to fall on his face. Symbolic though the dance may be, the two men part with ceremonious bows to one another.

In this sketch are present the elements of Laforgue's long story "Hamlet ou les Suites de la piété filiale,"[24] which was first published in three installments of *Vogue*, nine months before the poet's death. And a little later appeared *Moralités légendaires*, a volume of six stories, of which "Hamlet" is one.

Laforgue's *Sanglot de la terre*, his first volume of poems, is romantically self-pitying. Then, stirred by reading the philosophers, Hartmann and Schopenhauer, Laforgue found his own voice for his next volume, *Complaintes*. He blended an old popular form with contemporary feelings and idiom. But Laforgue was interested in imaginative prose as well as verse, and in 1885 he described the principle of his stories as "de vieux canevas brodés d'âmes à la mode."[25] He thought of several possible titles for the collection of stories: *Vieux canevas, Âmes du jour, Moralités légendaires, Fabliaux d'antan, Sachets éventés*. They all suggest his anachronistic spirit. Like the poetic *Complaintes*, the prose *Moralités* convey contemporary attitudes through an old-fashioned form, most strikingly in "Hamlet."

* Let us pluck hopelessly and undramatically; flesh ages after roses.

Laforgue's "Hamlet" takes the Prince "à la Yorick," with mocking jest. Victor Hugo in his Preface to *Cromwell* had invoked Shakespeare to support his mixture of the sublime and the grotesque, but Laforgue was better able to blend them in a work of fiction. Goethe had invoked Shakespeare as a poet who happened to write drama, but Laforgue wrote fiction of high dramatic potential. Goethe's Wilhelm Meister was a Hamlet enthusiast, but Laforgue's hero *is* Hamlet. Goethe uses Hamlet to structure the education of his hero, even while he is ironically criticizing that hero, but Laforgue fills his Hamlet with passions that are viewed half-critically by Hamlet *and* the tale's narrator. Goethe selects aspects of *Hamlet* to weave into his own complicated plot, and Laforgue selects aspects of *Hamlet* to weave into his own complex plot. Goethe-Wilhelm's description of the Prince is the most celebrated of innumerable passages of *Hamlet* criticism, whereas Laforgue's story of Hamlet is not well-known in France and is virtually unknown elsewhere. It combines a *paysage de l'âme* with dramatic events, colloquialism with stylized rhetoric, swift repartee and soliloquy bordering on stream of consciousness.

Laforgue was a post-Romantic writer who would be claimed by the Symbolists after his death, and yet his "Hamlet" contains a residue of classical drama in its unity of time and its development in five scenes: 1) Hamlet in his tower dwelling (with a flashback to Hamlet hunting); 2) Hamlet watching the funerals of Polonius and Ophelia; 3) Hamlet watching the performance of his own play; 4) Hamlet leaving his tower and his vengeful duty; 5) Hamlet in the graveyard where he is stabbed by Laertes. As the classical five acts depict the making of a hero, Laforgue's five scenes trace Hamlet's retreat from heroism. Dramatically conceived—over half the story is in dialogue—the scenes are related by a narrator who hovers over the action like a twentieth-century director, blocking, giving notes, and even throwing barbed comments at his hero.

The action takes place on July 14, 1601, which suggests a precursor to the fall of the Bastille. Symbolically, Hamlet's ivory tower will fall on Bastille Day, for its only inhabitant will die.

The story opens with a long description of the landscape, which is also a *paysage de l'âme* of the poetic and meditative prince. His legend demands that he execute vengeance, and its mythic rather than Shakespearean necessity is hinted at through Laforgue's use of names from Belleforest —Gerutha for Gertrude, Fengo for Claudius, Horwendill for King Hamlet. Across the bay lives the active Prince Fortinbras, but in rotting Denmark Prince Hamlet makes mock-heroic gestures. Into wax dolls of his mother and stepfather, he plunges a needle that he occasionally turns. That is one level of wish-fulfillment, and the second is the tragedy he has written, "The Murder of Gonzago."

From his tower, Prince Hamlet sees the sea through one small window and the forest through the other. He feels drawn to the sea with its infinite suggestiveness, and his first words reflect this: "Ah! me la couler douce et large comme ces flots. . . . Ah! de la mer aux nuées, des nuées à la mer! et laisser faire le reste. . . ."* (16) His soliloquy continues, expressing resentment at his fate, at Ophelia who loves him as a possession. Even as he watches the arrival of the players, Hamlet broods about the play that he began in order to spur his dull revenge, but continued for its own sake. His meditation is interrupted by a servant announcing the two principal actors and asking, on the part of Queen Gerutha, whether Hamlet intends to play a play in spite of the death of Polonius. So we begin to suspect that Hamlet is not entirely a dreamer-artist of Romantic nostalgia; he *has* killed Polonius.

The two actors enter—William and Ophelia (in French Ophélia differs by a letter from Ophélie, daughter of Po-

* Ah! to take it easy and wide like those waves. . . . Ah! from the sea to the clouds, from the clouds to the sea! and let the rest go. . . .

lonius). Laforgue's Hamlet is impatient with theatrical names—Ophelia, Cordelia, Lelia, Coppelia, Camelia—and he learns with relief that the actress is also called Kate. He explains his plot, which corresponds to Shakespeare's play within the play, except that the adulterous murderer is named Claudius.

The actors leave with his play, and the narrator comments: "Hamlet, homme d'action, perd cinq minutes à rêver devant son drame maintenant en bonnes mains."* (27) From the desire to trap his uncle-father, Hamlet extends himself into metaphysical speculation, and he utters a sentence that was to lie at the heart of Symbolism: "J'ai cinq sens qui me rattachent à la vie; mais, ce sixième sens, *ce sens de l'Infini*!"† (28; my italics) Romantic hesitation will give way to Symbolist *preference* for meditation over action, but Laforgue's Hamlet is torn between time and the timeless, life and infinity, action and contemplation. In spite of his sense of the infinite, Hamlet drives himself to vengeance: "En avant pardessus les tombes, comme la Nature!"‡ (29) Tombs mean corpses, and the first corpse is that of a bird, whose neck he wrings. Flinging the corpse away, Hamlet grazes the head of the caretaker's daughter, who declares her love of him and wishes to care for him. "Encore une," Hamlet dismisses her with promises, while the narrator provides a flashback of Hamlet's bloody but unheroic past.

Hunting in a forest, Hamlet has tortured helpless victims, pulling wings off butterflies, maiming snails, toads, and frogs, destroying anthills, birdnests, and flowers. And he has relished the suffering of animals he has victimized. After a siesta he washed his hands in their eyeballs. Like Camus' Caligula, Laforgue's Hamlet imitated the cruel ab-

* Hamlet, man of action, wastes five minutes dreaming about his drama now in good hands.

† I have five senses that bind me to life; but this sixth sense, this sense of the Infinite!

‡ Forward over the tombs, like Nature.

surdity of destiny, but then realized he was only an amateur, a provincial, compared to the cruelties of history. This Hamlet, with his adolescent excess, is thirty years old.

After the flashback, Hamlet becomes a *voyeur* at the funeral of Polonius, after which he engages the two gravediggers in conversation. Like Shakespeare's Hamlet, he takes up the skull of Yorick, but unlike Shakespeare's Hamlet, he learns that he is Yorick's brother, son of King Hamlet and a beautiful gypsy who never recovered from his caesarian birth. Revelation comes upon revelation when the gravediggers turn to a new grave, for Ophelia who is drowned.

Holding the skull of Yorick, Hamlet leaves the gravediggers in order to burst into a brilliant rhythmic soliloquy: "*Alas, poor Yorick*! Comme on croit entendre dans un seul coquillage toute la grande rumeur de l'Océan, il me semble entendre ici tout l'intarissable symphonie de l'âme universelle dont cette boîte fut un carrefour d'échos."* (39) Laced with the images of Shakespeare's Hamlet, and even his words—"*Good night, ladies*. . . . des mots, des mots, des mots!"—this soliloquy translates into modern idiom the obsession with death of Shakespeare's Hamlet. The monologue closes with a fantasy of his own death: "Quoi c'est donc là, là, ce jeune Hamlet si gâté, si plein d'une verve amère?"† (42) Paradoxically, the thought of death leads Hamlet to think of his life, but he is interrupted by the funeral cortege of Ophelia, and again he hides, *voyeur* of burials. He tries to pay a last tribute to Ophelia, offering ten years of his life if God will resuscitate her. No sign greets this extravagance, and Hamlet concludes that there is no God, or that he hasn't ten years left to live, inclining toward the former probabil-

* As the whole great murmur of the Ocean seems to be heard in a single sea-shell, I think I hear in this the whole unending symphony of the universal soul, for which this container was a crossroads of echoes.

† Oh, so there he is, this young Hamlet who was so spoiled, so full of bitter life?

ity. Again the narrator mocks him: "Hamlet, homme d'action, ne quitte sa cachette qu'assuré, bien entendu, que cette brute de Laërtes a filé avec toute l'honorable compagnie."* (46)

Feverishly bent on action, Hamlet dismisses thoughts of Ophelia in tears. He goes to the play rehearsal, where he finds Kate alone and in tears. He appreciates her beauty and thinks: "Oh, certes, si elle lui parle, si elle parle et côtoie l'hamlétisme sans y tremper, Hamlet est perdu! Perdu et gagné!"† (48) But Kate seems willing to dip into Hamletism and tells the Prince that she is so moved by his play that she is going to a nunnery. Hamlet basks in her admiration, questions her about theater life in the big cities, and decides that they will run away to Paris after the performance.

Back in his tower Hamlet soliloquizes briefly: "Je me moque de cette représentation et *de sa moralité* comme du premier amant de Kate!"‡ (52; my italics) The morality of Hamlet's legend demands vengeance, but he prefers to consecrate himself to artistic action. He melts the wax statues—neither one his parent—orders horses, and spits at the realistic paintings of his native Jutland.

The play within the play has the desired effect, as in Shakespeare, but Hamlet is less interested in vengeance than in hearing his words spoken by live actors, especially the beautiful and talented Kate. Leaving his stepfather to his own conscience, Hamlet flees with Kate. His first inquiry as man of action is to ask whether Kate has supped. As they ride past the cemetery, he is stung by a mysterious compulsion. He dismounts, explaining to Kate that he wishes

* Hamlet, man of action, does not leave his hiding-place till he is sure, of course, that that brute Laertes has taken off along with the whole honorable company.

† Oh indeed, if she speaks to him, if she speaks and skirts Hamletism without dipping into it, Hamlet is lost! Lost and won!

‡ I care as little about this performance and its morality as about Kate's first lover.

to pick a flower, a paper flower. However, he goes to Ophelia's grave where Laertes is keeping a vigil. Their exchange is brief and bitter, ending:

> Allons! Hors d'ici, fou, ou je m'oublie! Quand on finit par la folie, c'est qu'on a commencé par le cabotinage. —Et ta soeur!* (59)

Hamlet's three French syllables are at once a reference to the dead Ophelia and an untranslatable obscenity. A dog howls at the moon and "le coeur de cet excellent Laërtes (qui aurait plutôt mérité, j'y songe, hélas! trop tard, d'être le héros de cette narration) déborde, déborde de l'inexplicable anonymat de sa destinée de trente ans! C'en est trop! Et saisissant d'une main Hamlet à la gorge, de l'autre il lui plante au coeur un poignard vrai."† (59) Hamlet dies an animal's death—on all fours, vomiting blood, but he articulates defiantly in the Latin of Nero: "Ah! Ah! *qualis . . . artifex . . . pereo!*" Laertes flees after embracing the corpse. Kate discovers Hamlet's body and returns to the castle where her lover William beats her. "Et tout rentra dans l'ordre. Un Hamlet de moins; la race n'en est pas perdue, qu'on se le dise!"‡ (60) After giving us this excruciatingly individualized portrait, Laforgue implies that Hamlet is a type that is dispensable to the human race.

Laforgue's Hamlet is intermittently aware that he cannot escape his myth, and for all Laforgue's manipulation of that myth, he is faithful to its basic structure. A king's son, charged with avenging his father's murder and his mother's

* Come on! Get out, madman, or I'll forget myself! When a man ends up mad, it's because he began by play-acting.
And your sister!

† the heart of that excellent Laertes (who would rather have merited—I think of it, alas! too late—being the hero of this narrative) overflows, overflows with the inexplicable anonymity of his thirty-year-old destiny! It's too much! And gripping Hamlet's throat with one hand, with the other he plants a real dagger in Hamlet's heart.

‡ And order was restored. One Hamlet the less; the human race is not lost for that, let it be said.

infidelity, assumes an antic disposition. Within that framework, Laforgue uses Shakespearean details of Hamlet's studious youth, his fascination with theater, his haunting of graveyards, his mistrust of women, his solitude, and his irony. These are the warp and woof of Laforgue's "vieux canevas," but the "âme contemporaine" is his own. Laforgue gave Hamlet his own appearance, his interest in the unconscious, his etching instruments, his longing to be in Bohemian Paris, and perhaps his creative drive. Both Shakespearean and Laforguian are the range of Hamlet's imagery and the complexity of his irony.

Laforgue's subtitle guides the irony: "Hamlet ou les Suites de la Piété filiale." Filial piety demands vengeance, but because Hamlet is not naturally inclined to action—the Meister portrait and its Romantic extension—he tries to screw his courage to the sticking point by using words. In fictionalizing the horrible, horrible, horrible event (five times repeated in the text), Hamlet hopes to arouse himself to a bloody deed. So, too, by acting violently against weak victims, he hopes to arouse himself to a dangerous deed. Both hopes lead to his absorption in art at the expense of the living person and actual event; not only does he kill Polonius and reject Ophelia, but he experiences no grief at their deaths.

Moreover, Hamlet's art finally works against the vengeance it was summoned to inspire. Though his play bears the title of Shakespeare's play within the play, it weaves arabesques—Laforgue's Hamlet calls them *hors-d'oeuvre*—around that scene. In his own words: "Je refis la chose en vers ïambiques; j'intercalai des hors-d'oeuvre profanes. . . . Oui, je fouillais mes personnages plus profond que nature! je forçais les documents! Je plaidais du même génie pour le bon héros et le vilain traître!"* (20) Laforgue's Hamlet

* I redid the thing in iambic verse; I interpolated profane *hors-d'oeuvres*. . . . Yes, I mined my characters deeper than nature! I stretched the evidence! I pleaded with the same genius for the good hero and the wicked traitor.

translates vengeance from subject to form; he imbeds his filial piety in profane *hors-d'oeuvres*. Bending facts to create drama, he displays that "negative capability" for which Keats praised Shakespeare; his play abandons morality to put hero and villain on the same esthetic level. Four of his five quotations from or references to his play are irrelevant to its legendary morality. Hamlet playwright has been carried along the current of his own creation.

Kate's reaction to his play decides Hamlet to abandon filial piety and embark on life's profanity. In performance he feels detached from his stepfather and the Gerutha who is not his mother; though he confirms their guilt when King Fengo faints, he does not exult. Gathering up his manuscript, he flees with Kate, leaving the people and events that have fed his art. Hamlet turns his back on his legend. The results of his initial filial piety are the death of legend through dedication to art, even though that legend has defined his life.

In action and inaction Laforgue's Hamlet is aware of life's realities and his own inadequacies. Laforgue's narrator is even more aware of the hero's inadequacies, mocking Hamlet as both thinker and doer. Dying like an animal, Hamlet claims that he perishes as an artist, but the narrator undercuts that boast, denying that his loss will affect the human race.

Other ironies involve other characters. Hamlet's cynicism about women is exemplified in his callousness toward Gerutha and Ophelia, but Kate blends several women, thus inspiring Hamlet's substitution of art for heroism. Her life is not unlike that of the gypsy whom the gravedigger identifies as Hamlet's real mother. Kate plays Baptista in the play within the play and is thus a Gerutha figure. For a short while Kate (named Ophélie) is another Ophelia, but she sentimentalizes Hamlet's death, interpreting it as suicide in grief for his true love, Ophelia. Finally, Kate returns to her lover Will, a coarse insensitive fellow who thinks Hamlet mad and who beats her. The implication is that Kate is all women both to Hamlet and to *Will* Shakespeare, who will write the best-known offshoot of the legendary morality.

Laforgue critics have rarely appreciated his *Hamlet*, but its ambiguities are deep and reflective. Hamlet is at once a hero and a dandy who mocks heroism; he is both cruel and kind, and it is not at all certain that he is cruel only to be kind. He is a dilettante in several arts—he etches, he plays the organ, he models wax dolls—but an embryonic master of one, playwriting. He is fascinated and repelled by women, pretending to more experience than he has. Imprisoned in Denmark, he longs for the literary life of Paris. Hungry for certainty, he doubts all faiths but words: "Et puis, des mots, des mots, des mots! Ce sera là ma devise tant qu'on ne m'aura pas démontré que nos langues riment bien à une réalité transcendante."* (41) And always he is aware of his stance. Even more self-conscious than his ancestor, he thinks in theater metaphors. But on his way to a theater career, he is killed like an animal.

I like to think that Laforgue and his Hamlet would feel fulfilled by live performance of the story. Over half the tale is in dialogue form, so that adaptation is almost built into Laforgue's original. In 1939, just before World War II, Jean-Louis Barrault played in two dramas drawn from fiction, Knut Hamsun's *La Faim* and Jules Laforgue's *Hamlet* (the latter adapted and directed by Charles Granval). On a minimal set at the theater entrance Barrault entered, dressed as the dandy described by Laforgue. He interpreted the poet's dialogue "en gaîté . . . à la Yorick," though he made it clear that the jester was destined for death.

As a student under Charles Dullin, Barrault played Hamlet in the Morand-Schwob translation, but as a professional actor he feared the Shakespearean role. He has written: "Le personnage de Hamlet me hantait, mais je craignais de l'aborder. Le *Hamlet* de Laforgue était une bonne approche. C'est un *Hamlet* écrit, non par Shakespeare, mais

* And then, words, words, words! That will be my motto, as long as I haven't been shown that our languages echo a transcendent reality.

par un autre Hamlet."[26]* The substitution sounds facile, but Barrault himself did research in Laforgue's ironic poems in order to portray his Hamlet. By 1946 he felt ready for Shakespeare, in the Gide translation. I saw that production in 1949, when I was beginning to read Laforgue, and I thought then that Laforgue marked Barrault's Hamlet with an intelligence that bordered on madness, a self-awareness that spied on itself, an irrepressible mockery about what it cherished most.

Laforgue did not live as long as the thirty-year-old Prince who inspired him, but no one in the nineteenth century has captured so many facets of his fierce self-consciousness.

"Papa Hamlet" of Arno Holz (1863-1929) and Johannes Schlaf (1862-1941) was written only three years after Laforgue's *Hamlet*—in 1889—but it springs from and reflects another world.[27] The story is a landmark of German Naturalism, but it is virtually unknown outside Germany. "Papa Hamlet" was published as a translation from the Norwegian of Bjarne P. Holmsen. The very title deflates the Danish Prince, and the pseudonymous Scandinavian author would seem to imply regional authenticity for such deflation. The actual young German authors were convinced that a Naturalistic work could be published in Germany only by a foreigner, in the wake of Ibsen and Zola. The story's impact on young Gerhart Hauptmann was so strong that he dedicated to Bjarne P. Holmsen his first Naturalistic play, *Vor Sonnenaufgang*, which in turn inspired the two authors to write their own Naturalistic play, *Die Familie Selicke*. Hauptmann went on to success after success; Holz and Schlaf went on to failure after failure. The joint authorship undertaken in such friendship that neither would acknowledge as his own any part of "Papa Hamlet" dissolved in acrimonious enmity.

* The character Hamlet haunted me, but I was afraid to undertake it. Laforgue's *Hamlet* was a good approach. It is a *Hamlet* written, not by Shakespeare, but by another Hamlet.

Though each of them later claimed to be the more thoroughgoing realist, they created the fictional surroundings from those in which they were living in Berlin. Holz describes their working methods: "[Wir] einigten uns über ein Thema, durchsprachen dieses genau, Schlaf skizzierte danach die erste Niederschrift, und aus dieser formte ich dann das Definitive."[28]* When their separate identities were discovered, the authors said they could no longer tell who had contributed what to their work. However, in 1890 Schlaf published "Ein Dachstubenidyll" which contains the plot of "Papa Hamlet" without a hint of *Hamlet.* It must have been Holz who fleshed out the skeletal plot with Shakespeare.

Both the Schlaf sketch and the doubly authored story trace the deterioration of an actor, his wife, and their infant son. In the Schlaf sketch an omniscient narrator describes events in the past tense, of which the last paragraph may illustrate the rather smug style. At the age of six months the baby has died of a cramp.

> Ihr werdet es vielleicht sonderbar finden, dass der Verfasser einen Helden mit einer so lächerlich kurzen Lebensspanne gewählt hat: aber warum sollte eine Skizze nicht auch einmal einen so skizzenhaften Helden haben?
>
> . . . Von seinem Taten war nicht viel Spannendes zu berichten. Vielleicht waren seine Leiden seine Taten? Aber auch das ist zweifelhaft. Mögt ihr nach Belieben darüber urteilen, geehrte Leser!† (102)

* We agreed about a subject, talked it over thoroughly; Schlaf then sketched the first draft, and from this I wrote the definitive version.

† You may find it strange that the author chose a hero with such a ridiculously short life, but why shouldn't a sketch for once have a sketchy hero?

. . . There is nothing very exciting to say about his deeds. Perhaps his sufferings were his deeds? But even that is doubtful. Judge as you please, honored reader!

In "Papa Hamlet" the suffering of the infant and the brutality of the parents are intensified by a stylistic device implied in the title. Niels and Amalia Thienweibel have played Hamlet and Ophelia in provincial theaters; their infant is baptized Fortinbras. In five of the seven parts of the long story, quotations from *Hamlet* (Schlegel translation) are set against their miserable reality.

Instead of Schlaf's superior omniscient narrator, Holz adopts *Sekundenstil,* a second-by-second reporting of events as they happen. Thus the story's seven divisions are actually seven scenes (and an epilogue). As Holz wrote: "Keine Verse mehr, keine Romane mehr, für uns existiert nur noch die offene, lebendige Scene."* (110) As in Naturalistic drama, the dialogue seemed to be phonographically recorded (the phonograph was invented in 1887; the story was written in 1888), with its ellipsis, jargon, stammering, interruptions, incompleteness, repetition, non-verbal sounds, and pauses. Holz differed from Zola in believing that the truth of realism lay not in its subject matter but in its style. In our tape-recorded age we know that Holz's theory leads to deadly dullness. But in "Papa Hamlet" Holz is more brilliant than his theories because he juxtaposed to everyday inarticulacy the ringing rhetoric of Schlegel's *Hamlet.*

Niels Thienwiebel "der grosse, unübertroffene Hamlet aus Trondhjem" (19) carries a volume of Shakespeare in his torn dressing-gown, and he breaks into Hamlet-lines with and without provocation, as he waits to hear of his next *Hamlet* engagement. His slovenly, phlegmatic wife is "die reizende Ophelia." Papa Hamlet addresses the neighboring painter as Horatio, though his name is Ole, and the infant is actually baptized Fortinbras.

All scenes are set in the small Thienwiebel attic room. The first swift scene identifies Niels as an unemployed actor and the proud father of a newborn son; its dialogue consists of partial sentences. The second scene opens with the

* No longer do verses and novels exist for us, but only the open, living scene.

famous "Sein oder Nichtsein" soliloquy, which Niels is rehearsing in case he should be summoned to play *Hamlet.* But his recital is interrupted by the sordid details of housekeeping and nursing the infant in the fetid attic. When neighbor Ole-Horatio arrives with food and drink, the parents ignore the crying baby.

The third scene opens on Hamlet's words to Rosencrantz and Guildenstern in Act II, Scene 2—"I have of late—but wherefore I know not—lost all my mirth . . . ," but the prose passage is transposed into the third person, so that it becomes a narrated monologue.[29] This exalted description of Papa Hamlet contrasts with the pathetic reality of Niels posing as a dying warrior at the Academy of Art; this job supplies barely enough money to nourish the family, but he proudly rejects his wife Amalia's half-hearted offer to take in sewing. Instead, he begins to give three-month-old Fortinbras elocution lessons.

By the fourth section Amalia is sewing, and their poverty is aggravated by the approach of winter. Niels' increasingly incoherent thoughts are continually punctuated by lines from *Hamlet,* occasionally transposed to the third person of narrated monologue: "Oh, welch ein Schurk' und niedrer Sklav' er war!!" (36) Aided by alcoholic brews, Niels and Ole play various *Hamlet* duologues. When Ole falls asleep, Niels turns for repartee to his infant son, who continues to suck his rubber nipple. In the face of this indifference, Niels decides that his son is stubborn, and, dropping all reference to *Hamlet,* he prepares to beat the stubbornness out of the infant. But phlegmatic as she is, Amalia defends her six-month-old son.

The fifth section centers on a party, but an omninous note sounds in the opening *Hamlet* quotation: "Wirtschaft, Horatio! Wirtschaft! Das Gebackne vom Leichenschmaus gab kalte Hochzeitsschüsseln."* (42) The scene itself will reverse the direction, from a feast toward a funeral. Ole-

* Thrift, thrift, Horatio! the funeral baked meats/ Did coldly furnish forth the marriage tables.

Horatio has been so well paid for sign-painting that he finances a goose dinner in the Thienwiebel attic, with the landlady Frau Wachtel and pretty young Mieze as guests. Mieze takes Fortinbras on her lap, feeds him goose-fat and sugar to highlight his young life. After the adults have eaten and drunk themselves into a near-stupor, cigar-smoke fills the room and, as they play cards, the neglected infant begins to cry. Niels rises to box his ears, and this time his mother does not defend him. Fortinbras cries even more loudly, and his irritated father presses a pillow on his mouth. Ole and Mieze protest, and Niels orders them out. The little family is alone again: "Er stand da! Um seine Schultern die rote Bettdecke, in seiner Rechten das kleine blaugewürfelte Kopfkissen. Drüben, in der Ofenecke, die reizende Ophelia. 'Da! Nymphe!!' Er hatte ihr das Kissen ins Gesicht geschleudert."* (51)

Niels's brutalization progresses swiftly. In the short sixth section, the landlady demands her rent, and Niels leaves the attic for long hours at a time, at first to seek work, but soon to seek drinking companions. The narrator describes his conduct with a Shakespeare recollection: "Bevor nicht 'der Hahn, der als Trompete dient dem Morgen,' bereits mehrere Male nachdrücklich gekräht hatte, kam er jetzt selten mehr die Treppen in die Höhe gestolpert."† (53) Ophelia is no longer fair, and little Fortinbras is covered with a rash. The narrator closes this section with a generalization based on Shakespeare: "Der grosse Thienwiebel hatte nicht so ganz unrecht: Die ganze Wirtschaft bei ihm zu Hause war der Spiegel und die abgekürzte Chronik des Zeitalters."‡ (53)

The last section completes the degradation. On New

* He stood there. Around his shoulders the red bedcover, in his right hand the small blue-checked pillow. Over at the corner of the stove, the fair Ophelia. "There! Nymph!" He had flung the pillow into her face.

† Before "the cock, that is the trumpet to the morn" had crowed vigorously several times, he rarely stumbled up the steps.

‡ Great Thienwiebel was not entirely wrong: the whole economy of his home was the mirror and brief chronicle of the time.

Year's Eve Amalia coughs in bed, while the baby moans in its cold corner. Drunk, Niels enters with complaints—and no phrase from *Hamlet*. Undressing, he does not notice his Shakespeare on the table, opened to *A Midsummer Night's Dream*. Crawling into bed with his wife, he pulls the covers round him, and they exchange a few hopeless words. Through Amalia's broken phrases, we gather that she shifts Niels' amorous advances to attention to the crying baby. Brutally, Niels stuffs a rubber nipple into the baby's mouth, though he is screaming with a cramp. From the narrator's description of the room's objects and from the half-articulated phrases of the parents, we realize that the child has smothered, dead before the New Year. The modern Hamlet has slain his son.

The epilogue takes place a week later, when the body of Niels Thienwiebel is found frozen before a liquor store. The last two lines of the story combine a last Shakespearean echo with the clichés previously uttered by Niels or Amalia:

> Und seine Seele? Seine Seele, die ein unsterblich Ding war? Lirum, Larum! Das Leben ist brutal, Amalie! Verlass dich drauf! Aber—es war ja alles egal! So oder so!* (63)

It is a grotesque self-delusion for an unemployed actor to see himself as Prince Hamlet; substituting Shakespearean rhetoric for human feeling, he brutalizes his wife and smothers his child. The actor of the sensitive Prince becomes an insensitive monster, but that monstrosity reaches out to taint the whole Shakespeare tradition that ignores contemporary reality, to soar into fantasy. Not only do Niels' noble words clash with his own inarticulacy, but Shakespeare's noble words clash with hard facts and brutal

* And his soul? His soul, that was a thing immortal? Lirum, Larum! Life is brutal, Amalie! Depend upon that. But—after all it was all the same—this way or that.

deeds. The poetry indicts the poverty, and the poverty indicts the poetry.

On a metaphoric old canvas, Laforgue painted a searching and suffering modern soul, but Holz sketches ragged bodies suffering physically in modern urban life. The young Frenchman probes into the mocking modernity of the hero of soliloquies; the young German mocks him as an anachronism.

Sterne wove a Shakespearean descendant into *Tristram Shandy*. Goethe, Hauptmann, and Holz played Shakespeare's fiction against their own. Laforgue re-imagined Shakespeare's Hamlet (with a little help from Belleforest). In what is probably the best-known *Hamlet* offshoot, James Joyce (1882-1941) plays Shakespeare's fiction against his own, but he also infuses Shakespeare into his *Ulysses*.[30]

Completed when Joyce was forty, *Ulysses* reflects many years of pondering on Shakespeare. Richard Ellmann dates his equation of Shakespeare with King rather than Prince Hamlet from June, 1904—perhaps even June 16, 1904, later to enclose the action of *Ulysses*.[31] In 1913 he lectured on *Hamlet* in Trieste. In a 1918 love letter, Joyce compared himself to Shakespeare when he fell in love with the Dark Lady of the Sonnets. And in 1922 *Ulysses* was published by Shakespeare and Company.

The Shakespeare chapter of *Ulysses* begins:

> Urbane, to comfort them, the Quaker librarian purred:
> —And we have, have we not, those priceless pages of *Wilhelm Meister*? A great poet on a great brother poet. A hesitating soul taking arms against a sea of troubles, torn by conflicting doubts, as one sees in real life. . . . The beautiful ineffectual dreamer who comes to grief against hard facts. One always feels that Goethe's judgments are so true. True in the larger analysis. (184)

The ninth of the novel's eighteen episodes, "Scylla and Charybdis" in the Homeric framework, returns us to the mind of Stephen Dedalus after five successive chapters in that of Leopold Bloom. We enter Stephen's mind at two o'clock on the afternoon of June 16, 1904, when that young poet is in the office of Mr. Lyster, director of Dublin's National Library. Only at the end of the episode will Stephen leave the library, passing close to Bloom, but scarcely noticing him.

Ulysses has often been summarized, so that its plot is familiar to many who have not read it. Seventeen of the novel's eighteen parts trace the meanderings of Bloom-Ulysses and Stephen-Telemachus through Dublin, and the eighteenth part rollicks in the full, flowing stream of Molly Bloom's consciousness. The people are ordinary, the events ordinary and momentous—"birth, copulation, and death," to quote T. S. Eliot's Sweeney; or, more accurately, birth, ejaculation, and a funeral. But beneath and above and around the events of *Ulysses* is their verbalization. The characters, based on actual Dubliners, verbalize, and Joyce weaves verbal tapestries around them. Joyce's linguistic versatility is unparalleled, so that his novel has been misinterpreted as a book about language. But the virtuoso language remains an instrument for Joyce—a remarkably traditional instrument in that it tells a story, delineates characters, expresses and arouses emotion. What is untraditional about Joyce's language is its prismatic effect, showing different tones in different lights, as words probe into the life of the character, the cast of his mind, the heat of his heart, the novel's mythic and encyclopedic superstructure.

Joyce's *Portrait of the Artist as a Young Man* corresponds to Goethe's *Wilhelm Meisters Lehrjahre* in its narration of an education. Both authors rejected autobiographical first drafts, *Stephen Hero* and *Wilhelm Meisters Theatralische Sendung*, and both authors continued the adventures of their fictional heroes, feeding them on their own lives, but translating those lives into fiction. As middle-aged Goethe could become an elderly Faust as well as young Wilhelm Meister, middle-aged Joyce could become a Bloom approaching middle age, as well as young Stephen. Because both authors could transmute their experience into Meister and Stephen, Faust and Bloom, we care about the biographies of Goethe and Joyce. The subtle and complex relationship of creator to creation is the most passionately felt problem in the ninth episode of *Ulysses.*

Critics have found *Ulysses* such inexhaustible quarry that many have overlooked the sheer verve of its surface. Joyce preaches esthetics in *Portrait* and *Ulysses,* and he is a flamboyant practitioner of what he preaches, notably that "the dramatic form is reached when the vitality which has flowed and eddied round each person fills every person with such vital force that he or she assumes a proper and intangible esthetic life."[32] In these terms *Ulysses* is highly dramatic, and Stephen is early linked to Hamlet, the most celebrated character of English drama.[33] The first episode, with its tower by the sea, recalls Elsinore, and there are specific verbal parallels with Act I, Scene 4 of *Hamlet.*[34] Stephen and Hamlet are mourners in black, sad among smiling men. Both are ghost-haunted, and both disguise their suffering through the assumption of an antic disposition. Though both are meditative men, they figure in highly dramatic action. Joyce's Shakespeare chapter, centered on Stephen, is at once a tragedy of a disinherited prince (his name means crown), a comedy of literary manners, a sensational melodrama of adultery, a dialectical play of ideas, a farcical burlesque of scholarship, and a metaphysical problem play in the spirit of *Hamlet,* at once its subject and its model.

Mr. Lyster, a Goethe scholar, instantly confronts us with the Goethe-Meister view of Hamlet, which is at the root of nineteenth-century attitudes toward Shakespeare's play. Joyce's *Ulysses* takes place in 1904. Twenty-two-year-old Stephen, like successive generations of sensitive young men, feels his time out of joint, in esthetics as in ethics. Joyce couches Stephen's reaction to that time in dramatic fiction. His Shakespeare chapter is a two-act play, with a single setting, a short time-span, and a small cast of characters. Stephen is protagonist, George Russell (AE) main antagonist in Act I; Buck Mulligan is main antagonist in Act II. Stephen's sparring partners are the librarians Mr. Magee (John Eglinton) and Mr. Best, with the library's director Mr. Lyster intermittently present between the visits of three clients (one of whom is Bloom). Stephen ridicules Mr. Lyster's serviceable exits as being like the dance steps of Sir Toby Belch.

Joyce's play starts in mid-discussion, with Mr. Lyster's conjunction "And." An unrecorded remark has evidently prompted the director's conventional and sentimental pronouncement on *Hamlet*. The pronouncement is scorned by Stephen as a "twicreakingly analysis" (184) creakily outdated and secondhand. Stephen delays presentation of his own view, though we have earlier received hints of it.

In the first episode of *Ulysses* Buck Mulligan boasted to the Englishman Haines: "Wait till you hear [Stephen] on Hamlet." (16) "He proves by algebra that Hamlet's grandson is Shakespeare's grandfather and that he himself is the ghost of his own father." (18) The generations seem confused in Mulligan's mockery, and in the novel's second episode Stephen recalls his words with corrections: "He proves by algebra that Shakespeare's ghost is Hamlet's grandfather." (28) Father and ghost are common to both sentences, and they will combine to reinforce the basic theme of the ninth chapter—artistic creation.

In the first three episodes of *Ulysses* Stephen evokes *Hamlet* some dozen times so that we associate the two young men in black, each mourning a dead parent, each lonely among his own people. Though the library episode breaks only briefly into actual dramatic form, Joyce writes the drama of Stephen's downfall. In Act I Stephen seeks to impress his originality upon the Dublin literati, George Russell and the three librarians who write. But Russell is not sufficiently interested in Stephen to hear him out; he leaves the library with a snub. When Buck Mulligan arrives on the scene, Stephen thinks: "*Entr'acte.*" (197) In Act II Stephen replaces his thirst for literary recognition with one-upmanship; through he still displays learning, he knows he is shamming, and he answers Mulligan's wit with wit. The two acts are at once repetitious and incremental; Stephen fails in both. He does not impress George Russell; he does not subdue Buck Mulligan. In both acts he is greeted by smiles and laughter, so that he feels with Hamlet: "That one may smile and smile and be a villain." When Joyce's play is over, Stephen knows how easily it—and he—will be dismissed: "One day in the national library we had a discussion. Shakes." (215)

Unlike Wilhelm Meister, Stephen does not play Prince Hamlet on stage, and yet he too attempts a performance based on Shakespeare. Since Mulligan has early referred to Stephen on *Hamlet,* we know that the library presentation is not improvisatory. Mulligan uses the continuous present tense—"He proves by algebra"—suggesting that *Hamlet* may be a set-piece for Stephen, delivered on several occasions, varied to the particular impetus or audience. On June 16, 1904, Stephen was scheduled to deliver his Hamlet lecture to Mulligan and especially Haines at 12:30, but he has begged off with a cryptic telegram.

We do not know what launches the *Hamlet* discussion in the library office—perhaps Stephen's desire to publish a Shakespeare article in Mr. Magee's *Dana.* We suspect that Mr. Lyster's urbane admiration of Meister-Goethe, intended to comfort, will irritate Stephen. "A great poet on a great brother poet" leaves no room for the poet Stephen, and indeed Stephen will soon learn that he is excluded from an anthology of Irish poets being gathered by George Russell, Irish poet. On the other hand, the "ineffectual dreamer who comes to grief against hard facts" fits Stephen too snugly for comfort. Stephen therefore evokes Old Hamlet-Ghost-Shakespeare who came to grief against hard facts, but out of that grief he wrenched his plays. Stephen turns against Goethe's meditative figure, espousing instead a man of action whose plays are his acts.

Stephen builds his case slowly. Outwardly unmoved by Lyster's praise of Goethe, Stephen mocks him mentally in Shakespearean pastiche. He then absorbs praise of "Saxon Shakespeare's Hamlet," by the librarian John Eglinton (Mr. Magee). He reacts "superpolitely" to a Platonic Hamlet portrait by Platonic George Russell: "That model schoolboy [Aristotle] . . . would find Hamlet's musings about the afterlife of his princely soul, the improbable, insignificant and undramatic monologue, as shallow as Plato's." (186) Two birds with a single sentence, Plato and the meditative Prince, with a sideswipe at George Russell, AE.

The third librarian, Mr. Best, enters in time to catch Stephen's shaft and its followup: "Which of the two . . . would have banished me from his commonwealth?" (186) As Stephen's mind revolves around Aristotle, George Russell mentions Mallarmé, and Mr. Best shows his sophistication by citing Mallarmé on *Hamlet.* Accurately, he quotes: "*il se promène, lisant au livre de lui-même,*" and shows off his knowledge of French by translating: "*reading the book of himself.*" (187) But Mr. Best scarcely scratches the surface of the French Symbolist's 1896 essay, "Hamlet et Fortinbras," which describes the final bloodbath of Shakespeare's tragedy. Without any sense of Mallarmé's complexity, the two Irish librarians imply their superiority to the Frenchman described by Mallarmé, who advertises a provincial performance as "Hamlet ou le Distrait Pièce de Shakespeare." The second phrase is Mr. Best's addition to Mallarmé's text, and Stephen freely translates "le distrait" as "the absentminded beggar." (Stephen in the brothel will recall this translation: "*Le distrait* or absentminded beggar." [558]) "The Absentminded Beggar" is the title of a jingoistic Kipling poem, written to raise funds for the Boer War. While the librarians laugh at Stephen's translation, he recalls another phrase in the same Mallarmé piece: "Sumptuous and stagnant exaggeration of murder." (187)

With the Boer War in mind, bloodily supported by Kipling and Swinburne, Stephen delivers an attack on Hamlet, Shakespeare, and his own contemporaries:

> A deathsman of the soul Robert Greene called him. . . . Not for nothing was he a butcher's son wielding the sledded poleaxe and spitting in his palm. Nine lives are taken off for his father's one, Our Father who art in purgatory. Khaki Hamlets don't hesitate to shoot. The bloodbolstered shambles in act five is a forecast of the concentration camp sung by Mr Swinburne. (187)

Stephen's pronouns confuse poet, ghost, and prince. The first "him" and "he" refer to Shakespeare, but it is King Hamlet who "smote the sledded Polacks on the ice," and it is Prince Hamlet whose father is in Purgatory and whose task is vengeance, though seven deaths are the maximum that can be attributed to him. Most provocative is Stephen's extrapolation of Mallarmé's Hamlet (and perhaps Laforgue's?) to "khaki Hamlets" who "don't hesitate to shoot." Thus, bloodthirsty poets are the spiritual sons of butchers, among them Kipling and Swinburne who supported the Boer War, the latter defending the concentration camps into which the Boers were herded. Unlike Goethe-Meister's "beautiful ineffectual dreamer," Stephen's Hamlet-Shakespeare is an ugly and all too effectual doer. Harsh and somewhat shocking, Stephen's Hamlet-Shakespeare will become more sympathetic. But consistent will be the presentation of the poet as doer, firmly grounded in the facts of his personal and political life.

When Mr. Magee (John Eglinton) explains that Stephen's *Hamlet* is a ghost story, the young man "with tingling energy" defines a ghost as "one who has faded into impalpability through death, through absence, through change of manners." (188) By comparing Elizabethan London to contemporary Paris, and Stratford to virgin Dublin, Stephen implies that his ghost story will have resonances beyond literary history. Building on contemporary Shakespeare scholarship—"Work in all you know."—Stephen evokes a scene on a June day three hundred years ago. Shakespeare's company is playing *Hamlet*, with Shakespeare in the role of the Ghost "in the castoff mail of a court buck" (like Stephen in the cast-off shoes of Buck Mulligan). Stephen pictures a William Shakespeare who wrote his life into the tragedy *Hamlet* and a William Shakespeare who played his life as the Ghost Hamlet.

Stephen's *Hamlet* is based on selected items of Shakespeare's life and work, upon which he imposes coherence. (William Schutte has shown that he relies largely on the books of George Brandes, Sidney Lee, and Frank Harris.)[35] According to Stephen, the crucial and traumatic event in Shakespeare's life is his seduction at the age of eighteen by twenty-six-year-old Ann Hathaway. Pregnancy forces marriage, and a daughter is born, but Shakespeare never outgrows his feeling of inadequacy as a lover for a mature woman. Three years after his daughter is born, twins arrive —Hamnet and Judith—but there are no other children, for Shakespeare goes to London to become a playwright. Back in Stratford, Ann cuckolds him with his brothers Richard and Edmund, who become villains in William's dramas. As betrayed lover and husband, grieving father of a dead son, ghost by absence, Shakespeare vents his spleen in *Hamlet*: "To a son he speaks, the son of his soul, the prince, young Hamlet and to the son of his body, Hamnet Shakespeare, who has died in Stratford that his namesake may live for ever." (188) Only toward the end of Shakespeare's life, with the birth of a granddaughter, is there reconciliation, reflected in Marina, Perdita, and Miranda of the last plays. Young Stephen shows sympathy for a middle-aged Shakespeare whom he sees in his image as lonely and betrayed.

Stephen's portrait of Shakespeare as inept lover, unhappy father, and cuckolded brother arouses George Russell's outrage at "this prying into the family life of a great man."(189) Instead of retorting, Stephen meanders in his own thoughts, splitting into two voices about the hard fact of his debt to George Russell AE—"A.E.I.O.U." (190) In his mind the dialogue moves from Elizabethan into modern English. Aloud he bickers with Mr. Eglinton about Anne Hathaway, Picturing an old woman at the poet's deathbed, Stephen visualizes himself at his mother's deathbed.

In a pastiche of puns and literary phrases, Stephen evokes the Stratford cornfield seduction and Shakespeare's subsequent clumsiness with women: "His boywomen are the women of a boy. Their life, thought, speech are lent them by males. He chose badly? He was chosen, it seems to me. If others have their will Ann hath a way. By cock, she was to blame. She put the comether on him, sweet and twentysix. The greyeyed goddess who bends over the boy Adonis, stooping to conquer, as prologue to the swelling act, is a boldfaced Stratford wench who tumbles in a cornfield a lover younger than herself." (191) William Schutte has traced the passage to sonnet 135, one of Ophelia's songs, the clown song from *Twelfth Night, Venus and Adonis,* and *Macbeth.* While stringing these gems, young Stephen drools silently for his own turn in a cornfield.

But Platonic George Russell has had enough of seduction. He announces his departure, insensitive to Stephen's exclusion from the literary party to be held that night at Moore's, as from the literary anthology he is editing. Stephen thinks: "Cordelia. *Cordoglio.* Lir's loneliest daughter." (192) Stephen pities himself through two puns: Cordelia and the Italian word for sorrow; King Lear and Lir, Celtic god of the sea. Before leaving, Russell will not even promise to print Mr. Deasy's letter, as Stephen has requested.

With the celebrity gone, librarians Magee and Best both return to an equation of Shakespeare with Hamlet, but Stephen maintains his equation of creator with father-ghost. Rather than developing his viewpoint, he intensifies it with new images, rhythms, and references to the plays. He holds his diminished audience: "They list." (196) And since they list, Stephen guides his discourse toward the subject nearest his heart—the poet. Like a ghost, the poet Shakespeare "goes back, weary of the creation he has piled up to hide him from himself. . . . He is a ghost, a shadow now, the wind by Elsinore's rocks or what you will, the sea's voice, a voice heard only in the heart of him who is the substance of his shadow, the son consubstantial with the father." (197) Stephen's cadences dissolve creator into his creation into Creation, apprehensible only to an ideal audience. No longer concerned with "the porches of their ears," Stephen evokes a voice that can enter the heart directly when the son-creation is consubstantial with the father-ghost-creator.

It is to this poetic rendition of the poet, uttered without irony, that Buck Mulligan reacts with his ironic "Amen!" (197) Constitutionally unable to grasp Stephen's vision, he mocks Stephen who thinks: "Hast thou found me, O mine enemy?" (197)

From the first sentence of *Ulysses* Buck Mulligan is cast as Stephen's enemy, most pointedly through his cynicism. So now he calls the ghost—Hamlet and Holy—"the gaseous vertebrate." Stephen prophesies darkly that Mulligan will serve what he now mocks. Yet he himself is infected by Mulligan's mockery, so that he silently parodies the Apostle's Creed, but through this parody he formulates the same vision he has just evoked poetically—sufferer, creator, father, son, ghost, creation at one with the cosmos.

Ignoring Stephen's passion, Mr. Lyster is genial: "A most instructive discussion, Mr Mulligan, I'll be bound, has his theory too of the play and of Shakespeare. All sides of life should be represented." (198) All sides, sparked by Mulligan, deliver witty gleanings of Shakespeariana. Stephen reproves himself: "You're darned witty." (199) He imagines again the Stratford seduction while the others "talked seriously of mocker's seriousness."

Mulligan is prime mocker. He burlesques the Abbey Theatre writers. When a library attendant summons Mr. Lyster to help Mr. Bloom in the Reading Room, Mulligan is at once witty and anti-semitic, warning Stephen: "He knows you. He knows your old fellow." (201) Magee and Best spur Stephen to continue his Shakespeare saga, and he incorporates Mary Fitton and Penelope Rich into *Hamlet*, embellished with skewed testimony from the other plays. Under the surface brilliance, Stephen lives Shakespeare's pain, which he underlines by repetition: "Once spurned twice spurned. . . . Once a wooer twice a wooer." (202)

Stephen and Magee joke about the "secondbest bed" willed to Anne, Stephen modulating the librarian's words into rough blank verse. Though earlier Stephen had admitted marital reconciliation through a granddaughter, he now cites the second-best bed as proof of Shakespeare's lasting hostility to his wife. The argument gathers momentum, and the librarians seem increasingly caricatural to Stephen, who then draws a cruel caricature of Shakespeare as time-server: he writes *The Merchant of Venice* to profit from the anti-semitism inflamed by the Lopez case, *Macbeth* to cater to the taste of King James I for witch-burning, *Love's Labor's Lost* to jeer jingoistically at the Spanish Armada, *The Tempest* to celebrate the exploitation of the Bahamas, and *The Merry Wives of Windsor* to gratify the crude taste of Queen Elizabeth. Stephen then accepts John Eglinton's challenge to prove Shakespeare a Jew, and the librarian soon retreats to Russell's position—no prying into a great man's life.

Eglinton-Magee's embarrassment at his peasant father brings to Stephen's mind his own father, whom he associates with Bloom through Mulligan's earlier remark: "He knows your old fellow." (201) When Stephen rushed from Paris to his mother's deathbed, his father touched his hand and looked at him with eyes that wished him well but did not know him. "A father, Stephen said, battling against hopelessness, is a necessary evil." (207) Still on the theme of Shakespeariana, Stephen voices his meditations about artistic fatherhood: "When Rutlandbaconsouthamptonshakespeare or another poet of the same name in the comedy of errors wrote *Hamlet* he was not the father of his own son merely but, being no more a son, he was and felt himself the father of all his race, the father of his own grandfather, the father of his unborn grandson who, by the same token, never was born for nature, as Mr Magee understands her, abhors perfection." (208)

Through the generational doubletalk rings Joyce's theory of artistic creation. In *Portrait of the Artist* Stephen goes forth "to forge in the smithy of [his] soul the uncreated conscience of [his] race." By the time of the Shakespeare chapter of *Ulysses* Stephen holds forth on the artist creating that race—past, present, and future.

Mulligan responds with mockery, announcing that he is about to give birth to a play, and Stephen quickly links Shakespeare's family to ten of his plays, then moves on to Shakespeare's usurping and adulterous brothers. Only for death does Shakespeare return to Stratford of the cornfield sin. Stephen recapitulates his Shakespeare biography, falsifying facts, burlesquing his own delivery, and blending his own life into Shakespeare-Hamlet: "Where is your brother? Apothecaries' hall. My whetstone. Him, then Cranly, Mulligan: now these. Speech, speech. But act. Act speech. They mock to try you. Act. Be acted on." (211) Acted on, he continues with speech—the coincidence of Shakespearean names, the burden of banishment. His Shakespeare is now more clearly a lone creator transmuting his passion into his works. Finally, Stephen accepts Magee-Eglinton's compromise: "He is the ghost and the prince. He is all in all." (212) The phrase echoes Hamlet's praise of his father: "He was a man, take him for all in all."

But there is still a peroration: "The playwright who wrote the folio of this world and wrote it badly . . . the lord of things as they are whom the most Roman of catholics call *dio boia*, hangman god, is doubtless all in all in all of us, ostler and butcher, and would be bawd and cuckold too but that in the economy of heaven, foretold by Hamlet, there are no more marriages, glorified man, an androgynous angel, being a wife unto himself." (213) *Dio boia,* hangman god, the great leveller, makes us all equal—father and son and man and woman. As death levels all humanity, so the creator can blend its shifting facets, father and son, man and woman.

Stephen begins his *Hamlet* performance with deliberate provocation, but he ends it with a global and englobing celebration of creation. God the Creator and the artistic creator are "all in all in all of us." Stephen's theories, obliquely derived from his Shakespeare presentation, justify Joyce's artistic practice. The Shakespeare-Ghost-Hamlet equation is not to be taken literally, but it is to be taken seriously, as an expression of Joyce's esthetics. In the economy of that particular heaven, men play many roles, yet each is identifiably individual. Only after human beings are individuated do they become androgynous, intergenerational, and interchangeable. The process will reach its pinnacle in *Finnegans Wake,* but it is predicted in the Shakespeare chapter of *Ulysses*: Stephen is Shakespeare is Hamnet his son is Hamlet his creation is a creatively holy ghost.

In one of the earliest studies of *Ulysses* Stuart Gilbert pointed out: "The mystery of paternity, in its application to the First and Second Persons of the Trinity, to King Hamlet and the Prince, and, by implication, to the curious symbiosis of Stephen and Mr. Bloom, is ever in the background of Stephen's Shakespearian exegesis."[36] To these may be added the Third Person of the Trinity, the ghosts of Stephen's mother, Bloom's father, and the sons of Bloom and Shakespeare.

Bloom plays a very small role in the ninth episode of *Ulysses,* but in the long novel he too emerges as an analogue of Stephen's Shakespeare—seduced in a field, haunted by a ghost, father of a first daughter and a dead son, an ineffectual Don Juan, a moderately effectual businessman, a Jew in a nominally Christian world. In *Ulysses* Joyce creates tension through his contrast of Bloom and Stephen. Yet they are blended through the figure of Shakespeare-Ghost-Hamlet—orphans, exiles, mourners, wanderers, meditators, and would-be men of action.

After Stephen's peroration, Buck Mulligan shrieks "*Eureka!*" (213) While Stephen admits to not believing his own theory, Mulligan writes a brief *anti-Hamlet*: instead of an androgynous creator-creation, mere masturbation: "*Everyman His own Wife /or/ A Honeymoon in the Hand / (a national immorality in three orgasms)*." (216) Witty Buck leaves the library, followed by Stephen, who suffers a last snub when Magee reminds Mulligan of the Moore party, to which Stephen is not invited.

At the library entrance, Bloom passes between Stephen and Mulligan "bowing, greeting." (217) Stephen uses a rare first-person pronoun for a last thought stemming from *Hamlet*: "Here I watched the birds for augury." (217) Hamlet before his death defies augury, but Stephen seeks it, watching birds and imagining himself into his Greek myth, where he flies like Icarus, son of Dedalus. But there are no birds in Kildare Street. Only houses from which rise two plumes of smoke that suggest a last Shakespeare quotation: "Cease to strive. Peace of the druid priests of Cymbeline, hierophantic: from wide earth an altar.

> *Laud we the gods*
> *And let our crooked smokes climb to their nostrils*
> *From our bless'd altars*." (218)

The lines are lovely and multivalent. A victorious Cymbeline has bowed to Rome, so that the two countries may live in peace. Earlier in this episode, Stephen has castigated a bloody-minded bard-Hamlet, but his final words are hierophantic and harmonious. In the *Portrait* and earlier in *Ulysses* Stephen has associated creation with a sacrificial altar; now, soft flawed human smoke makes an altar of the wide earth, with the artist at once priest and Creator. Shakespeare the butcher's boy, through the consubstantial fatherhood of his creation, finally points toward the gods.

The Shakespeare chapter of *Ulysses* pivots on *Hamlet,* which is interpreted, extended, and wrenched to reveal marriage and parenthood, birth and death, physical and spiritual reality, artistic creation and global creation. The passion of Stephen's Hamlet rises from exile and paternity, so that he becomes a latter-day Ulysses. And in the list of correspondences drawn up by Joyce, the author parallels Shakespeare (along with Socrates and Jesus) with Ulysses.

In the Homeric analogy, the ninth episode is labeled "Scylla and Charybdis" with rock Scylla designated as Aristotle, Dogma, and Stratford; whirlpool Charybdis as Plato, Mysticism, and London. But *Ulysses* departs from the *Odyssey* in that Telemachus, as well as Ulysses, passes between the Scylla and Charybdis of the schema. Stephen-Telemachus hews closer to Scylla, defending Aristotle against Russell's Plato, the reality of dogma against Russell's mysticism, and the experiential trauma in Shakespeare's Stratford against its expression in the London plays. In Gorman's rendition of Joyce's scheme the technique of "Scylla and Charybdis" is listed as dialectic, and in the episode Stephen toys brilliantly with dialectic. But in the Lenati scheme the technique is listed as whirlpool, and Stephen nearly drowns his seriousness in a whirlpool of wit. At the risk of overliteralizing a metaphor, I suggest that Stephen faces the whirlpool of wit and the rock of whetstones. Stephen never comes close to Russell's Platonic whirlpool, which actually moves away from him when Russell leaves. But he is very close to the rock in the person of Mulligan, whetstone after whetstones, on whom Stephen continues to sharpen his wit. Stephen escapes that Scylla only because Mulligan accepts the invitation to Moore's from which Stephen is excluded.

At the end of the episode, Bloom passes between Stephen

and Mulligan. If the latter is the rock-monster Scylla, Stephen himself may be seen as a whirlpool of words. (Hamlet spoke "wild and whirling words.") Bloom glides between them, threatened only slightly by Mulligan's obscenities. As Ulysses-Bloom is also Hamlet-Shakespeare, Hamlet-Stephen is also Ulysses; both escape rock and whirlpool, to face new dangers in Circe's brothel.

In the "Scylla and Charybdis" episode, as Calvin Edwards has written: "The Homeric, Shakespearean, and Joycean mythologies converge—Ulysses: Shakespeare: the ghost: Bloom; Telemachus: Hamnet Shakespeare: Hamlet: Stephen; Penelope: Anne Hathaway: Gertrude: Molly; the suitors: Shakespeare's brothers: Claudius: Blazes Boylan—all become one."[37] The interpenetrating analogies add piquance to the mythic substratum of *Ulysses*—not only the titular Homeric myth but the shimmering Shakespearean surface, sprinkled with scholarship and erupting into drama.

Early in the novel, Joyce has prepared for Stephen's performance in the Shakespeare chapter, but he also associates Bloom with Shakespeare, both before and after that scene. Bloom often quotes Shakespeare, especially *Hamlet*—some forty phrases as opposed to three times that many for Stephen. Bloom varies Hamlet's most famous line as: "To enter or not to enter. To knock or not to knock." (688) and "To be or not to be wished for." (642) Other phrases from *Hamlet* occur to Bloom, which Schutte has listed.[38]

The separate *Hamlet* threads meet in the brothel, where Bloom and Stephen spend some time. Though each is involved in his own subconscious, they perhaps hear Lynch's remark "The mirror up to nature. (*He laughs.*) Hu hu hu hu hu hu." (567) Then follows the climactic scenic direction: "(*Stephen and Bloom gaze in the mirror. The face of William Shakespeare, beardless, appears there, rigid in facial paralysis, crowned by the reflection of the reindeer antlered hatrack in the hall.*)" Then Shakespeare speaks in Elizabethan pastiche, mocking Bloom as cuckold. When Bloom defends himself, Shakespeare responds: "(*With paralytic rage.*) Weda seca whokilla farst," which translates to *Hamlet*'s "None wed the second but who kill the first."

Many critics have remarked on the importance of this mirror-game; Sultan is eminently quotable: "No mystical communion but a point at which the fantasies of Bloom and those of Stephen coincide and roughly concur, the mirror incident marks that place in the chapter where the locus of its significant psychological action ceases to be the mind of the novel's older protagonist and becomes the mind of its younger one."[39]

In the afternoon library scene Shakespeare and his creations were interchangeable; in the late-night brothel scene Shakespeare and Joyce's creations are interchangeable: Martin Cunningham resembles the Bard physically; Bloom and Stephen are mirrored in Shakespeare, their spiritual analogue. The critics Calvin Edwards and William Schutte stress Shakespeare's beardlessness, paralysis, and antlerhood to argue against a redemptive significance in the meeting of Stephen and Bloom. But even if the mirror-Shakespeare is a paralytic clown, he is recognizably Shakespeare, as the clown Bloom is recognizably Ulysses. Joyce wants to have his heroic cake even while he eats it in a comic ecstasy of crumbs.

The mirrored image is not the only reminder of Shakespeare in the brothel. Stephen has already drawn a proportion between corrupt London and modern Paris, Elizabethan Stratford and virgin Dublin. It is in virgin Dublin that Stephen recounts the sexual anomalies of Paris, enhanced by mirrors. Drunken Stephen enacts a sex-show barker: "Enter gentlemen to see in mirrors every positions trapezes all that machine there besides also if desire act awfully bestial butcher's boy pollutes in warm veal liver or omelette on the belly *pièce de Shakespeare.*" (570) Stephen ends with the phrase from Mallarmé, but he has already reiterated his view of the interpenetration of art and life; the French can be translated as play of Shakespeare or (physical) piece of Shakespeare, androgynous (with belly) creator of live-r and little men (*homme*-lette).

In spite of his theory of the consubstantial father, Stephen rejects Bloom's fatherly advances. He demands his "augur's rod." Toward the end of the brothel scene as toward the end of the library scene, Stephen desires rather than defies augury. Again it eludes him, when he sickens at the hallucination of his emaciated, dead mother. He demeans his augur's rod by using it as a weapon against the chandelier, and Bloom paternally defends him from the brothel-mistress. Oblivious of Bloom's protective presence, Stephen utters his last line from *Hamlet,* quoting the Ghost: "Aha! I know you, grammer! Hamlet, revenge! The old sow that eats her farrow!" (595) The old sow is Ireland, and in order not to be devoured, Stephen-Hamlet-Joyce must take revenge through absence. The way to heed the Ghost's injunction is to become a ghost of absence.

This interpretation weaves Joyce into his fiction, since it is Joyce and not Stephen who accepts exile. Ellmann's biography (and most Joyce critics) affirm that this was Joyce's practice.[40] But Ellmann (and other critics) also show that Joyce's fiction is *fiction.* Like Goethe, Laforgue, and Hauptmann, Joyce used his own life to make art. Thus, *Ulysses* is a work of art to which Shakespeare and especially *Hamlet* contribute.

Ulysses is laced with puns, quotations, and paraphrases of Shakespeare; the library scene alone contains about a hundred references to *Hamlet.* More significant than quantity, however, is the quality of Shakespeariana, at once dramatic and thematic. Dramatic in the sheer conversational brilliance of the library scene, which can be appreciated with little knowledge of the references or background. Dramatic in the psychological reactions of Stephen, and his interaction with his opponents. Dramatic in the episode's cumulative development and climactic resolution through *Cymbeline.* The thematic quality is found in the marriage of the two main themes of the novel—familial relationships and artistic creation.

In the ninth episode of *Ulysses* Stephen makes a bravura performance of the Shakespeare theory in which he does not believe, and Robert Kellogg has made a succinct summary of it:

> According to the theory, the ghost's crying out for vengeance expressed Shakespeare's misery over Anne Shakespeare's adultery with his own brothers, Richard and Edmund. *Venus and Adonis* is evidence of Shakespeare's having been seduced originally by Anne, causing a wound to his sexual self-confidence that the sonnets document. In her sexual ascendancy over him Anne also lives on as Cleopatra and Cressida. *Richard III* and *King Lear* name the evil brothers Richard and Edmund. The death of Prince Arthur in *King John* is his son Hamnet's death. His mother's death resulted in the scene with Volumnia in *Coriolanus*, and her maiden name is preserved in the Forest of Arden. A reconciliation comes in the last plays, when Marina, Perdita, Miranda, and Imogene reflect the rebirth of family love in Shakespeare's own granddaughters. The aesthetic principle behind Stephen's theory is his belief that "his own image to a man with that queer thing genius is the standard of all experience, material and moral." In the discussion, he uses this principle to interpret the whole body of Shakespeare's work. Its main thematic significance in *Ulysses* derives, however, from its being also the aesthetic principle appropriate to an understanding of Stephen's and Joyce's life and art.[41]

The more we gloss Joyce's references, the more meaningful the novel becomes. But a half-century after its first publication, *Ulysses* appeals to a broader audience than professional Joyceans; it appeals to an audience that responds to the daily doings of the father of a dead son and of an adoptive son who is insensitive to his need; to the doings of a son who rejects a biological father and an adoptive father, but encompasses all creative fatherhood; to the doings of a mother-mistress-wife who finally affirms. Joyce's account of a day in June is not only a Homeric odyssey but also a Shakespearean tragicomedy, averting death though bringing some near it, and finally affirming a comic order.

There has been difference of opinion on the ultimate mode of *Ulysses*: comic or tragic? mocking or serious, or both? Though almost everyone is now agreed on "both," debate persists as to whether the novel ends comically or tragically.

Tragedy strikes me as foreign to Joyce, as to Goethe. But I do not go the whole cheery way to a happy ending, with the reunion of Ulysses and Penelope, with a Hamlet who avenges his father and inherits his kingdom. In *Ulysses* Joyce's tone recalls Laforgue's, both satirical and sympathetic to his protagonists. Bloom is more charitable and compassionate than anyone he meets; Stephen is brighter and deeper. But Ulysses-Bloom does not wield a mighty bow which nobody else can draw, and Stephen-Hamlet does not avenge even a symbolic murder. Stephen-Hamlet, using successive whetstones, has carved nothing significant with his knife-mind. He knows that he is still young and clumsy—the word "lapwing" is his burden—and yet he refuses a mentor-father to help him oust the usurper and establish his own identity. Stephen-Telemachus-Hamlet rejects a foster home which would make the novel's ending unmitigatedly comic, but the book does not end on that rejection. Instead, *Ulysses* moves away from *Hamlet* and the *Odyssey* to close on Molly's monologue of acceptance.

Molly is wife-mistress-mother-*tellus mater,* and her stream of consciousness accommodates several men, but it opens and closes on Leopold Bloom, her husband. Only toward the end does it admit Stephen too, with warmth. Wondering briefly why Stephen wouldn't stay the night, Molly soon plans for his next visit, when she will fill the house with flowers, as she was surrounded by flowers when Bloom wooed her as his mountain flower. Realistically, the three people must live in modern Dublin, but their day has recapitulated mythic patterns—of the *Odyssey*, of *Hamlet*, of eternal triangles.

Given Joyce's theory of creation, we may well imagine that we have not seen the last of Shakespeare in his work, and the name recurs as "Great Shapesphere" in *Finnegans Wake*. A study of Hamlet's role in that novel has yet to be done, and I am not the one who can do it. Until it is done, however, M.J.C. Hodgart's summary is useful:

> Dedalus-Hamlet is, like Telemachus, an avenger, and this correspondence is further developed in *Finnegans Wake*. Shem, who is the mother's boy of the twins, represents the workings of the Oedipus-complex: in fantasy he kills his father Earwicker, and also as Cain he kills Shaun-Abel, who is the father's representative and successor. This is elaborated in the story of how Buckley shot the Russian General, told most fully in Book II, ch. iii, which is paralleled by Hamlet's working himself up to kill Claudius. Wherever this theme is found, the quotations from *Hamlet* thicken.[42]

I am tempted to close this *Hamlet*-fiction section on *Ulysses*, a pinnacle of fiction, but it is only fair to include a few lesser examples. *Im Wirbel der Berufung* and *Lebenslauf eines dicken Mannes der Hamlet Hiess* by Gerhart Hauptmann and Georg Britting, respectively, were written after *Ulysses* as though *Ulysses* had never been written. And they are neither the last nor the least of Hamlet-fictions.

Georg Britting (b. 1891), German poet, journalist, short-story writer, based his one novel on *Hamlet*. The book started as a short story, "Das Landhaus," completed in 1926. The titular country house is the dwelling-place of Ophelia, whom Hamlet leaves court to visit. At the time of the story, they have a son Hamlet, but the Prince visits the country house from habit rather than passion. When Ophelia reproaches him for this, he has no answer. After he rides away, Ophelia drowns herself. The Prince returns only to arrange for her burial.

The story is related in leisurely fashion, with many repetitions and careful observation of seemingly irrelevant detail. As in some Expressionist writing, the emotions of the people are dispersed into the landscape. We hear nothing of the feelings of Ophelia or Hamlet, but rain drenches the country house, until the indifferent sun shines again.

Life goes on, and Hamlet's life goes on, giving to Britting's continuation its provocative title, *Lebenslauf eines dicken Mannes der Hamlet Hiess,* [*The Life of a Fat Man Named Hamlet*].[43] After Ophelia's suicide, Hamlet takes his son to court, where he has one loyal friend, the Horatio-figure Xanxres, as thin as Hamlet is fat. Together, they ride out to battle against the Norwegians, though Hamlet's inclination is to stay home and brood. The Shakespearean background is narrated by Britting:

> Sein Vater war tot, das musste er wohl sein, wenn König Claudius herrschen wollte, so klug war Claudius schon, und so klug war seine Mutter auch, die Königin, so klug waren beide gewesen, zu wissen, dass sie da einen toten Mann brauchten. Dem dicken Prinzen Hamlet stand auf einmal der Schweiss auf der Stirn. Es gab da eine Aufgabe, die ihm bevorstand, da war etwas zu tun, da war etwas ins reine zu bringen, und es war seine Sache, das zu leisten. Er wischte sich den Schweiss von der Stirn, er klopfte sich leicht auf die dicken Schenkel. Das später, zuerst den Krieg gewinnen!* (65-66)

* His father was dead, he had to be if King Claudius wanted to reign, Claudius was that smart, and also his mother, the queen, was that smart, they were both smart enough to know that they needed a dead man there. Suddenly there was sweat on the forehead of fat Prince Hamlet. There was a duty that faced him, there was something

The war is fought with old-fashioned armaments but a modern attitude. In spite of Hamlet's distaste for war, he orders the Danish attack in the name of Claudius, and they win a victory, but Xanxres is slain. The grotesquely fat Prince has to lie on his side to close the eyes of his only friend.

Back at the palace celebration, Hamlet subtly challenges his mother's second husband, his stepfather, to an eating contest. The fat Prince of insatiable appetite keeps offering morsels to King Claudius, and the latter downs them in a delirium of festive ceremony. Claudius knows that fat Hamlet is avenging his father's death, but he is helpless before the food and drink that seem to devour him.

King Claudius dies, and Hamlet inherits the throne. His son Hamlet falls in love with a commoner, Greta, and then repeats his father's amatory indifference; that girl too is driven to a desperate death. Ophelia's three brothers join Queen Gertrude to plot against King Hamlet. In the book's last chapter, father and son Hamlet—both fat—have renounced the throne and retired to a monastery. Father Hamlet is so fat that he cannot get out of his wheelchair, and the implication is that his incurable melancholy will lead shortly to his death. On the throne is Queen Gertrude, having outlasted two husbands, son, and grandson. At the book's end the monk Hamlet extinguishes a candle "und sah nun zum Fenster hinaus, wo man ein paar Sterne sah, und deswegen hatte er das Licht wahrscheinlich ausgedrückt, um die Sterne besser zu sehen."*

Physically and psychologically, Britting's Hamlet-portrait rests on Queen Gertrude's line: "He's fat and scant of breath." But the total portrait stems from Wilhelm Meister —a noble lonely soul faced with a task that weighs him

---

to be done, there was something to be set to rights, and it was his task to do it. He wiped the sweat from his forehead, he tapped himself lightly on his fat thighs. Later; first a war to be won.

* and now looked out of the window, where a few stars could be seen, and it was probably for this reason that he had extinguished the light, the better to see the stars.

down. Though Britting's Hamlet does exact revenge, though he fights in a war, his brooding melancholy is pervasive. Even his pathological appetite is a defense against gregariousness and accommodation. Incapable of sustained feeling for women, he inspires the self-sacrificing loyalty of Xanxres, and he achieves an understanding friendship with his son, who begins to resemble him. Having renounced the throne for the cloister, he finally gazes at the stars, communing with something larger than human affairs.

As mannered as the pseudo-poetic repetitions of Britting are the elegantly urbane descriptions of American James Branch Cabell (1879-1958). He bases *Hamlet Had an Uncle* (1940) on Saxo rather than Shakespeare, though he uses the Shakespearean form of the name Hamlet.[44] Gerutha is Gertrude, Fengon Claudius, and Horvendile old Hamlet. Cabell's hero is Hamlet's uncle Wiglerus, brother of Gerutha, third son of the king of Denmark, poet and connoisseur of women: "Because of my deficiency in moral earnestness, I exterminate human beings with less pleasure than—I admit frankly—I derive from begetting them." (68) Hamlet is Fengon's son, but the young Prince does not know that, and he is bent on vengeance for the death of Horvendile, whom he believes to be his father. Impetuous, stupid, and muscularly handsome, he is the very antithesis of the traditional Romantic Hamlet. Aided by a mischievous magician, he feigns madness and kills Corambus-Polonius. As in Shakespeare, King Fengon sends Hamlet to England to be murdered, but instead he marries the princess who was betrothed to his uncle Wiglerus. Hamlet then returns to Jutland and burns down the great hall with all its inhabitants. "In this pleasant vein of romantic irony, by killing his own father, did Hamlet avenge the death of his uncle." (112)

Hamlet then goes north to woo the warrior Queen Hermetrude for his wife's father, but, Tristram-like, he wooes for himself. After bloody wars, Wiglerus finds himself king of Denmark, and as such he feels that he cannot allow so impetuous an enemy as Hamlet to remain alive. On a bare hint from Wiglerus, Hamlet's new queen delivers her husband's head. Hamlet has boasted: "Honor is not merely a notion. . . . It is not a thing written idly in old legends. It is a commandment written very plainly in the heart of each man that lives, if only he be brave enough to read it. . . . I will not die tangled up in bed-covers, like cowardly Fengon. I will die with my manhood full upon me, as befits my brave father's son." (226) Hamlet actually dies at the hands of his wife's hired murderer who, on the suggestion of King Wiglerus, then kills the wife. Finally, Hamlet's uncle rules with common sense instead of honor. Urbanity is more attractive than honorable heroism, but both trivialise the Hamlet-myth, deriving from Saxo.

Three Tales of Hamlet by Rayner Heppenstall and Michael Innes also trivialise the myth.[45] In the first tale the journalist Heppenstall parodies Saxo. "The Fool's Saga" gnarls the complication of the play within the play by still another play. Hamlet is loved by four women: Thora his sister, Fyris his mistress, Hermintrude his queen, and Gertrude his mother, but he is finally killed by King Wiglek.

The other two tales are by Michael Innes, a mystery-story writer. In "The Hawk and the Handsaw" King Fortinbras and Lord Chamberlain Horatio applaud a play, Shakespeare's *Hamlet,* some forty years after Fortinbras ascends the Danish throne. But though they applaud, they express wonder about what really happened. A Dr. Mongo proves that the Ghost was a figment of Hamlet's imagination and the whole revenge plot a product of his insanity. However, since his aberrations placed Fortinbras on the throne, the ruler decides not to pursue his investigations.

The next story, "The Mysterious Affair at Elsinor," takes place a year later. A solicitor who persists in investigating that "mysterious affair" discovers that Fortinbras has manoeuvred events to rid himself of rivals to the throne. Slight as these stories are, they are symptomatic of a not uncommon modern distaste for Fortinbras. Rarely admitted to the theater before the end of the nineteenth century, Fortinbras is not today acclaimed as an acceptable ruler.

He does, however, desire justice in *Horatio's Version* by Alethea Hayter.[46] The author writes in her preface: "Most middle-brow theatre-goers probably react to the events of the play much as Horatio does. Perhaps, indeed, Shakespeare put Horatio into the play to stand for the audience. Like him, they sympathize with Hamlet without understanding him or approving of all his actions. I am one of them, and to those of my fellow theatre-goers who, like me, are also fond of detective stories, I dedicate *Horatio's Version*." (10)

Using the characters of Shakespeare's *Hamlet*, Hayter centers her novel on a court of inquiry about the sequence of events. The novel alternates between actual court testimony and Horatio's diary. A First Gentleman, who is apparently as loyal to the memory of Claudius as Horatio is to Hamlet, portrays the Prince as a homicidal maniac. Bernardo and Marcellus won't help clear the Prince's name because they will not break their oath of silence to him. At first, the presiding judge seems to discredit Horatio, and Hamlet's good name comes to hinge on the testimony of a Lady-in-Waiting, which conflicts with that of the First Gentleman, about Ophelia's death by drowning. But it grows evident that the First Gentleman, on orders from Claudius, allowed the poor mad girl to die, and Hamlet's case is won. The Presiding Judge Voltimand declares: "Horatio's version of the events has been shown to be the true one, and I congratulate him on his courageous persistence in bringing the truth to light." (101)

To clear Hamlet's good name, Horatio has broken his oath of silence. Doing penance in a monastery, Horatio wonders about his dead friend: "I never knew if he really, in his heart, cared about vengeance. Some of the time he did, but if he had really wanted it, why did he leave it so long? I sometimes thought I could divine what was in his mind, but I was never sure. No one will ever be sure about that." (106) It is an unassuming summary of many critical attitudes.

This study is entitled *Modern Shakespeare Offshoots*, but offshoot is a flimsy word for the three rich Hamlet fictions that constitute the mainstay of this section—*Wilhelm Meisters Lehrjahre*, "Hamlet ou les Suites de la piété filiale," and *Ulysses*. Though written in three different languages in three different centuries, the three works resemble each other in that their authors look within Shakespeare's Hamlet and within their heroes. They educate their fictional heroes to follow the Delphic "Know thyself." Laforgue's Hamlet tries to do this through his playwriting; Goethe's Wilhelm outgrows *Hamlet* as a textbook; Joyce's Stephen uses *Hamlet* as a springboard for his theory of creation, but he also sees that Prince Hamlet is his analogue.

Wilhelm Meister projects Hamlet as a pensive innocent who breaks under the strain of achieving active manhood. Wilhelm cannot see that Hamlet is his mirror-image; in spite of the Ghost's hints, Wilhelm languishes in theater adolescence, substituting what Carlyle called a "pasteboard apparatus" for action in the real world. Wilhelm Meister is an apprentice because he looks too intently, self-indulgently, inward; he graduates to mastership only when he fixes his eyes firmly on his surroundings, his very human surroundings.

Similarly, Laforgue's Hamlet is focused on himself rather than his vengeance. He isolates himself in an ivory tower, looking out at a landscape that mirrors his melancholy soul. And like Wilhelm he toys with a pasteboard apparatus—wax figurines and a play. He has translated his filial duty into the escapism of art, and yet that art finally inspires him with a different kind of activism. But his legend traps him, and he dies.

On the surface, Joyce's Stephen is the most passive of the three heroes. Without even a pasteboard apparatus, he wastes his wit in words to worthless companions. He idles away hours in bars and a brothel, unsung and unsinging.

He yearns for recognition by those who do not deserve to recognize him, and he rises to whatever trivial bait is offered him, hooked in stagnant waters. But beneath the sordid Dublin surface run the rich rivers of Western culture, containing *Hamlet.*

It is fitting that the three introspective fictional protagonists should be based on Shakespeare's most introspective hero, but their authors look more roundly than inward. Just as Shakespeare wrote a tragedy that ranged more widely than his Prince, the three fiction-writers were able to provide wider perspectives for their heroes. Goethe's narrative voice is like an ironic cone, narrowing as the novel progresses. Early, he patronizes Wilhelm, absents himself discreetly from certain scenes, implies a critique through narration of discrepancies between what Wilhelm says and does, or, more usually, does *not* do. Hamlet provides the subtlest clue of the narrator's ironic distance from Wilhelm, who anlayzes the Prince whom he does not appreciate as his analogue. Wilhelm tacitly rejects the Ghost's advice; he admires second-rate actors because the production revolves around him. But after Wilhelm puts aside the pasteboard apparatus, Goethe's narrative voice loses its ironic edge; Wilhelm's actions finally accord with his words, and he can see the larger world as well as his own microcosm. His last confrontation with the Ghost marks his new breadth. By the end of Goethe's novel, Wilhelm acknowledges that he doesn't deserve his luck; he has achieved humility.

No conic geometry can elucidate Laforgue's irony in his "Hamlet." Laforgue critics have noted that his own most cherished hopes were scathingly phrased in his poems, and the "Hamlet" also hides sincerity under its ubiquitous irony. But it would be too easy to dismiss the story as adolescent *Weltschmerz* disguised as cynicism. Because Laforgue's narrator is susceptible to passion and compassion, he takes refuge in cynicism, and as if the narrator fears his own sympathy for his hero, *he* takes refuge in cynicism. Though the flashback to Hamlet as a hunter is horribly sadistic, its very extravagance makes us suspect it as a pasteboard apparatus, along with wax dolls and a revenge play. On the one hand, the narrator scorns Hamlet, who also scorns himself for resorting to pasteboard apparatus; on the other, through the tears and talent of the actress Kate, that apparatus is able to dissolve and absorb mere filial piety. Laforgue's Hamlet is passive and active, restless in both states; he is both tender and cruel, traditional and modern, realistic and fantastic, excruciatingly self-aware and a mote in the universal unconscious. Different from Goethe's developing Wilhelm and his self-consistent Hamlet, Laforgue's Hamlet shimmers in the changing light, like the Impressionist painting his author loved. In contrast to Goethe, who distances us from Wilhelm through his ironic narrator, Laforgue foists an ironic narrator upon an ironic protagonist, yielding the postive of a double negative.

Joyce involves us in one of the most complex and condensed fictions ever written. Instead of a Hamletic mirror that reflects Wilhelm, or a shimmering Hamletic painting to dazzle the eye, Joyce presents a Hamlet that is both in and out of his hero's mind. In the ninth episode of *Ulysses* Shakespeare plays several roles, and so does Hamlet; though some of these roles are mutually exclusive, they are all contained within the stage of Stephen's mind, the second most important mind in the first half of the novel. In the last nine episodes, however, we often stray from these two minds, relying on a modern avatar of the omniscient narrator, but that narrator is not consistent in tone or attitude toward the characters.

In Stephen's mercurial mind, Hamlet appears as unwanted son, provincial leftover, military butcher, would-be ghost. But in the novel as a whole, with Bloom improbably quoting *Hamlet*, it is harder to pinpoint *Hamlet*'s meaning. Myriad-minded Joyce was working at once at the literal and symbolic levels of his novel. In one way, it is impossible to comment on a single phrase without having the whole vast canvas in mind; in another, the individual stitches seem to wander away from the tapestry in which they function. Stitches are the special province of professional Joyce scholars, but any attentive viewer can see Hamlet's shadow in the whole tapestry.

Stephen and Bloom are avatars of the Prince, mainly in loneliness and inactivity. Like Wilhelm, Stephen can project himself into Hamlet but, unlike Wilhelm, he can realize that he has done no deed. Bloom, on the other hand, is unaware of his Hamletism, and it is the reader who has to add the narrative hints to the fact that his deed is befriending Stephen. Both heroes blend physically in the beardless, paralytic clown-cuckoldom of William Shakespeare in the brothel mirror, and this forecasts the final event: they will be civil to one another, and they will part. The final detragification will take place outside their minds and outside their actions—in the liquid thoughts of Molly who links Bloom and Stephen through a background of flowers.

B. Drama: Digging at *Hamlet*

The nineteenth century, the century of Romanticism, brooded over Hamlet, who was plunged into fiction and drama. His shadow also darkened Büchner's Danton, Chateaubriand's René, Byron's Manfred, Pushkin's Boris, Vigny's Chatterton, Musset's Lorenzacchio, Browning's Sordello, Arnold's Empedocles, Villiers' Axel, and, in 1899, Strindberg's Eric XIV. On the nineteenth-century stage, *Hamlet* was invariably cut, sometimes adapted, and occasionally accompanied by dogs or horses. Few Englishmen went as far as eighteenth-century Garrick in his effort to rescue "that noble play from all the rubbish of the fifth act,"[1] but in Germany, the eighteenth-century actor-manager Schröder invented a happy ending for *Hamlet,* as did the playwright Ducis in France. Even when Dumas restored an unhappy ending in the nineteenth century, there were only three corpses (and a Ghost) in the final scene, with Hamlet himself condemned to live.

During the twentieth century, *Hamlet* adapters continued to raise their intrepid hands, and modern professional plays based on *Hamlet* fall into two groups, one written in nineteenth-century dramatic styles and the other in twentieth-century dramatic styles, often in the latest style at the time of their first performance. Predictably, plays of both groups explore only limited facets of the original, and they do so less searchingly and less resonantly than the fictions of Sterne, Goethe, Laforgue, or Joyce. Nor are *Hamlet* offshoots as inventive as the *Macbeth* transformations, *Ubu* or *him*; as provocative as Edward Bond's *Lear*; as dazzling as W. H. Auden's *Sea and the Mirror*; or as passionate as Aimé Césaire's *Une Tempête.*

In analyzing the first group of *Hamlet* offshoots—worn-out modes—I proceed not chronologically, but in the chronological order of the particular theater style. Thus, the most old-fashioned play of the group dates from 1949, but Percy MacKaye's *Hamlet Tetralogy* might have been written over a century earlier.

The American Percy MacKaye (1875-1956) was the son of a versatile theaterman, Steele MacKaye, and he dedicated his life to theater and literature, traveling to Europe at the turn of the twentieth century to familiarize himself with the new theater of Ibsen, Strindberg, and Hauptmann. During his long life, he wrote some twenty-five plays, as well as about a hundred volumes of miscellaneous prose and poetry. His *Caliban by the Yellow Sands* marked New York City's celebration of Shakespeare's tercentenary (of death) in 1916. But MacKaye did not return to Shakespeare until 1949, when he completed his tetralogy, *The Mystery of Hamlet, King of Denmark.*[2] In intention, that mystery should be the intrusion into human lives of mystical forces, personified by a magician, Gallucinius. In practical dramatic fact, however, the mystery proves to be King Hamlet's well-founded suspicion of adultery between his wife and his brother. Jealousy leads to King Hamlet's non-Shakespearean madness before his Shakespearean murder by

Claudius. And MacKaye's tragic tetralogy ends with Act I, Scene 2 of Shakespeare's *Hamlet*, on the Prince's words, "But break my heart, for I must hold my tongue."

Though the title points to mystery, the tetralogy abounds in violent romance, mixture of serious and comic, alternation of blank verse and prose, with incidental stanzaic forms. The first play of the tetralogy, "The Ghost of Elsinore," dramatizes Claudius' first murder; intending to kill the infant prince Hamlet, he attains Yorick's daughter. The second play, "The Fool in Eden," draws upon *Genesis* and Dante to frame the villainy of Claudius, who murders Yorick because he knows too much, but only after Yorick plays with seven-year-old Prince Hamlet. The third play, "Odin against Christus," set about twenty years later, seeks to elevate the Claudius-Hamlet rivalry to a mythic dimension. It is in this play that King Hamlet goes mad. The fourth play is summarized by its title, "The Serpent in the Orchard." Throughout all four plays, long sequences of blank verse alternate with commoners' prose intended to be comic. The whole was produced elaborately at the Pasadena Playhouse in 1949, and the text was printed the following year in a handsome deluxe edition. A single quotation should suffice to illustrate the blend of incompetence and pretentiousness. Hamlet soliloquizes:

> My father in heaven, dost thou behold my mother
> In hell? My mother, there, dost thou behold my father
> In the hell of beholding thee on earth? Do ye both
> Perceive your son, conceiving the woe of each—
> Woe, woven of memory and forgetfulness!—
> Horatio, methinks, I see thee bending
> O'er me, to gaze on me—and me, myself,
> Gazing on my father's and my mother's gazes,
> Drifting into darkness. —Hark!—Is it thee,
>   God-Father?—
> Silence . . . only Thy silence!

Percy MacKaye and Gerhart Hauptmann (1862-1946) were approximate contemporaries, but whereas the former received American acclaim as a theaterman, the latter was celebrated throughout the Western world—primarily as the father of Naturalist theater. And yet, it was Hauptmann who drew more often on the decidedly un-naturalistic Shakespeare—though not for naturalistic plays.[3] In 1899 he based his comedy *Schluck und Jau* on the frame play of Shakespeare's *Taming of the Shrew* (with an assist from the eighteenth-century Danish author, Holberg, who had also leaned on the Shakespearean comedy). Before World War I Hauptmann visited Stratford and commented about the particular affinity of Germany for Shakespeare. His 1921 play *Indipohdi* was influenced by *The Tempest*. In 1927 he was asked to prepare a version of *Hamlet* for the stage, and in 1930 he published that text in a de luxe edition, with illustrations by Gordon Craig. Though called a new translation—"neu übersetzt und eingerichtet von Gerhart Hauptmann"—the basic text is Schlegel's, to which Hauptmann added details from Saxo, Belleforest, and *Der bestrafte Brudermord*, as well as his own invention. His main changes are: 1) increased danger of war between Denmark and Norway, 2) increased importance of Fortinbras, who meets and supports Hamlet, 3) increased love of Hamlet for Ophelia, and 4) reworking of the final scene to open with Hamlet's "Sein oder Nichtsein" soliloquy and to close on Horatio's "Lasst schnell uns handeln, weil noch die gemüter / Der massen schnellen handeln günstig sind / Auf dass die feste hand des herrschers bald / Dem schwergeprüften lande frieden gebe / Es lebe Dänemark und sein neuer könig!"* (No capitalization of nouns in the original.)

Occupation with the various versions of *Hamlet* apparently caused Hauptmann to ponder the pre-play Prince during his student days at Wittenberg. In 1935, at seventy-

* Let us act swiftly because the people's hearts still favor swift action, so that the firm hand of the ruler may soon bestow peace on the severely tried country. Long live Denmark and its new king.

three, Hauptmann completed a transformation, *Hamlet in Wittenberg* in five acts and blank verse—a throwback to Romanticism by the father of German Naturalist drama.[4] From Shakespeare Hauptmann borrows Hamlet, Horatio, Rosencrantz, and Guildenstern. But he gives the Prince German friends, Wilhelm and Fachus. Mysteriously in the pay of Claudius is the Spaniard Don Pedro.

In the first scene Don Pedro tries to kidnap the beautiful gypsy Hamida, but a disguised Hamlet springs (unsuccessfully) to her rescue: "Ihr rührt sie nicht an, solange ein braver Wittenbergischer / Bursch und Lateinschüler noch eine gesunde Ader im Leibe hat."* Through a series of improbable coincidences, Hamlet and his companions subsequently rescue Hamida and her brother Lischka from a brothel, Hamlet wounding Don Pedro.

While his fellow-students Rosencrantz and Guildenstern spy on Hamlet for Claudius, the German Fachus declares loyalty to the Danish prince: "Ich bin ein Deutscher, beinahe hatt' ich gesagt: Wie Hamlet auch. Denn, er sei Däne oder nicht, er ist trotzdem deutsch in jeder Faser."† Whatever Hamlet's nationality, he is enthusiastic about theater, and he adds to the repertory of the local Wittenberg company his own play about King Cophetua and the beggarmaid. Under the guise of play-acting, Hamlet and his companions rescue the gypsy Hamida—again kidnapped—to play the beggarmaid.

Keeping Hamida prisoner, Hamlet grows increasingly morose and approaches a priest about marrying her. But Hamida is unhappy in her luxurious prison, and with Lischka, who has merely posed as her brother, she plots her escape. By the time Hamlet's friends report her faithlessness, he is no longer interested in her. Melancholy to the

* You don't touch her as long as an honest Wittenberg youth and Latin student still has his strength.

† I am a German—I almost said like Hamlet himself. For whether or not he is Danish, he is nevertheless German in every fibre of his being.

point of madness, he confesses to Horatio that he has seen his father's ghost: "Nun ja, wie du mich siehst, ich bin gehüllt / In meines Schicksals Schatten." In a banquet scene that recalls *Macbeth* Hamlet raves, imagining blood and ghosts. Brooding on his own destiny, Hamlet frees Hamida and Lischka.

At the end of Hauptmann's play news comes from Denmark that King Hamlet is dead, and the Wittenberg student is heir to the throne. German Fachus kneels to close the play: "Es lebe Hamlet! König Hamlet! Hoch!" But since Hamlet will never ascend the Danish throne, the last note is ironic.

Though the German playwright set Hamlet in the German university of Wittenberg at a time when it was racked by Luther's Hundred Articles, his play contains no hint of this excitement—social mobility, nascent nationalism, esthetic ambition, and intellectual ferment. Instead, his characters embark on a series of spirited but insignificant adventures—as in the short-lived drama of the Romantics.

Romantic drama was intended for educated audiences in legitimate theaters, so that melodrama was in part a reaction against it, but melodrama shared the suspense and noble motives of its rival. Simplifying morality, diction, and characters, it appealed to the new industrial proletariat of the nineteenth century, and it is still very much with us in the twentieth century—on the mass media. Though *The Hamlet of Stepney Green* by Bernard Kops (b. 1926) cannot be moved back a century as neatly as could the MacKaye and Hauptmann offshoots—it was written in 1956—its songs and simplicity relate it to melodrama.[5] Taking place among the lower classes, as melodrama did before naturalism, Kops's *Hamlet* seeks to exploit ethnic charm and comedy.

Written when Kops was thirty years old, *The Hamlet of Stepney Green* is his first of several plays to deal with the life of Jewish immigrants in London's East End—his own background. The Hamlet of Stepney Green is twenty-two-year-old David Levy, described in the List of Characters as "tall and intelligent. Wants to be a crooner." This desire estranges David from his mercantile surroundings. His father, Sam Levy, a herring salesman, addresses his son in the spirit of Shakespeare's Ghost: "My heart is jumping, all the bitterness of years I can taste in my throat. I've been poisoned by someone or something. What's the odds? By my life or my wife. But my wife was my life; so my life poisoned me, so my wife poisoned me." (124) David, like Hamlet, assumes the burden of revenge.

In Act II Sam's Ghost is visible only to his son, who is therefore thought to be mad—a view reenforced by what the scenic directions describe as his "*characteristic 'Hamlet' pose.*" When David perceives that his mother has erotic designs on the widower next door, his desire for revenge is spurred. But the tolerant Ghost counters: "You must encourage their romance if you want revenge." (151)

Act III opens on the wedding feast of widow and widower, "David . . . *looking more like Hamlet and very morose.*" (156) The fatherly Ghost comes to converse with his son.

David: What is the purpose in life? It seems senseless to me.

Sam: The purpose in life is to be aware that that question exists. What is the purpose in life? I wonder. I was borrowed from the darkness by your desire. I've been allowed to slip away for a few moments. I never had roots anywhere, Davey, and I'm still wandering. I love London so much that I hate leaving it, for ever and ever. If being a ghost means having a real pain in the heart then I am the biggest and most successful ghost that ever was. But I have the even greater desire to look for some other light; a light brighter than earth, a light I heard about in symphonies and poetry. I am dead and buried and live only in the imagination of a neurotic young man; you are fickle;

> you'll forget all about this, then I'll be really dead. (160)

Loyally, David protests that he will never forget. However, attracted by the girl next door, David decides to start life afresh, combining the herring business with crooning. Sam's Ghost blesses the young couple, laying Hamlet to rest: "Hamlet is dead and may flights of angels sing him down the stairs. He died two hours ago, when Mrs. Levy became Mrs. Segal; and I can go back whence I came." (168) Everyone else lives happily ever after, as in melodrama.

After such unabashed sentimentality in the 1950s, it is a relief to turn to the blend of sentimentality and cynicism in *Le Mariage d'Hamlet* of Jean Sarment (b. 1899).[6] Actor and playwright, Jean Sarment is forgotten today, but in the 1920s he appealed successfully to bourgeois audiences who wanted, through empathy with refined, sensitive, and ironic protagonists, to feel refined, sensitive, and ironic. His first play is about a prince who wins the love of an actress only when she believes he is *playing* a prince. His second play is about a rejected lover afflicted with madness and melancholy. Since Hamlet influenced these two plays, his third play introduces the Prince in his own name, drawing upon Laforgue as well as Shakespeare. (He later translated three Shakespeare plays, but not *Hamlet*.)

Le Mariage d'Hamlet (1922), like *Faust*, opens with a Prologue in Heaven, where Hamlet, Polonius, and Ophélie have for seventeen years been awaiting God's judgment. Abraham reports to God that they have been describing how differently they would behave, if they had their lives to live again. Mischievously, God decides to allow this, with perfect memory of the past.

The play proper then opens in a humble cottage where the trio is delighted with everything, especially the coming wedding of Hamlet and Ophélie. The latter has engaged a servant, and like Laforgue's actress, she is named Ophélia. Before the end of Act I, the prospect of bourgeois happiness begins to bore Hamlet, who responds to the unquestioning love of the servant Ophélia.

Act II takes place after the wedding of Hamlet and Ophélie. Polonius has drunk too much, and Hamlet has talked too much about his royal past, so that the wedding-guests think him mad. In fun, one of them dresses like a ghost, who summons Hamlet to avenge his grandfather's murder. Hamlet rises enthusiastically to the occasion: "Je savais bien qu'il devait rester quelque chose de pourri dans le royaume de Danemark!"* While Ophélie awaits Hamlet in their bridal chamber, he prepares to leave for Elsinore. Polonius tries to stop him, and Hamlet threatens him with a sword. The Prince departs, leaving a ring for the servant Ophélia and nothing for his wife Ophélie.

When Hamlet returns in Act III, Ophélie is on the verge of marrying an officer. In Elsinore, Hamlet has learned that he is the son not of a king but of a stableman. Polonius and Ophélie scorn him by offering him a job as swineherd. But the servant Ophélia persists in believing in his nobility, and the two commoners fall asleep in one another's arms. A drunken Polonius tries to seduce Ophélia, awakening Hamlet. All vengeful Prince, Hamlet strangles Polonius, and Ophélia assures him that he has behaved like "un grand Seigneur." However, Ophélie rouses the townspeople, who stone the servant couple to death. They die happy, convinced of Hamlet's royalty: "Messieurs . . . il faudra chasser ce mauvais palefrenier." And Ophélia sighs: "Mon roi!"

Sarment's *Mariage d'Hamlet* sprouted from a sentence of Laforgue: "Je reviendrai anonyme parmi les braves gens, et je me marierai pour toujours et pour tous les jours. Ç'aura été, de toutes mes idées, la plus hamlétique."† But Laforgue's Hamlet does not achieve bourgeois anonymity,

* I knew there must be something rotten left in the state of Denmark.

† I'll return anonymously among the good people, and I'll marry for ever and for every day. That will have been, of all my ideas, the most Hamletic.

which is merely a fleeting desire. And he does not live to marry.

When Jean Sarment played his own Hamlet in 1922, he dressed to resemble Jules Laforgue—"longue tête enfantine, cheveux châtains, front presque sacré, yeux étonnés et candides, bouche ingénue qui fait la moue, menton fuyant."* (26) Like Laforgue, Sarment endows his Hamlet with awareness of his own legend, and his play conforms in part to that legend—loving Ophélia, killing Polonius, dying violently. Despite these similarities, however, Sarment's Hamlet is a modern social climber. As a bourgeois, he is nostalgic for his royal surroundings. When he learns that he is not of royal blood, he loses his spirit. It is only with the return of belief in his royalty (fostered by Ophélia) that he acts forcefully and dies happy.

Laforgue's Hamlet reduces Shakespeare's, but he is firmly based on the Prince's power of irony and imagination. Sarment's Hamlet reduces that of Laforgue, perching precariously between swashbuckling Romanticism and ironic deflation. Neither playwright nor intellectual, Sarment's Hamlet is incapable of the inward search or the self-mockery of Laforgue's Hamlet, not to mention Shakespeare's.

These old-fashioned *Hamlets* can be conveniently pigeonholed—those of MacKaye and Hauptmann in Romanticism, Kops' in musical melodrama, Sarment's in *fin-de-siècle* Decadence. Two *Hamlets* of the 1950s pivot on that staple of realism, the adulterous triangle. Both these *Hamlets*, written in English, transplant their plots to contemporary realistic settings, but they seek to recall Shakespeare's characters through names, situation, and psychology.

Realism in the theater has to be more vivid and illusionistic than in any other art, but Alan Downer has usefully analyzed its three essential elements: realism of surfaces, realism of content, and inner realism, which may be called

* long childish head, chestnut hair, an almost holy brow, surprised and candid eyes, ingenuous pouting mouth, receding chin.

stage illusion, sociological credibility, and psychological credibility.[7] To this should be added realism of language. Most realistic plays are set in familiar living-rooms, where familiar middle-class characters talk about familiar social or psychological problems in familiar everyday language. Problem plays may have only the most tangential relationship to reality, but they have been played in realistic fashion for over a century.

This paragraph of definitions seems necessary to introduce two realistic *Hamlets*—*Return to Danes Hill* by Ashley Dukes, published in 1958,[8] and *Cue for Passion* by Elmer Rice, performed in 1958.[9] Remarkable is the fact that both authors had earlier—over a quarter-century earlier—practiced Expressionism, a highly anti-realistic form of theater. Yet each dramatist ended his playwriting career with a realistic offshoot of *Hamlet.*

Ashley Dukes (1885-1959) was an Englishman who studied in Munich in 1907-1908. After fighting against Germany in World War I, he was conquered by German Expressionist plays, Sorge's *Bettler* and Kaiser's *Von morgens bis mitternachts.* His translation of the latter was the first postwar German play to be performed in London, and to this day it is the best-known German Expressionist play in English-speaking countries. For most of his playwriting career, Dukes adapted experimental plays from French and German, but his original plays were confined to conventional realism.

Return to Danes Hill is a three-act "tragic comedy," set at the present time, in an English country house, Danes Hill. Gertrude and her second husband, Claude, await the return of her scientist son, Andrew, who has been gone for some time. Also present are an Archdeacon and his daughter Olivia, with whom Andrew has had an affair. When Andrew returns, he asks his mother about his father's death, whose shock he had experienced by what he calls "paranormal perception." Gertrude begs Andrew to free himself from the influence of his dead father: "The scholar, saint, contemplative, the gainer of himself and loser of the world! Oh, Andrew, let him not rule you! Break loose while there is time! Give yourself back to me! Living love has power as well! Living love is possession too! You are mine! You! *You*! He must not live again!" (44) But Andrew does not respond as she wishes.

In Act II Andrew reveals to his friend Horace his plan to convert Danes Hill into an "international meeting-ground at the top scientific level." In the meantime, Gertrude learns that Claude has been selling valuable books from the Danes Hill library, and Horace reveals to Gertrude that he has discovered Claude's thefts.

In Act III Andrew tries to win his mother to his plan for Danes Hill. Claude drunkenly discloses that Andrew's father knew of his long-standing affair with Gertrude. When Andrew absorbs this, when he realizes that Horace and Olivia have formed a new couple, he decides that Danes Hill cannot be his home. He undertakes another longterm scientific expedition, declaring that Danes Hill will be a prison for Gertrude and Claude. The son takes leave of his mother, who enunciates: "For you, knowledge and still more knowledge. For us, doom without penalty and death in life." (112) As often happens in realistic drama, her speech bears no relation to any words that people use in real situations. As often in realistic drama, melodrama lurks just below the surface. Virtuous Andrew commits himself to science, and the guilty couple is its own "doom without penalty," whatever that may mean. The good couple, Horace and Olivia, will apparently absent themselves not a moment from felicity. And what makes the mind reel is why the adaptor of *From Morn to Midnight, The Mandragola, The Celestina,* should reduce *Hamlet* to this prosaic and pretentious drawing-room.

The American playwright Elmer Rice is roughly contemporary with Ashley Dukes—1892-1967. His play *The Adding Machine* is probably the best-known American Expressionist play. Its locale is distinctly American, as is that of

Rice's more realistic plays. The last of these is the five-scene *Cue for Passion* (whose title comes from *Hamlet*). As in Dukes' play, the action takes place in the large living-room of a country house, but this one is located in Southern California. As in Dukes' play, the son of the household (now named Tony Burgess, perhaps to denote his demotion to the bourgeoisie) returns after a prolonged absence, but this prodigal has not received the news of his mother's remarriage, Grace to Carl. In this play, the Polonius-figure is a doctor rather than a clergyman, and his daughter is named Lucy rather than Olivia.

In Scene I Lucy describes to Grace her last meeting with Tony: "No real communication was possible in the state he was in. I'd never known him like that before. When he saw that I really meant no, he began raging and ranting, saying that all women are sluts, that all humanity is rotten, that the whole world and everything in it stinks on ice. Finally, I couldn't take it anymore [*sic*], so I ran upstairs, locked myself in, flopped on the bed and just plain passed out." (9) This is Ophelia's "My lord, as I was sewing in my closet" scene, updated and transplanted to Southern California. Rice's scene closes on the collapse of Tony, who buries his face in his hands when he learns of his mother's marriage to Carl.

In Scene II Carl tells Tony how his father died: while the two of them were playing chess, there was a mild earthquake that toppled a bronze bust of Tony (sculpted years ago by Carl) onto Tony's father, killing him instantly. This description is corroborated by the Horatio-figure, criminologist Lloyd Hilton, whom Grace has summoned. And finally, it is corroborated by Polonius-Dr. Gessler, who examined the body of Tony's father. Tony receives the news with a "grim facetiousness" that disturbs them all, and at the end of the scene the housekeeper Mattie (the only non-Shakespearean character) tells Lloyd that Tony never liked his father.

In Scene III a drunken Tony is so upset to learn that his

father was cremated that he loses a chess-game to Lloyd and moans about losing his queen. Tony then tries to convince the housekeeper Mattie that his father could not have died as described. Drunk and alone, he soliloquizes at some length, during which he thinks he sees his father's ghost. He sets up the chess-pieces and mutters: "The queen's gambit accepted. And it's your move, Tony, old boy." (67) He then slumps forward, unconscious.

In Scene IV, Tony arrives to tell Lucy to forget him, casually mentioning that he has been buying cartridges. She nevertheless leaves Tony, to set the stage for a mother-son colloquy, patterned on Shakespeare's closet scene. Tony tells his mother that he has always known that Carl was actually his father. When she vehemently denies this, he accuses Carl of having murdered his father. She counter-accuses Tony of an Oedipal love. That is Tony's "cue for passion," and, seeing Carl's silhouette at the window, Tony shoots—but misses Carl and wounds Dr. Gessler, as Hamlet wounds (and kills) Polonius in the original.

In the last scene Tony analyzes his conduct by the Freudian method that Ernest Jones applied to Shakespeare's *Hamlet*: "When I discovered that Carl had actually done what I'd always dreamed of doing—killed my father and married my mother, I felt even more agonized. . . . So that's why I couldn't go through with it. When I saw that silhouette against the curtain and thought he was snooping, I was swept by blind rage. So I pulled the trigger, yes—but I missed intentionally." (117) And to wrap it up neatly, criminologist Lloyd punctuates the Freudian analysis: "In other words you were unable to shoot yourself as personified by Carl. Which means that you really didn't want to commit suicide after all." (121) However, Tony's bizarre actions have apparently convinced Grace of Carl's guilt. Determined to free Tony, she urges him to depart and never see her again. They embrace for the last time, and Tony leaves. Grace informs Mattie that she is moving into Tony's room.

Although Rice's Tony is occasionally witty, most of the

language rests on shopworn realism in this Oedipal situation. In his autobiography Rice acknowledged his unfortunate intention: "I merely took the central situation of *Hamlet* and tried to examine it in the light of modern psychology. The play had a 'happy' ending, in the sense that the young protagonist comes to an understanding of his fixation and is thus enabled to shake off his bondage to his mother."[10]

These six lamentable *Hamlet* offshoots by six respected men of the theater constitute a group of stylistic throwbacks, even when their plays purport to take place in the present. In turning to the group of *Hamlet* offshoots styled in the idiom of their own day, we may begin with Eric Bentley's 1956 *H for Hamlet*.[11] As critic and reviewer, Eric Bentley (b. 1916 in England) has been a—perhaps *the*—major force in the maturing of American drama. Through essays, editions, and translations, he has educated a wide public to European dramatic masterpieces. In his impressive corpus of criticism, he has paid relatively little attention to Shakespeare, and yet he has drawn upon the Bard's most famous play. (Though *H for Hamlet* has not been published, I discuss it because Bentley has been so influential in professional theater, and because the play was written with the intention of professional production—an intention that still holds.)

Several critics have remarked on a similarity between Pirandello's *Henry IV* and *Hamlet*. Bentley substitutes Shakespeare's fictional Prince for the medieval emperor, while keeping Pirandello's basic plot. The 1922 Italian play opens on a long exposition about a masquerade in which a young man dressed as Henry IV fell off his horse and lost consciousness. Awakening, he believed he was Emperor Henry IV, and his wealthy sister incarcerated him with attendants to foster the illusion.

When the play proper begins, the sister (now dead) has engaged a psychiatrist to cure her brother by shock therapy involving two paintings of the masquerade—one of Henry IV and the other of the woman who loved-hated him, Matilda of Tuscany. Dressing as Matilda will be the woman of the masquerade and her daughter; the sister's nephew, who is engaged to the younger woman, will play the emperor when young. The madman will be cured by contrasting the young couple with the older woman whom he will relate to himself and his true identity. However, the plan goes awry since Henvy IV has known for eight years that he was not the emperor; the intended shock arouses his desire for the young woman, and when his successful rival for the older woman tries to stop him from embracing her daughter, the "sane" emperor kills him. In commenting on Pirandello's play, Bentley wrote: "Confusion here is presented confusingly, as indeed it is in the whole parallel between the modern young man and the Emperor Henry. One could wish that this Emperor were a man some conceivable audience would know about, so that they could recognize any parallels without effort. . . ."[12] Changing Henry IV to Hamlet, Bentley has provided the effortless recognition.

Bentley relocates the play in Elsinore, Long Island, and gives the protagonist the name James H. Denmark, where H stands for Hamlet. The Pirandellian paintings become statues of Hamlet and Ophelia. Bentley handles Pirandello's long clumsy exposition deftly, with the attendants Bernardo and Francisco initiating a neophyte as Reynaldo. The doctor becomes a caricature German who cures by what he calls "psychodramatic shock treatment." Moreover, Bentley's protagonist is the son of actors; he loves to act but hates the theater. In Dr. Sturm's words, "He wanted to act—but in private—and, here, he has his wish!" Since Shakespeare's tragedy provides two Hamlets, father and son, James H. Denmark enacts either role, as the mood strikes him, and in his first few minutes on stage, he plays both. Like Pirandello's false emperor, he philosophizes about existential reality as opposed to the roles people play. He challenges his twentieth-century visitors: "Cut me loose from that statue. . . . I want to *have* the life I missed, all of it, every moment of it."

Like Pirandello's emperor, Bentley's Hamlet-Denmark has a biographer, named William Shakespeare, whose account always seems to bog down in the middle of his fourth act. This time, however, Hamlet-Denmark forges through to the climactic word "revenge" in the soliloquy: "How all occasions do inform against me / And spur my dull revenge!" Bentley's revenge scene moves more swiftly than Pirandello's, but the gestures are identical. Knowing that his rival caused his "accident" twenty years ago, the protagonist plunges a sword into that rival, who dies screaming: "He's not insane." Hamlet-Denmark, looking at his attendants, closes the play: "That settles it then. We're here to stay." But whereas some Pirandello editions label the play a "tragedy," Bentley calls his play "a tragic farce" since the characters behave without dignity or nobility, and the protagonist perpetuates illusion by murder.

In a brilliant essay Bentley points out that Pirandello's *Henry IV* is grounded on psychopathological jealousy, but the play arouses doubt in reality. Pirandello's power lies in blending these intense passions with basic skepticism. When Bentley substitutes Hamlet for the obscure medieval Emperor, skepticism remains, but the passions no longer smolder because they are not present in Shakespeare's tragedy. Pirandello makes jealousy credible by superimposing Sicilian *dolce vita* on vague medieval history. The shift to jet-set America and Shakespeare's most famous play casts too bright a light on events. In Pirandello's murkiness lies dark power, whereas Bentley's more lucid construction generates light rather than fire.

Pirandello has influenced French theater more strongly than any other, and one of the first plays to show his influence is the 1924 *Mouchoir de Nuages* by Tristan Tzara (b. 1896).[13] A surprisingly coherent work for Dada, prescient in several theater techniques, the play has never been revived and is difficult to find.

Tzara himself has described it: "*Mouchoir de Nuages* est une tragédie ironique ou une farce tragique en quinze actes courts, séparés par quinze commentaires. L'action, qui tient du domaine du roman feuilleton et du cinéma, a lieu sur un tréteau placé au milieu de la scène."[14]* The entire set is a kind of box from which no actor leaves; when the actors are not "on," they apply makeup or change costume or comment on the action. The back wall, consisting of giant postcards on rollers, suggests changes of locale. These visible scene shifts and the omnipresence of the actors were new on the Paris stage of 1924.

Juxtaposed to the new techniques is the old plot of a love triangle; a banker, his wife, and a poet are played by actors who evidently used their actual names in performance. Wife falls in love with Poet, who is in love with poetry. Banker loses his money and falls in love with his own wife. Poet departs for an island in the colonies, where he is smitten by the mirage of his love for the Wife. Returning to Paris, he invites the married couple to a restaurant and to a performance of *Hamlet*. Act XII of Tzara's fifteen, on the ramparts of Elsinore, condenses three scenes of Shakespeare's *Hamlet* (in the Hugo translation). After the performance, the Banker is killed by two Apaches. Twenty years later the Wife rhapsodizes to her two sons who ask whether she is talking about the Poet or their father, the Banker. The final scene, set in a garret tended by a concierge who had played Ophelia in the play-within-the-play *Hamlet,* culminates in the Poet's suicide. The commentators indicate the high value of his soul while, covered by a veil, he ascends to heaven.

For all its truly inventive staging, *Mouchoir de Nuages* pivots on a lovers' triangle, and that is not the main subject of *Hamlet*; on the other hand, Hamlet's play within the play, *The Mousetrap* is focused on such a triangle. Hamlet's *Mousetrap* is played by professional actors, but the Poet's

* *Handkerchief of Clouds* is an ironic tragedy or a tragic farce in fifteen brief acts, separated by fifteen commentaries. The action, which partakes of the world of the serial novel and of the cinema, occurs on a platform placed at stage center.

Mousetrap—which is *Hamlet*—is played by actors from Tzara's frame play, the Poet himself enacting the Prince, a bit player Polonius, and the future concierge Ophelia. Even before *Hamlet* is grafted on to *Mouchoir de Nuages,* a commentator explains: "On joue Hamlet. Cette représentation est une souricière et une surprise. C'est le poète qui est et joue Hamlet. Vous me demanderez pourquoi; mais cela est le mystère du drame. Le public intelligent trouvera la clef le lendemain."*

Act XII of *Mouchoir de Nuages* runs together parts of three Shakespearean scenes—II, 1 (Ophelia's report to Polonius, beginning "My Lord, as I was sewing in my closet . . .); II, 2 (the Polonius-Hamlet dialogue followed by Hamlet's "I have heard that guilty creatures sitting at a play . . ."); III, 2 (the Hamlet-Polonius dialogue in which Polonius is willing to see in a cloud anything Hamlet suggests). Ending Tzara's brief act is Hamlet alone on stage declaiming: "Now could I drink hot blood / And do such bitter business as the day / Would quake to look on." In Tzara's next scene—Act XIII—the Banker is murdered. But the *Hamlet* scene itself sparkles with Hamlet's Dadaist fantasy. And after that scene, a Pirandellian spectator-actor comments:

> [Le Poète] est donc lui-même le fantôme et veut se venger. L'usurpateur est le Banquier. Mais comme il n'est que fantôme (car il aimait Andrée sous forme de mirage dans l'île) il ne peut rien faire et laisse la charge à Hamlet. N'ayant pas le temps de chercher et aussi par 'économie, économie,' le fantôme se confond avec Hamlet. Le Poète est donc à la fois le fantôme et Hamlet et joue les deux rôles. C'est la seule explication qu'on puisse donner à l'hameçon mensonge, car il n'y

* We are playing *Hamlet*. This performance is a mousetrap and a surprise. It is the poet who is and plays Hamlet. You will ask me why; but that is the mystery of the drama. The intelligent public will find the key the next day.

> en a pas d'autres, étant donné que les époux Banquier sont une famille fort convenable, carpe de la vérité, qui n'ont rien à faire ni avec le Roi ni avec la Reine vermoulus du Danemark.*

The poet Louis Aragon was present at the 1924 performance of *Mouchoir de Nuagès*, ranking it after Jarry's *Ubu Roi* and Apollinaire's *Mamelles de Tirésias* as "la plus remarquable image dramatique de l'art moderne."[15] And he adds that Tzara has supplied "une vue aiguë sur l'essentiel de Hamlet à ses yeux." In reading, however, one is struck not so much with a keen view as with parodic verve. Tzara draws his Poet-Hamlet-Ghost as much from the Symbolists as from Shakespeare, and he mocks a fair Ophelia who fails in her suicide attempt, to find comfort as a concierge.

"Le public intelligent" may, however, seek beyond Tzara's spirited humor, for another resonance of *Hamlet* in *Mouchoir de Nuages*. As Shakespeare's *Mousetrap* gathers energy from the vivid comments of Hamlet, so Tzara's *Mousetrap* gathers energy from the vivid comments of his spectator-actors. Tzara blends Shakespeare and Pirandello; his *Mousetrap* reaches out beyond the conscience of the King to the consciousness of modern art—suggesting the fragile boundary between fact and fantasy.

On fulsome praise of Tzara's *Mouchoir de Nuages* Louis Aragon closes his book, *Collages*. Deriving his definition from the visual arts, Aragon finds *Mouchoir* a superb example of the genre distinguished by "l'introduction d'un objet,

* So [the Poet] himself is the ghost and wants vengeance. The usurper is the Banker. But since he is a mere ghost (for he loved Andrée in the form of a mirage on the island), he can do nothing and leaves the task to Hamlet. Not having the time to search, and also because of "Thrift, thrift," the ghost blends with Hamlet. So the Poet is at once the ghost and Hamlet and plays the two roles. That is the only explanation that can be given for the illusory fish-hook, because there are no others, given the fact that the Banker couple is a very proper family, carp of truth, who have nothing to do with either the worm-eaten King or Queen of Denmark.

d'une matière, pris dans le monde réel et par quoi le tableau, c'est à dire le monde imité, se trouve tout entier remis en question."[16]* This is, of course, very different from Shakespearean collage, which attacks his text with scissors and glue; *Hamlet* becomes the reality introduced into the theater world of *Mouchoir*.

Mouchoir de Nuages foreshadows Brecht's estrangement effects through its insistence on the theater as theater—picture-postcard sets, real names of actors, and their candid assumption of roles. Even before Brecht evolved his own theory of theater, he was cool to Shakespeare because the bourgeois German theater respected the Bard as a classic, and he was especially critical of *Hamlet*, which was virtually venerated. Not long after Brecht's conversion to Marxism, he was asked to prepare *Hamlet* for radio broadcast, and surprisingly, he consented, but the script is lost. Using materials in the East Berlin Brecht archives, Rodney Symington has summarized the probable broadcast.[17] Less clearly epic than the *Macbeth* broadcast two years earlier—there is no Narrator—Brecht's version apparently portrayed a maniacal defender of feudalism. Brecht described rather than dramatized Shakespeare's first five scenes, and he shifted the order of many others. His final lines are extant, adding to and distorting those of Shakespeare's Fortinbras:

> Und so, sorgsam benutzend Schall zufälliger Trommeln
> Den Schlachtruf unbekannter Schlächter gierig
> aufnehmend
> Schlachtet er, durch solchen Zufall endlich ledig
> Seiner so menschlichen und vernünftigen Hemmung
> In einen einzigen schrecklichen Amoklauf
> Den König, seine Mutter und sich selbst.

* the introduction of an object, a material thing, taken from the real world, by which the painting (i.e. the imitated world) is totally called into question.

> Rechtfertigend seines Nachfolgers Behauptung
> Er hätte sich, wäre er hinaufgelangt, sicher
> Höchst königlich bewährt.* (GW VII, 3016-3017)

Hamlet would have been a fitting feudal king because his bloodbath promised royally!

Brecht never changed his view of a Hamlet who learned enough reason at Wittenberg to hesitate at feudal warfare, but who finally resumed his murderous feudal attitude. A century after the Young Germany movement, Brecht turned their Hamlet-conception topsy-turvy. For them, Hamlet's hesitation was the fatal flaw of the German intellectual; the humanistic revolutionary should act without hesitation. Brecht interpreted action as reaction, and hesitation as humanism. As one of his notes puts it: "Das Mittelalter mag in dem berühmten Zögern Hamlets Schwäche, in der endlichen Ausführung der Tat aber ein befriedigendes Ende gesehen haben. Wir sehen gerade dieses Zögern als Vernunft und die Greueltat des Schlusses als Rückfall. Allerdings drohen solche Rückfälle auch uns noch, und ihre Folgen haben sich verstärkt."† (GW XV, 334)

The passage is undated, but it may overlap with Brecht's *Messingkauf Dialogues*, written between 1939 and 1942, while the Brecht family were fleeing farther and farther from Hitler's expanding victories. When they were living in Stockholm, Helene Weigel gave acting lessons, and Brecht wrote several rehearsal scenes for her. The *Macbeth* exercise was a scene in which lower-class characters parallel the

* And so, making use of the sound of accidental drumbeats, greedily taking up the battle-cry of unknown butchers, by this accident finally free of his very human and reasonable hesitation, in a single horrible maniacal fit he slaughters the king, his mother, and himself, justifying his successor's assertion: "For he was likely, had he been put on, / To have proved most royal."

† The Middle Ages may have seen weakness in Hamlet's famous hesitation but a satisfactory outcome in the final completion of the deed. We see this very hesitation as reasonable and the atrocity of the conclusion as a relapse. Of course, such relapses still menace us, and their consequences have multiplied.

actions of the upper classes, but the *Hamlet* scene was to provide a new insight into the protagonist himself. In Brecht's words: "Die Fährenszene für den Hamlet, einzuschieben zwischen die dritte und vierte Szene des vierten Aktes, und die Rezitation des Schlussberichts sollen eine heroisierte Darstellung des Hamlet verhindern. Die bürgerliche Hamlet-Kritik begreift für gewohnlich das Zaudern Hamlets als das interessante neue Moment dieses Stückes, hält jedoch die Schlächterei des fünften Aktes, das heisst die Abstreifung der Reflexion und den Übergang zur 'Tat' für eine positive Lösung. Die Schlächterei ist aber ein Rückfall, denn die Tat ist eine Untat. Das Zaudern des Hamlet erfährt durch die kleine Übungszene eine Erklärung: es entspricht der neuartigen bürgerlichen Verhaltungsweise, die bereits auf dem politisch-sozialen Gebiet verbreitet ist."* (GW VII, 3014)

In Shakespeare's Act IV, Scene 3, Hamlet, having killed Polonius, feigns madness but assents to Claudius' plan to send him to England. For Brecht, Scene 4 is Shakespeare's climax; Hamlet learns that young Fortinbras is on his way to Poland to fight for a worthless piece of ground. Hamlet closes this scene with his fourth soliloquy: "How all occasions do inform against me" to "O, from this time forth, / My thoughts be bloody, or be nothing worth!" Thenceforth, bloodshed is inevitable.

Brecht's "Ferry Scene" is a duologue between Hamlet and a Ferryman, in the presence of an unnamed but trusted friend of Hamlet. The Ferryman explains to Hamlet that the fish business between Denmark and Norway is thriving

* The Ferry Scene for *Hamlet* (which is to be rehearsed between Scenes 3 and 4 of Act IV) and the recitation of the final report should prevent a heroic interpretation of Hamlet. Bourgeois *Hamlet* criticism usually takes Hamlet's hesitation as the interesting new factor of the play, and holds as a positive resolution the butchery of Act V, i.e. the cessation of thought and the transition to "Deed." But the butchery is a relapse, for the deed is a criminal undoing. Through the short rehearsal scene Hamlet's hesitation is explained; it springs from a new bourgeois attitude already disseminated in the politico-social realm.

under Claudius who, after some hesitation, has decided not to pursue the war against Fortinbras. Hamlet's friend, appalled, asks about their honor, and it is not the Ferryman but Hamlet who replies that this is a time of new ideals: "Das Blut riecht nicht mehr gut, ein Wandel des Geschmacks."* Shifting abruptly from prose to blank verse, however, Hamlet resumes his heroic role: "Füll das Kastell mit Schlächtern wieder, kehr zurück / Zur blutigen Tat, weil jener mit ihr anfing! / Oh, hätt er doch gezaudert! Hätt er doch!"† (GW VII, 3016) If Claudius had hesitated in murder as he has in warfare, Hamlet would not be honor-bound to engage in vengeance. But Hamlet's own hesitation in the face of the peaceful and profitable fish business will vanish in the next scene, after which he will imitate the rash honor of Fortinbras. Thus, the rehearsal scene pairs Hamlet and Fortinbras in bloody acts, whereas Claudius appears in more favorable light, having shifted from feudal slaughter to progressive capitalism. The scene is slight, of course, and would be uninteresting, were it not written by Brecht.

At about the same date as the rehearsal scene, Brecht wrote a sonnet about Hamlet, which expresses much the same sentiment:

In diesem Korpus, träg und aufgeschwemmt
Sagt sich Vernunft als böse Krankheit an
Denn wehrlos unter stahlgeschientem Clan
Steht der tiefsinnige Parasit im Hemd.

Bis sie ihn dann die Trommel hören lassen
Die Fortinbras den tausend Narren rührt
Die er zum Krieg um jenes Ländchen führt
"Zu klein, um ihre Leichen ganz zu fassen."

* Blood doesn't smell good any more. A change of taste.

† Fill the fort with butchers again; return to the bloody deed because the other one started it. Oh, if only he had hesitated. If only!

Erst jetzt gelingt's dem Dicken, rot zu sehn.
Es wird ihm klar, er hat genug geschwankt.
Nun heisst's, zu (blutigen) Taten übergehn.

So dass man finster nickt, wenn man erfährt
"Er hätte sich, wär er hinaufgelangt
Unfehlbar noch höchst königlich bewährt."*
(GW IX 608-609)

Several years later, in 1948, Brecht published his most coherent statement of dramatic theory, *Kleines Organon für das Theater.* In connection with the much-discussed *Verfremdungseffekt,* he takes the same attitude toward a Hamlet whose action is social reaction:

> Wählen wir als Beispiel . . . das alte Stück "Hamlet." Angesichts der blutigen und finsteren Zeitläufe, in denen ich dies schreibe, verbrecherischer Herrscherklassen, eines verbreiteten Zweifels an der Vernunft, welche immerfort missbraucht wird, glaube ich, diese Fabel so lesen zu können: Die Zeit ist kriegerisch. Hamlets Vater, König von Dänemark, hat in einem sie-

* Here is the body, puffy and inert
Where we can trace the virus of the mind.
How lost he seems among his steel-clad kind
This introspective sponger in a shirt!

Till they bring drums to wake him up again
As Fortinbras and all the fools he's found
March off to win that little patch of ground
'Which is not tomb enough . . . to hide the slain.'

At that his solid flesh starts to see red
He feels he's hesitated long enough
It's time to turn to (bloody) deeds instead.

So we can nod when the last Act is done
And they pronounce that he was of the stuff
To prove most royally, had he been put on.
(John Willett translation)

greichen Raubkrieg den König von Norwegen erschlagen. Als dessen Sohn Fortinbras zu einem neuen Krieg rüstet, wird auch der dänische König erschlagen, und zwar von seinem Bruder. Die Brüder der erschlagenen Könige, nun selbst Könige, wenden den Krieg ab, inden den norwegischen Truppen erlaubt wird, für einen Raubkrieg gegen Polen dänisches Gebiet zu queren. Nun ist aber der junge Hamlet vom Geist seines kriegerischen Vaters aufgerufen worden, die an ihm verübte Untat zu rächen. Nach einigen Zaudern, eine blutige Tat durch eine andere blutige Tat zu beantworten, ja schon willig, ins Exil zu gehen, trifft er an der Küste den jungen Fortinbras, der mit seinen Truppen auf dem Weg nach Polen ist. Überwältigt durch das kriegerische Beispiel, kehrt er um und schlachtet in einem barbarischen Gemetzel seinen Onkel, seine Mutter und sich selbst, Dänemark dem Norweger überlassend. In diesen Vorgängen sieht man den jungen, aber schon etwas beleibten Menschen die neue Vernunft, die er auf der Universität in Wittenberg bezogen hat, recht unzulänglich anwenden. Sie kommt ihm bei den feudalen Geschäften, in die er zurückkehrt, in die Quere. Gegenüber der unvernünftigen Praxis ist seine Vernunft ganz unpraktisch. Dem Widerspruch zwischen solchen Räsonieren und solcher Tat fällt er tragisch zum Opfer.* (GW XVI 695-696)

* Let us take as an example . . . the old play *Hamlet*. Given the dark and bloody period in which I am writing—the criminal ruling classes, the widespread doubt in the power of reason, continually being misused—I think that I can read the story thus: It is an age of warriors. Hamlet's father, king of Denmark, slew the king of Norway in a successful war of spoliation. While the latter's son Fortinbras is arming for a fresh war the Danish king is likewise slain: by his own brother. The slain king's brothers, now themselves kings, avert war by arranging that the Norwegian troops shall cross Danish soil to launch a predatory war against Poland. But at this point young Hamlet is summoned by his warrior father's ghost to avenge the crime committed against him. After at first being reluctant to answer one bloody deed by another, and even preparing to go into exile, he meets young

Despite a few errors of fact, Brecht interprets *Hamlet* excitingly, commenting more cogently on the Wittenberg education of the Prince than Hauptmann, who dramatized his university days.

Eric Bentley wrote Brecht that Hamlet did not slay his mother and himself, and Brecht admitted this but argued that Hamlet *brought about* their deaths. Moreover, he concluded: "The Hamlet interpretation is just an example of an *interpretation*—that is, certain emphases and displacements, possibly cuts, and even occasionally (not in this case) interpolations are needed."[18] However, Brecht's interpretation does require interpolation, so that the passage may be read as a scenario for a Brecht *Hamlet* adaptation.

Brecht has been grouped with modern *Hamlet* playwrights though his radio adaptation is not extant and his rehearsal scene is hardly modern in form. But the Marxist context is modern, and he may well have found an epic form to contain it. In histories of modern theater, Epic is usually followed by Absurd. Accordingly, the next *Hamlet* offshoot is absurdist in philosophy and form. *Rosencrantz and Guildenstern Are Dead* by Tom Stoppard (b. 1937) is the best known of modern *Hamlet* offshoots.[19] Tom Stoppard has written me that in 1964 he "wrote a few pages of pastiche blank verse about R & G, but abandoned the idea." Martin Esslin recollects that these few pages set the two courtiers on a ship for England; landing at Dover, they meet mad Lear crying "Kill kill kill kill kill kill," and are killed.

Some time after "abandon[ing] the idea," Stoppard must

Fortinbras at the coast as he is marching with his troops to Poland. Overcome by this warrior-like example, he turns back and in a piece of barbaric butchery slaughters his uncle, his mother and himself, leaving Denmark to the Norwegian. These events show the young man, already somewhat stout, making the most ineffective use of the new approach to Reason which he has picked up at the university of Wittenberg. In the feudal business to which he returns it simply hampers him. Faced with irrational practices, his reason is utterly unpractical. He falls a tragic victim to the discrepancy between such reasoning and such action. (John Willett translation) have pondered on Beckett's *Waiting for Godot,* which suggests the omnipresence of two main characters, their music-hall exchanges, and an unlocalized setting. From Jan Kott's "*King Lear* or *Endgame*" Stoppard may have taken the image of an absurd fate as the toss of a coin, the opening image of *Rosencrantz and Guildenstern Are Dead.* The "even chance" of salvation, which Beckett suggests through the two thieves in the Gospel of Luke, becomes Stoppard's head-or-tails of a coin; an absurd and somewhat ominous note sounds early in the play, when the coin falls heads some hundred successive times. The "even chance" lurches oddly.

In performance, the *Godot* quality of Stoppard's couple is evident in their music-hall exchanges, their games, their boredom, their lack of memory, and their general uncertainty about their condition. Except for their names, their connection with Hamlet is delayed. Once it is made, however, Shakespeare's *Hamlet* is woven around the omnipresence of the couple. About a third of the way into Stoppard's Act I, Rosencrantz and Guildenstern meet the Players. Some two-thirds of the way through the act, Hamlet, and Ophelia enter Stoppard's play. It is a curious entrance:

> *And* OPHELIA *runs on in some alarm, holding up her skirts—followed by* HAMLET.
>
> OPHELIA *has been sewing and she holds the garment. They are both mute.* HAMLET, *with his doublet all unbraced, no hat upon his head, his stockings fouled, ungartered and down-gyved to his ankle, pale as his shirt, his knees knocking each other . . . and with a look so piteous, he takes her by the wrist and holds her hard, then he goes to the length of his arm, and with his other hand over his brow, falls to such perusal of her face as he would draw it. . . . At last, with a little shaking of his arm, and thrice his head waving up and down, he raises a sigh so piteous and profound that it*

> *does seem to shatter all his bulk and end his being. That done he lets her go, and with his head over his shoulder turned, he goes out backwards without taking his eyes off her . . . she runs off in the opposite direction.* (35)

Stoppard's audience actually sees what Shakespeare's Ophelia describes in Act II, Scene 1. *Hamlet* is the script within which Stoppard's insignificant courtiers must play their games and their roles.

After the King and Queen have welcomed Rosencrantz and Guildenstern, the royal couple leave the stage to receive the ambassadors from Norway. Ros and Guil, as Stoppard calls them, are on their own again. At a loss, they ask each other questions and engage in impersonations, as do Beckett's Didi and Gogo, but Stoppard's pair often refer to their uncertain role in *Hamlet*—"Glean what afflicts him." Guil even plays at being Hamlet, so that Ros can understand his situation: "To sum up: your father, whom you love, dies, you are his heir, you come back to find that hardly was the corpse cold before his young brother popped onto his throne and into his sheets, thereby offending both legal and natural practice. Now why exactly are you behaving in this extraordinary manner?" (51) Soon the Prince himself enters, reading; he delights in taunting an offstage Polonius, and he closes Stoppard's Act I with his welcome to Ros and Guil, whom he cannot tell apart, even as they cannot tell themselves apart.

Stoppard's Act II opens later in Shakespeare's Act II, Scene 2, just before the arrival of the Players. Grounded on the music-hall dialogue of Ros and Guil alone, Stoppard's play rushes on into Shakepeare's Act III, Scene 1, whose "get thee to a nunnery" alternates with the Players' rehearsal of the dumbshow that they perform in Shakespeare's play within the play. However, Stoppard's Players go on to rehearse a pantomime of the murder of Polonius, then of two actors escorting Hamlet to England—"Traitors hoist by their own petard?—or victims of the gods?—we shall never know!" (82) Ros notices that the pantomime pair wear cloaks identical to his and Guil's, but the import of the mime eludes him. Stoppard's play then speeds through fragments of the first four scenes of Shakespeare's Act IV, punctuated by the music-hall duets of Ros and Guil, who, it is suddenly revealed, will escort Hamlet to England.

Stoppard's Act III is set on a ship at sea. On board are Ros, Guil, Hamlet. The inseparable couple read Claudius' letter, with its command that Hamlet's head be cut off. They are troubled by its contents, and yet it supplies their only *raison d-être*. As Ros sums up their situation:

> We, Rosencrantz and Guildenstern, from our young days brought up with him, awakened by a man standing on his saddle, are summoned, and arrive, and are instructed to glean what afflicts him and draw him on to pleasures, such as a play, which unfortunately, as it turns out, is abandoned in some confusion owing to certain nuances outside our appreciation—which, among other causes, results in, among other effects, a high, not to say, homicidal, excitement in Hamlet, whom we, in consequence, are escorting, for his own good, to England. Good. We're on top of it now. (111)

While the courtiers are asleep, however, Hamlet substitutes another letter for the original. Without Shakespearean license, the Players then emerge from barrels on deck. Without Shakespearean license, Stoppard's "HAMLET *clears his throat noisily and spits into the audience. A split second later he claps his hand to his eye and wipes himself.*" (116) The sight gag is venerable in music-hall, and it reduces Hamlet's already diminished stature in Stoppard's play. Returning to Shakespeare, Stoppard has pirates attack the ship. In the confusion, Hamlet disappears, leaving Ros and Guil with the Players. Though Ros and Guil discover the substitute letter that spells their deaths, they sail on toward England, an audience to the Players' enactment of various forms of death, including that of the two spies who wear the very cloaks of the courtiers, as did the friends of Hamlet in the earlier mime. Then, one after the other, Ros and Guil disappear from view, as the stage darkens to be lit up on "*the tableau of court and corpses which is the last scene of* Hamlet." (26) *Two* Ambassadors arrive from England, and the play ends on Horatio's Shakespearean reply to their report "that Rosencrantz and Guildenstern are dead."

The leading actors of the American company of *Rosencrantz and Guildenstern* had played minor roles in *Hamlet* productions, and Brian Murray declared: "There's nothing more meaningless than a meaningless Shakespeare character. . . . This strikes a blow for everyone who was ever puzzled by a minor Shakespeare part—the audience, the director, and, particularly, the actors. Now they have a chance to think about it."[20] One can readily sympathize with Shakespeare bit-players who have an opportunity to rise to stardom, but the problem lies in the way they "think about it."

Stoppard himself did his thinking through the absurdist twilight of Beckett's *Godot,* where the two central characters vainly seek meaning and thus carry the play's meaning. Ros and Guil are Stoppard's characters who vainly seek meaning and thus carry *his* play's meaning. In both plays, two friends ask each other questions, tell each other stories, play with puns, clichés, pauses, repetitions, and impersonations. Through it all, an inseparable couple confronts us with its stage presence, incapable of understanding it.

Like Beckett's Didi and Gogo, Stoppard's Ros and Guil wait and play. But more obviously than Beckett, Stoppard introduces philosophy into the music-hall patter of his pair; we hear about laws of probability and diminishing returns; about syllogisms, predictability factors, possible explanations, and a scientific approach.

Like Beckett, Stoppard sets a couple in a generalized human situation. Like Beckett's tramps, Stoppard's noblemen try vainly to understand that situation. Even more than Didi and Gogo, Ros and Guil lack certainty, memory, identity. Failing to seize important matters, they spend their time on trivia, and yet these trivia reflect human activities that are considered important. As in most couples, one member is brighter (Guil) and one more ingenuous (Ros). As in *Godot* (and in life) the range of experience moves from the gratuitous to the poignant. And as in *Godot*, many of the simple phrases are of extensible significance, reflecting on the human condition; identical in the two plays are "I forget," "Even chance," "Time has stopped," "It's the normal thing," "I'm going." Both plays mangle proverbs, and both plays contain jokes about falling trousers. The actors in both plays occasionally comment directly to the audience.

Implicit in both plays is the absurdity of death. Though Ros and Guil disappear from the stage (as opposed to Didi and Gogo), the English Ambassadors announce their *death*. And there are *two* English Ambassadors, identically dressed, as were Ros and Guil. The implication—never more than an implication—is that they will replace Ros and Guil in a new absurdist play that can lead only to death. In Stoppard's Act III death is the theme of the music-hall patter of Ros and Guil, and death is the theme of the Player scenes. Death is immanent, too, in the bone imagery of *Godot* as in the graveyard scene of *Hamlet*, but in *Rosencrantz and Guildenstern Are Dead* death is a constant subject of discussion and enactment.

In giving such explicit attention to death, Stoppard tries to have it two ways—heads and tails: on the one hand, Ros and Guil are Everyman, condemned to live and die they know not where or why. On the other hand, they are Rosencrantz and Guildenstern in Shakespeare's *Hamlet*, condemned by the hero to die because they have been false friends. Acceptance of their doom then becomes specific stupidity rather than mortal ignorance.

The loquacious Player explains to Ros and Guil: "I extract significance from melodrama, a significance which it does not in fact contain." (83) This is Stoppard's own technique. He has fragmented *Hamlet* into several melodramatic scenes and surrounded them by philosophic phrases and *Godot* echoes which seem to yield "a significance which [his play] does not in fact contain." One might argue that critics have thrust significance on Stoppard, who merely wanted to write a play, but his philosophic statements are not parody, and his death drive is not mere farce. Extremely skillful in dovetailing the *Hamlet* scenes into the *Godot* situation, *Rosencrantz and Guildenstern Are Dead* is a witty commentary rather than a theatrical exploration into either great work. We the audience never know more than Didi and Gogo, because Beckett knows no more. We know much more than Ros and Guil because we have absorbed *Hamlet.*

Martin Esslin's book has given wide currency to the phrase "Theater of the Absurd," but the words are not accurate for the phenomenon. The *DRAMA* of the Absurd flourished in the 1950s in small but traditional theaters, replete with proscenium, curtain, fixed seats, sets, props, costumes. Brecht's epic *THEATER,* with its emphasis upon the physical reality of the theater, introduced more radical changes in staging. In dramaturgy, however, the Absurd promulgated the theatrical viability of the ill-made play. Dramas of the Absurd are not plotless and characterless, as was often asserted, but the plots lack cause-and-effect coherence, and the characters lack rational motivation. Events happen disjunctively, and dialogue reflects that disjunction.

Immanent in tragedy is mathos-pathos, education through suffering. Shakespeare's tragic Hamlet returns from his sea voyage with a new understanding—"The readiness is all." The first group of old-fashioned *Hamlet* offshoots sympathetically portray a Hamlet who acquires a new understanding of himself—MacKaye's of his heavy heritage, Hauptmann's of irrational powers both within and outside him, Kops' of the necessity to blend aspiration and practicality, Sarment's of rising above bourgeois commonplaces,

Dukes' of the superiority of scientific investigation, Rice's of the crippling effect of an Oedipal complex. In contrast, the *Hamlet* offshoots in contemporary idiom tend to take a critical attitude toward the Prince, sometimes because he does not learn through suffering: Bentley's Denmark commits murder and lives fiction; Brecht's Wittenberg graduate rejects the new reason to retrogress into feudal bloodshed; Stoppard's Prince (though limited to Shakespearean lines) dallies with little people as though they were coins that might fall head or tail.

The next four offshoots, written between 1966 and 1970, exhibit fidelity to Shakespeare's words while radically altering their conception. Charles Marowitz, Joseph Papp, Paul Baker—all Americans—collage *Hamlet*, reordering lines and/or assigning them to different characters. Austrian Gerhard Rühm extracts Ophelia from *Hamlet*. Each of the offshoots is governed by a different attitude toward Shakespeare's tragedy.

Charles Marowitz (b. 1934) describes the origin of his *Hamlet* collage: "It started as a 28-minute condensation of *Hamlet* as part of the Theatre of Cruelty season at the LAMDA Theatre directed by Peter Brook and myself. There it was taken to be a 'clever exercise' and, in fact, was little more than that. But the problem it threw up made it difficult for me to leave it a Shakespearian charade. For the Festival of Experimental Theatres in Berlin [1966], I enlarged the play to an hour and built in certain views I held about the character and 'notion' of *Hamlet*."[21] (41) It is to these views that Marowitz dedicates some forty pages, introducing the published text of his first collage.

Marowitz writes many things about *Hamlet* in these forty pages, some of which had been written earlier—e.g., that Hamlet belongs to an old myth, that Hamlet is stronger in words than in action, that Hamlet and Fortinbras are like Jekyll and Hyde, that Ophelia is an erotic pawn in the chess of power politics, that the tragedy abounds in *buffo* routines. Explaining collage, Marowitz writes: "Directors have been finding 'new meanings' in the works of Shakespeare for centuries. . . . But what has remained sacrosanct in Shakespeare is the language, the structure, and the narrative. One of the questions behind the present undertaking is to discover to what extent one can juggle *those* elements and still maintain contact with what is essential in *Hamlet*. . . . One of the prerequisites for Shakespearian collage is the audience's general familiarity with the play. . . . I think the same would apply in the cases of *Macbeth, Othello,* and possibly *King Lear*." (14-15) By 1972, Marowitz had collaged *Hamlet, Macbeth,* and *Othello,* and possibly he will go on to *King Lear*.

"I despise Hamlet," writes Marowitz. "He is a slob, / A talker, an analyser, a rationalizer. / . . . You may think he's a sensitive, well-spoken fellow, but, frankly, he gives me a pain in the ass." (10) Marowitz evidently wanted to share that pain with his audiences. Though the sequence of scenes is not always clearly motivated, the beginning and especially the end of the collage portray Hamlet as "A talker, an analyser, a rationalizer."

The play opens on Hamlet and Fortinbras facing each other. After a few lines collaged from Act IV, Scene 4 of Shakespeare's tragedy, Hamlet accuses himself: "How all occasions do inform against me." The swift scene closes on the Ghost's injunction: "If thou hast Nature in thee bear it not." In turn, the Ghost, Fortinbras, Ophelia urge a passive Hamlet to action, while the court utters mocking sounds. Again the Ghost tries to spur Hamlet on, with other Shakespeare fragments intervening. Hamlet collapses into the arms of Rosencrantz and Guildenstern, who bear him to a pedestal. With a burst of energy, Hamlet begins to thrust a toy sword into imaginary victims (played by the real cast). One by one, the actors drop, and, surrounded by mock-corpses, Hamlet closes the collage: "From . . . this . . . time . . . forth / My thoughts be bloody or be nothing worth." "*Corpses, laughing hysterically, mock Hamlet with jeers, whistles, stamping and catcalls till final fade out.*" (97)

Marowitz cuts the cast to eleven, omitting Horatio, doubling Polonius with the Gravedigger-Clown—an old stage tradition. Since the collage is played rapidly, without intermission, one has the impression of invented scenes interpolated into the action, but the printed text shows that this happens rarely. Though Marowitz says that he intended to juggle language, structure, and narrative, he has assumed the basic Shakespearean narrative, he has remained faithful to the language, but he has violated the structure. He rearranges familiar scenes to sound like parodies—Hamlet in the Queen's closet, the play within the play, Claudius at prayer, the Laertes-Hamlet duel, and Ophelia's burial are played in that order, and serious impact is undermined by the staging. Hamlet swings into his mother's closet on a rope; the play within the play is a silent movie on a flicker-wheel; Claudius praying is an actor in a play, whom the court congratulates on his performance. While Claudius kneels, Hamlet stabs him three times; Claudius is unhurt, but Polonius falls dead. Hamlet and Laertes duel with toy swords, and a toy sword, having doubled as a pipe, is used by Hamlet to stab Rosencrantz and Guildenstern. Two extended non-Shakespearean scenes diminish Hamlet, though they use Shakespearean lines. Early in the play, there is a flashback to school (though in performance this is not evident as a flashback), with the Queen as teacher of a class consisting of Hamlet, Ophelia, Laertes, and the Gravedigger-Clown. The lesson is the advice of Polonius.

Toward the end of the collage Hamlet is placed on trial, with the King as judge, Fortinbras as his defense attorney, and Ophelia delivering testimony. At a climactic moment, the Ghost accuses Hamlet, and the King delivers his verdict: "Confine him. / Madness in great ones must not unwatch'd go." (89) The court disappears, leaving Fortinbras to advise Hamlet, but finally "*washing his hands of him completely*." (92) Thus does Fortinbras show the disdain of the man of action for the man of mere words. Hamlet confesses directly to the audience: "Yet I / A dull and muddy-mettled rascal . . . / Peak like . . . / John a' Dreams . . . and / can do nothing." (93) The court returns for Hamlet's final scene of impotence, strewing the stage with mock-corpses.

John Russell Brown summarizes the theatrical aspects of the collage: "Toys, games, rhythmic co-ordination, music-hall routines, fondling and brash sexuality, imitations of silent films, hysterical laughter and wordless responses from the whole cast, all are present and are used to provide sensational drama without the traditional aid of narrative or immediately meaningful structure."[22]

In a "Self-Interview," Marowitz drew far-reaching significance from his collage: "Our generation has a thing against the classics. They represent not only what we've been taught in school, but exist as the artistic embodiments of that paternalist society we are rebelling against at every turn."[23] The collage of the classic *Hamlet* was Marowitz' choice for the first production of his company at the Open Space Theatre in London, toward whose functioning he applied for a grant of twenty thousand pounds from the British Arts Council, a branch of the paternalist society that he is rebelling against, perhaps at not quite *every* turn.

A year after Marowitz presented his *Hamlet* collage in Berlin, Joseph Papp presented his *Hamlet* collage in New York City—1967.[24] Neither in his program nor in his preface to the published text does Papp use the word "collage," but today's theater world is a shrunken globe, and he had probably read about Marowitz's production, for both method and madness are similar.

Papp's published text is entitled *William Shakespeare's "Naked" Hamlet,* but in December, 1967, there was no nudity. On the contrary, the collage thrived on costume and business. The theater program declared: "This production aims radioactive ididium 192 at the nineteenth-century HAMLET statue and by gamma ray shadowgraphing seeks to discover the veins of the living original, buried under accumulated layers of reverential varnish. . . . Like all ventures into the unknown, the course we have taken is perilous. Tampering with a holy cow is dangerous business and can have dire consequences." In the second half of the twentieth century, however, there are very few, if any, holy cows, and dangerous business can be very good business. Especially when laced with variety. Besides collage, Papp's *Hamlet* used rock songs, elaborate gymnastics, local or contemporary allusions, and direct address to the actual theater audience.

Papp follows Shakespeare's plot-line more closely than Marowitz does. Like Marowitz, however, Papp interpolates scenes—Hamlet selling peanuts and balloons, Claudius chasing Hamlet around the theater. A few of Papp's devices are similar to Marowitz'; like the latter's Hamlet, Papp's Ghost enters on a rope swing; as the Marowitz Hamlet boots Guildenstern, Papp's Hamlet kicks Polonius—"Now cracks a noble heart." As Marowitz omits Horatio, Papp omits Fortinbras (an omission for which there is a long stage tradition).

In spite of such similarities, however, Papp and Marowitz differ in their attitudes toward the Prince. "I despise Hamlet," wrote Marowitz, and though Papp is not so personal, he finds the Prince sympathetic—"a 'put-onner' and a 'put-downer.' " Under Papp's direction, Hamlet was first played by Martin Sheen, with frequent assumption of a Puerto Rican accent—a reference to an oppressed minority in New York City. When the play toured in schools, Hamlet was played by black Cleavon Little, an obvious member of an oppressed minority. Though Papp's preface cautions against regarding Claudius as a villain, he was played like a combination of President Lyndon Johnson and a Greek junta general. Audience sympathy was always with the lithe, laughing, juvenile Hamlet, who played practical jokes on the other characters, with frequent excursions into the audience.

Before a word is spoken in Papp's collage, Hamlet and Claudius are recognizably protagonist and antagonist. Papp's play opens with rock music; when it stops,

> *One: The sliding doors are thrown open and some guards enter hurriedly pushing the Royal Bed on which* GERTRUDE *and* CLAUDIUS *are sleeping.*
>
> *Two: Two more guards rush on from the down-right tunnel rolling a plain wooden coffin which they leave at the foot of the Royal Bed.* HAMLET *is in the coffin, reading.* (41)

After khaki-clad guards challenge each other with flashlights across the darkened theater, Hamlet "*because he is cold, pulls the blanket off the Royal Bed to cover himself. . . . Claudius, in his sleep, groans and tries to retrieve the blanket.*" (43) Their tug of war begins.

Soon Horatio is thrown into their midst, in prison-stripes and handcuffs. During a whispered conversation between Hamlet and Horatio, the Prince remarks that he is reading a play *Hamlet* "an excellent play, well digested in the scenes, set down with as much modesty as cunning." (45) Polonius enters with his family and a ringing alarm clock. Claudius and Gertrude awaken, and the court ceremony begins.

Though Papp's *Hamlet* is not spoken as fast as Marowitz' (it runs some fifteen minutes longer—an hour and twenty minutes), it gives the effect of speed because of the frenetic physical activity. The actors must have studied the movies of the Keystone Cops, but the stage chases are not silent; into Shakespeare's lines, spoken (and printed) as prose, intrude modern colloquialisms. "Get him outta here," shouts Claudius, pointing to Horatio. When Hamlet tells Polonius that he can take his leave more willingly than he can take anything except his life, he actually says: "Except my wife. Except my *wife*? Except my *life*!" (74) Hamlet welcomes Rossencraft and Gilderstone (names from the First Quarto) "to Elsinore, to the castle, to New York City, to the New York Shakespeare Festival production of *Hamlet*!" (85)

When Hamlet shoots Claudius after the play within the play, Claudius yells: "What the hell was that?" With the actors using their real names, Hamlet and Claudius "ad lib" swearing at one another. The *pièce de résistance* features Martin Sheen as Hamlet delivering the "To be or not to be" soliloquy in Puerto Rican dialect, with Spanish insertions (not published).

Modern colloquialism blends with visual diversity to give a burlesque effect. For the first few minutes of playing time, Hamlet runs around in underpants and handcuffs. When he dresses, he wears a modern white suit, with black armband and beret. During the course of the action, he disguises himself as a peanut vendor, janitor, carpenter, motorcycle-rider, garbageman, and gravedigger, suiting gestures to each disguise. He is a mixture of "camp" actor and nightclub impersonator, always appealing directly to the audience, against the conspirators onstage.

In the last scene, the entire company plays Russian roulette. The printed text entitles this scene "Everyone Dies," but the deaths take time. Hamlet sheds his Puerto Rican disguise, announcing: "This is I, Hamlet the Dane," (149) and the guards reveal HAMLET THE DANE emblazoned on the back of their shirts. Each swiftly turning to fire, Laertes shoots Horatio, Hamlet shoots Laertes, Claudius shoots Gertrude. After being blindfolded, Claudius and Hamlet fire at each other several times but miss. Then Hamlet fires once, and, one by one, Claudius's bodyguards fall, Osric falls, the other guards fall. Claudius refuses to fall until Hamlet insistently points to the text of *Hamlet*, whereupon he lies down disgustedly. Hamlet points the gun at his own head, then offers it to a member of the audience, who pulls the trigger on Hamlet. Unharmed, Hamlet retrieves the gun and shows the spectator back to his seat. Then, throwing away the text of the play, Hamlet starts to run up the long stage staircase but trips and accidentally shoots himself. He picks up the book, reads: "The rest is silence," and lies flat at the top of the stage structure. After a scuffle,

Claudius is supposed to chase Hamlet offstage, and two guards enter, "*carry a huge funeral wreath with a picture of Hamlet on one side, and on the other 'R.I.P. Will Shakespeare.'* "

Second-guessing any shock reaction in the audience, Papp makes outrage impossible; there is only the barest of connections with "Will Shakespeare." Marowitz, directing for German and English audiences, capitalizes on their outrage, but Papp wooes an American audience with contemporary images. Though both directors have written rather ponderous introductions to their collages, it is hard to take the performances seriously. And unnecessary.

A third collage called *Hamlet ESP* was staged in Dallas, Texas, in 1970 by Paul Baker (who refuses to reveal his birthdate).[25] Of the three collages, Baker's adheres most closely to Shakespeare in following the order of his scenes and introducing no new lines. However, it *is* a collage, since lines are wrenched out of their original context, assigned to different speakers, and repeated for various rhythmic or psychological effects.

Except for the collage technique, the most distinctive feature of *Hamlet ESP* is the use of three different actors to play Hamlet, as Marowitz played three Macbeths in 1969. Shakespeare's lines are divided between the three Hamlets on no apparent principle, and they also speak lines of other characters—sometimes mimicking them, sometimes echoing them.

In his director's notes, Paul Baker states his basic production concept: "The main action of the play happens inside Hamlet's mind." (5) Accordingly, Hamlet relives each scene in his mind's eye, and one of the Hamlets plays the part of Hamlet, while the other two will play the roles of his fellow-actors.

Unlike Marowitz and Papp, Baker makes no pretentious claims but discusses practical production details. Having delineated his basic concept, however, he does not indicate how his visual details support that concept. The action is played on an enormous ramp, at the back of which are sideshow cutouts of the heads of Polonius, Laertes, King, and Queen. On each side of the ramp are "graffiti boards" with butcher's paper, on which the actors draw or write. Up left is a rock band, and downstage are two Mike Girls to insure amplification. A Prop Girl distributes properties as needed. The artifice of production is at all times evident.

The printed text lists twenty-six scenes and two intermissions, which might avoid the breathless effect of the other two collages. Working in Texas, Baker may not even have known the other two, for his production is a development of his own highly visual and physical theater. He accompanies the collaged lines with exaggerated mime—e.g., described actions are mimed when Ophelia recounts Hamlet's entrance into her closet or when the Queen describes Ophelia's madness. The Hamlets mockingly imitate the King, Polonius, Rosencrantz, Guildenstern, Osric. Occasionally, mime is naively mimetic, as when the Hamlets sink to their knees before Ophelia's "quite, quite down." Other visual effects are obtained through elaborate light-play, but it is not clear how these contribute to the "mental" conception.

Moreover, the "ESP" of the title seems inaccurate, since the theater relies not on extrasensory, but sensory, perception. Baker is known for his sophisticated use of stage space and his imaginative lighting. His actors have been praised for their skill in moving and speaking, but rock-band punctuation may inhibit them. The purpose of his collage seems not so much to reveal Hamlet's mind as to exhibit the artifices of the theater—carnival-booths, graffiti boards, and pervasive mime. Rather than revealing the mind of Hamlet, which Shakespeare accomplishes through an unprecedented number of soliloquies, Baker presents the Prince as a fragmented being.

These three *Hamlet* collages both value and devalue language. They value it because they offer Shakespeare's actual words, but they devalue it because the words are wrenched out of context, dominated by a governing conception, and subordinated to elaborate visual effects.

A German-language *Hamlet* offshoot of 1968 similarly values and devalues language; words come from the Schlegel translation of *Hamlet*, but they are situated in a new context and subordinated to the idea of theater. *Ophelia und die Wörter* was composed by Austrian Gerhard Rühm (b. 1930), a member of the Vienna Group that espoused "concrete" forms of all the arts.[26] Rühm has been writing concrete theater since 1954, and he elaborated its theory in 1962. (He uses no capitals.)

> das "neue theater" ist nicht eine als stil festgelegte form des theaters, es besinnt sich auf die elemente und das wesen des theaters und zerfällt daher auf grund der auswahl und anwendung dieser elemente, sowie bedingt durch die gegebenheiten des ortes (grösse, form und art des raumes) in mehrere grundtypen, die ihrerseits noch weiter differenziert sind. aber es ist gekennzeichnet durch eine grundtendenz: der realistischen ('konkreten') einstellung zum material. es handelt sich um die sinnlichen erscheinungsformen (vom menschen ausgehend), ihre beziehungen und deren wirkung.
>
> das problem der einheit von ort und zeit ist im realistischen (konkreten) theater nicht mehr gestellt. denn hier wird nichts vorgetäuscht, nichts beschrieben und nichts erzählt. es verhält sich so, wie es geschieht, und es geschieht jetzt und da, unter diesen oder jenen umständen (gegebenheiten). form und inhalt, darsteller und dargestelltes sind identisch. es ist immer gegenwart.* (278)

* the "new theater" is not a fixed form of theater; it reflects the elements and substance of the theater; on the basis of selection and application of these elements as well as through the actuality of the place (size, form, and kind of space), the theater can be divided into several basic types, which can be further subdivided. But it is recognizable by a basic trend: a realistic (concrete) attitude toward its ma-

In several of Rühm's shorter pieces this seems to be literally true, but in his plays based on classics, the new play depends upon familiarity with the old text. In 1965 Rühm played variations on two well-known Kleist plays, *Der Zerbrochene Krug* and *Kätchen von Heilbron*, and in each case he drew upon the entire drama for his relatively short works.

Kätchen is preceded by an epigram from Act IV, Scene 7 of Kleist's version: "Ich will dir sagen—(Sie kann nicht sprechen.)" (175) In Rühm's offshoot, Kätchen literally cannot speak, nor can anyone else in the play; the many characters perform silently. They present Kleist's intricate plot entirely through wordless gestures.

Ophelia und die Wörter is a *gegenstück* to *Kätchen* in that it consists entirely of Ophelia's words, and derivations or distillations from those words. Rühm's *Hamlet* transformation also begins with an epigram from the original (in Schlegel's translation):

> Polonius: Was leset ihr, mein Prinz?
> Hamlet: Worte, Worte, Worte.
> Polonius: Aber wovon handelt es?
> Hamlet: Wer handelt? (200)

Rühm's play is composed of words, but emptied of plot. It is divided into seven scenes separated by twenty-second blackouts. In *Ophelia und die Wörter* three different and discrete actions take place concurrently:

1. Ophelia plays the Shakespeare-Schlegel text in classical style. That is to say, she goes through her fives scenes, reciting her lines, but no one joins her in these scenes. (There are seven rather than five scenes because Shake-

---

terial. it deals with sensuous appearances (stemming from the human being), their relations and effects.

realistic (concrete) theater no longer poses the problem of unity of place and time. for here there is no pretending, describing, narrating. it happens as it takes place and it takes place here and now, in these or those circumstances (given conditions); form and content, actor and enacted are identical. it is always the present.

speare's Act IV, Scene 5 is broken into two scenes when Ophelia leaves the stage, and in Rühm's final scene Ophelia lies on a bench, silent.)

2. Over loudspeakers Ophelia's voice intones basic words abstracted from her lines—verbs in infinitive form, nouns referring to time, key objects, feelings. Ophelia pays no attention to this.

3. In a different stage area from Ophelia, two actresses in modern dress mime actions derived from Ophelia's words. (Rühm lists some forty verbs from which they may choose *ad libitum.*) They pay no attention to Opheila, or she to them. Their area of the stage is also that of concrete objects and of effects obtainable through a) projection of words for objects, b) projection of images of objects, c) presentation of actual objects, d) sonorization of words like bell or rain, e) lighting display for colors, f) a spray of scents. Each of these is triggered by a not necessarily relevant cue-word of Ophelia's.

The three simultaneous actions evidently work to convey an acute sense of Ophelia's descent into madness. The two modern actresses are literal antagonists of the classically performing Ophelia. It is their joint play, as well as the abstractions over the loudspeaker which enable us to participate in the madness. No longer do we watch with the Queen, pitying Ophelia; we are assaulted as she is by the inadequacy of language. On the one hand, signifiers screen off rather than reveal the signified; on the other, gesture and object are highly simplified.

In *Kaspar,* one of the most striking plays of the 1960s, Peter Handke's protagonist learns conventionality as he learns language. But Rühm's Ophelia cannot accept this accommodation to convention. As her emotional life develops from subservience to the men in her family, to victimization by the man she loves, to madness, and finally to death, that sequence of detachments is theatricalized through the disintegration of language. In the first scene, the loudspeaker is silent; there is apparently delay between the first naive pronouncement of words and the abstraction of thinking about them. In the seventh and last scene, classical Ophelia lies down to die on the stage bench; she is silent, but the loudspeaker blares words from her whole stage life, culminating in *zweifeln*—doubt. With the loudspeakers quiet, with Ophelia motionless, the word *Haupt* is accompanied by a smashed bust of Shakespeare; the word *Himmel* by a starry sky. Rühm has denied any interest in the metaphoric, but his images are not chosen by chance. The head gives way to the sky, bardolatry to the Milky Way. The classical heroine is still, but she has been torn between culture and nature, seeing and hearing, fragmentation and harmony, to end in doubt.

I should like to end this examination of modern *Hamlet* offshoots on Rühm's high note, and to all intents and purposes I will. *Hamlet* has not been as popular as *Macbeth* in the Alternative Theater, where texts are subordinated to group development. Emilio Galli's Group N (not called that at the time) began its psychophysical exploration with *Hamlet*. Galli chose the text because he felt that radical theater should attack the structures of theater, the cultural darling of the bourgeoisie, whose most cherished role is Hamlet. In his version, he therefore had sixteen Hamlets, to demystify the role while seeking its concealed myth.

Across the Channel in England, the Triple Action Theatre produced a seven-actor *Hamlet* based on a stage metaphor of a web. However, I prefer to discuss that version in the context of the development of the Triple Action Theatre, a fringe company largely devoted to Shakespeare offshoots. Given the highly physical orientation of the groups on both sides of the English Channel, and given the fact that their *Hamlet* offshoots lasted about ninety minutes in the theater, it is probable that Shakespeare's text was radically abridged in favor of scenic images.

Dramatic *Hamlet* offshoots fall short of the fiction of Sterne, Goethe, Laforgue, and Joyce. And they fall short, too, of dramas that lean on *Hamlet*—Musset's *Lorenzacchio*, Chekhov's *Uncle Vanya*, Büchner's *Danton's Death*, Strindberg's *Eric XIV*, Pirandello's *Henry IV*, and Byron's *Manfred*, to choose a random cross-national representation. Some modern *Hamlet* offshoots were written in outworn theater idiom, which would not *necessarily* preclude high quality; in fact, it does. *Hamlet* offshoots in modern modes —Dada, epic, absurdist, concrete, and collage are more spirited and perhaps more significant.

With the exception of Rühm's, all offshoots focus on the Prince, and perhaps their only common feature leads us back to Goethe and his portrait of the sensitive intellectual, for whom vengeful action was abhorrent. Sarment, Hauptmann, Tzara, Brecht, Kops, Dukes, and Rice strain against this view, exhibiting the Prince in active moments. Marowitz mocks Hamlet because of his non-action, and Stoppard because of his actions; Baker, Papp, and the Triple Action Theatre show him seizing rare opportunities to act, though surrounded by obstacles. In or out of Shakespeare, the Prince continues to tempt the actors, but perhaps the last word goes to Ophelia. Gerhart Hauptmann is the only author to have transplanted the Danish prince into both drama and fiction, and he provides suitable words on which to close this long chapter:

> Auf unzählige Weisen ist das Original [*Hamlet*] verstümmelt worden: durch gekürzte Aufführungen, durch Bearbeitungen, durch Vermischung verschiedener Stücke, Umstellung der Szenen, Veränderung der Namen, durch dilettantische und respektlose Verkleisterung enstandener Lücken, schauspielerische Zusätze und Eigenmächtigkeiten, und so fort und so fort.[27]*

* The original [*Hamlet*] has been mutilated in countless ways: through abridged productions, through adaptations, through mixing up of passages, reordering of scenes, changing names, through dilettantish and disrespectful filling in of original lacunae, through actors' additions, and other unauthorized changes, and so on and so on.

Chapter 4

Lear Come Lately

Hamlet and *Macbeth* are often contrasted, but *King Lear* looms as a lone pinnacle of Shakespearean tragedy. Staged less often than the other major tragedies, criticized more severely, *King Lear* was rarely regarded as Shakespeare's masterpiece—before the twentieth century. But especially since World War II, its agonies and cruel humor have hit home. For this reason the tragedy itself, rather than offshoots, has spoken directly to contemporary audiences. No important fiction has embraced *Lear* as it has *Hamlet*, and very few dramatists have used *Lear* as a springboard for their own plays. However, a number of writers have been so passionately caught up in *Lear* that their comments form a minor genre of essayistic offshoots, outside the mainstream of professional *Lear* scholarship. Exceptionally, then, this chapter on *King Lear* will venture away from drama and fiction, into the essays of imaginative writers. But not at its beginning.

Shakespeare blended documents with fiction and drama to arrive at the complications and complexities of his *King Lear*. The Annesley family squabble, various accounts of the Lear legend, Sidney's *Arcadia*—any of these may have started Shakespeare on his own *Lear*. Kenneth Muir's summary of the sources of *King Lear*—"a play, a prose romance, a chronicle, two poems and a satirical pamphlet on exorcism"[1]—may be particularized as the anonymous play *King Leir*, Sidney's romance *Arcadia*, Holinshed's *Chronicles*, Spenser's *Faerie Queene*, *A Mirror for Magistrates*, and Harsnett's *Declaration of Egregious Popish Impostures*.

Perhaps the germinating work was the anonymous play *King Leir*, for Shakespeare's *King Lear* is unique among his tragedies in having as source an extant drama. The basic story of the anonymous *Leir* resembles a fairy-tale more than a drama: a king had three daughters of whom the youngest alone was fair and loving and good. The king favored his bad children and mistreated the good. In most versions of the story, the king comes to appreciate the good child, and the two generations harmonize happily. So in *King Leir*. Through eight scenes of the chronicle play Leir divides his kingdom between Gonorill and Ragan, disinheriting Cordella, who is then wooed and won by the Gallian king in disguise. The two elder daughters mistreat Leir, who is faithfully served by his courtier Perillus. Cordella and her husband come upon Leir and Perillus as starving outcasts. Father and daughter are reconciled; the Gallian forces defeat those of the wicked sisters; and all is apparently well that ends well.

Shakespeare impressively individualizes the characters of the chronicle play; he underlines the theme of filial ingratitude (and loyalty) through addition of the Gloucester subplot; he invents the storm on the heath with the rending trio of madman, mock-madman, and fool—inner chaos reflected in nature's chaos. Shakespeare transforms a sequence of mildly suspenseful events into a tragedy of cosmic resonance. The phrase "cosmic resonance" can be easily said, but only a few tragedies literally attain it, preeminently *The Oresteia* and *King Lear*.

Though *Lear* towers in its own stature, comparison with *Leir* illuminates Shakespeare's genius and his craftsmanship, hard as it is to draw a boundary line. W. W. Greg, that pioneer scholar, has listed some forty parallels—mainly verbal—between the old *Leir* and Shakespeare's tragedy.[2] By far the majority consist of such ordinary phrases that Shakespeare needed no source for them. On the other hand, three important images do seem to derive from *Leir*: the king likens Goneril to a fiend, he kneels to Cordelia, and he compares himself to a pelican, which, in the old play, "kills itself to save her young one's lives." Shakespeare's Lear moans: " 'Twas this flesh begot / Those pelican daughters."

What makes Shakespeare Shakespeare is complexity of conception wringing us through the most varied language of English dramatic literature, or perhaps of any literature. And in that respect, comparison of *King Lear* to *King Leir* is almost ludicrous. In the old play neither idiom nor rhythm varies with the speaker, whereas Shakespeare's *Lear* is his supreme achievement in linguistic variety—ceremonious blank verse, staccato pentameters, ballads, dialect, and amazingly flexible prose. The bad sisters' mellifluous speech at once distinguishes them from tongue-tied Cordelia. Kent is immediately recognizable by the bluntness to which Cornwall will later call attention. Edmund is cynically elegant, and his father is trifling and superficial. Edgar speaks four distinct idioms: ingenuous nobleman, mad beggar, country bumpkin, mysterious challenger. The Fool, in contrast, is consistently plainspoken in vocabulary but gnomic in meaning.

Shakespeare reaches his greatest breadth and depth in the speech of Lear. At first formal, Lear's words soon shake the elements. Even as he fears madness, Lear erupts into the broken rhythms and pregnant wisdom of his madness. With contrition, he acquires a new simplicity of syntax and vocabulary.

Leir's last lines scarcely hint at those of Lear.

> Thanks (worthy *Mumford*) to thee last of all,
> Not greeted last, 'cause thy desert was small:
> No, thou hast lion-like laid on to-day,
> Chasing the *Cornwall* king and *Cambria*:
> Who with my daughter, daughters did I say?
> To save their lives, the fugitives did play.
> Comme, sonne and daughter, who bid me advaunce,
> Repose with me awhile, and then for *Fraunce*.[3]

The mechanical quality of rhyme, repetition, alliteration, negatives, and question tinge this final ceremony with an almost comic note. The single stale image—"lion-like"—

confirms the dull statements of the lines which are stiffened into pentameters.

Lear's final lines earn their agony (as I interpret them, disagreeing with Bradley's "Redemption of King Lear"):[4]

> And my poor fool is hanged: no, no, no life?
> Why should a dog, a horse, a rat, have life,
> And thou no breath at all? Thou'lt come no more,
> Never, never, never, never, never.
> Pray you undo this button. Thank you, sir.
> Do you see this? Look on her! Look her lips,
> Look there, look there.

The three questions of the passage bear on mortality. The word "fool" has been much discussed, but it too bears on mortality. Since the fool was a pet like an animal in the court, it prepares for the animals in the following line, who share mortality with human beings.

In these lines the tragedy's hundreds of negatives rise to a final crescendo—no, no life, no breath, no more, culminating in the five "nevers" and "undo." Only the homely "button" and the negatives "never" and "undo" provide respite from the throbbing monosyllables. Yet the speech seems to grow painfully from the opening declaration and the immediate question. Another question with its midline caesura is followed by a prediction with its five daring nevers. A request and a courteous response lead to the climactic four-syllabled question, the double spondee "Do you see this?" The liquid *l*s in the four "look"s and "lip"s then loosen into sobs that finally break the pentameter pattern.

Dramatically, the seven lines of Lear's last speech divide into three parts: the opening line is at once a statement and question about Cordelia's death; the next two and a half lines form a question and a hammered negative answer, addressed to the Cordelia who is "thou" to Lear; the last three lines are addressed to an anonymous "you," at first politely, then in anguish. The domestic animal imagery of the first three lines are balanced in the second three lines by the stage reality of Lear's button and Cordelia's lips. The button is at once a humble prop and the crucial object in father Lear's empathetic imitation of death by hanging; he wants his button loosened because he imagines the tightening noose. Finally, we cannot know whether Lear dies in hope that Cordelia's lips are moving, or in despair at their cold fixity. For we cannot see beyond Lear's last words to the infinite resonance of the adverb "there." This final simplicity has been earned through Lear's imperious syntax as an absolute ruler, his hyperbolic curses as a mistreated father, his surrealistic associations as a madman, his ironic morality as a mad judge. The beauty of these last household words can hardly be borne.

However, their beauty has not always been appreciated. In 1681 Nahum Tate amended *King Lear,* eliminating this speech. (He followed this adaptation by less radical alterations of *Richard II* and *Coriolanus.*) Many actors declared their preference for Tate over Shakespeare, and audiences were not given the choice. Tate's *Lear* (with minor modifications) held the London stage for one hundred fifty-seven years. However, it did not hold the boards firmly, since Genest lists only twenty-one different productions during that time, and only one between 1788, when King George III had his first attack of what was thought to be madness (but was actually porphyria), and 1820, when he died. Tact precluded staging of a play about a mad monarch, even though George III appreciated the parallel between Lear and himself.

Tate's *Lear* was produced by such celebrated actors as Spranger Barry, John Kemble, David Garrick, and even Edmund Kean, who tried to restore an unhappy ending, but not that of Shakespeare. For dubious reasons. Hawkins' *Life of Kean* quotes his "invariable exclamation" on being admired as Othello: "The London audience have no notion of what I can do until they see me over the dead body of Cordelia."[5] In 1823, encouraged by Hazlitt's and Lamb's essays against Tate's adaptation, Kean killed Cordelia so as to bend over her dead body, but Shakespeare's *Lear* (still much modified) lasted three unpopular performances before Kean returned to Tate. Only in 1838 did William Charles Macready play Shakespeare's *Lear*—with some misgivings, a female Fool, a forked lightning, and a conceptual unity that boded ill for Tate's scissors and paste.

Tate himself could not have known how long his adaptation would play, and he explained it with some modesty. Admiring Shakespeare, he merely wished to curb the Bard's extravagance and disorder, but he did pride himself on one major change:

> 'Twas my good Fortune to light on one Expedient to rectify what was wanting in the Regularity and Probability of the Tale, which was to run through the whole, a *Love* betwixt *Edgar* and *Cordelia*; that never chang'd a Word with each other in the Original. . . . This method necessarily threw me on making the Tale conclude in a Success to the innocent distrest Persons: Otherwise I must have incumbred the Stage with dead Bodies, which Conduct makes many Tragedies conclude with unseasonable Jests.[6]

Prefiguring melodrama, Tate imposes a black-and-white morality upon Shakespeare's characters: the bad are all bad, and the good almost all good. Bad Edmund commits adultery with bad Goneril, he plots to rape good Cordelia, and he plans to marry bad Regan. It is bad Goneril who orders the execution of good Lear and good Cordelia; bad Edmund knows no contrition when he dies. Tate drops the Fool, tempers Lear's curses, and sentimentalizes the reunion with Cordelia: "O pity, Sir, a bleeding Heart and cease / This killing Language." Lear helps to reverse his fortunes by slaying two soldiers who threaten Cordelia, and, after giving his restored kingdom to Edgar and Cordelia, he dissuades Gloster from suicide:

> No. *Gloster*, Thou hast Business yet for Life;
> Thou, *Kent* and I, retir'd to some cool Cell
> Will gently pass our short reserves of Time
> In calm Reflections on our Fortunes past,
> Cheer'd with relation of the prosperous Reign
> Of this celestial Pair . . . ,

who are of course Cordelia and her faithful Edgar. The latter closes the play with a ringing "Truth and Vertue shall at last succeed."

It is easy to laugh at Tate. The surprise is that, given his biases, he retained the storm scene, the blinding of Gloucester (probably offstage), the cliff scene, and many images of animals and procreation, which must have been repugnant to his sensibility. During Tate's hegemony Dr. Johnson wrote: "Cordelia, from the time of Tate, has always retired with victory and felicity. And, if my sensations could add anything to the general suffrage, I might relate, that I was many years ago so shocked by Cordelia's death, that I know not whether I ever endured to read again the last scenes of the play till I undertook to revise them as an editor."[7] In Germany, A. W. Schlegel remonstrated: "[Cordelia's] death has been thought too cruel; and in England the piece is so far altered in acting that she remains victorious and happy. I must own, I cannot conceive what idea of art and dramatic connection those persons have who suppose that we can, at pleasure, tack a double conclusion to a tragedy; a melancholy one for hard-hearted spectators, and a merry one for souls of softer mould."[8] All the same, Schlegel did not choose to translate *King Lear*. But the best known attack on Tate (by then long dead) is Charles Lamb's: "Tate has put his hook into the nostrils of this Leviathan for Garrick and his followers, the showmen of the scene, to draw the mighty beast about more easily. . . . Lear is essentially impossible to be represented on a stage."[9]

On the American stage Tate lasted even longer than in England, and as in England, literary men turned to the text rather than the theater—most creatively Herman Melville in the middle of the nineteenth century. Nevertheless, it was the stage impact of Fanny Kemble as Lady Macbeth that caused Melville to return to Shakespeare's plays, which he bought in a seven-volume edition with large type. Under the influence of those plays, writing in the margins of the still extant volumes, Melville changed his romantic whaling narrative into *Moby-Dick*. F. O. Matthiessen has illuminated the mammoth novel as a Shakespearean tragedy: Ahab is a Lear whose madness leads to no purgative sympathy, and Pip is a Fool whose wisdom is ignored,[10] as Melville was virtually ignored during his lifetime.

By the middle of the nineteenth century Shakespeare's *King Lear* was back on the English-speaking stage, but it was performed least often of the major tragedies. At the turn of the twentieth century, *King Lear* was used as a whipping-boy by the most eminent nineteenth-century novelist, Leo Tolstoy (1828-1910). Always hostile to Shakespeare, Tolstoy at the age of seventy-five undertook to reread all the plays, and this exercise confirmed his negative opinion of the Bard. His "Shakespeare and the Drama" originated in the request of an American friend, Ernest H. Crosby, for a preface to his article on Shakespeare and the working classes (which said in effect that Shakespeare was against the working classes). The preface grew to double the length of the article, and after its publication in Russian in 1906, Tolstoy closely followed the English translation, which appeared that same year in the influential *Fortnightly Review*.[11]

Tolstoy's Shakespearophobia erupts early in his long, fourteen-part essay: "I felt an irresistible repulsion and tedium [on reading Shakespeare], and doubted as to whether I was senseless in feeling works regarded as the summit of perfection by the whole of the civilized world to be trivial and positively bad, or whether the significance which this civilized world attributes to the works of Shakespeare was itself senseless." (4) In attempting to demonstrate Shakespeare's inferiority, Tolstoy focuses on *King Lear*, marshaling favorable opinions by Dr. Johnson, Hazlitt, Hallam, Shelley, Swinburne, Hugo, Brandes. Tolstoy proposes to summarize Shakespeare's *Lear* "as impartially as possible," but it seems not to be possible, since pejorative comments often intrude—"inflated characterless style," "naively absurd and unnatural," "a special kind of storm such as there never was before," "inflated and incessant ravings," "tedious and monotonous ravings," "difficult to follow the action."

After his impartial summary, Tolstoy begins the discreditation: Lear and Gloucester are incredibly gullible, the disguises are not convincing, and, to sum up: "But it is not enough that Shakespeare's characters are placed in tragic positions which are impossible, do not flow from the course of events, are inappropriate to time and space—these personnages, besides this, act in a way which is out of keeping with their definite character and is quite arbitrary." (52)

Tolstoy then turns to the old anonymous *King Leir*, whose characters are "strikingly weakened and deprived of force by him [Shakespeare], as compared with their appearance in the older drama." (56) Like Tate before him, Tolstoy plumps for poetic justice: "The older play also terminates more naturally and more in accordance with the moral demands of the spectator than does Shakespeare's, namely, by the King of the Gauls conquering the husbands of the elder sisters, and Cordelia, instead of being killed, restoring Leir to his former position." (63) Insensitive as Tolstoy may appear, his attack against "exaggeration of events, exaggeration of feeling, and exaggeration of expression" forces *Lear*'s admirers to come to terms with the drama's unparalleled immensity.

Generalizing from the inadequacies of *Lear* to those of Shakespeare, Tolstoy moves in on the nineteenth-century German critic G. G. Gervinus, and from that base, tries to demolish the man whom he considers the most pernicious of Bardolators, Goethe (who also praised the old *Leir*). Because Goethe was irreligious, says Tolstoy, he admired Shakespeare, who shared his hedonistic attitude. German critics, seeking a non-French model, followed Goethe's lead, thus repudiating the religious wellspring of drama. (Tolstoy says nothing of Herder or Lessing, Germans who preceded Goethe in admiring Shakespeare.)

Bardolatry stemming from Goethe has had two disastrous effects: "First, the fall of the drama, and the replacement of this important weapon of progress by an empty and immoral amusement; and secondly, the direct depravation of men by presenting them false models for imitation." (118) Among the imitators, Tolstoy mentions Schiller, Hugo, Pushkin, Ostrovski, and Alexei Tolstoy. Grouping these as Shakespeareans, Tolstoy is vituperative about the most nefarious legacy of the Bard—an inability to distinguish between good and evil: "And the error of extolling an insignificant, inartistic writer—not only not moral, but directly immoral—executes its destructive work." (123) After this energetic condemnation, Tolstoy concludes somewhat anticlimactically: "First, having freed themselves from this deceit, men will come to understand that the drama which has no religious element at its foundation is not only not an important and good thing, as it is now supposed to be, but the most trivial and despicable of things. Secondly, having freed themselves from this hypnotic state, they will recognize that, while there is no true religious drama, the teaching of life should be sought for in other sources." (124)

At the time he fired this volley against Shakespeare, Tolstoy was the world's most celebrated novelist, and he was eager to have the piece translated into English, so as to demolish the Bard on his home ground. There he found support from England's most fiery dramatist, George Bernard Shaw, who had written a decade earlier: "No man will ever write a better tragedy than *Lear*."[12] However, when Tolstoy's friend and translator, V. Tchertkoff, asked Shaw for a comment to accompany book publication of the Crosby-Tolstoy essays, Shaw obliged, though he had not read either essay. He repeated what he had often said in his reviews of Shakespeare productions: that Shakespeare had small philosophy and less morality, but that he made beautiful word music. After publication of the slim volume, Shaw and Tolstoy exchanged a few letters, but by 1945 Shaw could dismiss Tolstoy on *Lear*: "Tolstoy declared that the original Lear is superior to Shakespear's rehandling, which he abhorred as immoral. Nobody has ever agreed with him."[13]

After Tolstoy's death in 1910, his anti-Shakespeare piece was retranslated for inclusion in his complete works. Before reading it, G. Wilson Knight (b. 1897) saw *Timon of Athens* as a virtual biography of Tolstoy, who "lived the very history that Shakespeare traced out for him three centuries earlier."[14] (246) Knight, a college professor turned actor, playwright, and director, couples Tolstoy's adverse criticism with that of Robert Bridges, saying that both men were reacting intelligently against romantic and psychological Bardolatry. Moreover, he finds them correct within the limitations of their vision, but then proposes to expand that vision to see Shakespeare's grand design.

Agreeing with the two Shakespearophobes that the Bard's characterization is often incredible, Knight maintains that it varies with the design:

> In *Othello* and *Coriolanus* the persons are very firmly differentiated and fairly "natural"; in *Timon of Athens,* firmly differentiated but scarcely "natural" in the usual sense; in *Antony and Cleopatra* "natural" but not very solidly differentiated; in *King Lear,* and still more in *Macbeth,* often both "unnatural" (in the sense of "remarkable" or "strange") and slightly differentiated. But in all these greater plays the whole vision is primary: human realism, sometimes natural, sometimes unnatural, only exists in vassalage to this poetic vision. (287)

Agreeing, too, with "the rugged beauty of Tolstoy's gospel" (297) Knight nevertheless exonerates Shakespeare from Tolstoy's charge of lacking religious essence. Citing recurrent images such as tempests and music, Knight imposes his well-known religious design on Shakespeare's oeuvre:

> We must understand the disorder-philosophy of the Histories, the death-forces in *Hamlet* and *Macbeth* embattled against life, the Christian ethic of *Measure for Measure,* the purgatorial vision of *King Lear,* the accomplished paradise of *Antony and Cleopatra.* And beyond those we shall be directed to the birth and resurrection dramas of the Final Plays; recognizing therein true myths of immortality caught from the penetralium of mystery by one of the few greatest writers of the world. (296-297)

From the same basic religious premise, Tolstoy and Knight come to polar evaluations of the Bard.

Over a decade later, in 1947, George Orwell (1903-1950) calls Tolstoy's attack on *Lear* "a prolonged exercise in misrepresentation."[15] In his "Lear, Tolstoy, and the Fool" Orwell himself makes some astounding assertions: "*Lear* is one of the minority of Shakespeare's plays that are unmistakably *about* something." (42) "Shakespeare had a considerable streak of worldliness in him, and if he had been forced to take sides in his own play, his sympathies would probably have lain with the Fool." (47) "In his sane moments Lear hardly ever makes an intelligent remark." (49) More central to Orwell's basic argument is his dogmatic statement: "The subject of *Lear* is renunciation, and it is only by being wilfully blind that one can fail to understand what Shakespeare is saying." (43) Orwell then declares climactically: "The most impressive event in Tolstoy's life, as in Lear's, was a huge and gratuitous act of renunciation." (44) And somewhat anticlimactically: "His exaggerated revulsion from sexuality was also distinctly similar to Lear's." (45) Orwell interprets Tolstoy as a religious fanatic who used his heavy guns on the humanist Shakespeare because the latter threatened his life style. The failure of Lear's renunciation mirrored the failure of Tolstoy's own, which the Russian nobleman could not and would not admit. Orwell concludes that the final test of a literary work is not philosophy but survival. And Shakespeare's works have survived. Similarly, Tolstoy is remembered not for his attack on Shakespeare but for *War and Peace* and *Anna Karenina.* However, Orwell does not explain why he chose to write about that attack rather than the novels of the great Russian author.

George Woodcock attempts that explanation, speculating on Orwell's biography as Orwell speculated on Tolstoy's. In *The Crystal Spirit* he summarizes his argument:

> [Orwell] in his youth if not in his old age—followed the example of Lear and Tolstoi in attempting a major act of renunciation. He gave up his career in the Indian service, which was probably no great sacrifice, but he followed it up by his deliberate descent into the lower depths of destitution; for a period . . . he contemplated a permanent renunciation of his past and of all his claims to social advantage. Afterwards, like Tolstoi, he realized that he had acted on mistaken motives, and that the impression he had first gained of having crossed the great gulf of cast was an illusion. The history of Orwell was as "curiously similar" to the history of Tolstoi as Tolstoi's history to Lear's, and what appears to be violent disagreement is really an unwilling and unadmitted recognition of moral affinity.[16]

We might be watching one of Genet's whirligigs: under the appearance of a moral essay on Shakespeare, Tolstoy hides the reality of his personal frustration; under the appearance of a critical essay on Tolstoy, Orwell hides the reality of *his* personal frustration. The Russian and the Englishman become other faces of Lear, but at least we are spared the suggestion that Shakespeare is Lear.

In contrast to this biographical continuum running through Tolstoy, Shaw, Knight, Orwell, and Woodcock, is the psychomythic approach of Sigmund Freud (1856-1939). While Freud was perfecting his psychoanalytic techniques, he published occasional short papers, one of them based on a choice among three caskets.[17] The father of psychoanalysis relates *King Lear* to all men rather than to the biographical quirk of a few.

In this piece Freud considers various fairy-tales along with two Shakespeare plays, *The Merchant of Venice* (to which his title obviously refers) and *King Lear* (whose relation to his title he explains). Freud had already interpreted dreams of containers as symbols of women, and he now finds that Shakespeare's comedy resembles his tragedy in that both pivot on a scene in which a man chooses among three women or women-symbols (caskets). He traces Shakespeare's theme to its source in *Gesta Romanorum,* moves on to the opening scene of *King Lear,* then summarizes such analogues as Paris and the Greek goddesses, Cinderella and her sisters, Psyche and her sisters. Working through myth and fairy-tale, Freud points out that the third woman is not only beautiful but also silent, and that silence often symbolizes death.

After a short digression on the Three Fates, Freud interprets the several tales he mentions. When the hero chooses the silent beauty, he is choosing death, but since no one *chooses* death, this seeming choice is an inversion of the inevitable, when death claims the hero.

Though Freud ranges over many myths in this short article—as Jung, Campbell, and Levi-Strauss were to do after him—he concludes on *King Lear.* Remarking parenthetically that he does not deny the drama's two lessons—that one should not abdicate responsibility and that one should not fall prey to flattery—Freud insists that the overpowering effect of the tragedy lies deeper. Lear, an old and dying man, is nevertheless unwilling to renounce the love of women: "Nun denke man an die erschütternde letzte Szene, einen der Höhepunkte der Tragik im modernen Drama: Lear trägt den Leichnam der Cordelia auf die Bühne. Cordelia ist der Tod. Wenn man die Situation umkehrt, wird sie uns verständlich und vertraut. Es ist die Todesgöttin, die den gestorbenen Helden vom Kampfplatze wegträgt, wie die Walküre in der deutschen Mythologie. . . . Der alte Mann aber hascht vergebens nach der Liebe des Weibes, wie er sie zuerst von der Mutter empfangen; nur die dritte der Schicksalsfrauen, die schweigsame Todesgöttin, wird ihn in ihre Arme nehmen."* (36-37)

Ideally, Freud on *Lear* should be paralleled by Marx on *Lear,* but since Marx did not comment on that tragedy, we may substitute Bertholt Brecht, self-declared admirer of Marx. Unlike other Shakespearean tragedies, *Lear* never became a springboard for a Brechtian rehearsal scene. But he devotes several pages to *Lear* in *Der Messingkauf,* critical dialogues that were written between 1939 and 1942. Four speakers in these dialogues represent various Brechtian attitudes about the theater of the future, presumably in a happy Marxist land; they are designated by profession—Philosopher, Dramaturg, Actor, Actress.

The four of them speak for four nights, and Shakespeare figures in the conversations of the second and third. On the earlier evening the Philosopher sees no necessity to get rid of beautiful old plays, but they must be performed from a historical distance. Empathy with Lear must be avoided, but it is not necessary to attack him. The Dramaturg explains:

* Now think of the shattering final scene, one of the tragic summits of modern drama: Lear carries Cordelia's body on the stage. Cordelia is Death. If we reverse the situation, it becomes comprehensible and familiar to us. It is the goddess of death who carries the slain hero from the battlefield, like the Valkyrie in German mythology. . . .

But the old man vainly grasps at the love of woman, as he first received it from his mother; only the third Fate, the silent goddess of death, will take him in her arms.

> Man kann die Bediensteten des überall abgewiesenen Königs zeigen, ein kleines Häuflein, das nirgends mehr genährt wird und ihn verfolgt mit ihren stummen Vorwürfen. Ihr Anblick müsste Lear peinigen, und das würde einen guten Grund für seine Raserei abgeben. Die feudalen Verhältnisse müssen einfach gestaltet werden.* (GW XVI, 592)

What is necessary is arousing the historical sense of the audience.

On the third night the Dramaturg admires Lear's death scene (of which Brecht's translation is apparently in the Berlin Brecht Archives). It is praised for its realism.

> Nehmt die Stelle, wo *Lear* stirbt! Dies "Pray you, undo this button: thank you, Sir!" In die Verwünschungen drängt sich ein Wunsch, das Leben ist unerträglich, und dann drückt noch die Kleidung; was gelebt hat, war ein König, was stirbt, ist ein Mensch. Er ist ganz zivil ("thank you, Sir"). Das Thema wird voll abgehandelt, im kleinen und im grossen. Der Enttäuschte stirbt, Enttäuschung und Sterben werden gezeigt, sie decken sich nicht ganz. Es wird keine Verzeihung gewährt, aber Freundlichkeiten werden entgegengenommen. Der Mann ist zu weit gegangen, der Dichter geht nicht zu weit. Die Vernichtung des Lear ist vollständig, der Tod wird noch überraschend als Spezialschrecken demonstriert, Lear stirbt wirklich.† (GW XVI, 616)

* The servants of this generally unwanted king could be shown as a little group which no longer gets its meals anywhere and pursues him with dumb reproaches. Lear would have to wince at the sight of them, and that would be a good enough reason for him to lose his temper. You just have to show the feudal conditions. (62-63)

† Take the scene where Lear dies: his "Pray you, undo this button: thank you, Sir!" A wish insinuates itself among his maledictions; life has become intolerable, and on top of that his clothes are too tight; it was a king that lived, a man who dies. He is quite polite: ("thank you, Sir"). The subject is fully covered in detail and in outline. A disappointed man is dying: dying and disappointment are shown, but

"Disappointment" is a curious understatement for Lear's final moments. And if death is demonstrated as a "special horror," it would seem to be the death of Cordelia rather than Lear, of whom Kent says: "He hates him / That would upon the rack of this tough world / Stretch him out longer." Moreover, "really" about a stage death is a curious adverb for Brecht, arch-enemy of illusion in the theater.

Earlier in *Der Messingkauf* the Brechtian Philosopher has grouped Shakespeare's tragedies as pictures of the decline of feudalism. Paradoxically, the decidedly un-Marxist Marshall McLuhan (b. 1916) takes a not dissimilar view of *King Lear,* but he prefers feudalism to capitalism. McLuhan's *Gutenberg Galaxy* opens with an interpretation of Shakespeare's *King Lear,*[18] and a note summarizes his view of the tragedy: "*King Lear* is a working model of the process of denudation by which men translated themselves from a world of roles to a world of jobs." (345)

In McLuhan's Prologue, which introduces his pattern of juxtaposing quotations from widely various sources, he states that *The Gutenberg Galaxy* "begins with the interplay of cultures via commerce and ends with the dissolution of the tribal state, even as it is dramatized by Shakespeare in *King Lear.*" (17) Even after the idiosyncratic readings of *Lear* that have filled this chapter, it is somewhat startling to learn that *that* is what Shakespeare was dramatizing in *King Lear.*

McLuhan means to startle. He defines Lear's "darker purpose" as specialization. Edmund, Goneril, and Regan are also specialists, manifesting competitive individualism. Goneril and Regan "are cued for particular occasions, streamlined by fragmentation of sense and motive for exact calculation. They are like Lear, avant-garde Machiavels, able to deal explicitly and scientifically with occasions."[19]

---

don't quite coincide. There's no question of forgiveness, but friendly actions are not rejected. The man has gone too far, not so the dramatist. Lear's destruction is complete; there is a startling last demonstration of death as a special horror; Lear really and truly dies. (80-81)

In contrast, Kent, Edgar, and Cordelia are autonomous centers. Shakespeare and McLuhan are on their side in this modern morality play: "*King Lear* is a kind of medieval sermon-exemplum or inductive reasoning to display the madness and misery of the new Renaissance life of action." (26)—the life of action which began with Gutenberg's invention of printing.

McLuhan views cultural history as an exemplum or morality play in which Virtue is played by pretribal habits or modern electronic Wholeness, while Vice snarls in individualism or alphabetic specialization. Traditionally, Virtue and Vice engage in a Psychomachia for the soul of Everyman. According to McLuhan, Vice has had the upper hand for over four centuries, but Virtue is now rearing a powerful electronic head. During the reign of Vice, however, McLuhan cites four literary works as prophetic warnings against the Gutenberg Inferno: Rabelais' *Gargantua,* Cervantes' *Don Quixote,* Pope's *Dunciad,* and Joyce's *Finnegans Wake.* Though *The Gutenberg Galaxy* opens on the opening scene of Shakespeare's *King Lear,* though Hamlet's most famous soliloquy emerges as "an indispensable point of reorientation between the old oral and new visual cultures . . . pitting 'conscience' against 'resolution,' " (191) McLuhan does not elevate Shakespeare to his hagiography.

McLuhan has summoned an enviable range of Gutenberg stars with which to damn the Gutenberg galaxy, and perhaps he has read them less reductively than he has read *Lear.* In such reduction, he follows the Tolstoy pattern. Faltering beneath the ethical complexity, theatrical intensity, and verbal variety of Shakespeare's *Lear,* these writers fasten on a facet of the complex tragedy, reducing it to a virtual sermon. But as Marvin Rosenberg writes in his *Masques of King Lear*: "Any spectator who prefers a 'meditation or oration' . . . will do better in a church."[20]

Despite limitations, however, the passion of response to *King Lear* indicates its powerful impact in the twentieth century. *Hamlet* has inspired more imaginative offshoots, and *Macbeth* more theater experimentation, but *King Lear* has provoked probing minds. No professional critics have been—can afford to be—as reductive as Tolstoy, Orwell, or McLuhan, and yet they tend to cleave to one of two interpretive poles: 1) *Lear* as redemptive tragedy, whose best known spokesman is A. C. Bradley: "Should we not be at least as near the truth if we called this poem *The Redemption of King Lear,* and declared that the business of 'the gods' with him was neither to torment him, nor to teach him a 'noble anger,' but to lead him to attain through apparently hopeless failure the very end and aim of life?"[21] Bradley's question posits an "end and aim of life." 2) In contrast, Jan Kott writes in *Shakespeare Our Contemporary*: "Tragedy is the theatre of priests, grotesque is the theatre of clowns. . . . In both Shakespearean and Beckettian *Endgames* the *Book of Job* is performed by clowns."[22] Bradley's view tended to influence theater productions of the first half of the twentieth century, Kott's of the second. (His book appeared in French in 1962.)

Performance texts followed Shakespeare with relatively minor revisions, and offshoots are rare. I have found only five, but they are markedly different from one another. The first, a throwback to nineteenth-century dramatic form, was published in 1915; the last, performed in 1973 by the Triple Action Theatre, will be discussed in that context. Of the other three, one is trivial, one almost non-verbal, and the third—by Edward Bond—is an attempt at modern tragedy.

King Lear's Wife by Gordon Bottomley (1874-1948) was first published in 1915 in a volume of Georgian poetry, and it received a London production the following year, directed by John Drinkwater and starring Lady Beerbohm Tree as Queen Hygd, Viola Tree as Goneril.[23] *King Lear's Wife* precedes Bottomley's *Gruach* in inventing a past for Shakespearean characters; like *Gruach,* it imposes psychological coherence on Shakespeare. Implicitly, *King Lear's Wife* seeks to answer the question of Shakespeare's Lear:

"Is there any cause in nature that makes these hard hearts?" The title suggests Bottomley's answer: King Lear's wife.

Queen Hygd, King Lear's wife, is "not born for wedlock." Frigid and demanding, she has failed to warm her family with love, and she is on her deathbed as the play opens. King Lear and his mistress Gormflaith dally before the sleeping queen, and the young commoner tries on the queen's crown. Offstage, the unwanted child Cordelia cries. Oblivious of the child, King Lear's wife awakens in time to see the guilty pair tiptoe out of her room, her crown on the head of the king's mistress. Queen Hygd staggers out of bed, utters half-delirious condemnations, and dies in the arms of her daughter Goneril, who has just entered. When the king returns, his daughter accuses him: "Yes, she had long been dying in her heart. / She lived to see you give her crown away; / She died to see you fondle a menial."

When the king leaves, Goneril forces Gormflaith to return the crown to the dead queen, then forces the young woman out. Back at the dead queen's bedside, Goneril shows her father a bloody knife and boasts that she has just killed his mistress. King Lear refrains from punishing her because she taunts him with Gormflaith's infidelity. Lear's last words reveal his powerlessness before his eldest daughter: "I thought she had been broken long ago: / She must be wedded and broken, I cannot do it." The play closes on a cynical conversation between two serving-women washing the body of King Lear's dead wife—reminiscent of the Blind Man and the Fool in Yeats' *On Baile's Strand*.

Like Yeats, Bottomley apparently wished to inject a modern note into an old legend—a combination he abandoned for *Gruach*. Like the later transformation, this one attempts a psychological rationale for the Shakespearean characters, but there is even less continuity than in the later play. Bottomley's Lear is a philandering weakling, his Goneril a proud avenger, his Cordelia a whimpering child. And yet the play is predicated on reasonable psychology: the king philanders because his wife is old and cold; the queen dies because she is envious of her rival; Goneril kills because she is jealous of her royalty; Gormflaith becomes the king's mistress because she is ambitious; Cordelia cries because she is neglected. All is neat, comprehensible, and too simply credible. The surface realism of the psychology blends badly with the blank verse that lacks distinctive imagery or rhythms. Though produced during World War I, the play is redolent of a more leisurely period that was patient with undramatic verbiage.

Some forty years later, the Lear story is reduced to utter triviality in Robin Maugham's comedy, *Mister Lear* (1956).[24] Roughly modeled on Somerset Maugham, the celebrated uncle of Robin (b. 1916), the titular protagonist is never so named in the play itself. He is Walter Craine, famous author and father of three daughters (who may owe something to the author's three sisters). The elder two are schemers, and the youngest is fair and good. The butler Harold Kent has saved Walter's life in World War I and evaluates the three daughters at their proper worth.

Lear's partition of the kingdom becomes Craine's partition of his large London house before he departs to work on a Hollywood film. The two elder daughters remodel the house while young Jane is on a hiking trip. Other details of the plot bear small relation to *Lear*, but in the last of the three acts an Edmund-Edgar character emerges in the person of Walter's secretary, Peter Stacey. The two elder daughters woo him, but he loves young Jane, as Nahum Tate invents a love between Edgar and Cordelia. And like Tate's play, *Mister Lear* ends happily some three centuries later, in 1956. A wealthy woman proposes to Walter, and Peter wins fair Jane. And that will be the last trivial transformation discussed in this book.

Into this chapter, which has already broken out of my self-imposed English-French-German boundary, I introduce an Italian *Lear*. For two reasons: 1) words are unimportant in the conception of the Gruppo Sperimentazione Teatrale; 2) the production has been televised, taped, and distributed in Europe. The GST, as it is called, was founded by Mario Ricci (b. 1932) in 1964 and is thus one of the most durable examples of fringe theater. As important as the small group of actors has been the active participation of visual artists in their productions. And yet, several performances have been based on texts, such as the 1966 *Gulliver's Travels* or the 1971 *Moby-Dick.*

King Lear, their most popular production, was conceived in 1969.[25] As in much work of fringe theater, it developed from improvisations to include four highly visual scenes: 1) the frivolous activities of Lear's court, 2) the civil war, 3) Lear's madness, 4) Lear's death. Each of these scenes develops gesturally around a seeding image: 1) a merry-go-round, 2) a puppet show, 3) hammer and anvil, 4) black drawings on white paper. The first two scenes are highly colored, whereas the last two are confined to black and white. All actors mime their scenes while a tape plays about five per cent of Shakespeare's text, in Italian.

Mario Ricci's description of the opening scene indicates how slenderly the performance depends upon Shakespeare. "The scene opens with one black treelike object in the center of the stage. The walls are entirely black. Six figures in highly colored costumes walk onstage, one by one, in very dim light, carrying white shields. The shields fade in and out of the light as the actors take their places. One light then comes up strong on one of the six figures, lighting his face from the side. Lear appears, and while the light comes up very slowly, he places a cardboard sandwich on each figure. The sandwiches are made of four cardboard squares with different fragments of Lear's person painted on them in black and white. One by one, the figures hang their white shields on the black tree, then disappear. The light dims again, and the same process is repeated, except that the figures carry colored lances, which are placed one by one in metal slots at the base of the shields, so that the end result is a canopy and poles of a merry-go-round. Then the same figures enter, riding brightly colored wooden hobby-horses, and they take their places at each of the six poles. At a given signal on the tape (medieval music and the words of the first scene of Shakespeare's *King Lear*) the merry-go-round begins to turn, and the figures burst into chatter and laughter. Lear enters, stands in the middle of the stage, and distributes apples, which are eaten by the people on the merry-go-round. The merry-go-round in motion is illuminated by colored slides—a carpet of daisies, slices of watermelon, a plate of beans, a fish on yellow paper, a large ripe tomato, a series of bicycle tires hanging in a bicycle shop. A thunderclap is heard on the tape, and the merry-go-round stops. Brusquely, one of the figures dismantles his portion of the merry-go-round and rides off with a pole and piece of canopy transformed again into lance and shield. The others do the same in groups of two and three. The king is left alone. Thunder is followed by the taped sound of rain, and Lear exits carrying the merry-go-round tree."

The Shakespearean text is subordinated to, if not drowned in, grouping, gesture, sound, color. As in much Alternative Theater work, narrative and character are replaced by visual and sonic structures. But these structures have their own meaning. Unlike Shakespeare's tragedy that circles from a full ceremonious stage back to a full but depleted stage, the GST four scenes move from busy stage to Lear alone. Color and motion finally dissolve into a solitary old man.

Though Mario Ricci (b. 1932) and Edward Bond (b. 1934) are almost exact contemporaries, the latter is a playwright who presents a full and finished text to his director. Born into an English working-class family with agricultural background, Bond is not enthusiastic about his formal schooling, but he is enthusiastic about Shakespeare. He said in an interview:

> My education really consisted of one evening, which was organized by the school. They took us along to a

> play at the old Bedford Theatre in Camden Town. We saw Donald Wolfit in *Macbeth,* and for the very first time in my life—I remember this quite distinctly—I met somebody who was actually talking about my problems, about the life I'd been living, the political society around me. . . . Now it's not true that God is concerned every time a sparrow falls to the ground, because he couldn't bear it, but it is true that Shakespeare cared. Of that I have absolutely no doubt—even about this man Macbeth, who perhaps was like Hitler. And so I got from that play a sense of human dignity—of the value of human beings.[26]

Bond began his creative writing with verse, but he soon turned to plays "because it was towards the end of the 'fifties, and there was a great feeling about the theatre, and also partly because of the experience of *Macbeth,* so that one's mind naturally thought in terms of confrontations and speeches."[27] Bond discarded some fifteen plays before sending *The Pope's Wedding* to London's Royal Court Theatre, which produced it inexpensively in 1962. In 1971 *Lear* opened—the fifth of Bond's plays to be staged at the Royal Court.[28] In 1974 his continued concern with the Bard took the form of a play about the spiritual and physical death of Shakespeare, *Bingo.*

In an interview Bond explained his compulsion to re-view Shakespeare's *King Lear*:

> [*King Lear*] is a play for which (it's a stupid thing to say) for which I have enormous admiration, and I've learnt more from it than from any other play. But the thing is I'm afraid that we use the play in the wrong way; as a society we use the play in a wrong way. And it's for that reason I would like to rewrite it so that we now have to use the play for ourselves, for our society, for our time, for our problems.[29]

Though the feeling is contemporary, Bond's *Lear* takes place in an indefinite time; his set and costumes are rather general; his scenes shift from open space to prison and back to open space again. It is mainly through language that Bond conveys the contemporary relevance of *Lear*.

The basic story of the two *Lear*s is similar: a king-father is violently opposed by two power-hungry daughters. But there is no loving third daughter to rescue him, for Bond's Cordelia is not Lear's daughter. In a radical change from Shakespeare, Cordelia becomes the wife of the only man who befriends a defeated Lear, the Gravedigger's Boy about whom Bond has written: "That, incidentally, was the image from which the play grew—this image of the Gravedigger's Boy. In some senses he is much older than Lear, and Lear recognizes this—he has been in his grave, and Lear, who is a very old man, has still to go towards it."[30] Bond no longer remembers how or why the image of the Gravedigger's Boy (which suggests *Hamlet* rather than *Lear*) inspired a play about Lear and his daughters in civil war, but the sustained companionship-opposition of Bond's couple recalls the Shakespearean King and Fool. However, Bond dramatizes the pair as an old man who grows in self-knowledge while the young man's ghost ages and decays.

Shakespeare's *King Lear* contains the most complicated plot of his major tragedies, and though Bond virtually jettisons the Gloucester story, he too weaves complications. His own summary of the play's action is thematic and Hegelian: "Act One shows a world dominated by myth. Act Two shows the clash between myth and reality, between superstitious men and the autonomous world. Act Three shows a resolution of this, in the world we prove real by dying in it." (xiv) But Bond's plot develops through eighteen scenes (as opposed to Shakespeare's twenty-six) in three acts, and this diffuses his delineation of both myth and reality.

Theatrically, the myth is symbolized by a wall, toward the building of which Bond's Lear drafts his kingdom's manpower. As the play opens, a wall worker has died in an accident, but there can be no accidents in a totalitarian country. Lear suspects sabotage behind accidents, and sabotage implies a saboteur, who has to be publicly executed. A scapegoat is chosen, and King Lear orders his execution, firing the gun himself. Lear's mythology has convinced him that the wall can protect his country against his enemies, but he does not see that he is buying security for his country at the inflated price of the welfare of its inhabitants.

Lear's daughters seem to oppose his ruthlessness, but only for part of the first scene. Named Bodice and Fontanelle, they plot to marry Lear's enemies, the dukes of Cornwall and North. And once married, they war against their father's forces. Very soon, however, they turn against their husbands. The once loving daughters, the barely loving wives are imbued with Lear's drive for power, but they ornament that drive with cruel invention. Lear's cruelty springs from self-imposed necessity, but that of his daughters is wantonly sadistic. They supervise the maiming of Lear's adjutant, Warrington, whom each of them has secretly wooed. Bond's Fontanelle is lustfully exuberant as she orders ingenious torments, but Bodice knits systematically, controlling the procedure. Before the daughters are killed —within minutes of one another—their partnership turns to enmity, as in Shakespeare.

Lear defeated and hunted is sheltered by a gravedigger's son, a simple man who hid from Lear's conscription to the wall's labor force. The troops of Lear's daughters shoot the Gravedigger's Boy and rape his pregnant wife, Cordelia, but Lear, unrecognized, is not harmed. A village carpenter, in love with Cordelia, shoots the marauding soldiers. Cordelia and the carpenter will form a nucleus of resistance in civil war.

By Act II Lear is his daughters' prisoner, and mad. In a swiftly rigged trial, his daughters try to trap him into self-accusation, but like Shakespeare's Lear, he proves himself wise in madness. Like Shakespeare's Cordelia, Bond's commands an army, but unlike her predecessor who wars through love, she wars in fierce hatred. And unlike Shakespeare's Cordelia, she is victorious; her forces take Lear prisoner—a second time—and he is joined in jail by his daughter Fontanelle, and then Bodice. Cordelia's husband, the carpenter John, orders the onstage execution of both Lear's daughters. As Shakespeare's Cornwall blinds Gloucester but does not kill him, the carpenter grants permission for the blinding but not the killing of Lear, who then begins to see the folly of his past. Bond's Lear is tortured pointlessly and efficiently by someone who believes that such actions will advance his career. The blinded, bleeding ex-monarch turns for relief to the ghost of the Gravedigger's Boy, who had befriended him when alive. By the end of Act II Cordelia too has fallen prey to the myth of security through power, and she has ordered the resumption of work on the wall. Blind Lear hopes to reach her with his new insight about the futility of power: "I must stop her before I die!" (67)

After the pain of the first two acts of Bond's *Lear*, Act III poses a deceptive harmony though offstage Cordelia rules the kingdom, and her government drafts labor to build the wall. At the old home of the Gravedigger's Boy Lear speaks out against government tyranny, and men journey to hear him. But Lear's oasis cannot be tolerated in a power-oriented world. Cordelia arrives to inform Lear that he must be silent if he does not wish to be tried and executed. In the home of the Gravedigger's Boy, where Cordelia was once reluctant to shelter refugee Lear, she delivers the deadly message to the ex-king, oblivious of the presence of the ghost of her ex-husband, who begs Lear to speak of him. When Cordelia leaves, Lear tells his caretaker couple that he has a journey to make. When Cordelia leaves, the Ghost of the Gravedigger's Boy goes offstage, where he is attacked by his own pigs; stumbling onstage, he dies a second time.

The play's final scene shows Lear at the wall, as in the opening scene, but acting differently. Instead of sacrificing a life to build the wall, Lear now sacrifices a life to unbuild it, and that life is his own. He shovels down five loads of dirt before he is shot—by a farmer's son who has been drafted.

Shakespeare's *King Lear* inspired Bond's father-daughter conflict and King-Fool relationship, but the primary resemblance is in the growth of the tragic hero. Shakespeare's King Lear moves from self-pity, to contrition toward Cordelia, to compassion for the Fool, to "Poor naked wretches, whereso'er you are," and, finally, to kneeling to Cordelia. Bond's Lear experiences a comparable progression: looking at the disfigured face of mute Warrington, he confronts his own mortality. He lies to protect the Gravedigger's Boy, and he agrees to harbor his ghost. After the death of his daughters, he acknowledges his responsibility for their cruelties. He writes anti-wall letters to Cordelia, and he offers asylum to deserters from the wall: "I came here when I was cold and hungry and afraid. I wasn't turned away, and I won't turn anyone away." (74) However, when soldiers seize the deserters, Lear does turn people away, and, in spite of the opposition of the Ghost of the Gravedigger's Boy, he resolves on political activism. Unlike the ambiguous death of Shakespeare's king, which has been viewed as redemptive by Bradley and as grotesque by Kott, the death of Bond's Lear is a muted affirmation. He has no significant effect on the wall, but he makes an unbuilding gesture. He is blind, but wall-workers see his gesture. He is shot at the end of the play, but as the workers leave the stage, "*One of them looks back.*" (88) That look is a faint promise that others may imitate Lear's hard-learned heroism. We cannot know whom, for unlike Shakespeare, Bond provides us with no positive characters such as Kent, Edgar, and Albany. The redemptive note is faint indeed.

However, the mathos-pathos of the hero, his self-knowledge through suffering, his sanity through madness, his vision through blindness (Bond combines the separate afflictions of Shakespeare's two old men in his Lear)—these are central to both tragedies. Similar, too, is the way in which elements of comedy serve to intensify the tragic impact. Shakespeare's tragedy contains disguises, word play, slapstick, satire, and the dissociated ramblings of the false madman Edgar and the true madman King Lear. Bond exposes us to scenes of such violence that he risks a reaction of laughter, as in *Guignol*; but he converts that risk into the mixed tone of his torture scenes: the sadistic daughters are grotesque caricatures when they torture Warrington, and the nameless orderly is another grotesque caricature when he removes Lear's eyes. Bond thus supplies us with a repetition of the blinding of Gloucester, and in both scenes there is a complex effect of intensification and mitigation of the horror through the caricatural nature of perpetrators. Outside these scenes of specific torture, the slaughter of war is mixed with the crude humor of the slaughterers: "An' I'll 'ave 'er reekin' a pig blood. Somethin' to write 'ome t' tell mother." (31)

Grotesque humor, tragic conception, and dramatic structure are Bond's largest debts to Shakespeare. Other reminiscences are less important, and yet they cause the play to achieve resonance. The partition of the kingdom, the mock-trial in the hovel, the blinding of Gloucester, and the father-daughter imprisonment are incorporated into Bond's scenes.

The opening scene is closest to Shakespeare, whose King Lear evades responsibility by dividing his kingdom. Bond's Lear, in contrast, assumes responsibility by building a wall to prevent division of his kingdom. In both scenes the king is misled by the politic rhetoric of his daughters, and both scenes end on the scheming of two disloyal daughters. Bond's Warrington, like Shakespeare's Kent, tries to advise the headstrong king. But the absence of a third honest daughter means that Bond's Lear has to work out his own destiny.

In Act II, Scene 1 of Bond's *Lear* the daughters of the defeated mad monarch rig up a pseudo-trial, but his insane words indict them, and this recalls the fantasy trial of

Shakespeare's mad King Lear in Act III, Scene 6. As has already been mentioned, Bond splits Gloucester's blinding into two different torture scenes. In the first Lear's daughters order a soldier to maim Warrington; though the soldier does not rebel as does Cornwall's nameless servant, he does evince disgust, "What a pair!" (14) By the time Lear is blinded in Act II, there is no one to express disgust or disapproval; even the Gravedigger's Boy's Ghost merely says: "Surely you've suffered enough." (64)

In Act V, Scene 3 of Shakespeare's tragedy, a sane Lear speaks in tender images to the Cordelia with whom he has recently been reunited: "Come, let's away to prison. / We two alone will sing like birds i' th' cage. / . . . . So we'll live, / And pray, and sing, and tell old tales, . . . and we'll wear out, / In a walled prison, packs and sects of great ones / That ebb and flow by th' moon." These lines will echo in Bond's two prison scenes. When Lear is jailed by his daughters, he is joined by the tender ghost of the Gravedigger's Boy, who in turn is able to summon the ghosts of Lear's daughters as young girls; but the harmony is soon disturbed by notes of death. It is Lear who is responsible for his daughters' early knowledge of death, and though he is mad, he faces this guilt, promising the ghost of the Gravedigger's Boy in words that recall those of Shakespeare's Lear reunited with Cordelia: "We'll help each other. Cry while I sleep, and I'll cry and watch you while you sleep." (42)

As in this scene, there are other phrasal reminders of Shakespeare's tragedy. Both kings are obsessed by their daughters' ingratitude. King Lear tries to explain Mad Tom's poverty: "Didst thou give all to thy daughters?" Bond's Lear explains the comfort to be found with the Gravedigger's Boy: "No daughters! Where he lives the rain can't be wet or the wind cold." (18)

In the mock-trial of *King Lear* the mad monarch as judge orders: "Then let them anatomize Regan, see what breeds about her *heart*." (My italics.) This leads to the literal anatomization of Fontanelle in Bond's *Lear*. Performed surgically by the orderly who will blind Lear, the operation is at once horrifying and farcical as in *Guignol.* The efficient surgeon is a chilling caricature. Though the neat display of Fontanelle's organs is incredible, Lear's reaction is moving: "So much blood and bits and pieces packed in with all that care. Where is the . . . where . . . ?" (59) Shakespeare's line has suggested not only the dissection but the unnamed heart.

In the movement of Bond's Lear from political defeat to private life to political passion to heroic action that seeks no power, he learns pity, as does Shakespeare's Lear through the storm on the heath. Bond stresses the education of his Lear through bald and non-Shakespearean repetition of the word "pity." When Lear first meets the Gravedigger's Boy, he thinks of pity as a commodity: "I know you have no pity to sell." (17) When he is mad and on trial, he looks in a mirror and thinks he sees an animal: "Who shut that animal in a glass cage? O God, there's no pity in the world." (35) Much later, on his way back to the home of the Gravedigger's Boy, he meets the farmer's son who will shoot him, and he exclaims: "I'd never seen a poor man! You take too much pity out of me, if there's no pity I shall die of this grief."(66) It is because Lear can feel pity and arouse pity that he does not die—yet. In his last meeting with Cordelia, he preaches: "Our lives are awkward and fragile and we have only one thing to keep us sane: pity, and the man without pity is mad." (84) Significant is the first person plural; not the royal "we" but the "we" of collective guilt that can be expiated only by collective compassion.

Bond has dramatized the moral education of his Lear. But no one is Shakespeare, and though Bond achieves an impressive Lear, his very stature dwarfs the other characters. The Gravedigger's Boy, the Fool-analogue which was Bond's starting image for his play, remains an image rather than a character. Matter-of-factly attractive when alive, shockingly killed, he wears his ghostly attire clumsily. Like Shakespeare's Fool, he is both protective of and protected by Lear; he is the king's affectional bond during his purgative madness. And yet, his ghost's dialogue does not quite focus his "instinctive sort of life." He evokes sympathy through his visible deterioration, but he is difficult to situate in Lear's growth.

Cordelia, on the other hand, is all too schematic and easy to situate. Like Shakespeare's Cordelia, she appears in only four scenes. But Shakespeare early dramatizes Cordelia in her tongue-tied tenderness, whereas Bond's Cordelia exhibits a taciturn sulkiness even before she is raped. Bond has said: "Cordelia in Shakespeare's play is an absolute menace. I mean, she's a very dangerous type of person, and I thought that the other daughters, though I'm not excusing them, were very unfairly treated and misunderstood."[31] Presumably, Bond found Shakespeare's Cordelia dangerous because she translated her wrongs into an avenging army. He implicitly condemns his Cordelia for translating *her* wrongs into an avenging army, but in that translation she becomes "a very dangerous *type* of person" rather than a person.

Conversely, the other daughters may have been "unfairly treated" by Shakespeare, but they are frighteningly credible, as generations of actresses have shown. Bond's daughters, in contrast, are caricatures. Bodice (which covers the heart) and Fontanelle (which provides an outlet for secretions) are sadistic monsters: they turn against their father in the first scene, they betray their husbands in the second, they betray one another in the third, and they supervise the torture of Warrington in the fourth. Killed within minutes of one another in the middle of the play, it is they who indulge in much of the stage violence for which Bond is notorious. "My plays are all concerned with the problem of violence," he has said, "because it is *the* consuming problem—the one that will decide what happens to us all."[32]

Shakespeare's *King Lear* is a violent tragedy, but unlike his apprentice work *Titus Andronicus*, the violence is credible and necessary in a context whose immensity is conveyed through language. And in language as in tragic conception, Bond imitates and challenges comparison with his peerless predecessor.

Bond's prose is at once distinctive and contemporary. Like Shakespeare, he abounds in imagery of vision, of animals, of a maimed human body. Shakespeare's *King Lear* bristles in over a hundred negatives, and Bond's *Lear* also resonates in negatives, especially the Shakespearean "nothing." Like Shakespeare's Lear, though less insistently, Bond's characters repeat the verb "kill"—in speech as in action.

Most strikingly drawn from Shakespeare's tragedy is Bond's animal imagery. When his Lear is powerful, he refers to his people as sheep and to his enemies as wolves. In defeat, Lear speaks of himself as an animal: "The night is a black cloth on [my daughters'] table and the stars are crumbs, and I am a famished dog that sits on the earth and howls." (17) While learning to savor bread, Lear reflects: "The mouse comes out of his hole and stares. The giant wants to eat the dragon, but the dragon has grabbed the carving knife." (18) Looking at himself in a mirror, Lear exclaims: "Who shut that animal in that cage? . . . O God, there's no pity in this world. You let it lick the blood from its hair in the corner of a cage with nowhere to hide from its tormentors. No shadow, no hole! Let that animal out of its cage." (35) Witnessing his daughter's autopsy, he remarks: "She sleeps inside like a lion and a lamb and a child. . . . Did I make this—and destroy it?" (59) Blinded, he meets the farmer's son who will later shoot him: "A wolf, a fox, a horse—they'd run away, they're sane. Why d'you run to meet your butchers? Why?" (66) And, restored to sanity, Bond's Lear ends his parable of a man's voice in a bird's body: "And just as the bird had the man's voice the man now had the bird's pain. He ran round silently waving his head and stamping his feet, and he was locked up for the rest of his life in a cage." (75) Having decided to act on the wall, Lear tells his protectors: "Now I have only one more wish—to live till I'm much older and become as cunning as the fox, who knows how to live. *Then* I could teach you." (85) Bond is not Shakespeare, of course, but Lear's sustained animal imagery concretizes the great Shakespearean line: "Unaccommodated man is no more but such a poor bare forked animal as thou art."

Like *King Lear,* much of *Lear* takes place out of doors, close to the elements, but it is of earth that we are most aware in the modern tragedy—earth and its human and animal inhabitants. Lacking a storm, *Lear* follows *King Lear* in a smaller water image—tears. Early in both plays the monarch is ashamed of unmanly tears. Late in Shakespeare's play, King Lear is reunited with Cordelia, crying out: "Thou art a soul in bliss; but I am bound / Upon a wheel of fire, that mine own tears / Do scald like molten lead." Bond's Lear speaks to Cordelia in abstractions, but after she leaves and the Gravedigger's Boy is dead, he returns to imagery: "I see my life, a black tree by a pool. The branches are covered with tears. The tears are shining with light. The wind blows the tears in the sky. And my tears fall down on me." (86)

No longer an animal, Lear is now a tear-nurtured tree. Shakespeare's final re-establishment of social order is paralleled by Bond's integration of his Lear into a natural order, before the old man decides on his last political act. It is through tears that the light shines, and the human is linked to the cosmic when tears become the rain that nourishes a tree. In Shakespeare's tragedy, suffering has led to Lear's wisdom and to ours, even if we "Shall never see so much, nor live so long." In Bond's tragedy, suffering leads to Lear's action, which springs from a new awareness of a self that has shed tears.

Most impressive in Bond's transformation of Shakespeare's tragedy is his range of tone and idiom so that the emblematic arises from the familiar. As in Shakespeare's tragedy, simple daily negatives reach out to annihilate the cosmos. Shakespeare's two opening scenes focus on Nothing, and Bond also works Nothing into two scenes. After Bond's Lear watches the dissection of his daughter, he cries out guiltily: "I destroyed her! I knew nothing, saw nothing, learned nothing! Fool! Fool! Worse than I knew!" (60) His self-recognition as a fool points to the beginning of wisdom.

Acclaimed as a wise man, Lear expresses self-awareness in a crescendo of negatives: "I'm buried alive in a wall. Does this suffering and misery last forever? Do we work to build ruins, waste all these lives to make a desert no one could live in? There's no one to explain it to me, no one I can go to for justice. I'm old, I should know how to live by now, but I know nothing, I can do nothing, I am nothing." (80) Noteworthy is the shift from the past tense in the earlier scene to the present tense as he nears his death: "I knew nothing . . . I know nothing." Lear has to become nothing—neither king nor father nor comforter of a ghost—before he can know and do something.

Lear's final self-knowledge is immediately followed by his deed of political defiance, and the simplicity of his last words renders his death movingly. Digging the wall down, he says: "I'm not as fit as I was. . . . But I can still make my mark." (87-88) Shot, he grasps his shovel and says "One more" before he is killed. The two syllables are as loaded as Shakespeare's "Look there!" Bond's words affirm that his Lear has gone beyond Nothing. His shovelful of earth will not be the last thrown from the wall; Lear will not be the last rebel. There is always the possibility of "One more."

Chapter 5

Peopling the Isle with Calibans

The Tempest was created by Shakespeare to harm no one. His last comedy reflects his tragic themes but strips them of peril: brother plots against brother, as in *King Lear*; usurper conspires against the rightful ruler, as in *Macbeth*; a young prince is tested, as in *Hamlet*; young lovers meet obstacles, as in *Romeo and Juliet*. Any or all of the four plots of *The Tempest* might have ended tragically: two conspiracies involving two realms (Naples and Setebos), the love story of Miranda and Ferdinand, the separate servitudes of airy Ariel and earthy Caliban. But magic prevents tragedy. Magician Prospero is practical and metaphysical, matchmaking and puritanical, stern and forgiving, cruel only to be kind. He imposes the happy ending.

The Tempest should have been Shakespeare's last play. His friends Hemming and Condell placed it first in the Folio, editing it with unusual care, and it has been universally admired by subsequent editors and actors. Like the major tragedies, it has never been long absent from the stage—in some form, but critics have labored it less than the tragedies or the problem comedies. *The Tempest* has often been read as Shakespeare's biography; he stands tall and proud as father, magus, master of ceremony and morality. Together, Prospero and his creator come to career-end: "And deeper than did ever plummet sound / I'll drown my book." Though *Henry VIII* mars that grand dual finale, it offers no offshoots. *The Tempest* is Shakespeare's last play to provoke a flurry of offshoots, and they focus on Caliban rather than Prospero.

The stage history of *The Tempest* versions parallels a history of the English theater.[1] The first production by Shakespeare's company may have been staged at the newly leased private theater, the Blackfriars, with its seats for all spectators, its artificial lighting, and its expanded room for musicians. In 1611 and again in 1613 *The Tempest* was played in an elaborate court setting. After the English Civil War, Shakespeare's play was displaced by the Davenant-Dryden adaptation, which then became the basis for an opera by Purcell. The Davenant-Dryden adaptation was the most popular play on the Restoration stage.

A cluster of *Tempest* offshoots is summarized by Ashley Thorndike:

> [*The Tempest*] has given rise to many imitations, adaptations, and sequels. Fletcher copied its storm, its desert island, and its woman who had never seen a man [in *The Sea-Voyage*]. Suckling borrowed its spirits [in *The Goblins*]. Davenant and Dryden added a man who had never seen a woman, a husband for Sycorax, and a sister for Caliban. Mr. Percy MacKaye has used its scene, mythology, and persons for his tercentenary Shakespearian Masque. Its suggestiveness has extended beyond the drama, and aroused moral allegories and disquisitions. Caliban has been elaborated as the Missing Link, and in the philosophical drama of Renan as the spirit of Democracy, and in Browning's poem as a satire on the anthropomorphic conception of Deity.[2]

My account of modern *Tempest* offshoots begins where Thorndike ends, with the 1864 publication of *Caliban upon Setebos* by Robert Browning (1812-1889).[3] The poem appeared in the volume entitled *Dramatis Personae,* and it gives us a vivid portrait of the slave of Shakespeare's drama. Written after Browning's own dramas, the dramatic monologue broods similarly upon the self. Nineteenth-century audiences, fed on melodrama, rejected such static subjects in the theater, but the poem has been widely acclaimed and might well prove useful to an actor playing Shakespeare's Caliban.

Caliban's language distinguishes Browning's poem, but he was not the first poet to respond to Shakespeare's verse lines for the "salvage and deformed slave." Dryden thought that Caliban proved Shakespeare's "copiousness of invention."[4] (34) Nicholas Rowe wrote "That Shakespear had not only found out a new Character in his Caliban, but had also devis'd and adapted a new manner of Language for that Character." (35) John Warburton summarized: "It was a tradition, it seems, that Lord *Falkland*, Lord *C. J. Vaughan*, and Mr. *Seldon* concurred in observing, that *Shakespear* had not only found out a new character in his *Caliban*, but had also devised and adapted *a new manner of language* for that character." (48)

A century later Robert Browning devised and adapted a new manner of language for *his* character, grounded in the natural life of the island, an elliptical grammar, and such Elizabethan turns of phrase as forsooth, wroth, it liked him, it nothing skills. Browning's Caliban refers to the Shakespearean characters of Prospero and Miranda, and to characters who do not actually appear in Shakespeare's play, Caliban's mother Sycorax and her god Setebos. Browning's title has a double meaning; *Caliban upon Setebos* is at once the character on the island, and the speaker discoursing on his god. Like Shakespeare's character, Browning's Caliban is an ignoble savage—cowardly, cruel, envious, but possessed of keen senses and a vivid imagination.

Browning prefaces his poem with an epigraph from Psalm 50: "Thou thoughtest that I was altogether such an one as thyself." And that *is* what his Caliban thinks—that God is such an one as he. The idea of an anthropomorphic deity is at least as old as the Bible, but it was sparked into new relevance by the publication in 1855 of Darwin's *Origin of Species*. For sophisticated believers, faith could no longer be based on the natural world. But Browning's Caliban is an unsophisticated believer, rooted in the natural world, and conceiving Setebos in his own image. Browning's Caliban utters his monologue in the darkness of his muddy cave and, unlike other Browning monologues, it is addressed to no one; most specifically, it is not addressed to Setebos, from whom Caliban wishes to conceal his irrepressible ruminations.

Browning's first blank-verse paragraph (of twelve), set off in brackets, sets the scene as background for "Letting the rank tongue blossom into speech." That speech is spoken by Caliban mainly in the third person, for he disclaims his own words. Use of the third person, or verbs without subject, or voiceless printed apostrophes suggest Caliban's fear of a vengeful Setebos who "made all we see, and us, in spite."

Occasionally, however, Caliban forgets caution, and the "I"s peal forth.[5] The first one does not sound until three verse paragraphs (after the opening bracketed passage) expose Caliban's *Genesis*; his god Setebos has created the world because He was cold and uncomfortable, at once scornful and envious of what was not Himself. Then, in the first of six lapses into the first person, Caliban imagines himself as a drunken and powerful creator; he would create a clay bird, and if the clay foot snapped off, if the bird implored him in pain, he might "give the manikin three legs for his one, / Or pluck the other off." So does Setebos act by caprice.

But Setebos is dominated by his God, the Quiet. In conceiving the omnipotent Quiet—"all it hath a mind do, doth" —Caliban briefly uses the first person for the second time. More interesting is his third use—the pronoun "my"—in a kind of play within the monologue. Caliban pictures the universe as a Chinese box: the Quiet makes Setebos dance to its whims, and Setebos in turn rules over Prospero, who dominates Caliban. Though Caliban may imagine himself creating a clay bird, he often plays at being Prospero, replete with book, wand, and robe; a crane is his Ariel and a lumpish sea-beast his Caliban. A four-legged serpent is his

Miranda, and she is not only his daughter but "*my* wife." (my italics)

Despite such brief rebellious lapses into the first person, Caliban realizes his affinity to Setebos. Seven times during the course of the poem, he describes his own caprice and cruelty, only to end with the telling comparison: "So He." Since Setebos has created all beings in weakness, Caliban's fourth lapse into the first person describes the strong organism Setebos might have created in his stead, the Hercules-Caliban that might have been.

During the course of his monologue Caliban grows bolder in his resentment of the Setebos-world. His second to fifth paragraphs begin with " 'Thinketh," but the eighth and ninth graduate to " 'Saith." Caliban is aware that he is uttering words. In the ninth paragraph he conveys his envy of Prospero, the favorite of Setebos, through his fifth eruption into the first person.

Contrary to what his mother thought, Caliban believes that nothing will ever change; beyond this life is nothing, and in this life "the best way to escape His ire / Is, not to seem too happy." Playing at not seeming too happy, Caliban breaks into his last, boldest, and most extended use of the first person. If he is overheard, he will cut his finger off, sacrifice his best kid, let apples rot on the tree, give his "tame beast" (Miranda?) to the orc, and dance round a fire with a hymn of praise: "What I hate, be consecrate / To celebrate Thee and Thy state, no mate / For Thee; what see for envy in poor me?" Then, lapsing into wishful thinking, he wonders whether Setebos may not "doze, as good as die."

His hope is rudely interrupted in the last verse paragraph, set off in brackets, like the first. But whereas the opening bracketed passage sets a scene, the last paragraph depicts Caliban reacting to an event—a punitive tempest, presumably sent by an angry god whom Caliban hastens to propitiate. Shakespeare's Caliban called himself a "thrice-double ass" for worshipping "this dull fool" Stephano;

Browning's Caliban chides himself: "Fool to gibe at Him!" And he offers his own unhappiness in penance. However, it is token unhappiness, short of what he expansively promised. Instead of cutting a finger off, he bites through his upper lip; instead of sacrificing a kid, he lets the quails fly by; instead of letting the luscious apples rot on trees, he will refrain from eating whelks for a month. "So he may 'scape!"

Browning creates a vivid being, well versed in his natural surroundings, observant of the parts of his body, sensuous with all five of his senses. Though Caliban speaks in simple sentences, we have to work through his elliptical lines (that omit pronouns and auxiliary verbs) as though reading a foreign idiom. But this estranging effect, as in Brecht, finally underlines his basic familiarity. The critics seem to agree that Browning intended to satirize anthropomorphic religion, and he probably meant us to feel superior to his direct and childlike Caliban. But Caliban resembles most of us in the vehemence of his passions, the craftiness of his cowardice, and his accurately anthropomorphic imagination. Though he is over a century old, his lack of inhibition is modern, and he predicts the modern center of *Tempest* offshoots—the savage and deformed slave.

Robert Browning is a nineteenth-century English poet rarely read outside the classroom, and Ernest Renan is a nineteenth-century French philologist-philosopher rarely read even in the classroom. In his own century, however—his dates are 1823-1892—Renan was a man of some celebrity. Educated to the priesthood but turning against the Catholic Church, sympathetic to the French Second Empire but reconciling himself to the establishment of the Republic, achieving notoriety through his *Life of Jesus* (1863), and mellowing into reminiscences, Renan was a controversial figure in his own time and country. Considerably attenuated, some of the controversy is reflected in his *Tempest* transformations, written in 1877 and 1879.[6]

Directly after the French defeat in the Franco-Prussian

War, Renan vented his disappointment in a series of *Dialogues philosophiques*; the dialogue form, stemming from Plato, can accommodate differing and even conflicting philosophic attitudes, as may be seen in various works by St. Augustine, Berkeley, Descartes, and Malebranche. Soon Renan shifted from philosophic dialogue to drama: "Puis je trouvai que le dialogue ne suffit pas, qu'il y faut de l'action: que le drame libre et sans couleur locale, à la façon de Shakespeare, permet de rendre des nuances beaucoup plus fines."* (372) But though Renan claims to need action, many of the events of his plays take place offstage, and he himself admits that his dramas are "à mille liens de toute pensée de representation scénique."[7] (373)

Renan read *The Tempest* in Émile Montégut's prose translation of 1867, and he explains the reason for his own transformation: "Prospero, duc de Milan, inconnu à tous les historiens; Caliban, être informe, à peine dégrossi, en voie de devenir homme; Ariel, fils de l'air, symbole de l'idéalisme, sont les trois créations les plus profondes de Shakespeare. J'ai voulu montrer ces trois types agissant dans quelques combinaisons adaptées aux idées de notre temps."†[8] (39) Though Renan's play has dated, his approach has not—Shakespearean types "adapted to the ideas of our time." Renan specifically designates Ariel as idealism, but in the play Prospero tends to speak for the idealistic, cultured, aristocratic aspect of man—a man much like Renan himself. His Caliban represents Renan's view of democracy.

Renan's transformation shuttles between Prospero's study at the Chartreuse de Pavie and the government seat at Milan. In Act I a drunken Caliban screams for liberty and

* Then I found that dialogue is not adequate, that there must be some action in it; drama which is free and without local color, in Shakespeare's manner, allows you to render much more subtle nuances.

† Prospero, Duke of Milan, unknown to all the historians; Caliban, ill-formed creature, still unpolished, in the process of becoming human; Ariel, son of the air, symbol of idealism, are Shakespeare's three most profound creations. I wanted to show these three types acting in some combinations adapted to the ideas of our time.

is reproached by Ariel, while Prospero occupies himself with spiritual research. Act II resembles Renan's dialogues in that diverse philosophical and political opinions are uttered by various non-Shakespearean characters, including Faust and Wagner. In the second scene of this act, Ariel creates a magic spectacle in which gods of steel defeat the old Olympian gods. In spite of the warning of Gonzalo that Milan is on the point of revolt, Prospero retires to his study in Pavie. Revolt indeed breaks out in Act III, and Caliban quickly assumes leadership with the cry "Guerre aux livres." By the end of the act, he is in control of the government, occupying Prospero's palace, and viewing his old master with a new sympathy: "J'étais injuste pour Prospero; l'esclavage m'avait aigri. Mais maintenant que je couche dans son lit, je le juge comme on se juge entre confrères."* (413)

Browning's Caliban plays at being Prospero, and Renan's Caliban imitates Prospero by deciding to respect property, culture, and beauty. Like Prospero, he resolves to "faire le bonheur de l'humanité." In Act IV Prospero sends Ariel to retake the ducal throne but, effective against Alonso, Ariel is powerless against the people: "Là où Caliban peut tout, nous ne pouvons rien. . . . Tout ce qui est apparence pour les yeux, tout ce qui est idéal, non substantiel, n'existe pas pour le peuple. . . . Le peuple est positiviste."† (420-421) Some Milanese nobles advise resistance, others acceptance. When a monk of the Inquisition condemns Prospero, and when Caliban's representative defies the monk, Prospero exclaims: "Ma foi, vive Caliban!" In Act V Caliban refuses to deliver Prospero to the Inquisition, and he welcomes Gonzalo as his adviser. The pardoning spirit of Shakespeare's Prospero is inherited by Renan's Caliban. But the

* I was unfair to Prospero; slavery had made me bitter. But now that I sleep in his bed, I judge him the way colleagues judge each other.

† Where Caliban can do everything, we can do nothing. . . . Everything that is merely appearance for the eyes, everything that is ideal and not substantial, does not exist for the people. . . . The people are positivists.

scene closes on the reflections of the Prior of the Chartreuse, who praises a Caliban in whose regime Prospero may live and perhaps even rule again. In his working draft, Renan noted: "On a voulu montrer ici ce que Shakespeare n'admettait pas, que Caliban était susceptible de faire des progrès."[9*]

Originally, Renan's play ended there, but at the suggestion of his friend, the Russian novelist Ivan Turgenev, the philosopher wrote a new ending: "La mort d'Ariel . . . doit terminer tout, comme un bel accord."[10†] (33) Prospero therefore frees Ariel, who recognizes that his freedom is his death. Once Prospero has consented to be soiled by real events, pure idealism dies. This was a favorite theme of Renan, and upon it he closes his play, with a swan song by Ariel.

During the long play itself, however, it is the vulgar energy of Caliban that raises the dialogue above abstraction. And it is because Caliban loses his cynical positivism that Renan's sequel to *Caliban, l'Eau de Jouvence* (1879) makes duller reading. Renan sets forth his purpose: "Tâchons de trouver un moyen d'enterrer honorablement Prospero et d'attacher Ariel à la vie, de telle façon qu'il ne sait plus tenter, pour des motifs futiles, de mourir à tout propos."[‡] (441) In this philosophical drama, Prospero's name is changed to Arnaud, who, living in the Avignon of the popes, seeks the titular elixir of youth. He finds it in the idealism represented by Ariel. Republican Caliban rules offstage, and only at the play's end does Prospero declare: "La source de Jouvence est dans notre coeur. C'est l'idéal qui ne laisse pas vieillir. La force qui ressuscite, c'est la

* I wanted to show what Shakespeare did not grant, that Caliban was capable of making progress.

† Ariel's death . . . should conclude the whole, like a beautiful harmony.

‡ Let us attempt to find a means of burying Prospero honorably and attaching Ariel to life, in such a way that he no longer will feel the temptation, for futile reasons, to die at every turn.

pureté de notre âme."* That purity is symbolized by Ariel as a beautiful maiden, who is reconciled to a repentant Caliban. Aged Prospero equates the elixir of life with the dignity of dying whenever one wishes. Smiling at the happy Ariel-Caliban couple, Prospero chooses his moment, but his death is marred by his ancient enemy, the cardinal of the Inquisition, who announces that he will drown the corpse. If the body is found, a suicide will be reported; if not, it will be a kidnapping by the devil. And the play ends, not on Prospero's happy death, as the end of life's elixir, but on the power of the Church, triumphantly and hypocritically singing an innocent child's song: "Sur le pont / D'Avignon, / C'est là que l'on danse, / Sur le pont / D'Avignon, / Que l'on danse en rond." (521) Caliban was capable of growth in Renan's first transformation of *The Tempest,* and this provided a reprieve for Prospero. But in the second philosophical drama, Prospero is finally and fatally vulnerable. Nevertheless, Ariel and Caliban have joined forces, and perhaps a new idealism can be born of their union, so that all human beings can "danse[nt] en rond."

These nineteenth-century offshoots of *The Tempest* indicate how early Caliban attracted aspects of the modern imagination—reaction to fundamentalism, reaction to popular democracy. The first twentieth-century offshoot resembles Renan's *Caliban* in presenting Shakespeare's savage and deformed slave as a symbol for the common people. Though it is no more dramatic than Renan's philosophical drama, it was specially composed for performance. *Caliban by the Yellow Sands* by Percy MacKaye (1875-1956) is the most ambitious of all Shakespeare theater offshoots, since it involved about 2,500 performers, playing before an audience of 135,000 at New York City's Lewisohn Stadium; and 5,000 before 250,000 spectators in seventeen performances at Harvard Stadium. *Caliban by the Yellow Sands* was written to celebrate the tercentenary of Shakespeare's death.[11]

* The fountain of youth is in our hearts. It is the ideal that prevents aging. The force that resurrects is the purity of our soul.

With World War I decimating Europe, a group of Americans decided to honor Shakespeare on these shores, and MacKaye was chosen to create the vehicle.

Percy MacKaye was the son of theater innovator Steele MacKaye, the descendant of an old American family dedicated to public service. *Caliban* was intended to celebrate Shakespeare and the theater, as well as to render the public service of involving in a common project New York City's several races, religions, and economic strata. MacKaye designated his work as a masque, a form of community drama, "a means and method for promoting the virtues of neighborliness and cooperation."[12] MacKaye believed that the modern masque would yield "an art more sensuous, sane, and communal than the theatre has ever known." (xxv) His text was to be blended with music, dance, and the most elaborate outdoor staging ever seen. The text itself centered on four *Tempest* characters transplanted into "a plot and conflict which are my own conception." (xv) MacKaye's plot and conflict are virtually the same, for Caliban is an Everyman figure tempted by Lust, Death, and War (the last especially relevant in 1916), but finally saved by Prospero, Ariel, and particularly Miranda. This skeletal plot, written largely in blank verse, served as the excuse for lavish spectacle; the three acts are introduced by mime interludes of three periods of theater—Antiquity, Middle Ages, and Elizabethan England. The acts themselves are irregularly punctuated by nine scenes from Shakespeare plus an invented Morality play. A table may indicate the structure.

PROLOGUE

Ariel-Caliban conflict. Caliban attacks Miranda, who is rescued by Prospero. Spirits of Ariel drive Caliban into his cave.

First Interlude, Antiquity. Egyptian, Greek and Roman pantomime.

ACT I (dominated by Lust)

Prospero shows Caliban

Inner Scene 1 from *Antony and Cleopatra.*

Caliban is delighted. Prospero lends Ariel his staff to produce

Inner Scene 2 from *Troilus and Cressida.*

Caliban, again delighted, requests the staff but is refused. However, Miranda dresses him in splendid attire and waves the staff to produce

Inner Scene 3 from *Julius Caesar.*

Caliban, echoing the cry of Brutus: "Awake, Romans, Awake," seizes the staff and produces a "scene of mingled riot and orgy," which ends in a vision of a giant cross, whereupon

Inner Scene 4 shows St. Agnes, a lamb, and a shepherd.

Caliban is contrite as the act ends.

Second Interlude, Middles Ages. Mimes of Faust, the Field of the Cloth of Gold, and Commedia dell'Arte.

ACT II (dominated by Death)

Caliban wants to dance on the yellow sands, but Death calls him, and Prospero tries to give him courage by producing

Inner Scene 5 from *Hamlet.*

Caliban does not want the Prince to follow the Ghost, and yet he himself follows Death, while Prospero shows Miranda

Inner Scene 6 from *Henry VIII.*

Prospero retires to his study, and Ariel conjures lovers in

Inner Scene 7 from *Romeo and Juliet* and *A Winter's Tale.*

Miranda sickens, and Death claims her. An alarmed Ariel calls Prospero, who promises to revive her.

Third Interlude, Elizabethan. Folk Festivals.

ACT III (dominated by War)

Prospero revives Miranda, and Caliban puts aside his gray

Death-tainted garments. Miranda pleads with Prospero to be gracious to Caliban, and they both don green garments to see

Inner Scene 8 from *As You Like It*.

Caliban thanks Miranda, who teaches him the meaning of selfless love. But War lures Caliban, who is nevertheless entranced by

Inner Scene 9 from *Henry IV* and *Merry Wives of Windsor*.

Caliban identifies with a plagued Falstaff, and Miranda conjures

Inner Scene 10 from *Henry V*.

Caliban, armed with Prospero's hood and staff, challenges Prospero, whose "unhooded features reveal their likeness to Shakespeare's." (139) Caliban overcomes the Bard, Ariel, and Miranda, but Prospero-Shakespeare announces: "My art that builds the beauty of the world." (141)

EPILOGUE

Though Caliban triumphs over the trio, he needs and pleads for their visions. Miranda seconds his plea—"Master?"—and Shakespeare-Prospero closes the spectacle with the well-known "Our revels now are ended" speech.

On the huge playing areas of the stadiums, however, the sleep-rounded life was large rather than little. Theater celebrities participated: Isadora Duncan, John Drew, Robert Edmond Jones. A mammoth production in terms of personnel, *Caliban by the Yellow Sands* is a verbal dwarf, and many of the words were apparently lost to the audience. Nor do reviewers celebrate MacKaye's announced theme: "Caliban seeking to learn the art of Prospero—is, of course, the slow education of mankind through the influences of coöperative art, that is, of the art of the theatre in its fullest scope." (xvii)

Today it is easy to scoff at MacKaye's grandiose but simplistic conception; there were probably scoffers even in

1916, since some performers put on a burlesque, *Caliban Jr.* Nevertheless, the enterprise achieved its purpose of populous participation in a theater event. Not only was every night sold out, but the run had to be extended and then moved to Harvard Stadium.

An unusual incident in American theater history, *Caliban by the Yellow Sands* is scarcely more inspired than the same author's *Hamlet Tetralogy*. The obligatory blank verse is often blank in the worst sense—replete with noble sentiments and Elizabethan nonce-words, as was not unusual in nineteenth-century poetic drama. Ariel's address to his Spirits will suffice as an example:

> O Spirits, I have dreamed, but Death has closed
> My sight in darkness. Spirits, I have begotten
> Sweet Joy, but Lust hath drowned her in his wine. (13)

Only in Caliban's lines does MacKaye rise above the maudlin, sometimes leaning on Browning for an elliptical syntax:

> Am seed of Setebos:
> Am Caliban: the world is all mine isle:
> Kill what I please, and play with what I please;
> So, yonder, play with him: pull out his wings
> And put 'em back to grow.—Where be *thy* wings,
> Spring-i'-the-air? (18, to Miranda)

Unfortunately, Caliban learns Prospero's style; his last words are "hoarse with feeling." Perhaps they were eclipsed by the elaborate play of lights upon the vast arena.

With the next *Tempest* offshoot, we plunge into mid-twentieth century. "The Sea and the Mirror" is often considered the major work of the poet W. H. Auden (1907-1973).[13] Born in York, England, educated at Oxford, Auden won early fame as the spokesman of English Leftist intellectuals. In 1939 he moved to the United States, and shortly afterward he moved back into the Anglican faith of his family. "The Sea and the Mirror" (1944) subtitled "A Commentary on Shakespeare's Work," obliquely reflects that faith.

The commentary takes dialogue form, with each of the Shakespearean characters speaking his piece. In technical virtuosity, these pieces resemble the "Oxen of the Sun" chapter of James Joyce's *Ulysses.* But rather than tracing the *growth* of English poetry, as Joyce traces that of prose, Auden creates a *variety* of rhythms and patterns for the Shakespearean characters.

Monroe Spears admirably summarizes the situation of the long poem in dialogue form:

> There is the implicit setting of a theater, after a performance of *The Tempest*; the Stage Manager addresses the Critics in the Preface, and the Prompter echoes the last speech. In the first scene, Prospero, packing up to leave the Island, bids farewell to Ariel; in the second, the rest of the cast, on a ship taking them back to Italy from the Island, speak *sotto voce* to each other and to the audience. They are all still in the world of the play, but at the same time are sufficiently detached from it to comment on its meaning and on their future lives; in some sense they are leaving the Enchanted Island of the art work and emerging into "real" life. The last of them, Caliban, addresses the audience directly and develops explicitly the speculations about the relation between Art and Life suggested both by the play and by the dual roles the other characters have just been playing.[14]

Spears reproduces a diagram from Auden's early draft of the work which serves nicely as an introduction to its themes:[15]

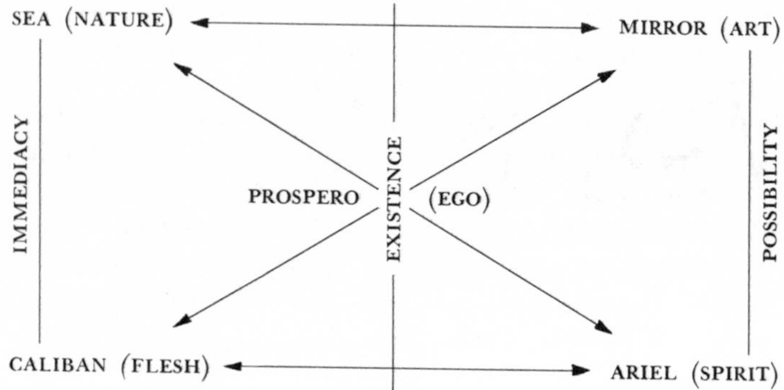

At the end of Shakespeare's comedy, Prospero has meted out his pardons, and the Europeans board the ship for Naples. So in Auden, but Auden's Caliban speaks from some undesignated limbo which is also a theater, since he addresses an audience. That fiction, a theater in a book, is the initial invention of the poem: "Preface (The Stage Manager to the Critics)." The poem proper follows in three parts: I. Prospero to Ariel; II. The Supporting Cast, Sotto Voce; III. Caliban to the Audience. An Epilogue balances the Preface: "Postscript (Ariel to Caliban, Echo by the Prompter)." Each of the characters is distinguished by an individual voice, or at least by an individual verse form, but the verse is also marked by Auden's own stylistic traits—ellipsis, specialized vocabulary, clever metaphors, aphoristic generalizations, heavy reliance on verbs and nouns as opposed to adjectives and adverbs. Caliban alone speaks in prose, which parodies the convoluted style of Henry James.

Auden's ostensible theme, as the working diagram indicates, is the relationship of Art to Nature or Life. The Stage Manager's Preface enunciates this in four ten-line stanzas of intricately rhymed trimeters. Beginning with the metaphor of Art as a circus, the Stage Manager goes on to pose questions about the purpose of Art, and he concludes with a pastiche of Shakespeare that gracefully suggests how the Art-Life dichotomy will lead to more universal dichotomies —Time-Eternity, This World-Other World.

> Well, who in his own backyard
> Has not opened his heart to the smiling
> Secret he cannot quote?
> Which goes to show that the Bard
> Was sober when he wrote
> That this world of fact we love
> Is unsubstantial stuff:
> All the rest is silence
> On the other side of the wall;
> And the silence ripeness,
> And the ripeness all. (352)

On this side of the wall is the "stuff / As dreams are made on"—both Life and the Art that feeds upon it. But on the other side of the wall is the eternity that appears to us as silence. The ripeness is a mystic whole beyond mere experience or expression.

In the poem proper, Prospero alone has two voices. The first sounds in elegiac couplets, the mourning rhythm. Unmetrical and stress-rhythmed, they reveal Prospero's artistic past, which has brought the other characters to self-knowledge. But Prospero also speaks three lyrical stanzaic passages (italicized in the text) that interrupt his meditative couplets. The first stanzaic interlude expresses colloquial cynicism about the ability of art to depict ideals: "Dare even Pope or Caesar know / The price of faith and honour?" (355) When the couplets continue, Prospero wonders about the future of Ariel, his magical servant. Then he shifts to the human realm, aware that neither Antonio nor Caliban has expressed contrition, and aware of his own responsibility:

All by myself I tempted Antonio into treason;
  However that could be cleared up; both of us know
That both were in the wrong, and neither need be
    sorry:
  But Caliban remains my impervious disgrace. (356)

Prospero does not dwell on this "disgrace." Instead, he predicts the future of the Europeans, with some irony about their limited vision. His second stanzaic interruption wittily incites Ariel to formulate fictions that will screen out reality: "But should you catch a living eye, / Just wink as you depart." (357)

Resuming the elegiac couplets, Prospero faces a future without Ariel, mere living without writing (the situation that Henry James found unimaginable for the Shakespeare he equated with Prospero). In his last stanzaic interruption Prospero asks Ariel for a last song. No longer the artist, Prospero is merely an old man, but he pleads for art "To man, meaning me, / As now, meaning always, / In love or out, / Whatever that mean, / Trembling he takes / The silent passage / Into discomfort." (359) Though "discomfort" is an understatement for the uncertainties of spiritual experience, the "trembling" is accurate.

The Second Section, devoted to monologues of the several Shakespearean characters, displays Auden's dazzling virtuosity: Antonio speaks in terza rima, Ferdinand a Petrarchan sonnet, Stephano a ballad, Gonzalo twenty-line stanzas of trochaic tetrameter, Adrian and Francisco a couplet, Alonso twelve-line stanzas in syllabic rhythm, the Master and Boatswain six-line ballad stanzas, Sebastian a sestina, Trinculo trimeter quatrains, and Miranda a villanelle. Some of these forms seem to harmonize with Auden's characterological conceptions; all of them amaze the ear. Moreover, after each of the speakers, Antonio expresses his unrepentant dissent in five-line stanzas of invariant rhyme-words, which delineate his situation: Prospero, my own, know, Antonio, alone. Prospero and Antonio, "Creation's O," are forever in opposition.

In this second section of "The Sea and the Mirror" Antonio speaks first and last. He defines his function to Prospero: "As I exist so you shall be denied." (361) Mephistophelian, he prevents complacency on the part of Prospero. By his mocking, repetitive stanzas, Antonio undermines Ferdinand's love, Stephano's appetite, Gonzalo's reasoned acceptance of faith, the mere entertainment of Adrian and Francisco, the suffering wisdom of Alonso, the unreflective diurnal round of the Master and Boatswain, the accidental repentance of Sebastian, the sad jests of Trinculo, and the harmony evoked by Miranda through suppression of bad fairy-tale characters. Remarkable is Auden's economy that catches the spirit of the Shakespearean characters, and extends it through his rendition of their different idioms and rhythms.

In this swift run-down of rhyme patterns, and of themes, I have presented the Shakespearean characters in Auden's order. That order moves from the denying spirit of Antonio to the total harmony of Miranda, by way of Ferdinand's almost Platonic love, Stephano's sensuality, Gonzalo's intellectuality, Alonso's hard-earned humility, and Trinculo's tragicomedy. The two brief duets—Adrian-Francisco and Master-Boatswain—provide comic relief while rounding out the existential background. By the end of the Second Section, Auden has re-enforced Shakespeare and expanded his concept. The characters have achieved some measure of self-awareness, and, except for Antonio, they have shown contrition.

In the three-part structure of "The Sea and the Mirror" the mirror of art dominates Part I, spoken by the artist-magician Prospero. The sea of passionate experience is central to Part III, spoken by the "savage" Caliban. But Part II is the civilized human domain, vulnerable to magic but not governed by it; always threatened by evil from within.

Various as the human beings are, the graduation from corrosive Antonio to joyful Miranda suggests that they have been ennobled by Prospero's art—all but Antonio. Perhaps the furthest extrapolation from Shakespeare is Trinculo; listed as "a jester" in the Folio text, Shakespeare's Trinculo is a drunken sot who displays no wit, whereas Auden's jester springs from the modern clown tradition that evokes laughter through a breaking heart.

Auden also develops Alonso beyond the Shakespearean sketch, in the longest verse sequence of these separate soliloquies. Aware that he is dying, Alonso addresses advice to his son Ferdinand. Only at the end of Alonso's monologue do we learn that he has been writing aloud—a last will in a double sense. Alonso cautions his son about the vanity of kingship, and yet he insists on the necessity for performing the office responsibly. Alonso places kingship in an eternal perspective, in the context of which sea and desert are comparably infertile, the one evocative of dry cerebration and the other of teeming sensuality. Spurning both, Alonso finally summons images from *The Winter's Tale*—music, statue—to signal the end of his letter and the beginning of his religious life:

> Read it, Ferdinand, with the blessing
> Of Alonso, your father, once King
> Of Naples, now ready to welcome
> Death, but rejoicing in a new love,
> A new peace, having heard the solemn
> Music strike and seen the statue move
> To forgive our illusion. (368-369)

Alonso's whole letter, in intricately rhyming twelve-line stanzas, absorbs the sea-change strangeness of Shakespeare's enchanted island to suggest Alonso's movement toward another realm, "a new love, / a new peace."

The Second Section of "The Sea and the Mirror" shows Auden's consummate craftsmanship, though critics have slighted it in favor of the Third Section. But "Caliban to the Audience" relates Auden's work to the other *Tempest* offshoots considered in this chapter. Auden devotes over half his poem to Caliban's discourse, and the style of that discourse has been widely admired as a parody of Henry James. It is possible that Auden knew James' introduction to *The Tempest* (1907), in which, equating Prospero with Shakespeare, he wonders: "What manner of human being was it who *could* so, at a given moment, announce his intention of capping his divine flame with a twopenny extinguisher, and who then, the announcement made, could serenely succeed in carrying it out?"[16] The usual view of the late Jamesian style is that it permits exquisite nuance, but Auden uses it to force close reading of his difficult, witty text.

As was mentioned earlier, Caliban's language has fascinated writers from the seventeenth century onward, but Auden alone endows Shakespeare's "salvage and deformed slave" with a highly erudite, syntactically difficult prose—almost the obverse of his Shakespearean idiom. Auden's natural man speaks erudite language, his oral address is veiled by his difficult syntax, and his message is allusive and elusive.

Auden's Caliban is certainly *not* a savage and deformed slave, but it is difficult to say what he *is*. In Auden's early working diagram, he is designated as "Flesh," but he is a good deal more than that. Just as the sea and mirror images acquire extended meanings in the first half of Auden's poem, Caliban hides several meanings beneath his consistently Jamesian syntax, and Auden suggests the separation of these meanings through the use of three separating asterisks in the printed text. Basically, Caliban takes three different attitudes, but the third is further subdivided. 1) Speaking to the audience, Caliban presumes to speak *for* them—"for the present I speak your echo"—and as such, he challenges Shakespeare's interweaving of life and art, which decorum would separate. 2) Caliban then does an about-face and speaks in Shakespeare's name—"a special message for our late author . . . to any gay apprentice in the magical art." (384) He limns an imaginary biography of the artist who begins his profession in joyous control of Ariel but ends in being stubbornly defied by Caliban. 3) Finally, Caliban "on behalf of Ariel and myself" (390) addresses the audience on the nature of reality, which he finds to be ultimately religious. Thus, in his three parts Caliban successively approximates Natural Man, Artist, and Man of Faith.

In spite of the three asterisks to provide pause between parts, Caliban's arguments are hard to follow, since they are offered through ironic roles, couched in convoluted sentences, screened by sustained metaphors and personifications. In Caliban's first part, for example, Caliban-as-Audience makes extended reference to "Him" as Caliban and "Her" as the Muse. Pages of pronouns race by without antecedent; yet without antecedents, the argument is impenetrable. Moreover, with brilliant prestidigitation, Auden enlists Hamlet's phrase about art—"mirror [held] up to nature"—to criticize the artist Shakespeare for indecorously introducing Caliban into the domain of the Muse. A single sentence near the end of this part epitomizes the attack:

> Are we not bound to conclude, then, that, whatever snub to the poetic you may have intended incidentally to administer, your profounder motive in so introducing Him to them among whom, because He doesn't belong, He couldn't appear as anything but His distorted parody, a deformed and savage slave, was to deal a mortal face-slapping insult to us among whom He does and is, moreover, all grossness turned to glory, no less a person than the nude august elated archer of our heaven, the darling single son of Her who, in her right milieu, is certainly no witch but the most sensible of all the gods, whose influence is as sound as it is pandemic, on the race-track no less than in the sleeping

> cars of the Orient Express, our great white Queen of Love herself? (383)

It is an enthralling sleight-of-hand, equating love with savage drives, and leading to the question: "Is it possible that, not content with inveigling Caliban into Ariel's kingdom, you have also let loose Ariel in Caliban's?" (383) At the beginning of his monologue, Caliban has introduced himself as the "begged question," and he concludes this section with the question "Where is Ariel?"

Before answering, however, he speaks in the name of the author to the would-be artist. His artistic biography recalls Prospero's autobiographical introduction. Both artists enjoy the services of Ariel but, unlike Prospero, the fictional magician tries to dismiss his servant, only to be confronted with Caliban, "the dark thing you could never abide to be with." (390) In this part, too, pronouns are subtly deployed, for though Caliban pretends to speak at Shakespeare's command, he soon assumes the first person singular and reproaches the fictional artist with relegating him, Caliban, to an inferior position. Yet he closes on the hope of "our both learning, if possible and as soon as possible, to forgive and forget the past, and to keep our respective hopes for the future, within moderate, very moderate, limits." (390) Unlike Shakespeare's Caliban, and differently from Renan's, Auden's has acquired a sense of pardon.

In the third and longest section of his monologue, Caliban addresses himself to the audience at large on the subject of "the Journey of life—the down-at-heels disillusioned figure." (391) But he proceeds to divide his audience into two groups—the majority who choose Caliban as their guide, and the élite who choose Ariel. Caliban-guide will lead to chaos and disaster, and Ariel to "perpetual emergency and everlasting improvization." (397) The opposing forces here would seem to be the sensuous versus the spiritual life.

After three asterisks, Caliban sums up the undesirability

of either way cut off from the other. Returning to the theater in which he is addressing the audience, Caliban admits that he and Ariel have performed shabbily, and yet in the very inadequacy of performance one comes to realize: "There is nothing to say. There never has been. . . . There is no way out. There never was." (402) All the actors can hope for is a hint of "the real Word which is our only *raison d'être*." Finally, "it is just here, among the ruins and the bones, that we may rejoice in the perfected Work which is not ours." Life *and* art must be traversed in order to be transcended, en route toward the Divine. Caliban closes on an aphorism of eternal harmony: "The sounded note is the restored relation." (403)

Fortunately, however, it is a more melodious rendition of that note that concludes the long poem—Ariel's verses to Caliban, with an Echo by the Prompter. Ariel affirms his love for Caliban. Each of his stanzas ends with an "i" sound—reply, cry, sigh, and the "I" of the Prompter (whose function, paradoxically, is to echo rather than prompt), which sounds like "Aye." The first person singular consents to blend art and experience, the sea and the mirror. But implicit in Prospero's farewell to Ariel, Alonso's letter to his son, the love poems of Ferdinand and Miranda, and Caliban's address to the audience is stress on the ultimate importance of a religious goal.

Auden's debt to Kierkegaard's thought has been acknowledged and studied. He has written about Kierkegaard and edited an anthology of his writings. In "The Sea and the Mirror," however, Auden uses Kierkegaard with a difference. The long poem does not dramatize three stages of human development—esthetic to ethical to religious. Rather, the pre-religious life consists, for the poet, of an intricate interweaving of experience and expression. Then comes a time of stock-taking (which some critics interpret in the light of Auden's own biography) when the inadequacies of both art and life must be confronted and an effort made to fix one's eyes on the religious domain—"the smiling secret," "O Light," "the real Word."

Conveying the main themes of "The Sea and the Mirror" is also betraying them—the more so for a poem that deliquesces into its myriad patterns, rhythms, and images. Auden has created his own Enchanted Island in which the Art-Life dichotomy is more or less in focus, but sea and mirror blind with reflections upon reflections. It is easy to lose oneself in a patch of iridescence, as in a patch of Impressionist canvas, but it is more rewarding to back off and appreciate the whole. Auden's "Sea and the Mirror" is a singularly dramatic whole, in which each character progresses toward self-knowledge, but through Caliban we all progress, if not to self-knowledge, at least to self-interrogation. We may not follow Caliban—of all people!—to the final "restored relation," as we may not follow Dante to the multifoliate rose, but we are numb if we do not feel the intensity of his "Journey of life," no longer a "down-at-heels disillusioned figure" in Auden's shimmering hands.

"The Sea and the Mirror" has been staged as an afterpiece to Shakespeare's *Tempest*. In Oxford, in 1968 and again in 1969, each actor played first the Shakespearean then the Audenesque role, with director Frank Hauser speaking the Stage Manager's Prologue. Several reviewers thought the actors were more skillful in the modern version, and even the redoubtable Irving Wardle of *The Times* (who found Caliban's address "sheer coyness") admitted that the whole "takes on unlooked for authority on the stage."[17] Moreover, he continues: "Harold Lang, red-eyed and baleful as the preaching Caliban, conveys the spirit of a well-reasoned argument where little exists." However, *much* argument exists when Caliban is caught in several contemporary dilemmas.

Though Auden's "Sea and the Mirror" was written in 1944, it was not staged until 1968, and free Shakespeare staging undoubtedly made this possible. A month after the relatively unheralded Oxford performances, one of England's best-known Shakespeare directors produced an experimental *Tempest* in London. Peter Brook (b. 1925), an Oxford graduate, was a professional director by the age of twenty, a director of Covent Garden Opera at twenty-six, one of the directors of the newly organized Royal Shakespeare Company in 1962, and founder in 1971 of the International Centre of Theatre Research, based in Paris. He has been widely acclaimed for his productions of Shakespeare—*Love's Labor's Lost* in 1947, *Titus Andronicus* in 1954, *King Lear* in 1962, *A Midsummer Night's Dream* in 1970, and a French *Timon* in 1974. Though he produced *The Tempest* in 1957 (with John Gielgud as Prospero, Alec Clunes as Caliban), he returned to that play in 1968, with experimentation in mind.

Spurred by the French actor-director Jean-Louis Barrault, Brook assembled a multi-national group of actors to explore such questions as: "What is theatre? What is a play? What is the relationship of the actor to audience? What are the conditions which serve all of them best?"[18] In selecting *The Tempest* as the vehicle for such research, Brook wished to investigate whether Shakespeare's text "could help the actors find the power and violence that *is* in the play; whether they could find new ways of performing all other elements which were normally staged in a very artificial way . . . and whether the actors could extend their range of work by using a play that demanded this extension."(245) When one poses questions in this way, one is likely to "find" affirmative answers.

As the performance site, Brook chose the London Roundhouse, today equipped with conventional theater seats, but then evidently bare. On that ample floor the actors engaged in improvisations, and they finally formalized certain scenes for performance. As Margaret Croyden describes it:

> The plot [of *The Tempest*] was shattered, condensed, deverbalized; time was discontinuous, shifting. Action

> merged with collage, though some moments were framed and, as in a film, dissolved and faded out. Whenever Shakespeare's words were spoken, they were intoned and chanted. Brook tried to strip the play of preconceived language patterns connected with classical interpretations of Shakespeare. In addition, he was interested in finding the relationship of the audience to actors in a new kind of space and what responses and experiences are possible when all conventions are dispensed with. (246)

Not quite *all* conventions, since the story line of *The Tempest* did govern the performance. However, a few characters disappeared—Alonso, Antonio, Gonzalo, Sebastian—and Sycorax became visible as a large woman-witch. Prospero, played by English actor Ian Hogg, wore a white Karate suit; Ariel, played by Japanese actor Katsuhiro Oida, wore a ceremonial kimono. All the other actors wore black leotards. The audience surrounded the actors on three sides but allowed for a wide horizontal playing area. Vertical action was given scope through the use of large mobile pipe scaffoldings.

As in much subsequent experimental work, the action went forward without a break. For clarity, however, the action may be divided into scenic sequences.

1. Actors and audience mill around the large open area, and then the actors begin informal, game-like warm-ups.

2. The actors move to the center of the floor and group themselves in pairs, performing the mirror exercise to the sound of their own humming.

3. The actors turn toward the audience, each stiffening his face into a mask and uttering non-verbal animal sounds.

4. The play begins, as in Shakespeare, with a tempest. Part of the actors play the ship, and part the passengers. Ariel creates the storm by using "the sleeves of his kimono as

wings with which he calls forth the spirits; his speech (a combination of Japanese words and non-verbal sounds) and powerful No foot movements call up the wind, rain, and thunder." (247) The crew moans: "Lost, all is lost."

5. Miranda and Prospero converse, ametrically speaking the Shakespearean lines. Miranda moves impatiently about the wide playing area and climbs the scaffolds.

6. The exhausted passengers land on the island.

7. Ferdinand and Miranda meet and fall in love, embracing in a rocking position.

8. The rest of the cast, in pairs for the mirror exercise, mock them by imitation.

9. The Europeans regain their strength, learning again to use their senses. Almost incomprehensibly, they chant the phrases "brave new world" and "how beauteous is man."

10. High on a scaffold, Sycorax gives birth to a black-hooded Caliban, who is almost immediately captured by Prospero.

11. Enacting the Shakespearean line "You taught me language," Prospero teaches Caliban the meaning of the words "I," "you," "food," "love," deliberately hurting his pupil in the lesson on the last word. Then Caliban learns "master" and "slave," which leads him to escape.

12. Against a background of percussive sound, Caliban climbs up the scaffolds, pursuing Miranda to rape her, and bellowing: "I am subject to a tyrant."

13. Captured and imprisoned, Caliban roars with frustration while Ariel moans: "Ah, ah, brave new world," and the chorus mocks "how beauteous is man."

14. Caliban escapes and takes command of the island dwellers. He and his mother direct a sexual orgy.

15. The cast forms a pyramid on the scaffolds, Sycorax pinioning Ariel at the base, and Caliban at the apex.

16. The pyramid crumbles into a pack of dogs attacking Prospero sexually, to the accompaniment of obscene noises.

17. Ariel arrives with brightly colored trinkets to bribe the dog-pack.

18. The cast improvises games which are transformed into the Ferdinand-Miranda wedding ceremony. For this event, the audience seated on the scaffold platforms is wheeled swiftly on to the playing area.

19. The wedding over. Prospero says with a double meaning: "I forgot the plot." The actors mirror his loss of memory.

20. *The Tempest* epilogue is recited, each actor mouthing a phrase and slipping away.

21. As the words "ending," "despair," "relieved," "by prayer" sound in the distance, the light shines brightly on the empty playing space.

The Roundhouse *Tempest* adaptation predates most of the New Theater experiments with *Macbeth* and *Hamlet.* Several of its experimental procedures were to become customary in a relatively short time—emphasis upon the physical as opposed to the verbal, and upon the spontaneous as opposed to the structured, free use of playing space rather than traditional actor-audience separation, absence of set, costumes, and props, story line blurred in favor of images emerging from actors' improvisations, ready eruption of the violent and the sexual.

Radically different is Aimé Césaire's *Une Tempête,* rooted in the political consciousness of the Third World, and centered on a militantly black Caliban.[19] Aaron the Moor, Joan the Frenchwoman, and Shylock the Jew argue against a modern liberal Shakespeare without prejudice against color, nation, or religion. None of these characters is as evil as Richard III, true-blue Englishman, but these characters exude their malice genetically as Richard does not.

Black Othello is ambiguous. Nobler than the Moor of Shakespeare's source, Cinthio, he has almost always been a commanding figure on the stage. In the twentieth century T. S. Eliot and F. R. Leavis attacked his motives, so that later critics have debated whether the Moor is noble, as eighteenth-century critics debated whether he was Black. The latter question flared up in nineteenth-century theater when the American Negro Ira Aldridge, billed as "the African Roscius," played Othello in London's Covent Garden in 1833. He later played other Shakespearean roles and produced a transformation of *Titus Andronicus*, focused on a heroic Aaron.[20] But he apparently did not think of playing Caliban. Toward the end of the century, another Black actor, Morgan Smith, played Shakespearean roles, notably Othello, in England. But no other Black Othello reached the professional stage until Paul Robeson enacted the Moor in 1930, and sporadically for some twenty years thereafter.

Unlike Othello and Aaron, Caliban is not designated as Black in Shakespeare's text. Shakespeare may have been reading tales of shipwreck in the West Indies, whose inhabitants are non-white. Caliban's name probably derives from "Carib," meaning a savage of the New World (from which "cauliban," a Romany word meaning blackness.

Frank Kermode, editor of the Arden edition of *The Tempest*, summarizes Shakespeare's play: "The main opposition is between the worlds of Prospero's Art and Caliban's Nature. Caliban is the core of the play."[21] The classical scholar, Bernard Knox, reads the play in the classical tradition of comedy, in which the domestic problems of the master are solved through the intrigue of the slaves.[22] During the play, Prospero calls Caliban a slave four times. Yet

Caliban has been a coveted role on the English stage, and several actors have first played Prospero, then shifted to Caliban. In a celebrated interpretation, Beerbohm Tree played Caliban "biting at a raw fish, fanning flies from Stephano, and ultimately, alone on his island, watching the full-rigged ship as it faded on the horizon towards Italy."[23]

Until the twentieth century, however, Caliban was white. The first Black Caliban I can discover was ex-boxer Canada Lee, in Margaret Webster's New York production of 1945. (Canada Lee began his acting career in Orson Welles' Voodoo *Macbeth* of 1936.) Lee resented his slavery and snarled at his master, often confronting him in the fighter's defensive crouch, from which he could (but never did) spring to attack. After Lee, there have been a number of Black Calibans on the stage, though he is still more often portrayed by whites.

It is possible that the Black poet Aimé Césaire knew something about this background of Blacks playing Shakespeare when, at the suggestion of director Jean-Marie Serreau, he adapted *The Tempest* for a Black cast. Born in Martinique in 1913, Césaire had a very different view of his native land from that advertised in tourist brochures. He describes it in his best-known poem *Cahier d'un retour au pays natal*.[24]

Escaping gladly from his own background, Césaire went at age eighteen to Paris, first on scholarship to the Lycée Louis-le-grand, then to the prestigious École Normale Supérieure.[25] At the lycée he met the Senegalese Léopold Sédar Senghor about whom he later said: "Quand j'ai connu Senghor, je me suis dit africain." The two young men in 1932 founded a review *L'Etudiant Noir*, which attempted to cut across national and class lines, uniting Black students on the basis of their color. *Négritude* was born.

A man of prodigious energy, Césaire has committed his life to both poetry and politics. For many years he was mayor of Fort de France, Martinique, and a delegate to the

French National Assembly. For many years, he has been recognized as one of the major poets of the French language. In 1956 he adapted for theater a 1946 poem, *Et les chiens se taisaient*. He has explained the shift: "J'ai voulu expliciter à mon peuple ce que ma poésie contenait."[26] In 1963 he wrote *La Tragédie du roi Christophe,* which French director Jean-Marie Serreau staged.[27] The two men, Black and white, from Martinique and from Paris, worked together in harmony and enthusiasm. Serreau had often been the first to direct plays of the French avant-garde, but he dedicated the last ten years of his life to founding a Paris-based Third World theater group, whose name he often changed. At the time of his death in 1973, it was Théâtre de la Tempête, after Césaire's adaptation.

Césaire has commented on his adaptation in an interview:

> I was trying to "de-mythify" the tale. To me Prospero is the complete totalitarian. I am always surprised when others consider him the wise man who "forgives." What is most obvious, even in Shakespeare's version, is the man's absolute will to power. Prospero is the man of cold reason, the man of methodical conquest—in other words, a portrait of the "enlightened" European. And I see the whole play in such terms: the "civilized" European world coming face to face for the first time with the world of primitivism and magic. Let's not hide the fact that in Europe the world of reason has inevitably led to various kinds of totalitarianism. . . . Caliban is the man who is still close to his beginnings, whose link with the natural world has not yet been broken. Caliban can still *participate* in a world of marvels, whereas his master can merely "create" them through his acquired knowledge. At the same time, Caliban is also a rebel—the positive hero, in a Hegelian sense. The slave is always more important than his master—for it is the slave who makes history.[28]

Césaire's intention is to depict Caliban's slavery more graphically than Shakespeare does. Shakespeare's Prospero tells Miranda: "We cannot miss him [Caliban]: he does make our fire, / Fetch in our wood, and serves in offices / That profit us." Césaire dramatizes profit in its ugly modern meaning—white exploitation of Black labor.

Like Genet's play *Les Nègres*, written for Black actors, Césaire's *Une Tempête* is based on playing roles. But Genet's play is an entertainment to camouflage an offstage revolution, whereas Césaire shows a revolution erupting onstage, in the person of Caliban. Unlike Genet's mocking actors, Césaire's actors work in an "atmosphère de psychodrame," each Black choosing his role by putting on a mask. The implicit assumption, as in psychodrama, is that the role will effect a cure of the actor. For the most part, each actor plays a Shakespearean character, but the strongest plays a natural force, a tempest. Césaire's director says: "Il me faut une tempête à tout casser." Quite literally, this tempest *does* break everything apart—not only the ship's hierarchy but the racial and cultural hierarchy of European tradition.

Césaire approached Shakespeare intending to adapt him radically for a Black company, and yet he uses more of Shakespeare's plot than do the other *Tempest* offshoots, as demonstrated by the following table:[29]

Césaire		*Event*	*Shakespeare*	
I	1	tempest	I	1
I	2	exposition (Prospero to Miranda) Prospero's orders to Ariel and Caliban	I	2
II	1	Ariel-Caliban debate	no such action	
II	2	magic banquet	II, 1 and III, 3	
II	3	Antonio-Sebastian plot	II, 1; III, 3; V, 1	
III	1	Ferdinand-Miranda plot	II, 2; III, 1	
III	2	Caliban-Stephano-Trinculo plot	II, 2; III, 2	
III	3	nuptial masque	IV	1
III	4	glittering apparel trick	IV	1
III	5	Prospero pardons the Europeans and frees Ariel	V	1

Césaire's only new scene is an Ariel-Caliban debate in which the former espouses gradualism and the latter revolt. But the new scene is not Césaire's most significant change, which is obscured by the table.

Shakespeare's Prospero pardons the Europeans in his final scene, after Ariel has expressed compassion for them. Césaire also delays the formal pardon till the last scene, but Césaire's Prospero *decides* to pardon the Europeans in Act I, Scene 2, after the first sign of Caliban's defiance. Prospero's celebrated forgiveness becomes a necessary expedient of white rule.

Though Kermode and others have seen the Prospero-Caliban opposition as the center of Shakespeare's play, Césaire stresses that centrality by paring away much of the dialogue of the other characters. The European plots are effectively terminated by the end of Césaire's Act II. In Ariel's words: "Aussi, tournons la page! Pour clore cet épisode, il ne me reste plus qu'à vous convier tous, au nom de mon maître, aux réjouissances qui doivent marquer aujourd'hui même les fiançailles de sa fille Miranda."* (49) In Césaire's Act III the play-long conflict between Prospero and Caliban comes to a head, and Césaire changes Shakespeare's ending. The Europeans depart for Italy, but Prospero remains on the island, with Caliban: "Et maintenant, Caliban, à nous deux!" (91) Time passes, denoted by a half-lowering of the curtain. In the last scene Prospero is weak and old; shouting that he will defend civilization, he shoots in all directions. Suddenly he feels cold and cries out for Caliban (presumably to fetch wood for a fire). But the time of slave labor is over, and from offstage comes the voice of Caliban singing: "LA LIBERTÉ OHÉ, LA LIBERTÉ!"

One might dismiss Césaire's adaptation as mere agitprop, and yet his play is not simplistically constructed about a

* So let's turn the page! To close this episode, nothing remains for me to do except to invite you all, in the name of my master, to the festivities that are to celebrate the engagement of his daughter Miranda on this very day.

heroic Black Caliban and an evil white Prospero. Prospero *is* evil and white, but that evil is conditioned by his "civilization"—the despoiling of unindustrialized countries by Western capitalism. His magic is crassly materialistic, and Césaire weaves this modern reality into the basic fabric of his adaptation. Thus, Césaire's Prospero explains in his exposition that he was ousted from Milan because he had discovered prospective colonies, and his enemies "ourdirent un complot pour me voler cet empire à naître." (20) (That *complot* appears to owe something to Renan, with whose work Césaire is familiar: like Renan's Prospero, Césaire's is hounded by the Inquisition, but the persecution has a philosophic basis in Renan, an economic basis in Césaire, since Prospero is dethroned through a church-state pincer plot.)

Prospero is villainous because he supports the privileged position into which he was born. Caliban, in contrast, is not a ready-made Black hero; he has to educate himself to revolt, and he does so in the irreverent mocking idiom of today's young Blacks. The Stephano-Trinculo confederacy is the last step in his education; when he learns to scorn them, he is ready to face Prospero alone. And yet, he cannot bring himself to kill Prospero.

Césaire's structural changes are less theatrical than his textural changes, which infuse an ideological vehicle with vigorous speech.[30] In the very first scene, Shakespeare's mariners are impudent to their titled passengers, and Césaire underlines that impudence, but also their courage. At the end of the scene, Shakespeare's nobles pray offstage, except for Gonzalo, while onstage the sailors drown their fear in drink. Césaire has the nobles sing a hymn onstage while the sailors busily luff. (The sailors do not reappear in Césaire's play, so that we do not hear their restored Shakespearean deference to the aristocrats.)

In the second scene, Miranda's distress is similar in both plays, but Prospero comforts her differently in each play. Césaire has him draw a self-portrait of a martyred and benevolent preserver of both justice *and* property: "Nous manigançâmes la tempête à laquelle tu viens d'assister, qui préserve mes biens d'outre-mer et met en même temps ces sacripants en ma possession."* (22) But when Prospero speaks to Ariel and Caliban (separately), he becomes a stern master, even threatening the latter with "la trique." Prospero is literally two-faced, presenting the fair one to Miranda and quite another to his slaves. Elsewhere in Césaire's play, Prospero merely feigns sternness to the Europeans, in order to dominate them. "Puissance" is his leitmotif. Thus, after depriving the Europeans of the magic banquet, as in Shakespeare, Césaire's Prospero then insists that they eat: "Qu'ils se sentent manger dans ma main comme des poussins. C'est une marque de soumission que j'exige d'eux."† (43) When they are clearly in his power, at the end of Césaire's Act II, Ariel announces his master's all-European pardon. And when Prospero is satisfied that Ferdinand is obediently chopping wood, he orders Caliban to finish the job. Angered at the Caliban-Stephano-Trinculo plot, Césaire's Prospero orders Ariel to attack them with anti-riot gas.

Though Césaire consistently darkens Prospero (to use the habitual white metaphor!), he also colors other characters. Caliban's growing spirit of independence is central. His very first word is "Uhuru," the African cry of liberty acquired by former slaves. Césaire traces Caliban's acquisition. Rebellious against Prospero, Caliban thinks to make common cause with the poor Europeans. But when Trinculo and Stephano bicker over the brightly colored garments, Caliban rejects them more forcefully than in Shakespeare. Near the end, he bursts into laughter when Gonzalo tries to convert him to Christianity. And at no point does he express contrition to Prospero.

The different Shakespearean characters display modern

* We rigged the tempest you just saw, which saves my overseas property and at the same time puts these scoundrels in my power.

† Let them feel they're eating out of my hand, like chicks. It's a sign of submission that I demand of them.

sentiments for the nameless island that resembles Césaire's own Martinique. Ariel and Caliban (separately) express their attachment to their native land. Ariel does not inveigh against the tree in which Sycorax imprisoned him: "Après tout j'aurais peut-être fini par devenir arbre. . . . Arbre, un des mots qui m'exaltent!"* Caliban breaks into verse in equating the island with his mother: "Et je te retrouve partout: / Dans l'oeil de la mare qui me regarde, sans ciller, / à travers les scirpes. / Dans le geste de la racine tordue et son bond qui attend. / Dans la nuit, la toute-voyante aveugle, / la toute-flaireuse sans naseaux!"† (26) Among the Europeans, Gonzalo is most appreciative of the island, which he wishes to keep unspoiled so that tourists can profit from it. His utopia is indebted neither to Shakespeare nor to Montaigne: "Qu'ils restent ce qu'ils sont: des sauvages, de bons sauvages, libres, sans complexes ni complications. Quelque chose comme un réservoir d'éternelle jouvence où nous viendrions périodiquement rafraîchir nos âmes vieillies et citadines."‡ (41) At the lower European level, Stephano and Trinculo are indifferent to the island, but, as in Shakespeare, they wish to profit from its inhabitant, Caliban, whom they address in *petit nègre*. Though Prospero does not specifically praise the island, he feels himself its sole protector, expressing this in verse: "Sans moi, qui de tout cela / saurait tirer musique? / Sans moi cette île est muette. / Ici donc, mon devoir. / Je resterai."§ (90)

* After all, maybe I would have ended by becoming a tree. . . . Tree, one of the words that inspires me!

† And everywhere I find you again: / In the eye of the pond that looks at me, without blinking, / through the rushes. / In the motion of the twisted root and its leap that waits. / In the night, the blind all-seeing, the all-smelling without nostrils!

‡ Let them remain what they are: savages, good savages, free, without complexes or complications. Something like a reservoir of eternal youth where we might periodically come to refresh our aged and urban souls.

§ Without me, who out of all that / would know how to draw music? / Without me this island is dumb. / Here then, my duty. / I shall remain.

Césaire fits both lovers and gods into a contemporary capitalist context. Prospero matches Miranda to Ferdinand in order to protect his empire from the threat implicit in Caliban's defiance. Ferdinand is pleased that Miranda catches him cheating at chess, for she will need that ability in Europe, where everybody cheats. At their nuptial masque, Juno wishes riches for the young couple, and Ceres lack of poverty. Only after they speak does Iris mention "pure love." Into their midst bursts the only character newly introduced by Césaire, the African god-devil Eshu, who mocks his white colleagues with obscenities. Before him the white goddesses are helpless, but Prospero understands that Black god and man are united against him: "Par cette insubordination, c'est tout l'ordre du monde qu'il remet en cause. La Divinité peut s'en moquer, elle! Moi, j'ai le sens de mes responsabilités!"[31*] (71)

It is through his control of language that Césaire conveys these distinctive nuances. He uses colloquial French prose for the body of the play, thus robbing the Shakespearean aristocrats of their noble verse. But he captures the rough impudence of the sailors, the longwindedness of Gonzalo, the witty word-play of Antonio and Sebastian, and the drunken stupidities of Stephano and Trinculo. Prospero's language has been aptly analyzed by Peter Rohrsen: "Césaires Prospero redet apodiktisch, unduldsam gegen jeden Widerspruch. Charakteristische Redeformen sind Flüche, Befehle, Verbote und herrische Grundsatzerklärungen und nur gelegentlich Fragen oder erzählende Passagen. Die Isolation des autoritären Tyrannen wird so in beinahe jeder seiner Äusserungen deutlich gemacht."[32†] In

* By that insubordination, he calls into question the entire world order. A god can afford not to care about it! But I have a sense of my responsibilities!

† Césaire's Prospero speaks apodictically, impatient with all opposition. His typical speech-patterns are curses, orders, interdictions, lordly explanations, and only occasionally questions or narrations. The isolation of the authoritarian tyrant is thus articulated in almost all his expressions.

general, Prospero pontificates to his white subordinates and barks at the Blacks.

It is of course to Caliban that Césaire gives his most lyrical lines, and that lyricism is based, like Césaire's own poetry, on the African tradition that affirms the magical efficacy of words, at once things and signs. Caliban's first word onstage is "Uhuru," the African cry of liberation. He curses Prospero before he can be cursed, and he denies the relevance of the white man's language: "Tu ne m'as rien appris du tout. Sauf, bien sûr à baragouiner ton langage pour comprendre tes ordres: couper du bois, laver la vaisselle, pêcher le poisson, planter les légumes, parce que tu es bien trop fainéant pour le faire."* (25) Caliban's rebellion begins with the rejection of his name; he will no longer answer to "Caliban," anagram of "cannibal," but "X," the man whose name has been stolen. Of his four songs, two celebrate liberty and two the African god Shango.

It is mainly through songs that Césaire indicates a level of sensitivity beyond the colloquial surface. He knows better than to try to translate "Full fathom five" or "Where the bee sucks." Instead, he composes lyrics for the several characters: Ariel's lyrics evoke the strange seascape; Ferdinand's his sadness at his work; Stephano and Trinculo sing sailors' drinking songs. But it is Caliban who is most musical, as it is Caliban who is most poetic.

The poet Césaire allows only three of the Shakespearean characters to erupt into verse—Caliban, Ariel, and Prospero. The famous "Our revels now are ended" speech has no counterpart, but when Caliban declines to kill a defenseless Prospero, the latter declares: "Et maintenant, finie la comédie!" (79) It is time for the final scene in which the three characters speak verse, but not predictably. When Prospero frees Ariel, the former slave breaks into lyrics of

* You haven't taught me anything at all. Except, of course, to jabber your language in order to understand your commands: cut the wood, do the dishes, catch the fish, plant the vegetables, because you're far too lazy to do it.

brotherhood with slaves everywhere: "Je laisserai tomber / une à une / chacune plus délectable / quatre notes si douces que la dernière / fera lever une brûlure / dans le coeur des esclaves les plus oublieux / Nostalgie de liberté!"* (83) Caliban refuses Prospero's offer of peace and breaks into verse of purely political import: "Et je sais qu'un jour / mon poing nu, mon seul poing nu / suffira pour écraser ton monde!"† (88) In answering political verse, Prospero boasts to Caliban of his accomplishments—the white man's burden—and complains of lack of appreciation: "Mais tu m'as toujours répondu par la rage et le venin, semblable / à la sarigue qui pour mieux / mordre la main qui la tire de la nuit / se hisse au cordage de sa propre queue!"‡ (91) When the curtain is lowered to rise again on an aged Prospero, Césaire specifies: "*Ses gestes sont automatiques et étriqués, son langage appauvri et stéréotypé.*"§ (91) In that impoverished language he announces an invasion of opossums, to whose meaning he has just given the key. Caliban is offstage at the last, but he has earlier enunciated—not in verse but in prose—the meaning of the Black-white opposition: "Qu'un animal, si je puis dire, naturel, s'en prenne à moi le jour où je pars à l'assaut de Prospero, plus souvent! Prospero, c'est l'anti-Nature. Moi je dis: A bas l'anti-Nature! Voyez, à ces mots, notre hérisson se hérisse? Non, il rentre ses piquants! C'est ça, la Nature! C'est gentil, en somme! Suffit de savoir lui parler! Allons, la voie est dégagée: En route!"** (74-75) At the last, Caliban merges with Nature offstage.

* I will let fall / one by one / each more delectable / four notes so sweet that the last one / will arouse a burning / in the hearts of the most forgetful slaves / Nostalgia for liberty!

† And I know that one day / my fist, my bare fist alone, / will be enough to crush your world!

‡ But you have always answered me with rage and venom, like / the opossum which the better / to bite the hand that takes it from the dark, / hoists itself up the rope of its own tail!

§ His gestures are automatic and spare, his language impoverished and stereotyped.

** That a natural animal—if I can say that—should attack me on the

Césaire's title is *A Tempest,* and the opening scene specifies the atmosphere of psychodrama. Black actors may have been cured of a colonial complex through role-playing. But a tempest "à tout casser" will occur and recur as long as white man enslaves the Black.

Over the past hundred years, through six *Tempest* offshoots, Caliban has emancipated himself. Though not always intended to be sympathetic, he emerges to the modern eye as an Everyman figure. Browning apparently took a condescending attitude toward his Caliban, and yet the palpable cunning of his savage can elicit a feeling of kinship. Caliban's propitiation of his god Setebos resembles Pascal's wager: the Almighty being unknowable, one might as well wager on faith.

Faith and skepticism are also relevant to Renan's *Caliban.* Like his English predecessor, the French philosopher takes a condescending attitude toward his mob leader, but the vulgarian defends an élite Prospero against totalitarian orthodoxy. And similarly, MacKaye's Caliban learns to appreciate Prospero's theater. Both Calibans—French and American—respond to love, and through love to a universal brotherhood. Both plays are naive and abstract, unredeemed by the sensuous specifics of Browning's island. Nevertheless, three sensitive and educated gentlemen—English, French, American—were drawn to Shakespeare's savage and deformed slave as an intelligent and educable Everyman.

With Auden's Jamesian Caliban, we enter another world and time. And yet the Everyman resonance is heard again. Auden's Caliban represents raw experience unmediated into art, and yet he is more responsive than most Europeans to an ultimate spiritual reality. He alone is aware of life as process, for which Auden's virtuoso verses are metaphors.

day I set out to storm Prospero, no way! Prospero, he's the anti-Nature. I say: Down with the anti-Nature! You think, at these words, our hedgehog bristles? No, he draws in his quills! That's what Nature is! It's kind, in short! Just have to know how to talk to it! Come on, the route's cleared; let's go!

Peter Brook, who might have read Auden at Oxford, theatricalized an almost inarticulate Caliban, who also represents raw experience. Like many well-educated men of today's theater, Brook has turned against the education that nourished him; his *Tempest* actors therefore explore the primitive man and the primitive actor, before convention fixed his behavior. And the most primitive is Caliban, who expresses neither spiritual sensitivity as in Auden, nor regret as in Shakespeare. But Caliban's honest rendition of his strongest drives mirrors those drives in us.

Educated Aimé Césaire also stresses the natural honesty of his Black Caliban, who opposes Prospero on grounds of economic exploitation disguised as culture, ecological exploitation disguised as progress, standardization of language disguised as literacy—all summed up in the white man's burden that results in the Black man's crucifixion. Césaire's Caliban may seem anachronistic in his desire to return to nature, but it is to his own nature that he wishes to return—a nature rich in myth, metaphor, and affectional bond. The Everyman figure is explicitly Black in Césaire's adaptation of *The Tempest*, but with white exploiters clinging to their exploitation, some whites aspire to Negritude, so as to emulate the honest dignity of the Black Everyman.

I am surprised by my own polemical note, after this examination of offshoots of specific Shakespeare plays. But the note arises directly from the material, each play having yielded its own pattern of derivatives. *Macbeth* offshoots accumulate into a history of non-realistic theater forms, from the mythological farce *Ubu* to group creations of the Alternative Theater. *Hamlet* is probed most deeply in fiction —Sterne, Goethe, Laforgue, Joyce at its pinnacles. Dramatic replays of *Hamlet* fall into two main kinds, a residue of nineteenth-century poetic drama and a mishmash of more recent trends, including realism. *King Lear* inspired few offshoots but spurred essayistic controversy that reflects the lives of the essayists. And finally, the *Tempest* offshoots occasionally recall the Prospero-Shakespeare equation—in MacKaye and Auden—but always present Caliban as a modern Everyman.[33]

Chapter 6

Triple Action Theatre

Vertical might describe the organization of the last few chapters, i.e., climbing the chronological rungs of offshoots of a specific Shakespeare play. The next few chapters will be horizontal—striding through several Shakespeare offshoots by a single author, and in this particular chapter that author is director Steve Rumbelow, founder of the Triple Action Theatre of Britain.

Rumbelow (b. 1949) was trained in the visual arts, and when he turned to theater, he conceived of it as moving sculpture in space. Though he had not at that time—1966—read Artaud, his ideas resemble those of other Alternative Theater groups whose esthetic derives from the French theater prophet. Thus, Margaret Croyden's description of the Living Theatre Artaudian spectacles is applicable to Rumbelow's productions: "Enacted in a *mise-en-scène* fugue rather than in a naturalistic linear form, the pieces relied on dense metaphors rather than on plot. The action, sequentially and spatially arranged, was built on juxtaposed physical configurations made with the actors' own bodies."[1] Unlike most Artaudian groups, however, Rumbelow's has not become anti-verbal. On the contrary, Rumbelow finds that poetic drama—and pre-eminently Shakespeare—provides the widest scope for varied and rhythmic movement in space. Most of his productions have been based on Shakespeare's plays, which he does not hesitate to adapt according to his needs.

The needs have changed over the years. In 1966, when Rumbelow first thought of exploring theater as living sculpture, he decided to acquire familiarity with the new medium by working at the Bristol Old Vic (where he progressed from stagehand to stage manager), and by directing Sunday night experimental productions in Worthing. Moving to London, he became a stage manager for the Royal Shakespeare Company. In 1968 he observed some of the rehearsals of Peter Brook's experimental *Tempest* at the Roundhouse. At about this time, too, he met Morgan Sheppard, who had attended Grotowski's workshops and was promulgating their exercises. He decided to leave the Royal Shakespeare Company and found his own group. Sculpture in space was to be created by subjecting actors to an amalgam of rigorous exercises derived from workshops of the Grotowski type and from Rumbelow's own experience in ballet, boxing, kendo, rugby, and yoga.

Rumbelow chose the name Triple Action Theatre with a double meaning in mind. He felt that most theater consisted of two-dimensional rendition, almost recitation of texts, and he proposed instead a dynamic exploration of three spatial dimensions—triple action. He also hoped to have three theater groups—triple action: one would probe myths through physical means, as private research rather than public performance; another would dilute such research for performance before an uninitiated public; the third would present to more specialized audiences physicalization of classical texts. Only the last group has been realized, though the intention of the second group has been met in that the explorations have resulted in performances before thousands of spectators—mainly in English university towns, but also on tours of Holland and Poland.

Rumbelow founded the Triple Action Theatre with a Shakespearean base, and Shakespeare has continued to be his primary source of material. Rumbelow's first production, *Macbeth* in 1969, tried to fuse the three kinds of approach implied by the desire for three groups. His eighteen actors had had some training in modern dance, and Rumbelow invented exercises for three months of intensive workshops before turning to the play. Many movements were inspired by Legeti's music for *2001 Space Odyssey,* though the music was dropped for the performance. Cutting the text severely, the Triple Action *Macbeth* elides each scene into the next. As became habitual in Triple Action Theatre, sets and props consist mainly of actors' gestures. The actors are dressed in differently colored body-stockings, ghosts in white. The Three Witches are visible at all times, sometimes uttering sounds that approximate Gaelic or Saxon words, sometimes forming such scenic items as a rock, a bed, or a throne.

In performance, flats create suggestive shadows before any actors appear, though some actors—soldiers—have been "planted" among the spectators. As lights come up on the playing area, Macbeth and Banquo charge at the planted actors, symmetrically arranged as if in battle formation. The two warriors shatter that order while onstage the Witches chant "Fair is foul and foul is fair." In a Witch-formed throne an ailing Duncan then praises Macbeth and Banquo, while a sinister Seyton lurks at the edge of the stage.

In the next highly stylized scene Macbeth and Lady Macbeth reach for the sky. They then perform as hosts of a scarlet banquet, before the murder of Duncan. During the murder they speak their lines to the accompaniment of owl-hooting by the rest of the cast. Macbeth the killer takes center stage for a silent scream. Seyton acts as a diabolic Porter, and a ghost-figure accuses Macbeth gesturally and rhythmically until Lady Macbeth pretends to faint. All lines are Shakespeare's, much abridged and sometimes re-arranged.

Duncan's murder is stressed by nonverbal accompaniment, and Banquo's murder is mimed, with irregular flashing lights limning the assassination. During the post-murder banquet the white ghost of Banquo takes center stage, while the guests disperse throughout the auditorium. As Macbeth twists and grimaces in a kind of epileptic fit (borrowed, no doubt, from *Othello*), Banquo does a Kabuki-type dance on his back, to suggest the ultimate triumph of his dynasty.

In Lady Macbeth's sleepwalking scene the whole cast

forms an immense spider. They toss Lady Macbeth high in the air, and when she falls, they seem to swallow her up, as she emits a one-note scream. This scream is prolonged while the rest of the cast becomes an army of accusing ghosts. Suddenly, Macbeth finds himself alone at center stage, with Lady Macbeth's scream still resonating. The ghosts then throw the sinister figures of Ross and Seyton into the first rows of the audience (into collapsible seats).

The Macbeth-Macduff confrontation is an animal battle, with Macbeth a bear ("bearlike I must fight the course") and Macduff a panther. They carry no weapons, and they exchange unguarded blows. Macduff kills Macbeth by sinking his teeth into his throat. In the final scene the Witches strip Macbeth and paint his body white. Still bearlike, he is chained to a post while the ghosts carry out the body of Lady Macbeth, to Gregorian chanting. The Witches freeze, and Macbeth delivers the "Tomorrow and tomorrow and tomorrow" lines. At the last a single spot illuminates Macbeth's anguished face and a Witch hovering over him in the position of the strutting player of *commedia dell'arte.*

Rumbelow opened his Triple Action Theatre on an ambitious note with this eighteen-actor *Macbeth.* Though the group played to good houses in London and Holland, they could not meet expenses, much less support themselves, and they dispersed after the production. With considerably reduced casts, Rumbelow turned to other works—*Lord Byron, Experiment One—Tragedy,* Byron's *Manfred, Oedipus,* and a *Faust* synthesized from Marlowe, Goethe, and *Manfred.* After film and television stints to recoup his finances, in 1971 Rumbelow produced *Everyman* and *Julius Caesar.* He feels that *Everyman* was his first production to achieve his aim of blending the rhythms of a spoken text with physical movement so demanding that the actor cannot slip into the inhibitions of the intellect. But it was after *Julius Caesar* that the British Arts Council made a three-year grant to the group. Between that sum and English tours the Triple Action Theatre became almost self-sustaining in 1971. That is to say, six actors managed to salvage about four pounds a week. However, they had to support themselves at other jobs when they were not performing. Each year the group has added to its repertory, relying mainly on Shakespeare.

Julius Caesar, performed with a cast of five, extended the physical-verbal blend of the Triple Action Theatre, and it also drew on Rumbelow's painterly training. Each scene begins as a brightly colored Roman wall-painting, brought to life by a clownlike Casca, who is played by a woman. Brutus and Cassius are sharply contrasted physically, so that each of their scenes becomes a sculptural duel that terminates in the bright stillness of the painting.

The Triple Action performance begins almost where Shakespeare ends—a battle scene up through the death of Cassius. The slow build to Caesar's murder thus takes on a retrospective quality. The murder itself differs from Shakespeare's, as shown by the scenic direction: "Casca strikes Caesar. Caesar runs screaming around the spectators. Cassius and Casca run after him, beating him with their fists and shouting taunts. Caesar runs for protection to Brutus, who strikes him." Caesar dies, crying out: "Et tu, Brute? Then fall, Caesar!" Marc Antony's funeral oration follows. Then, in a swift shift to the battle scene with which the performance opened, the ghost of Caesar thrusts at Brutus, who dies with a speech that Rumbelow composed.

The Triple Action Theatre's approach to Shakespeare has taken on a certain consistency. Rumbelow chooses the play because it suggests to him an image that becomes obsessive, and in the workshops the actors physicalize the image, however oblique its relation to the text. Their *Tempest* started with Stephano as a bowler hat, *Hamlet* with the prince in a subterranean cavern, *Richard II* with overlapping circles, *Richard III* with a vortex. Sometimes the image is not retained in the final production. While the group improvises on the image, Rumbelow shapes the text and devises workshop exercises to physicalize the text. After varying workshop periods, the group moves into specific scenes as chosen by Rumbelow. During the course of rehearsals, both text and physicalization undergo changes, but the form is set some two weeks before opening. However, modifications may be made even after opening.

In 1972, four years after observing Peter Brook's adaptation of *The Tempest*, Rumbelow produced his own version, and it is closest to the original of all his Shakespeare productions. The Program Note summarizes the basic concept: "At night, Alonso (King of Naples) and his confederates surprise Prospero (Duke of Milan), his court magician Ariel, and his daughter Miranda. The party thrusts Prospero, Ariel, and Miranda into an open boat, and Caliban (Alonso's fool) deals Prospero a fatal blow. Ariel gives comfort to the dying man by conjuring a fantasy at the moment of death. Prospero dreams of revenge but through the process of the fantasy learns the virtue of forgiveness. The fantasy disintegrates in chaos, and Prospero dies."[2]

The seizing and stabbing of Prospero are performed in mime, and a Prospero-Ariel duologue of short lines (invented by Rumbelow) introduces the storm-scene of the Shakespearean *Tempest*. The rest of the performance uses almost all Shakespeare's scenes, but they are cut for swift action. Visually, Prospero derives from Blake's paintings of God; standing on ten-inch boots that look like rocks, he becomes part of the island. Ariel, in contrast, is based on ancient Egyptian art, with shaven head and pointed beard. Stephano and Trinculo are clowns with red noses and bowler hats, and Caliban is a cross between cat and baboon. As Prospero's fantasy dissolves in the final scene, the various characters back out to the sound of rhythmic laughter until Ariel and Prospero are alone on stage. Ariel recites the "Our revels now are ended" speech to Prospero, who addresses the Shakespearean Epilogue directly to Ariel, concluding: "As you [Ariel] from crimes would pardoned be, / Let your indulgence set me free."

Unlike *The Tempest*, the Triple Action Theatre *Hamlet*,

also produced in 1972, is an example of reworking through radical staging. On a rope-web seven actors will jockey for position. Dressed alike, they wear black leotard tights and gray string vests that look like chain-mail or the scales of giant insects. These seven actors play nine parts, Claudius doubling as Ghost, Polonius as Gravedigger. As in some more traditional productions, there is no Fortinbras, Reynaldo, Osric. In some ninety minutes of playing time, lines are drawn from almost every Shakespearean scene, with occasional interpolations of Rumbelow's own material. But the text is of course severely tailored to the theater metaphor—a web of intrigue upon which moments of entrapment are played.

When the Triple Action *Hamlet* opens (with Shakespeare's Act I, Scene 2), Claudius sits like a spider, bloated and menacing at netcenter while Hamlet-fly hovers perilously at its edge. In Hamlet's confrontation with the Ghost, the former is trapped head downmost on the net. Polonius often balances on all fours as he licks appropriate boots for advancement. When Claudius prays and Hamlet ponders killing him, their respective positions on the ropes hold them in equilibrium. In the "To be or not to be" soliloquy the ropes bind Hamlet's wrists and ankles so that he is trapped into paralysis, suspended in midair. Mad Ophelia falls head first from high on the web into a rigging at the side, which serves as a graveyard. In a spectacular finale Laertes and Hamlet dive out of the rope-net onto the stage floor, to duel with rope-whips. As they fight, deaths succeed each other, two bodies—the King and the Queen—falling into the cemetery side-rigging. And afterwards Laertes and Hamlet. Horatio intones "The rest is silence" and summons the dead to rise as ghosts, who collectively recite the collaged closing lines:

> Diseases desperate grown,
> By desperate appliance are relieved
> Or not at all; we are but a

Sharked up list of lawless resolutes
For food and diet to some enterprise
That hath a stomach in't
And blest are those
Whose blood and judgment are so well co-medled,
That they are not a pipe for Fortune's finger
To sound what stop she please.

Nineteen seventy-three was a year of unprecedented activity for the Triple Action Theatre—three Shakespeare adaptations (*Richard II, Richard III, King Lear*) and a new *Faust*, which they eventually played in repertory. For these productions the actors remained at a stable seven—six men and one woman. Two of the men, Dave Walsh and Nigel Watson, had evolved a sensitive method of rhythmic communication, and the 1973 productions allowed for several scenes *à deux*.

The group views *Richard III* as their final piece developed from research into a blend of colorful flamboyance, declamatory speech, and strenuous physical movement. Though the Program Note indicates that the action should be viewed as taking place in the megalomaniacal mind of Richard, this is not evident in performance. The actors are dressed in differently colored tights, men's heads shaved into diabolic horns, and their faces heavily made up in red, black, and white, suggesting both clowns and devils. Most of the lines are spoken rapidly and loudly so that they are difficult to comprehend, but the highly physical actions make the power plays unmistakable. Without a controlling image, such as the web of *Hamlet, Richard III* is shaped by lights, color, and mirrors. The young princes' heads are enclosed in large cardboard diamonds, suggesting playing-card helplessness. The Richard-Anne courtship is highlighted in pantomime against a background of mirrors. The sinister alliance of Richard and Buckingham (Walsh and Watson) eliminates rival after rival—Hastings dies under blinding light—and they laugh in cadence to supply transition between scenes. In ripple-lighting Richard is crowned with an iron ring of spikes, and after the coronation his bare shoulders are covered by black leather pads inset with nails. He mocks while Buckingham dies before a mirror. In the final scene ghosts laugh at Richard, and the last battle trembles with St. Vitus' dance until Richard is seized with death's rictus.

The Triple Action *Lear* is called *Leir Blindi,* which is Icelandic for "blind clay"—a phrase that summarizes the Absurdist meaning of the production. Rumbelow's seed-image was a gigantic white beard from which the other characters would emerge. But before cutting the Shakespearean text for physicalization, Rumbelow visited Eugenio Barba of Odin Teatret, talked to him at length, and saw his *Min Fars Hus*. Deeply moved, Rumbelow decided that Triple Action Theatre work should be simplified and intensified. Though he had not yet read Jan Kott's "*King Lear* or *Endgame*," he and his group, out of their own development, were moving in a Beckettian direction.

The Triple Action Theatre productions use very simple sets and few props, but *Leir* is unique in doing without makeup or lighting. The set is a bare floor, and throughout the performance, except for matches and candles, the space retains a natural darkness. The audience enters the darkened playing area while the actors, wearing shapeless sackcloth garments, are bowed like monks over votary candles. When the audience is seated, the candles are blown out, and the darkness becomes a chaos of cacophonous noises. Slowly, very gradually, a breathing rhythm intrudes upon, then orders the sounds. A man is expelled onto the stage, falling in fetal position. He will prove to be Leir. Then Gloucester is born to the accompaniment of rhythmic panting. For each character there is an increase of light and volume of breath. With six actors on stage, a writhing Gloucester speaks the opening lines, Shakespeare's "These late eclipses of the sun and moon. . . ."

Leir's kingdom is not divided, but Leir, Kent, and Edmund-as-Servant enact Leir's humiliation at Cornwall's castle. When Kent is put in the stocks, two actors form the stocks. Kent is also the Fool, so that the relationship between Leir and his servant is multivalent. During the storm Leir rides on his servant's back. The storm itself is theatricalized through extraordinarily simple means. In the stage darkness four actors manipulate a large sackcloth to create a wind, while two other actors periodically light matches and throw them across the stage. Through these occasional glimmers of light, these uneven currents of air, Leir's words are sensed as well as heard: "Blow, winds, and crack your cheeks!"

The storm abates. Two candles flicker to reveal two men huddled together in what may be a hovel, but the candle's shadows give the effect of many men, as in the Kosintzev film of *Lear*. Gloucester and Edgar join the shivering pair, and Gloucester shrieks a non-Shakespearean: "I curse thee, Edmund." This dissolves into the Dover cliff scene, Edgar leading his blind father. Father and son use only about half dozen of Shakespeare's exchanges, and when Gloucester jumps off the cliff, he falls in slow motion, then slumps suddenly. There is a moment of absolute stillness before Edgar finds him. Leir wanders into this scene, and the two old men meet again as in Shakespeare. The reunion is followed by a choral chant, and a panning motion of candles highlights them tenderly before Leir expires. Edgar then reveals himself to Gloucester, who gropes toward him but collapses before he can embrace his son.

In a Resurrection motif both old men step forward, their lighted faces radiant, but when they retire with their candles, darkness again claims the stage, and we hear the cacophonous noises of the play's beginning. As at the beginning, the rhythm of breathing orders the chaos; two figures are expelled, no longer Leir and Gloucester, but Kent and Edgar. The implication is that the whole cycle will be played again, that man's life from birth to death is repeated in each generation, with its suffering, blind actions, and momentary joys.

Leir Blindi contrasts markedly with the almost baroque *Macbeth* played five years earlier, but Rumbelow had to explore his own means and way to this recent simplicity. The seven Shakespeare adaptations are stages along that way, but these are not the only productions of the company, which has remained fairly stable over the past three years. Their work on Shakespeare nevertheless shows that the Bard provides viable material for the Alternative Theater.

Chapter 7

Shaw *versus* Shakes

By describing the Shakespeare offshoots of Rumbelow, Shaw, Brecht, and Beckett in that order, I deliberately flout chronology, for several reasons. As in the chapters on the separate plays, there is no building through the years; one playwright's way with Shakespeare is not necessarily the heritage of the next generation. The last playwright/director chronologically, Steve Rumbelow, is not the climax of a progression through Shaw, Brecht, and Beckett, though these playwrights have influenced him. Moreover, by upsetting chronology, I can juxtapose chapters of marked contrast. Thus, Rumbelow's highly physicalized offshoots (whose scripts nevertheless limit themselves very largely to Shakespeare's own words) oppose Shaw's highly verbal offshoots (whose scripts are merely sprinkled with Shakespeare quotations). Between Shaw and Rumbelow, a theater revolution took place. At the turn of the twentieth century, Shaw wished to link life, literature, and theater more closely than was customary, whereas Rumbelow some seventy years later strains to separate theater from literature, only sometimes bringing it closer to life.

When Shaw began his revolution, he was twice the age of Rumbelow when he began his (*toute proportion gardée*!). And since Shaw's medium was more verbal, he polemicized his revolution with a wit that slashed at Victorian smugness. Against Shakespeare he waged a pitched battle, but it was only one battle in Shaw's war on stereotypes—stereotypical melodrama that bore no relation to the social problems of modern urban industrialism, stereotypical production that bore no relation to the way modern men and women actually behaved. Once Shaw's war was won, he was a genial victor, exacting no booty from the Bard.

"When I began to write," Shaw told his biographer, "William was a divinity and a bore. Now he is a fellow-creature."[1] Shaw implies that Shakespeare became a fellow-creature *because* Shaw began to write. And the implication is valid, for Shaw's Shakespeare criticism focused not on the Bard's life—in the Victorian manner—but on his craftsmanship. Shakespeare became a fellow-creature of *Shaw's,* in that he too wrote plays for a given audience under given circumstances.

George Bernard Shaw lived for nearly a century (1856-1950), and his Shakespeare comments span over half that lifetime. He read a paper on *Troilus and Cressida* in 1884, and he wrote a puppet play *Shakes Versus Shav* in 1949. Between those dates he reviewed many Shakespeare productions, and he prefaced many of his own plays with comments on Shakespeare.[2] A book-length study is needed on the subject of Shaw and Shakespeare, though several essays are available.[3] Most critics are agreed on the relative consistency of Shaw's attitude toward Shakespeare, based on a few axioms: Shakespeare's content was trivial, his philosophy pessimistic, his form often admirable, and his word-music unparalleled. The blend of trivial, pessimistic, admirable, unparalleled suggests a certain ambivalence about Shakespeare, however consistent that ambivalence may have been. When defending Shakespeare against actor-managers, Shaw exalted the text. As a champion of Ibsen's drama, Shaw lashed out against Shakespeare's ideas. In *Our Theatres in the Nineties* Shaw admitted: "I postulated as desirable a certain kind of play in which I was destined ten years later to make my mark (as I very well foreknew in the depth of my unconsciousness); and I brought everybody: authors, actors, managers, and all, to the one test: were they coming my way or staying in the old grooves?"[4] Ibsen was coming Shaw's way (indeed, leading the way), but Shakespeare was staying in the old grooves. Hence his barbs at the Bard. Both barbs and exaltation remain delightful reading, but I shall bypass that delight to focus on Shaw's

Shakespeare offshoots. These should, however, be viewed in the context of Shaw's reactions to Shakespeare through his long life.

"Shakespear was like mother's milk to me," Shaw told his biographer;[5] and he wrote that same biographer: "I go back to Shaigh, the third son of Shakespear's Macduff. Hence my talent for playwriting."[6] With nature and nurture derived from Shakespeare, Shaw claimed that by the age of ten he "had an extensive repertory of [Shakespeare] quotations years before it ever occurred to [him] to read a play through."[7] The Shakespeare quotations were memorized from *Cassell's Monthly Magazine,* where verses footnoted each lavish illustration of Shakespeare. Shaw graduated from these excerpts to Lamb's *Tales from Shakespeare,* and then to the plays themselves.

While he was living in Dublin, Shaw's mother initiated him into musical concerts; his father took him to the theater to see melodramas, farces, and Shakespeare's plays, usually interpreted by Barry Sullivan. Some seventy years later (in 1947) Shaw paid tribute to the Irish actor: "[Sullivan] kept Shakespear and the tradition of great acting alive in these islands whilst in fashionable London Shakespear 'spelt ruin' for theatre managers."[8]

During Shaw's lean years in "fashionable London," from the age of nineteen to forty-two, he maintained a devotion to Shakespeare. "When I was twenty," he wrote in a celebrated review of *Cymbeline,* "I knew everybody in Shakespear, from Hamlet to Abhorson, much more intimately than I knew my living contemporaries." (55) While in his twenties, Shaw became a member of the New Shakespeare Society, and in 1884, at thirty he prepared a paper on *Troilus and Cressida,* which has only recently been published.

In choosing as his subject *Troilus and Cressida,* Shaw shows his interest in a Shakespeare problem play—unusual for the time. He analyzes the play and situates it in Shakespeare's development. Often Shaw attributes to Shakespeare the opinions of his characters, and he tries to penetrate Shakespeare's mind: "When [Shakespeare] created Troilus, he was just young enough to enter into his feelings; just old enough to despise them; and not old enough to have reached that indulgent but imperfect memory of them which he had when he drew Ferdinand in the Tempest."[9]

Shaw reserves his main point for the end of his talk: "In finding out the vanity of the Trojan war, [Shakespeare] found out, like the writer of Ecclesiastes, the vanity of all things, and with this discovery he must have felt that instead of being at the end of his career he was only at the beginning of it. The access of power which ensued can only be imagined by considering carefully the great gap between Henry V and Hamlet. But Shakespeare's growth did not progress by leaps and bounds. There must be a bridge across that great gap. And the only bridge which fits it is Troilus and Cressida, with its cynical history at one end and pessimistic tragedy at the other."[10] Seven years later, in his 1891 *Quintessence of Ibsenism* Shaw holds to this view: "Shakespear, in *Hamlet*, made a drama of the self-questioning that came upon him when his intellect rose up in alarm, as well it might, against the vulgar optimism of his *Henry V*, and yet could mend it to no better purpose than by the equally vulgar pessimism of *Troilus and Cressida*."[11]

While a free-lance journalist in the 1880s, Shaw spent long hours in the Reading Room of the British Museum, where he met Tom Tyler, who was the first to suggest that Shakespeare's Dark Lady of the Sonnets was Mary Fitton. On this surmise Tyler based a lengthy introduction to a new edition of the *Sonnets*, which Shaw reviewed anonymously and favorably.

As art critic and music critic for *The World* and *The Star*, between 1888 and 1895, Shaw occasionally lashed out at the Bard, in accordance with his philosophy: "In this world if you do not say a thing in an irritating way, you may just as well not say it at all, since nobody will trouble themselves about anything that does not trouble them."[12] Shaw proceeded to trouble Victorian bardolators—bardolatry is his neologism—with his impudence toward the Bard.

It was above all during three years as drama critic of Frank Harris's *Saturday Review* that Shaw achieved a *succès de scandale*. Under the initials G.B.S., he reviewed nineteen Shakespeare productions. He sparked through London with such sentences as: "With the single exception of Homer, there is no eminent writer, not even Sir Walter Scott, whom I despise so entirely as I despise Shakespear when I measure my mind against his." (54) By and large, however, Shaw attacks Shakespeare less often than he defends him against actors and managers, championing him against the cuts of Henry Irving and the elaborations of Augustin Daly. Quite consistently, Shaw maintains that he loathes Shakespeare's philosophy though he loves his word-music.

Knowing many of the plays by heart, Shaw expresses a somewhat unusual taste for the time. Though he agrees with many predecessors that *Hamlet* is Shakespeare's best play, he pronounces *Coriolanus* his greatest comedy, *Julius Caesar* a political melodrama. He prefers the problem plays—*Troilus and Cressida, All's Well That Ends Well,* and *Measure for Measure*—to the popular comedies *As You Like It, Twelfth Night,* and *Much Ado About Nothing,* which he denigrates as potboilers. Shaw finds *Henry V* jingoistic, *Othello* melodramatic; he praises Verdi's *Falstaff* more highly than *The Merry Wives of Windsor*. He calls Richard III "the Prince of Punches," and he attacks *Cymbeline* as "stagey trash of the lowest melodramatic order."

After Shaw stopped reviewing in May, 1898, to devote himself to playwriting, he concerned himself less often with Shakespeare, though he was sometimes spurred by a particular performance—Forbes Robertson's Richard III in 1903, Mrs. Patrick Campbell's Lady Macbeth in 1921, John Barrymore's Hamlet in 1925. The latter occasioned a letter to the American actor: "I wish you would try it [*Hamlet* uncut] and concentrate on acting rather than on authorship, at which, believe me, Shakespear can write your head off."[13]

Sometimes Shaw's prefaces bristled with references to the Bard, as in the 1903 Epistle Dedicatory to *Man and Superman*; coupling Shakespeare and Dickens, Shaw denigrated both: "I read Dickens and Shakespear without shame or stint; but their pregnant observations and demonstrations of life are not co-ordinated into any philosophy or religion. . . . The truth is, the world was to Shakespear a great 'stage of fools' on which he was utterly bewildered. . . . He must be judged by those characters into which he puts what he knows of himself, his Hamlets and Macbeths and Lears and Prosperos. If these characters are agonizing in a void about factitious melodramatic murders and revenges and the like, whilst the comic characters walk with their feet on solid ground, vivid and amusing, you know that the author has much to shew and nothing to teach."[14] Perhaps this is what Shaw most resented about Shakespeare—that there was nothing he could learn for his own stagecraft, as he could from Ibsen.

When Shaw achieved a good measure of success, he mellowed toward the Bard, and one of his last attacks came in 1906, in answer to a request from the English translator of Tolstoy. The Russian novelist's attitude toward Shakespeare has been described in the chapter on *King Lear* offshoots; Shaw was unfamiliar with Tolstoy's essay but replied in similar spirit: "As you know, I have striven hard to open English eyes to the emptiness of Shakespeare's philosophy, to the superficiality and secondhandness of his morality, to his weakness and incoherence as a thinker, to his snobbery, his vulgar prejudices, his ignorance, his disqualifications of all sorts for the philosophic eminence claimed for him." Shaw proceeds to accuse Shakespeare of accepting a ready-made morality, instead of seeking a new one. He then warns Tolstoy that English critics will charge him with stigmatizing "our greatest poet as a liar, a thief, a forger, a murderer, an incendiary, a drunkard, a libertine, a fool, a madman, a coward, a vagabond, and even a man of questionable gentility. You must not be surprised or indignant at this: it is what is called 'dramatic criticism' in England and America."[15] It is hard to be angry at such irreverent wit; it is harder today to take it seriously.

Most of the slings and arrows of outrageous Shavian wit flew at the Bard at the turn of the twentieth century, and from that time too dates Shaw's most problematical Shakespeare offshoot. Problematical because I cannot prove that Shaw's *Caesar and Cleopatra*, completed in 1898, derives from Shakespeare's *Julius Caesar* and *Antony and Cleopatra*. Other Shakespeare offshoots are easily traceable to the Bard: lines in the dramatization of *Cashel Byron's Profession* in 1901, *The Dark Lady of the Sonnets* in 1910, burlesque scenes from *Macbeth* in 1916, *Cymbeline Refinished* in 1937, and *Shakes Versus Shav* in 1949.

The genesis of *Caesar and Cleopatra* is obscure. In March and again in May of 1897, Shaw saw Shakespeare's *Antony and Cleopatra* with Louis Calvert and Janet Achurch (in Manchester and in London). His review begins: "Shakespear is so much the word-musician that mere practical intelligence, no matter how well prompted by dramatic instinct, cannot enable anybody to understand his works or arrive at a right execution of them without the guidance of a fine ear." (15) No one would quarrel with this, but the main thrust of Shaw's critique is characterological: "Cleopatra says that the man who has seen her 'hath seen some majesty, and should know.' One conceives her as a trained professional queen, able to put on at will the deliberate artificial dignity which belongs to the technique of court life." (17) Shaw finds that Miss Achurch lacks such dignity, and he charges her with "drop[ping] from an Egyptian warrior queen into a naughty English *petite bourgeoise*, who carries off a little . . . greediness and a little voluptuousness by a very unheroic sort of prettiness. . . . When the bourgeoise turns into a wild cat, and literally snarls and growls menacingly at the bearer of the news of Antony's marriage with Octavia, she is at least more Cleopatra." (18) When Shaw came to create his sixteen-year-old Cleopatra, she became both English *petite bourgeoise* and Egyptian kitten who scratches to kill.

Summing up his critique of the principals, Shaw writes: "Here, then, we have Cleopatra tragic in her comedy, and Antony comedic in his tragedy. We have Cleopatra heroically incapable of flattery or flirtation, and Antony with a wealth of blarney in every twinkle of his eye and every fold of his chin." (20) In a bright spirit of contradiction, perhaps, Shaw makes his Cleopatra the obverse of this. It is impossible to know whether he specifically aimed at an anti-Shakespearean hero and heroine, but within a few months of seeing this Shakespeare production (on September 8, 1897) he wrote Ellen Terry that he was thinking of a play on Caesar and Cleopatra.

In October, 1897, Shaw reacted favorably to Forbes Robertson's interpretation of Hamlet and later said that he wrote the part of Caesar for him. In January, 1898, Shaw saw the Beerbohm Tree production of *Julius Caesar,* and his adverse reaction may have influenced his own conception of the Roman hero: "There is not a single sentence uttered by Shakespear's Julius Caesar that is, I will not say worthy of him, but even worthy of an average Tammany boss." (110)

This review elicited such indignant response that Shaw happily offered a rejoinder: "A fortnight ago I ventured to point out in these columns that Julius Caesar in Shakespear's play says nothing worthy, or even nearly worthy, of Julius Caesar. The number of humbugs who have pretended to be shocked by this absolutely incontrovertible remark has lowered my opinion of the human race. There are only two dignified courses open to those who disagree with me. One is to suffer in silence. The other, obviously, is to quote the passage which, in the opinion of the objectors, is worthy of Julius Caesar. The latter course, however, would involve reading the play; and they would almost as soon think of reading the Bible." (116)

A few months later, Shaw was hard at work on his own play. In spite of two operations on a foot-bone and marriage to Charlotte Payne-Townshend (on June 1, 1898) Shaw finished the play by the end of the year. Forbes Robertson did not play Caesar in the first performance (necessarily swift for copyright reasons); Mrs. Patrick Campbell circumvented Shaw's intention by playing a vixenish coquette. The play was published in 1901 as the second of *Three Plays for Puritans,* and for it Shaw wrote his well-known preface "Better Than Shakespear?" (Only in 1912 did he write the "Ra Prologue" usually played today.)

As one of the *Three Plays for Puritans, Caesar and Cleopatra* was intended by its self-styled Puritan author to be unromantic—Puritan being Shaw's antonym of Romantic. He eliminated from his play love and revenge, those staples of Romantic theater. And he did so by dramatizing Cleopatra's first meeting with Caesar, after which hero and heroine do *not* fall in love. Shakespeare's strong, handsome, sensual Antony is replaced by Shaw's keen, balding, intelligent Caesar. Shakespeare's unwithered and infinitely various Cleopatra is replaced by a charming and capricious adolescent. Instead of opposing the worlds of Rome and Egypt, Shaw sets his play in a picturesque and anachronistic Alexandria. Instead of driving toward the double tragedy, Shaw ends on a comic note that nevertheless predicts Shakespeare's tragedy; Caesar promises to send Cleopatra a handsome young hero, Mark Antony.

Caesar and Cleopatra is the only Shaw play he designated "A history," and critics have debated the veracity of his claim. Shaw drew up a long list of historical sources for the program of the copyright performance of the play, which he footnotes: "Many of these authorities have consulted their imaginations, more or less. The author has done the same."[16] Shakespeare is not among the authorities listed, but the Bard may nevertheless have been in his mind.

In his Preface, "Better Than Shakespear?" Shaw asserts: "It will be said that these remarks can bear no other construction than an offer of my Caesar to the public as an improvement on Shakespear's. And in fact that is their precise purport." (215) Toward that improvement Shaw enlisted the help of the nineteenth-century German historian, Theodor Mommsen. Other possible sources have been suggested, but it is improbable that Shaw needed them.[17] Shaw considered himself a spokesman for his age, and he felt that his age was better able than Shakespeare's to appreciate Caesar.

Shaw's Caesar is at once an "improvement" on Shakespeare's Caesar and a reaction against his Antony. Since Shakespeare's *Julius Caesar* is a tragedy of betrayal, Shaw insists that none of Caesar's followers will betray him, though he gives them ample opportunity. A general of strategy rather than strength, Shaw's Caesar is eager for the economic gains of his conquests.

At three points in his play Shaw might have been directly influenced by Shakespeare's Caesar, but twice he reacts against that portrait. Shakespeare's Cassius, belittling Caesar, describes saving his life while swimming, whereas Shaw's Caesar leads his forces in swimming to capture an island. Shakespeare's Caesar is a cultured man who condemns Cassius for loving neither plays nor music, whereas Shaw's Caesar is a practical man who captures a city by sacrificing the great library of Alexandria.

More important, however, is the similiarity between the two Caesars. When Artemidorus attempts to warn Shakespeare's Caesar—"O Caesar, read mine first; for mine's a suit / That touches Caesar nearer. Read it, great Caesar!" —Caesar seals his own doom when he replies: "What touches us ourself shall be last served." Shaw's Cleopatra tries to persuade Caesar to defend the palace against the mob aroused by the murder of Pothinus, warning him: "You will perish yourself." Rufio turns on her sharply: "Now, by great Jove, you filthy little Egyptian rat, that is the very word to make him walk out alone into the city and leave us here to be cut to pieces." Only Rufio's pleading (and Lucian's news) persuades Caesar to save them all, including himself. In both Shakespeare and Shaw, Caesar places his cause above himself, but Shakespeare's hero thereby brings about his own tragedy and Rome's. Shaw's hero, in contrast, staves off tragedy by shrewd pragmatism.

Consciously or unconsciously, Shaw wrote his "history" in reaction to (and against) Shakespeare's two Roman tragedies. *Caesar and Cleopatra* displays his most creative use of the Bard. His preface shows his awareness of being the Bard's competitor, and twentieth-century theaters have alternated productions of Shakespeare's *Antony and Cleopatra* with Shaw's *Caesar and Cleopatra,* most notably as played by Laurence Olivier and Vivien Leigh.

After the 1898 *Caesar and Cleopatra,* Shaw put Shakespeare to mere yeoman service in *The Admirable Bashville* of 1901. Because of imperfect copyright laws, dramatized versions of Shaw's novel *Cashel Byron's Profession* were reaping profits in the United States. In order to protect his rights, Shaw dramatized the novel within a week, saying that blank verse went faster than prose for his old-fashioned romantic plot. The footman Bashville loves and serves highborn Lydia Carew, who is also loved by the prizefighter, Cashel Byron. After five acts, the play ends with a double wedding—Lydia to Cashel, and Cashel's actress mother to a nobleman. Only the admirably self-effacing Bashville is unrewarded, but he will perhaps become a champion prizefighter.

As Shaw acknowledges in his Preface, the play is the kind of romantic comedy he inveighed against; perhaps for this reason it lacks wit, but some humor emerges from burlesquing Shakespeare. Cashel Byron spouts Shakespeare because his mother is an actress: "My earliest lesson was the player's speech / In Hamlet; and to this day I express myself / More like a mobled queen than like a man / Of flesh and blood. Well may your cousin sneer! / What's Hecuba to him or he to Hecuba? Before a crucial prizefight, he exclaims: "There's a divinity that shapes our ends / Rough hew them how we will. Give me the gloves." But the fair Lydia scorns his profession: "I say begone. Oh, tiger's heart / Wrapped in a young man's hide, canst thou not live / In love with Nature and at peace with Man?" With Lydia's persuasion and Cashel's own discovery of his noble birth, the hero finds that he can "live / In love with Nature and at peace with Man." He prophesies the championship of the admirable Bashville and retires from the ring.

Shaw also sprinkles Shakespeare quotations upon the prose play, *Doctor's Dilemma,* and in 1910 he puts Shakespeare himself into a playlet, to speak a few of his own lines. With *The Dark Lady of the Sonnets* Shaw hoped to raise money for a Shakespeare Memorial National Theatre. Perhaps because *The Dark Lady* was thin fare on a fund-raising occasion, Shaw wrote a sketch for the program note, entitled "A Dressing Room Secret." That secret mocked the main tenet of nineteenth-century Shakespeare criticism—his ability to create characters. And Shaw makes his point through a brief story set in a theater dressing-room. When Iago complains to the costumier that he doesn't look like a character, the latter agrees that he is not a character. A bust of Shakespeare affirms this iconoclastic opinion, admitting that the Bard has always botched his villains, particularly Iago. Lady Macbeth thereupon interrupts with complaints about her costume, and again the bust confesses that he couldn't convey her villainy because "she turned into my wife." The bust then describes how Falstaff grew beyond his control, so that he had to "make that old man perish miserably." Finally, the bust sneezes and falls to the floor in fragments.

As Shakespeare criticism, the sketch is negligible, but it was probably intended to set the anti-bardolatrous mood for Shaw's playlet in which Shakespeare is a character. The performance did not raise much money, and Frank Harris afterwards charged Shaw with plagiarizing his own play on the Dark Lady. When Shaw's play was published, it was preceded by a preface over twice the length of the play, which itself is called "a brief trifle." Shaw denies plagiarism "because Frank conceives Shakespear to have been a broken-hearted, melancholy, enormously sentimental person, whereas I am convinced that he was very like myself."[18] With this double-edged sword, Shaw admits both modern playwrights into the Order of the Bard.

In *The Dark Lady* the likeness of Shakespeare to Shaw rests upon a gift for witty retort. The character Shakespeare, played by Harley Granville-Barker, appropriated lines from the speech he heard around him—from a Beefeater, from Queen Elizabeth, and from the Dark Lady. For all that, however, most of words of Shaw's Shakespeare sound like Shaw rather than Shakespeare. Though the playlet has often been performed—most interestingly, perhaps, at the instigation of James Joyce in Zurich, 1918—it *is* "a brief trifle." But the Preface contains Shaw's most extended appreciation of Shakespeare: he wrote great parts for actors, he did not scorn the poorer classes (*pace* Crosby and Tolstoy), he was misunderstood in his own time, he was never self-pitying. Most significant is Shaw's admission that Shakespeare saw the world "if not exactly as Ibsen did (for it was not quite the same world), at least with much of Ibsen's power of penetrating its illusions and idolatries."[19] The preface shows Shaw's power, once above the battle, of penetrating the world's bardolatries to arrive at deeper appreciation of Shakespeare.

In 1916, while World War I was destroying Europe, Shaw struggled with his darkest play, *Heartbreak House*; he took refuge in comic relief by burlesquing scenes from *Macbeth*. His "Macbeth Skit" combines Scenes 5 and 7 of Act I of Shakespeare's tragedy. Lady Macbeth speaks the Shakespearean lines, but her husband replies in modern English prose: "Your language is beyond me, my dear girl. . . . I never met a woman who could talk over my head as you do."[20]

In March, 1916, Shaw recast Act V, Scene 8, Macbeth's

fight with Macduff, into a brief fictional sketch.[21] For most of the scene, Shaw concentrates on the mind of Macbeth, laboriously extrapolating from Shakespeare's action-packed lines. The burlesque notes are relatively faint until Macduff's fury focuses on Macbeth's faulty imagery, misusing "dam" for poultry. Macbeth's "strange discursiveness" blesses him with a swift death: "he felt his foe's teeth snap through his nose and his foe's dirk drive through his ribs." Shaw concludes with a mock-tribute to Shakespeare's villain-hero: "Macbeth was born before his time. Men call him a villain; but had the press existed in his day, a very trifling pecuniary sacrifice on his part would have made a hero of him. And, to do him justice, he was never stingy."

Like *The Dark Lady* Preface, burlesque indicates Shaw's new mellowness toward Shakespeare, and by 1920 Shaw even admitted debts to him. Called a Shakespeare-thief, he boasted of it: "Shakespear's crude Gratiano is Benedick, Berowne, and Mercutio, finally evolving through Jaques into Hamlet. He is also my Smilash, my Philanderer, my John Tanner. . . . I play the old game in the old way, on the old chessboard, with the old pieces, just as Shakespear did. And the amazing fact that I have ever been mistaken for anything else is due solely to the ignorance of literature prevalent among journalists who have no time for reading, and, indeed, no taste for it: an ignorance which enables managers to mutilate, travesty, and misrepresent Shakespear without detection or rebuke."[22] Shaw and Shakespeare tower together over journalists and managers.

Nevertheless, in 1937, Shaw altered *Cymbeline*'s last act in a way that might be described as mutilation, travesty, and misrepresentation. In 1896 his review of *Cymbeline* had established him as the Bardicide, but by 1937 his eminence was such that the Stratford Memorial Theatre would have played his revised end of *Cymbeline*, were it not for the abdication of King Edward VIII. Shaw's princes were prepared to follow the lead of the modern king, but the modern English theater was not prepared to tolerate this in a play.

In a preface, Shaw rationalizes his revision: "Cymbeline, though one of the finest of Shakespear's later plays now on the stage, goes to pieces in the last act" which is "a tedious string of unsurprising *dénouements* sugared with insincere sentimentality after a ludicrous stage battle." (62-63) Shaw claims to rewrite Act V "as Shakespear might have written it if he had been post-Ibsen and post-Shaw instead of post-Marlowe."[23] (64) One of Shaw's incidental remarks seems particularly apt in an examination of Shakespeare offshoots: "I shall not deprecate the most violent discussion as to the propriety of meddling with masterpieces. All I can say is that the temptation to do it, and sometimes the circumstances which demand it, are irresistible." (65) Who could ask for a better epigraph for his crime?

In revising *Cymbeline*'s Act V, Shaw went the way of many modern directors who omit the battle description, the Vision masque, and/or the lengthy recognitions. Shaw compresses Shakespeare's five scenes into one, and he reduces the number of lines to one-third, keeping eighty-nine of the original. Shakespeare's verse has the leisurely charm of improbable revelation that an audience nevertheless expects, but Shaw's verse is deliberately flat and businesslike, meaning no more than it says.

Shaw's single scene is set on "*A rocky defile,*" after the Roman-British battle. The Queen and her doctor disappear from Shaw's version, which opens on the defeat of the Romans. Posthumus enters and recites his soliloquy over the bloody handkerchief. Iachimo then enters and discloses his identity. Both men praise Imogen, whom they believe dead, whereupon they fight: "Let's cut each other's throats." (71) They are interrupted by the entrance of the Cymbeline family (still unknown to one another), and that entrance is followed by a recognition scene between Imogen and Posthumus, after which Iachimo clears her fair name. Continuing the "unsurprising *dénouements,*" Belarius reveals the princely identity of Imogen's brothers and Cymbeline's sons, who declare their lack of kingly ambition.

> *Guiderius*: I abdicate, and pass the throne to Polydore.
> *Arviragus*: Do you, by heavens? Thank you for nothing, brother.
> *Cymbeline*: I'm glad you're not ambitious. Seated monarchs do rarely love their heirs. Wisely, it seems. (76-77)

Iachimo then recommends Posthumus to Imogen, who reclaims her husband with something less than rapture: "I must go home and make the best of it / As other women must." (78) The reigning monarch, old Cymbeline, closes the act with Shakespeare's lines.

Shaw cuts and undercuts Shakespeare's sensational revelations—"Each one here, / It seems, is someone else." (77)—and he also dilutes the poetry into a metered prose. Not quite a burlesque, the new ending was taken so seriously in 1937 as to preclude production.

A dozen years later, in 1949, Shaw paid a final half-mocking tribute to Shakespeare in a ten-minute sketch, *Shakes Versus Shav*. The playlet opens on the rage of Shakes against an imposter Shav who "dares pretend / Here to reincarnate my very self." (276) They spar; first Shav is knocked down, then Shakes. When Shakes challenges: "Couldst write Macbeth?" Shav replies: "He has been bettered / By Walter Scott's Rob Roy." (277) Macbeth and Rob Roy appear, the latter cutting off the head of the former, who retires to Stratford with head under his arm. Shakes then challenges: "Where is thy Hamlet? Couldst thou write King Lear?" (278) And Shav answers that he has done so in *Heartbreak House*, from which we are shown an illuminated transparency.[24] Shakes accuses Shav of stealing his words, for he speaks Shakespearean pastiche in the sketch, and Shav pleads: "Peace, jealous Bard: / We are both mortal. For a moment suffer / My glimmering light to shine." (279) A light shines for a moment, and then Shakes concludes the sketch with the words of Macbeth: "Out, out, brief candle!" The playlet ends in darkness, and Shaw's long life ended fifteen months later.

In sheer number of years Shaw's attention to Shakespeare was remarkable, spanning well over half a century. He early familiarized himself with the plays, both in performance and—a rare accomplishment then as now—in full text. Shaw's knowledge of all Shakespeare's lines emboldened him to express unconventional opinions as a reviewer. He praised the problem plays at the expense of the romantic comedies; he stressed the pessimism rather than the nobility of the tragedies. He reviewed productions with the text in the eye of his mind, so that he inveighed against directors' cuts and actors' alterations. He followed nineteenth-century taste in considering *Hamlet* Shakespeare's greatest play, but he predicted twentieth-century taste in his high valuation of *King Lear.* He flouted Romantic tradition in showing scorn for Shakespeare's mind, but he followed that tradition in admiring Shakespeare's psychology. Once Shaw left reviewing for playwriting, he measured his dramaturgy against the Bard's, and he was happy to find that they were worthy rivals.

Archibald Henderson's biography calls Shaw *Man of the Century*. Mainly through the work of Martin Meisel,[25] however, Shaw looms large as a man of the *nineteenth* century, and for all his contradictory assertions, this is true, too, of his Shakespeare commentary. His favorite Shakespearean actor remained Barry Sullivan, whose melodramatic incantations can almost be heard through Shaw's praise. Shaw's favorite Shakespeare plays were those that seemed to harmonize with the plays of Ibsen, a late nineteenth-century playwright. Shaw's irresistible wit spanked Victorian bardolatry, but witty spankings—Harris, Chesterton, Wilde—were a turn-of-the-century sport. It was only after Shaw had persuaded a growing audience to reject romantic melodrama of the earlier nineteenth century in favor of realistic problem plays of the later nineteenth century that he was able to view Shakespeare appreciatively. His Preface to *The Dark Lady* deserves to be as well known as his "Better Than Shakespear?"

Rather than sustaining a Shaw-Shakespeare dialogue through the decades, Shaw first absorbed Shakespeare's word-music, later attained notoriety through impudent reviews of Shakespeare productions, then proclaimed triumph in self-declared competition with the Bard. Shaw did not interrogate Shakespeare so much as remold him into the image he needed—first into an anti-Ibsen and last into a proto-Shaw.

Shaw's tepid Shakespeare offshoots are far less vigorous than his Shakespeare commentary, often delivered in polemic heat. But even the ephemeral offshoots help us view Shakespeare as "a fellow-creature," though not so spirited a fellow-creature as emerges from Shaw's Prefaces. Only in *Caesar and Cleopatra* did Shaw challenge Shakespeare—perhaps unconsciously—and he did so by shifting the ground of combat; his Caesar is not faced with conspirators; his Cleopatra is too young for grand passion. A detailed study of Shaw's relationship with Shakespeare might be entitled "Reviews, Burlesques, and Reading between the Lines."

It would be sad not to close a Shaw chapter with a quotation from Shaw—which I therefore draw from the 1898 Preface to his first volume of (unpleasant) plays:

> It is only within the last few years that some of our younger actor-managers have been struck with the idea, quite novel in their profession, of performing Shakespear's plays as he wrote them, instead of using them as a cuckoo uses a sparrow's nest. In spite of the success of these experiments, the stage is still dominated by Garrick's conviction that the manager and actor must adapt Shakespear's plays to the modern

stage by a process which no doubt presents itself to the adapter's mind as one of masterly amelioration, but which must necessarily be mainly one of debasement and mutilation whenever, as occasionally happens, the adapter is inferior to the author.[26]

Chapter 8

Brecht Changes Shakespeare

> B: Ich denke, wir können Shakespeare ändern, wenn wir ihn ändern können.* (GW XVI, 879)

Bert Brecht, an admirer of Shaw, succinctly expressed a sentiment resembling the Shaw quotation that closed the last chapter. Both authors imply that a playwright has to be a giant to tread on Shakespeare's stage. Though Shaw's witty Shakespeareana still delights, his creative offshoots are pygmy ventures. There is a comparable disparity between Brecht's criticism of Shakespeare and his creative offshoots.

Brecht (1898-1956) wrote this chapter's opening quotation in 1955, a year before his death, while analyzing the opening scene of Shakespeare's *Coriolanus*. The words occur in a dialogue between four people, and their speaker is B, who often sounds like Brecht. Fittingly, since Brecht had been trying to change Shakespeare for some three decades.

In our earliest record of Brecht's response to Shakespeare, he turned his back on him. As twenty-five-year-old Dramaturg of the Munich Kammerspiel, he toyed briefly with adapting *Macbeth*, but instead he and collaborator Lion Feuchtwanger adapted Marlowe's *Edward II*. In sharpening Marlowe's tragedy about the downfall of a socially irresponsible king, Brecht made his first and last stage adaptation of a classic until his return to Germany after fifteen years of political exile. But this is not to say that he ignored Shakespeare during the interval.[1] In 1925 he expressed admiration for Erich Engel's class-oriented production of *Coriolanus*, which set him to thinking about what he was to

* B: I think we can change Shakespeare if we *can* change him.

call "epic theater." In 1927 and 1931 Brecht adapted *Macbeth* and *Hamlet* for the radio, but neither script is extant.

In 1931 Ludwig Berger of the Berlin Völksbühne asked him to arrange *Measure for Measure* for performance, and, after a few years, Brecht produced *Die Rundköpfe und die Spitzköpfe*. Before the triumph of Hitler, Brecht had an idea for a Julius Caesar play, which he discussed with Erwin Piscator. What he produced, however, was an unfinished novel, based mainly on Livy. In 1942, in Hollywood, he thought this suitable for a film but finally published it as a long story "Caesar und sein Legionär." (Actually, there are two stories taking place on the two days before Caesar's assassination; one story is told from Caesar's viewpoint and the other from his legionnaire's viewpoint.) Before Brecht came to America, while living in Stockholm, he drew upon Shakespeare for rehearsal scenes, and in 1941 the Bard contributed to his *aufhaltsame Aufstieg des Arturo Ui* and to an idea for a film about *Hamlet der Wiezenbörse*. In 1942 he thought about a modern Timon, "die Tragödie eines gigantischen Schimpfers . . . der sich der Verführung durch die Caritas nicht zu erwehren weiss und ruiniert wird."[2]* Back in Europe in 1948, he proposed a *Lear* project to his long-time co-worker, Casper Neher. He was intermittently occupied with *Coriolanus* during the 1950s.

From 1920 to 1956, as Brecht developed from a Bohemian cabaret-habitué to the most influential theaterman of the Western world, he commented on Shakespeare. In his book on Brecht and Shakespeare, Rodney Symington analyzes Brecht's references to nineteen Shakespeare plays. To no other author did Brecht pay such sustained homage, though the homage is often critical.

Several scholars have examined Brecht's response to Shakespeare. Helge Hultberg and Rodney Symington, who have had access to unpublished materials in the East Berlin Brecht Archives, have written overviews of the relation-

* the tragedy of a colossal badmouth . . . who doesn't know how to defend himself against the seduction of *Caritas* and is ruined.

ship; they come to rather different conclusions.[3] Hultberg finds Brecht hostile to Shakespeare because he desired to replace heroic dramaturgy with other models; Symington finds Brecht appreciative of various facets of Shakespearean staging. Though mediation between these scholars was not the purpose of the French theater critic Bernard Dort, he can help us understand their opposition: "Alors qu'il [Brecht] rejette l'idéologie shakespearienne et sa vision tragique de l'univers, Brecht accepte les formes du théâtre élisabéthain qui lui apparaissent, par référence à sa propre expérience et à ses propres préoccupations, comme une anticipation du théâtre épique."[4]* Agreeing with Dort, John Fuegi has analyzed Brecht's use of Elizabethan theater techniques in his major plays *Mother Courage, The Caucasian Chalk Circle*, and *Galileo*.[5] Brecht's epic dramaturgy drew upon the freedom of Elizabethan dramaturgy.

Drama is a unique genre in that its language is both spoken and written, but the critic usually confines his study to the written word. In Brecht's case such confinement is misleading, since he scorned the idea of dramatic finality. When he arrived at a workable version of a play, he published it as a *Versuch*, an experiment. After publication, he would make changes during rehearsal, through reasoned substitutions rather than frenzied inspiration. His *Versuche* were intended to undergo experimentation in the laboratory of theater rehearsal. But cut off as Brecht was from German theater during his fifteen years of exile, he nevertheless continued to write, revise, and, occasionally, produce. Thus it is hard to agree on a definitive text for some of Brecht's plays.

With Brecht's first extant Shakespeare offshoot, we fall into a textual puddle. When Ludwig Berger of the Berlin Volksbühne asked Brecht to compose a *Measure for Mea-*

* While Brecht rejects Shakespeare's ideology and his tragic vision of the universe, he accepts the forms of the Elizabethan theater, which, given his own experience and preoccupations, appear to him like an anticipation of epic theater.

sure promptbook in 1931, the playwright made notes for what would have been his second preparation of a classic for the stage (after *Edward II*). However, his own approach gradually drove Shakespeare undergound, and by 1933 he had written *Die Spitzköpfe und die Rundköpfe,* which he planned to publish as a *Versuch,* according to his habit. The play was in galley-proof when the Reichstag burned and Brecht fled from Germany. A refugee in Denmark, he revised the play for a 1936 production in Copenhagen. The two drafts have been published, and the earlier stages of his work have been studied in some detail by the East German scholar Werner Mittenzwei.[6]

In 1931, when Brecht meditated on Shakespeare's play, he noted: "Mass für Mass gilt für viele als das philosophischste aller Shakespearischen Werke, es ist zweifellos sein fortschrittlichstes. Er verlangt von den Hochgestellten, dass sie nicht nach anderem Masse messen, als sie selbst gemessen sein wollen. Und es zeigt sich, dass sie nicht von ihren Untertanen eine moralische Haltung verlangen dürfen, die sie selber nicht einnehmen."[7]* Brecht's analysis is reductive, but moral measure based on class distinction becomes Brecht's literal point of departure from Shakespeare; those in high places are contrasted with underlings not by Shakespeare but by Brecht.[8]

With this dichotomy at its center, Brecht's adaptation gradually became a transformation. He began with the Baudissin translation into which he wished to inject events of contemporary Germany, but he found it difficult to combine Shakespeare and Hitler. Mittenzwei, who has examined his many efforts, wrote: "selten hat er ein Werk so oft umgearbeitet wie dieses."[9] And Rodney Symington traces Brecht's changing conceptions through his changing titles:

* For many people *Measure for Measure* is valued as Shakespeare's most philosophical work; it is undoubtedly his most progressive. It demands that those in high places measure others by the same standards as they themselves would wish to be measured by. And it turns out that they should not demand from their underlings a moral code that they themselves do not embrace.

"Schon die Titel der verschiedenen Fassungen zeigen, wie Brecht seine Konzeption des Stückes geändert hat: so z. B. MASS FÜR MASS ODER DIE SALZSTEUER NACH SHAKESPEARE. . . ; in der nächsten Fassung wurde dieser Titel aus dem Manuskript gestrichen und Brecht schrieb: REICH UND REICH GESELLT SICH GERN NACH SHAKESPEARE. . . ; 1932 entfernte sich Brecht in der nächsten Fassung noch mehr von Shakespeare. DIE SPITZKÖPFE UND DIE RUNDKÖPFE (nach Motiven aus Shakespeares MASS FÜR MASS. . .); in der nächsten Fassung (Bühnenfassung) verbindet er zwei frühere Titel: DIE SPITZKÖPFE UND DIE RUNDKÖPFE ODER REICH UND REICH GESELLT SICH GERN. . .—jetzt fehlt allerdings jede Erwähnung Shakespeares."[10]*

Brecht's early outline, published by Mittenzwei, retains Shakespeare's act structure as well as many of his scenes, but the Duke's motivation has shifted from morality to economics: "Der Herzog übergibt angesichts eines allgemeinen Bankrotts seines Staates die Regierung dem Herrn von Angeler."[11]† The next scene shows divergent reactions of upper- and lower-class characters, but the main line of action still follows Shakespeare's main plot. Only a few scenes of this early plan were actually developed, when Brecht abandoned it for a new version that would more directly reflect events in contemporary Germany. He completed this draft and planned to publish it before production, as a *Versuch*, an experiment, which he introduced: "Das Schauspiel 'Die Spitzköpfe und die Rundköpfe' oder

* The very titles of the several versions show how Brecht changed the conception of the play, e.g. *Measure for Measure or the Salt-Tax, After Shakespeare*; in the following version this title was crossed out, and Brecht wrote *The Rich Stick Together, After Shakespeare*; in 1932 Brecht brought his next version even further from Shakespeare. *The Peakheads and the Roundheads* (on themes from Shakespeare's *Measure for Measure)*; in the next draft—for the stage—he joins two earlier titles, *The Peakheads and the Roundheads or The Rich Stick Together*, now indeed dropping any mention of Shakespeare.

† Faced with his country's general bankruptcy, the Duke gives the government to Mr. von Angelo.

'Reich und reich gesellt sich gern' ist der 17 der 'Versuche.' Dieses Schauspiel ist auf Grund von Besprechungen entstanden, welche eine Bühnenbearbeitung von Shakespeares 'Mass für Mass' bezweckten. Der Plan einer Erneuerung von 'Mass für Mass' wurde während der Arbeit fallen gelassen."* (GW III, Anmerkungen 1) Not completely abandoned, however, for Brecht retained Shakespeare's story of a substitute ruler who rigorously applies the letter of the law. With his eye on current events, he converted the substitute ruler into a Hitler-figure, about whom Brecht had been collecting anecdotes, caricatures, and newspaper clippings, which are now in the East Berlin Brecht Archives.

In keeping with his early note on Shakespeare's play, Brecht dramatized a double standard of morality toward those in high places and toward underlings. To this end he intruded a peasant into Shakespeare's demimonde, which he changed to the world of small businessmen who formed the bulk of Nazi supporters. The peasant, a man of independent initiative, resembles Kleist's Michael Kohlhaus, who demanded his rights so inflexibly that he became a monster. (Mittenzwei states that Brecht also drew upon the case of Jean Calas, who was executed in 1762 but subsequently defended by Voltaire from the charge of killing his son rather than seeing him convert to Catholicism.)

In the *Versuch* version Brecht divides his cast into Czuchs and Czichs, or Roundheads and Peakheads, which corresponds to Nazi division into Aryans and Jews. Brecht's main Roundheads are his Regent, the Adviser, the deputy Angelas, and the peasant family. The principal Peakheads are Shakespearean Isabella and her rich brother, but Brecht swells his cast with non-Shakespearean clergy, attorneys, and shopkeepers, as well as a peasant army that resists the government, on the verge of economic ruin.

* The play *The Peakheads and the Roundheads or The Rich Stick Together* is the 17th of the *Experiments.* This play originated in discussions having as their purpose a stage adaptation of Shakespeare's *Measure for Measure.* In the course of work, the plan of modernizing *Measure for Measure* was abandoned.

Transplanting the action to Lima, Peru, Brecht begins his *Versuch* with the appointment of a substitute ruler. The Regent, the largest landholder of Peru, will temporarily replace himself by Tomaso Angelas because he fears to impose a salt tax (which will hit the poor very hard) while a peasant army threatens the government. In order to defeat that army and force collection of the salt tax, the Regent permits Angelas to promulgate his racial theories. Angelas in power speaks in blank verse and Hitler's phrases. Modified from *Measure for Measure* is Angelas's condemnation of a Peakhead landlord for seducing the Roundhead daughter of a peasant. Late in Brecht's play the Peakhead's sister Isabella offers to purchase her brother's life with her chastity, though Angelas has indicated no desire for her. Instead of Shakespeare's bed-trick, Brecht substitutes a Roundhead whore for Isabella, and she is raped by soldiers under the orders of Angelas, who refuses to rescind the death-sentence against the Peakhead landlord. But the return of the Regent returns the *status quo ante*. The landlord will go free, and the united landlords will support the no longer threatened government. A slightly lower salt tax will be enforced. During a banquet at the end of the play, rebel peasants are hanged.

Brecht's Shakespeare offshoot presents the Roundhead-Peakhead distinction as a cloak for the rich-poor distinction. Brecht's Angelas is even more rigid than Shakespeare's Angelo, but he does not lust for Isabella. Though Brecht's Angelas is a tool of the landowners, he does not know that, and he believes his own racial demagogy. He does not accommodate his measures to the situation, condemning Peakheads whether the peasant army is winning or losing. The landlords, in contrast, back him only when they cannot control the peasants; once they no longer need him, they call for the return of the Regent. In his final ouster, Brecht's Angelas exhibits a certain dignity: "ich, der für Recht war gegen arm und reich / hab arm und reich jetzt gegen mich.

O Undank!"[12*] He pleads against mercy for the Peakhead landlord: "Lasst mich nicht gehn, umringt von spitzigen Köpfen / den Spitzkopf zu befrein! Der Mensch ist schuldig!"[13†] Only at the end does he accept the Regent's abrogation of the division between Peakheads and Roundheads.

I know of no production of Brecht's *Spitzköpfe und die Rundköpfe,* with its fifteen scenes and long tirades of blank verse whose parodic intention is not always clear. The play as a whole wavers uncertainly between parody of Nazism and celebration of revolt; its center shifts erratically between an unscrupulous peasant whose lack of class-consciousness leads to his downfall and a scrupulous deputy-ruler whose lack of class-consciousness leads to *his* downfall. Though *Die Spitzköpfe und die Rundköpfe* was in galley-proof when Brecht fled from Germany, it was not actually published (in German) during Brecht's lifetime.

As an exile in Denmark, Brecht revised the play for production in German at a small Copenhagen theater. The fifteen scenes were cut to eleven. The salt tax was dropped and the Sickle Revolutionary Army strengthened. The unscrupulous peasant, renamed Callas, became the central character, and the Angelo-figure was weakened. Of this version Mittenzwei writes: "[Brecht] nahm jetzt der Figur des Angelo alle Züge subjektiver Ehrlichkeit, idealistischen Wollens und ihre tragische Note und liess die Züge des skrupellosen Demagogen und brutalen Herrschers deutlich hervortreten."[14‡] Mittenzwei is stating intention rather than fact, however, for Brecht took away more than he emphasized. Angelo Iberin, as the Hitler-figure is finally called,

* I stood for right 'gainst poor and rich, and now / Both poor and rich oppose me—ungratefully.

† O do not make me, ringed by peaky heads, / Set the Peakhead free. The creature's guilty.

‡ Brecht now took away from the Angelo-figure all traits of subjective honesty, idealistic desire, with their tragic tone, and emphasized the traits of the unscrupulous demagogue and brutal ruler.

speaks in only three of the eleven scenes. Not so clearly the unscrupulous demagogue and brutal ruler that Mittenzwei describes, Angelo becomes a mere instrument whereby the landlords control the peasants. Though Brecht said that his *Versuch* had already abandoned *Measure for Measure,* his *Rundköpfe und die Spitzköpfe* departs further from its Shakespearean source, so that his recent English translator claims that "the original is hardly noticeable except to the informed."[15]

Once informed with *Measure for Measure,* however, one can hardly fail to notice the structural dependence of *Die Rundköpfe und die Spitzköpfe* on Shakespeare: a ruler appoints a substitute and disappears. The substitute enforces the letter of the law so that a man is condemned to death, but he can perhaps be saved through the sacrifice of his sister's chastity. A substitute replaces the sister as sex-object, and a second substitute replaces the brother as victim. The ruler returns and restores order.

This summary shows how Brecht follows Shakespeare's plot, but it fails to show how Brecht's lower-class plot reflects pointedly upon the economic immorality of "measure for measure." In effect, Shakespeare's main plot becomes Brecht's sub-plot, and the Callas family usurps center-stage. Moreover, Brecht's substitute ruler does not desire Isabella, his substitute bed-partner resembles Shakespeare's Juliet more than his Marianna, and the substitute victim is the play's main character. In sharpest contrast to Shakespeare, the Duke's final restoration of order is an *un*happy ending, by Brecht's moral measure.

In Brecht every substitution has its price, and it is money that finally distinguishes Shakespeare's dark comedy from what Brecht called a *Greuelmärchen* or horror tale. Brecht drops the smoldering virtue of Angelo and pushes him into the background. Brecht drops the pitiless virtue of Isabella and has her seek convent life as an ivory tower. Brecht drops the teasing voyeurism of "the old fantastical duke of dark corners" who makes Shakespeare's problem play so problematical. Instead, Brecht's horror tale rests on the fact that "Reich und Reich gesellt sich gern," in the untranslatable pun of his subtitle. The rich and the government are good companions because they are two sides of the same cold coin.

Die Rundköpfe und die Spitzköpfe is set in the land of Yahoo, a pejorative name taken from Swift's *Gulliver's Travels*. Since the country is threatened by peasant revolt, a Hindenberg type of Regent turns the government over to a Hitler type of Angelo Iberin, whose racial theories will hopefully destroy peasant class unity. When a Peakhead landlord, De Guzman, is accused of seducing the daughter of his Roundhead tenant, Callas, Angelo Iberin condemns him to death, and that sentence temporarily assuages peasant unrest. In the flush of Angelo's new regime, Callas appropriates two horses of the condemned landlord and thus becomes a local hero. In the meantime, De Guzman's sister Isabella, who wants to enter a convent, learns that she might be able to save her brother's life by yielding her virtue to the prison-commander, who never appears onstage. She comes to the brothel for lessons on behavior in bed, but the brothel mistress convinces Isabella to save her virtue and pay the Roundhead whore, Nanna, to take her place. Shortly afterward, De Guzman's lawyers persuade Callas to take his place at the gallows, though they assure him a pardon will be forthcoming. It comes, not from Iberin, but from the returned Regent. In the final scene, landlords and government officials share a sunrise banquet, while peasant rebels are prepared for execution. The returned Regent offers a toast to the *status quo*. And yet the last visual image is a mysterious red sickle painted on the whitewashed wall, so that Brecht's horror tale ends on a note of revolutionary hope.

In spite of the structural similarities to *Measure for Measure*, Brecht's *Rundköpfe und die Spitzköpfe* borrows only one scene from Shakespeare—the meeting of the condemned brother and the sister who has it in her power to save him. Shakespeare's Claudio-Isabella scene occurs in Act III, Scene 1, or about halfway through the play. Claudio first reacts indignantly to the idea of Isabella's sacrifice, but then he realizes: "Death is a fearful thing." Brooding on that fearful thing, he pleads:

> Sweet sister, let me live.
> What sin you do to save a brother's life,
> Nature dispenses with the deed so far
> That it becomes a virtue.

Isabella is outraged:

> O you beast,
> O faithless coward, O dishonest wretch!
> Wilt thou be made a man out of my vice?
> Is't not a kind of incest, to take life
> From thine own sister's shame? What should I think?
> Heaven shield my mother play'd my father fair,
> For such a warpèd slip of wilderness
> Ne'er issued from his blood. Take my defiance,
> Die, perish. Might but my bending down
> Reprieve thee from thy fate, it should proceed.
> I'll pray a thousand prayers for thy death,
> No word to save thee.

and even more harshly:

> Thy sin's not accidental, but a trade;
> Mercy to thee would prove itself a bawd,
> 'Tis best that thou diest quickly.

She is unaware that the Duke has been listening to their conversation.

Brecht's Isabella is very much aware of the presence of the De Guzman family lawyers, who do not believe that the death sentence will be implemented in the face of Sickle Army losses. But De Guzman himself is fearful, and he pleads with his sister:

> Kurz, das nackte Leben muss
> Gerettet sein und als das Höchste gelten.*
> (GW III, 1005)

As in Shakespeare, Isabella is horrified:

> Wie sprichst du, Bruder! Der mich ansprach, war
> Ein Mensch von tierischem Aussehn.†

With sudden and surprising self-criticism, her brother counters:

> Wie seh ich aus?
> Die Pächterstochter sah mich vielleicht tierisch.
> Natürlich ist's nicht leicht, doch meinst du, ihr
> War's leicht, mit mir zu sein? Sieh diesen Bauch.
> Und sie war jung wie du.
> *Isabella*: Und du hast es verlangt?
> *De Guzman*: Ich hab's verlangt.
> *Isabella*: Nun gut, so wisse, Bruder
> Wenn es von mir verlangt würd: ich tu's nicht.
> *De Guzman*: Ich hab's verlangt! Und er verlangt es auch!
> Und's ist auch nicht nur meine Sach'! 's ist deine!
> Wenn man mich hängt, zahlt dir kein Pächter Pacht
> Und deine Keuschheit liegt am freien Markt.
> Sie will bezahlt sein, und das liegt an dir!
> *Isabella*: Um alles bitt mich, Bruder, nicht un das!
> *De Guzman*: Stell dich nicht an! Und spiel hier nicht die Heilige!
> Mich hängen sie, und weder für die Hur
> Noch für die Betschwester will ich gehängt sein. Schluss!

* In brief, this life / Must be saved and valued as the highest good.

† What say'st thou, brother! The man accosting me / Looked like an animal.

Isabella: O Bruder, nur die Not macht dich so schlecht!
*Sie läuft weg.**

Shakespeare's imagery fastens sin to sex, intensifying the moral conflict within brother and sister. Brecht repeats the word *tierisch*, but this is a statement rather than an image of bestiality, while his imagery derives from economics. This is grist for his central theme but not for the credibility of the brother-sister conflict. Instead of sexual images, Brecht's brother and sister refer to sexual intercourse as *es* and *das*. The colloquial quality of these pronouns jars with the blank verse to give a parodic effect, and yet Brecht apparently wishes De Guzman's self-reproaches to be taken seriously. In this one residual scene from Shakespeare, Brecht seems uncertain of his tone.

More skillful is his writing in two different areas—the various social levels and the adventures of the peasant Callas. Brecht captures Shakespeare's vigor in the demimonde, and he also gives insights into groups of landlords, peasants, lawyers, religious figures, storm troopers. In swift exchanges Brecht makes these figures more credible than De Guzman and his sister Isabella. On the other hand, the amoral peasant Callas is more charming than horrifying. He takes his destiny into his own hands rather than join the

* How do I look? / Maybe the tenant's daughter saw in me / An animal. It's hard, but dost not think / She found it hard to be with me and my paunch? / She's young as thou.
Isabella: And didst thou then demand it?
De Guzman: I did demand it.
Isabella: Well, then, brother, know,
If it's demanded me, I won't perform it.
De Guzman: I did demand it! And he demands it too!
And it's not only my affair! It's thine!
If they hang me, no tenant pays thee rent,
And thy virginity can seek its price.
It must be paid, and that depends on thee!
Isabella: O brother, ask me anything but that!
De Guzman: Make no fuss and do not play at sainthood!
They're hanging me, and neither for a whore
Nor bigot will I stand a hanging. Period.
Isabella: O brother, desperation makes you bad.
She runs away.

rebellious peasants. A drunken Callas predicts the camaraderie of Brecht's drunken Puntila, and his pragmatism looks forward to the canny self-preservation of Brecht's masterly Azdak. But the theatrical charm of Callas contradicts Brecht's moral intention, which is to condemn an individual initiative that betrays its class. For Callas is the hero-villain of Brecht's play; if he (and, implicitly, his kind) had banded together with other peasants—Roundheads *and* Peakheads—a sickle would have decorated a victory flag instead of being surreptitiously scrawled on a wall.

Begun as a modernization of *Measure for Measure*, Brecht's *Rundköpfe und die Spitzköpfe* was completed in exile, when the Nazis were firmly in power, and World War II was only three years in the future. Between starting and finishing his play, Brecht left his homeland with no prospect of return. In the company of other German refugees, he propagandized to bring about Hitler's downfall. Though he may have drawn some comfort from his anti-Nazi activity, he must have been frustrated by his distance from theater. With the opportunity of an amateur production of *Die Rundköpfe und die Spitzköpfe*, he eagerly took part in rehearsals and attended to details of staging. He later published his Notes, where he first used the neologism *Verfremdung* (which I translate as "estrangement," rather than the usual "alienation," which has too many associations with the metaphysics of existentialism). More important than the word are the new techniques that Brecht delineated. At the very time when he was occupied with direct diatribes against the Nazis, he underlined the parable form of his play. To this end, he wrote a Prologue. Four of the seven actors take the stage in street clothes, but the Regent and Callas, each holding a pair of scales, are wearing costumes. The Regent balances two doll Roundheads against two Peakheads, and Callas balances two pieces of fine clothing against two rags. The scales thus show measure for *un*measure. The Regent explains that in times of crisis one skull may weigh more than another, whereas Callas explains that fine clothes always weigh more than rags. The Stage Manager then instructs the actors to don their heads and costumes. The Prologue breaks dramatic illusion before it is created, as with the device of a narrator.

In other notes on the play, Brecht mentions the importance of social *gestus* in building a role. He discusses self-contained scenes which he estranges through inscriptions, sound effects, actors' direct address to the audience. In the passionate brother-sister scene, he tries to avoid sympathy by drenching the principals in rain. Brecht also uses other estranging techniques—above all twelve songs. And in the two trial scenes the audience is expected to reverse the corrupt stage verdict.

Brecht's notes on the Angelo-figure indicate his continued problems:

> *Angelo Iberin* wurde mit keiner äusseren Hitlerähnlichkeit ausgestattet. Schon die Tatsache, dass er in gewisser Weise ein sehr idealisiertes Abbild eines Rassepropheten ist (was für die Parabel ausreicht), verbot dies auch dort, wo es die Polizei nicht verboten hätte. Jedoch wurden einigen Gesten, teilweise nach photographischem Material, verwendet. So sind die beiden Verbeugungen vor dem Vizekönig (in 1 und 11) ohne Einsicht in solches Material kaum zu bringen. Das Weinen des Iberin, der (in 11) ein grosses Taschentuch herauszog, als ihn die Rückkehr des Vizekönigs angezeigt wurde, erschien vielen als allzu naive Darstellung, es ist jedoch ein charakteristischer und verbürgter Zug solcher Figuren, ebenso die demagogische Verwertung der Erschöpfung nach den grossen Reden. Iberins Behandlung des Mikrophons (in 7) erlangte sogleich eine gewisse Berühmtheit, der Schauspieler zeigte die beinahe erotische Beziehung des Iberin zu diesem Instrument.* (GW XVII, 1085-1086)

* Angelo Iberin was not given any external Hitler-traits. Even if the police had not forbidden it, this would have been forbidden by

On the one hand, Brecht sees him as a parabolic figure, and on the other, as psychologically credible, and undermining both are such touches as the erotic orientation to the microphone and the Charlie Chaplin use of a giant handkerchief.

For all his care, Brecht's parable was not favorably received in Copenhagen in 1936. Anti-semitic groups picketed the small theater, and critics felt that the play's class and racial problems were no concern of Denmark. Brecht seems never to have undertaken another production, and the Berliner Ensemble has never produced it. It is very rarely played.[16]

The main failure of *Die Rundköpfe und die Spitzköpfe* is Brecht's appallingly simplistic view of Nazi persecution of the Jews. Elaborate pointed masks endow the whole problem with an exotic quaintness. This may be appropriate for tenth-century Caucasians, but it is insensitive at a time when the real Peakheads were crowded into concentration camps, with their refined tortures.

Politically skeletal, the play is theatrically overloaded. Brecht wallows in estrangement techniques among which he would later learn to select the most suitable to the particular play. These new procedures burden an already heavy plot—the *Measure for Measure* story of substitutions, the *Michael Kohlhaus* story of an independent peasant, a country in the throes of civil war, a street of small shopkeepers, hypocrisy of religious orders, corruption of law courts, and the alliance of *Reich* and *Reich,* realm and riches. There are too many minor characters and too few in-

---

the fact that he is in some sense a very idealized portrait of a racial prophet (which suffices for the parable). Nevertheless, several gestures were borrowed in part from photographic documentation. Without insight into this, the two bows before the Regent (in Scenes 1 and 11) are scarcely conceivable. It seemed to many an overly naive presentation when Iberin was notified of the Regent's return and he cried and pulled out a large handkerchief; but this is a characteristic and authenticated feature of such figures, as well as their demagogic display of exhaustion after big speeches. Iberin's handling of the microphone (in Scene 7) immediately attained a certain notoriety; the actor showed Iberin's almost erotic attraction to this instrument.

sights into major characters. Above all, Brecht's language is sluggish, rarely achieving his distinctive salty economy. Yet the play merits this lengthy attention because it illustrates how Shakespeare can lead a major playwright astray. Brecht read into Shakespeare the class basis for meting out justice, and he proceeded to dramatize this by departing from Shakespeare. Given his thematic interest, he would have done better to drop Shakespeare completely, as he apparently thought he did. But the central brother-sister scene remains, serving neither his theme nor his transformed plot. The second version of *Die Rundköpfe* is less sprawling than the *Versuch,* and from its production Brecht was able to refine his estrangement techniques for his great parable plays.

In 1932, when Brecht began to adapt *Measure for Measure,* he tried to annihilate Hitler through stage ridicule. Though he believed that he abandoned Shakespeare in the process, the Bard occasionally came to his mind in these early years of exile. In 1934, Brecht implicitly compared himself to Shakespeare in a conversation reported by the critic Walter Benjamin: "Von meinem Standort kann ich nicht zugeben, dass Shakespeare grundsätzlich eine grössere Begabung gewesen sei. Aber auf Vorrate hätte er auch nicht schreiben können. Er hat übrigens seine Figuren vor sich gehabt. Die Leute, die er dargestellt hat, liefen herum. Mit knapper Not hat er aus ihrem Verhalten einige Züge herausgegriffen; viele gleich wichtige hat er fortgelassen."[17]*

In 1936, when *Die Rundköpfe und die Spitzköpfe* was performed, Brecht could still view Hitler as a temporary evil, but each successive year eroded that view. World War II broke out in 1939, but Brecht continued to write—sketches, plays, theater theory. In the very year of the war,

* In my situation I cannot admit that Shakespeare is basically a greater talent. He couldn't write from cold storage either. After all, he had his figures before him. The people he presented were all around him. With great difficulty he drew several traits from their behavior; he dropped many that were just as important.

Brecht worked at his Messingkauf dialogues while his wife, Helene Weigel, taught acting at a Stockholm theater school. For her use, Brecht composed actors' exercises based on *Macbeth, Hamlet, Maria Stuart, Romeo and Juliet,* a dialogue between Homer and Hesiod, and on the German round song that Beckett was to translate into French and English to open the second act of *Waiting for Godot.* In the chapters on *Macbeth* and *Hamlet,* those scenes were examined, teaching the actor estrangement from a heroic role. As set forth in Diderot's *Paradox sur le Comédien* the actor plays better when he is able to view his role critically. Cumulatively, however, the actions of the character acquire complexity; as Walter Sokel explains it:

> Primacy belongs to character in so far as the actor always has to show that the character could always have acted differently than he actually did. He transcends the actual plot by virtue of his conceivable possibilities, which have been narrowed and crystallized into the acts he has chosen. The primacy of the character's action, on the other hand, rests on the fact that it is the actions that make the plot. Thus, in a sense, for Brecht, character becomes the victim of plot. For the plot which is the product of his choices is also the judgment on him.[18]

This is the *raison d'être* of Brecht's brief rehearsal scenes. As was noted earlier, Brecht's *Macbeth* scene parallels Shakespeare's scene of Duncan's murder, the key scene of the plot in which the protagonist chooses the evil that will both define and judge him. Through the distance obtained by the parallel (involving different but analogous characters), the actor (and through him the performance audience) criticizes his role.

Brecht's *Hamlet* and *Romeo and Juliet* rehearsal scenes, however, suggest how different the heroes' actions might have been; the actual plot therefore implies an adverse judgment on their conduct. So that each of the young lovers may be judged separately, Brecht writes two rehearsal scenes. In the first, Romeo dispossesses his old tenant-farmer so as to give the land to Rosalind as a parting gift. The old man pleads his need, but Romeo can think only of his new passion, whose decorum demands a parting gift for the old. When the old man protests that he is being treated like an animal, Romeo calls him an animal and drives him out, but he will return in the background of the balcony scene.

In Juliet's scene she seems to treat her maid like an equal, as both girls speak of their new loves. But the maid has a rival, and if she doesn't meet her lover that very night, she may lose him. Juliet obligingly gives her the night off—until she sees Romeo sneak into her garden. Then she needs the maid to conceal her own tryst; if the maid makes noise in her room, the watchman below will not suspect that Juliet has left the room for the balcony. When the hour strikes for the lovers' meeting of the maid, she faints.

It is often said that the nobility of Shakespeare's protagonists leads to their downfall, but Brecht shows that the young lovers are ignoble in their selfish passions. These scenes, which Brecht called *Zwischenszene,* were to be rehearsed between scenes 1 and 2 of Act II of *Romeo and Juliet.* Brecht's scenes show that Romeo and Juliet are alike in their self-indulgence, disregarding the pain they inflict on their social inferiors. Actors rehearsing these "between-scenes" would necessarily take a critical attitude toward the tragic lovers.

Brecht was after larger game in his own plays, which he continued to write, though without access to a theater. World War II continued to rage in Europe, and America seemed the only safe place for him. While waiting in Finland for a visa, Brecht wrote a play on the rise of Nazism, which he had apparently been mulling over for years, since Walter Benjamin's Journal for September 27, 1934, mentions

Brecht's plan for "Ui eine Satire auf Hitler im Stil der Historiographen der Renaissance." By 1941, the style had changed to a parody of heroic drama, but Hitler remained at the center of *Der aufhaltsame Aufstieg des Arturo Ui.* Its Chicago setting may have sprung from Brecht's hope for production in America, but the play was neither produced nor published during Brecht's lifetime—in America or elsewhere.

Hitler and not Shakespeare was the seed of *Ui,* but Shakespeare soon lent support to it. For planned publication, Brecht wrote a note: " 'Der aufhaltsame Aufstieg des Arturo Ui,' 1941 in Finnland geschrieben, ist ein Versuch, der kapitalistischen Welt den Aufstieg Hitlers dadurch zu erklären, dass er in ein ihr vertrautes Milieu versetzt wurde. Die Verssprache macht das Heldentum messbar."* (GW IV, Anmerkungen 3) The last cryptic sentence seems to imply that the aura of heroism is as hypocritically anachronistic as heroic blank verse. But Brecht's notes testify to his difficulty in writing metrically. He tried to rationalize its roughness as suitable to these rough heroes but his friend and co-worker Margarete Steffin felt that the *Verfremdungseffekt* would be lost unless the verse scanned. His reaction was an even more elaboate rationalization of blank verse that remained rough.

Like Holz in "Papa Hamlet," Brecht mocked a heroic verse tradition, but the former set it against impoverished modernity whereas Brecht set it against capitalist villainy, or rather he cloaked capitalist villainy in pseudo-heroic blank verse.

The sixteen-scene play describes sixteen steps of Ui's rise to power, and Brecht's notes show how carefully he based his gangster scenes on events between 1929 and 1938 when,

* *The Resistible Rise of Arturo Ui,* written in Finland in 1941, is an effort to explain to the capitalist world Hitler's rise, by transferring him to a milieu familiar to that world. The verse renders heroism measurable.

after the murder of Chancellor Dollfuss of Austria, Hitler received ninety-eight per cent of the Austrian vote. Earlier, Brecht had problems in theatricalizing Hitler as both powerful dictator and capitalist pawn, but Arturo Ui is a more common phenomenon, a perfectly legal gangster. He himself understands: "Vor Polizei / Und Richter muss ich erst geschützt sein, eh / Ich andre schützen kann. 's geht nur von oben."* (GW IV, 1741)

It is not clear whether Brecht intended any surface resemblance between Ui and Hitler. But it is clear that Brecht conceived of a mythical Chicago as the ideal locale for his "ignobled" hero. He had already used that milieu in his 1924 *Im Dickicht der Städte,* 1929 *Happy End,* and 1931 *Die Heilige Johanna der Schlachthöfe,* and its resonances are audible in *Mahagonny.* In those plays, there is, as Martin Esslin suggests, a covert sympathy for the free-wheeling lawlessness that contrasts with the surface legality of European bourgeois life.[19]

Like *Die Rundköpfe und die Spitzköpfe, Arturo Ui* opens with an estrangement device, an Announcer who introduces four major characters—Dogsborough, Givola, Giri, and Arturo Ui. The last of these elicits a Shakespearean comparison:

> Wem fällt da nicht Richard der Dritte ein?
> Seit den Zeiten der rotem und weissen Rose
> Sah man nicht mehr so grosse
> Fulminante und blutige Schlächterein!† (GW IV, 1722)

But the figure onstage is maudlin and inarticulate, lacking Richard's high brilliant style.

* I need / Protection from policemen, yes, and judges / Before I can protect. Protection comes / Only from the top.

† Who won't think of Richard three?
In Wars of Roses white
And red we last did see such great
Bloody fulminating butchery.

Like *Die Rundköpfe und die Spitzköpfe, Arturo Ui* is set at a time of national crisis, and as in the earlier play, a capitalist lackey is appointed to deal with the crisis, but only in *Ui* does the lackey become the dictator. Arturo Ui, "ein Sohn der Bronx," steps to power exactly as Adolf Hitler, Austrian paperhanger, rose to power. Unlike that of the first Shakespeare offshoot, where the basic structure resembled *Measure for Measure,* the structure of *Ui* is governed by actual events, and the Shakespearean borrowings are textual.

The first extended reminiscence derives from *Julius Caesar,* and it is important to Brecht's meaning. Though the gangster Ui acquires power by his strong-arm tactics, he wants respect and respectability as well. To this end he takes lessons from a ragged Shakespearean actor on how to walk, stand, sit, and finally speak, like a stage hero. In the Berliner Ensemble production, Ekkehard Schall literally grew and increased his power of projection under the tutelage of the Shakespearean actor, whose lesson terminates with Mark Antony's funeral oration in the Schlegel translation. But when Ui orates, Brecht makes insidious changes that mock the hero-dictator—especially the substitution of the word *tyrannisch* for the often-repeated "ambitious." Shakespeare's final line is "What cause withholds you then to mourn for him?" But Ui omits "for him," so that the line becomes: "Was für ein Grund hält euch zurück zu trauern?" (GW IV, 1773) Mourning will be pervasive.

In the next scene Ui harangues a crowd with a long speech full of hypocritical noble intentions. He has learned his lesson and will deliver several orations, always imitating an outworn rhetoric, and implicitly marking someone's funeral.

Brecht's best-known Shakespeare parody is his Scene 13, in which Ui woos Betty Dullfeet over the coffin of her husband whom he has murdered, as Richard III wooed Lady Anne over the coffin of *her* husband whom he had murdered. But to appreciate the full flavor of this scene, one also has to know Goethe's *Faust I*, which is parodied in Brecht's Scene 12. Goethe's Mephistopheles woos Martha while Faust seduces Gretchen in a garden. Brecht's quadrille takes place not in a garden but a gangster's flowershop, and the two couples are the brawny gangster Givola and boy-sized Dullfeet, Ui and Mrs. Dullfeet. In stichomythic rhymes, the two gangsters make veiled threats to Mr. and Mrs. Dullfeet. As Ignatius Dullfeet pales with terror, Ui and his wife arrive at an entente cordiale; Betty Dullfeet intones a platitude: "Freundschaften, die in Wind und Wetter reifen," and Ui, placing his hands on her shoulders, replies: "Ich liebe Frauen, welche schnell begreifen."* (GW IV, 1818) Ui closes the scene with a curt unstated order to his henchman: "Mir missfällt der Mann." [Dullfeet]

The next scene opens on Dullfeet's coffin. Though Betty Dullfeet spurns Ui's offer of "protection" and condemns his crimes, we cannot quite forget his hands on her shoulders in the previous scene. By the play's final scene, when Ui is wooing the voters of Cicero-Austria, she is speaking in his behalf.

In the interim—Scene 14—a ghost of Roma-Röhm appears to Ui, and critics have traced it variously to *Macbeth, Julius Caesar*, or *Richard III*. However, Brecht's Ghost preaches at some length, as though he, too, had taken lessons from an old Shakespearean actor. The Ghost frightens Ui only momentarily, and by the last scene he gains control of Cicero, as of Chicago. His final oration to the crowd reels off a list of other American cities begging for "protection." It is *their* funeral oration that the tyrant Ui finally delivers.

Brecht wrote *Der aufhaltsame Aufstieg des Arturo Ui* in a few weeks in 1941, then did not touch it again during his six years in America, or on first returning to Europe. Shortly before his death, he revised it for publication and eventual production; at that time he made notes insisting that

* Friendships that through storm and wind can grow.
I like a lady who is quick to know.

the gangsters must be ridiculed in order to rob them of the romantic aura of great criminals. In 1958 the Berliner Ensemble tried to carry out his wishes. The ensemble acting and the impeccably relentless tempo have been widely admired, but the tone is problematical in spite of Brecht's note on his comic parable.

More pointedly than in his *Heilige Johanna,* Brecht uses a pseudo-noble style to show up ignoble characters. His moral condemnation is implicit (and occasionally explicit) against the gangsters of a mythical Chicago that is meant to mirror the capitalist world. But comic or not, the villain hero is always a moral problem. Shakespeare's Richard III and Macbeth usually elicit a certain sympathy that tends to undercut moral condemnation by the audience. In playing Ui for the Berliner Ensemble, Ekkehard Schall displayed a not unlovable clumsiness reminiscent of Charlie Chaplin's Dictator (who was also not unlovable), so that it was hard to summon horror at his rise. Laughter sounded in both the East Berlin Theater am Schiffbauerdamm and the Guthrie Theater production in New York City. Brecht saw no incompatibility between such laughter and moral condemnation. He wished to destroy the Nazi hagiography through ridicule, and he wished moral condemnation of their crimes. Medieval audiences, scholars tell us, were at once amused and terrorized by stage devils. If this is true, can modern audiences also blend their reactions? Can criminals elicit moral condemnation when they appear in comic guise? The classical theory of comedy holds that laughter can correct *faults,* but the faults of Brecht's comic figures are ruthless murders.

In both his Shakespeare transformations, *Die Rundköpfe und die Spitzköpfe* and *Der aufhaltsame Aufstieg des Arturo Ui,* Brecht hoped to deflate fascism with the barb of ridicule, but his first Hitler-figure took on such heroic qualities that his dramatic role had to be severely pruned. The second Hitler-figure is a caricature gangster arousing affectionate laughter rather than horror. In Brecht's third major Shakespeare offshoot, *Coriolanus,* he again treated a figure whose heroic resonance he wished to destroy, and this time he avoided comedy.

After fifteen years of exile, Brecht returned to Germany in 1948. On a liberal subsidy from the East German government, Brecht helped found the Berliner Ensemble. Much preoccupied with practical theater problems—among which was his desire to establish a viable classical repertory—Brecht limited his playwriting to adaptations. In April, 1951, he started to translate Shakespeare's *Troilus and Cressida* but soon shifted to *Coriolanus,* on which he worked sporadically until December, 1952, leaving it almost complete.

Unlike *Die Rundköpfe* and *Ui, Coriolanus* begins without estrangement. But as at the beginning of those two plots, a country is in a state of crisis, and a strong man rises to quell unrest. In *Die Rundköpfe* the strong man was a controllable temporary expedient; in *Ui* he was an uncontrollable gangster; in *Coriolanus* he is self-indulgently but efficiently representative of the patrician warrior class.

Brecht's purpose in changing *Coriolanus* was to convert a tragedy of pride into a tragedy of illusion, since Coriolanus believes himself to be indispensable. His self-delusion is fostered by success at the battle of Corioli, but it is shattered by his failure in the battle for Rome—failure of military prowess and failure of nerve. Against the hero's self-delusion Brecht pits the self-reliance of the oppressed Plebeians. All his changes bear upon this antithesis: elimination of details that show Coriolanus as other than an efficient fighting-machine; addition of details that present the Plebeians as wronged, aware, and finally brave and united.

Brecht's changes in Shakespeare's opening scene predict those throughout the play. In Shakespeare we first hear a Plebeian opinion of the hero: "First, you know Caius Marcius is chief enemy to the people." Brecht underlines this: "Cajus Marcius wird uns mit Waffengewalt entgegentreten.

Werdet ihr davonlaufen oder werdet ihr kämpfen?"* Another Plebeian replies: "Wir werden ihn totschlagen.—Er ist der Hauptfeind des Volkes."† (GW VI, 2397) The enmity is instantly concretized, and its cause is revealed as the high price of food, which Coriolanus will not alleviate. The Plebeians complain about their grievances rather than Coriolanus, but they do not whine. They display more humor and more realism than in Shakespeare, for one of Brecht's great strengths as a dramatist is his ability to sketch a popular milieu in a few remarks—the shopkeepers in *Die Rundköpfe,* the vegetable merchants in *Ui,* the Plebeian craftsmen of *Coriolanus.*

When Menenius enters, Shakespeare's Plebeians tease him about being long-winded, and Brecht increases the teasing. The famous belly parable proves his long wind but also his Patrician allegiance, since it conceals the entrance of Caius Marcius escorted by armed men, and it calms their outrage. In Brecht as in Shakespeare, Coriolanus gratuitously insults the Plebs. In Brecht as in Shakespeare, Coriolanus mocks their complaints about hunger and unjust distribution of food. Shakespeare's Coriolanus announces that the Plebs have been awarded five tribunes, but Brecht's Coriolanus receives this news by private messenger, and the two—not five—tribunes enter almost immediately with the senators who announce the new war.

Perhaps the most telling change in the first scene occurs at its end. The people's tribunes, Brutus and Sicinius, speak more briefly than in Shakespeare, but they speak like responsible representatives, worried about their people. Shakespeare's Brutus seems personally envious of Coriolanus, whereas Brecht's is thinking of his people's welfare:

> Half all Cominius' honors are to Marcius,
> Though Marcius earned them not; and all his faults

* Caius Marcius will meet us with force of arms. Will you run away or will you fight?

† We'll knock him dead; he's the people's main enemy.

To Marcius shall be honors, though indeed
In aught he merit not.

Solch eines Mannes Schwert
Ist mehr, als seine Laster schaden, wert.*

Chapter One of this book indicated Brecht's structural changes to *Coriolanus*, so that commentary may now be confined to textual variants. In Brecht's Act II, Scene 3, after the victory at Corioli, Coriolanus sues for votes. Mockingly, he asks the common people their trades, and when one citizen says that he is a gardener, Coriolanus asks what his trade teaches in statecraft. The gardener replies with a different lesson from the belly parable's: common vegetables, and not a royal rose, make for a healthy garden. But the lesson is lost on Coriolanus.

Only in a Brechtian song does Coriolanus reveal his attitude more candidly and with more insight than in his dialogue:

Hier seht ihr Cajus Marcius Coriolan
Bei dem Versuch, sich Hinz und Kunz zu nahn.
Er hat römische Adler zu verkaufen
(Bitte die lieben Kleinen, sich nicht um die Federn zu raufen!)
Ich bitte die Herrn, von Amtes wegen
Die Finger in meine Wunden zu legen.
Gegen ein kleines Almosen bin ich bereit
Zu jedwedem Dienst. Tretet heran! Letzte
Gelegenheit!† (2441-2442)

* The sword of such a man / Has greater worth than his defects can harm.

† Here stands C. Marcius Coriolan
Trying to please the common man
He's selling the Roman eagle here
(Don't fight over the feathers, children dear!)
Gentlemen, my wounds. These. And these.

When Coriolanus refuses to give Volscian corn to the Plebeians, they turn against him and banish him from Rome. He joins Aufidius in warring against Rome, but the Plebeians never regret their expulsion. On the contrary, they arm against him, with Cominius agreeing to give them weapons. When the Patrician women wish to sue for peace, Sicinius does not trust them and sends a Plebeian woman with them.

The reunion of the Coriolanus family is Brecht's main change in Shakespeare. Though mother and wife threaten suicide if he sacks Rome, their plea is very different from that in Shakespeare, for Volumnia reports on a different Rome:

Unersetzlich
Bist du nicht mehr, nur noch die tödliche
Gefahr für alle. Wart nicht auf den Rauch
Der Unterwerfung! Wenn du Rauch sehn wirst
Dann aus den Schmieden steigend, die jetzt Schwerter
Wider dich schmieden, der dem eignen Volk den
Fuss auf den Nacken setzen will und dafür
Sich seinem Feinde unterwirft. Wir aber
Der Glanz und Adel Roms
Muss nun die Rettung vor den Volskern
Dem Pöbel danken oder deinen Volskern
Die Rettung vor dem Pöbel!* (2492)

Look closely. Touch them if you please.
I'll serve you for a penny; I'll dance
Attendance. Gather round! Step up! Last chance!

* You are no longer indispensable
Merely a deadly threat to all. Don't expect
To see submissive smoke. If you see smoke
It will be rising from the smithies forging
Weapons to fight you who, to subject your
Own people, have submitted to your enemy.
And we, the proud nobility of Rome
Must owe the rabble our salvation from the
Volscians, or owe the Volscians our
Salvation from the rabble.

His mother is in an untenable position, and she places her son in an untenable position. It is not even clear whether he yields to her pleading or to her picture of a Rome that might very well defeat him.

The new final scene comes from Plutarch rather than Shakespeare. But Brecht is no more hesitant about twisting the works of the Greek than of the Elizabethan. In Plutarch the Roman Senate grants that the family of Coriolanus wear mourning for ten months, the maximum period permitted by law. Brecht has his Brutus reject the family request to wear mourning, and he thereby ejects Coriolanus and his class from the new people's republic of Rome. Brecht's final scene punctuates the uselessness of a military technician in a peace-loving community.

Though Brecht did not live to direct his *Coriolan*, he apparently used Shakespeare's version "as something of a training-ground for the younger dramaturgs and assistant directors. . . . They were divided into groups of two or three, says Peter Palitzsch, and set to analyze the story, check the translation, and suggest cuts and changes."[20] Brecht himself provides an insight into this work in a dialogue that he wrote in 1954 about the first scene of Shakespeare's *Coriolanus*. That dialogue takes about twice the number of pages as the scene itself.

The four speakers bear the initials B for Brecht, P for director Peter Palitzsch, R for dramaturg Käthe Rülicke, and W for director Manfred Wekwerth (who later was one of the directors of Brecht's *Coriolan*). In their examination of the opening scene of Shakespeare's tragedy, the four Marxists draw upon Plutarch and Livy, as did Shakespeare. The modern theatermen are concerned about the Plebeians, who have traditionally been shown as comic and cowardly in the bourgeois theater. In contrast, this group wants to show how daring it is to forge a unity of the Plebs. When the commentators turn to the hero, B remarks: "Ich finde, dass ihr bei der Behandlung der Fabel von Anfang an darauf bestanden habt, auch in den Genuss des Vergnügens an der Tragödie des Volks zu kommen, das einen Helden gegen sich hat. Warum nicht dieser Neigung folgen?"* (GW XVI, 877) Brecht had of course followed that inclination to the extent of basing his adaptation upon it. Brecht's four theatermen constantly express admiration for Shakespeare's dramaturgy, especially his realism, as opposed to his rather anti-Shakespearean comments over the course of the years.

Since the Berliner Ensemble staged the Messingkauf Dialogues with considerable verve, one can imagine staging the *Coriolanus* dialogue as a curtain-raiser to the play, Shakespeare's or Brecht's. Several of the remarks are as quotable as the barbs of Shaw (whom Brecht admired for his wit).

Though Shakespeare provides the material, the interpretation is more exclusively class-conscious, as is B's prediction of revolt. B commits a scholarly error: "Ich mache darauf aufmerksam, dass wir in den Shakespeareausgaben keine Regiebemerkungen haben oder solche, die vermutlich später eingefügt wurden."† (878) Though later editors have added scenic directions to Shakespeare, we do find them in the Folio.

As the four theatermen warm to their description of the growing rebellion, W asks: "Können wir den Shakespeare ändern?" and B replies: "Ich denke, wir können Shakespeare ändern, wenn wir ihn ändern können. Aber wir haben ausgemacht, zunächst nur über Änderungen der Interpretation zu sprechen, damit unsere analytische Methode als auch ohne Zu-Dichtung anwendbar erscheinen kann."‡ (879) The ironies are delicious: W, who asks whether they can change Shakespeare, will fifteen years

* Judging from the way you've treated the story it seems to me that you've insisted all of you from the first on smacking your lips over the tragedy of a people that has a hero against it. Why not follow this inclination? (258)

† Let me emphasize that no edition of Shakespeare has stage directions, apart from those presumed to have been added later. (258)

‡ W: Can we change Shakespeare?

B: I think we can change Shakespeare if we *can* change him. But later direct Shakespeare's *Coriolanus* by heavily re-interpreting the text. B, who replies that they will change only through interpretation, has just revised Shakespeare's text into his own play.

When W asks why B is willing to show the development of the Plebeians but no development in the hero, B answers in terms of his own Coriolanus: "Vielleicht, weil er keine rechte Entwicklung hat. Seine Wandlung vom römischsten der Römer zu ihrem grössten Feind geschieht gerade deshalb, weil er der gleiche bleibt. . . . Bei unserer ersten Durchsicht sahen wir das Tragische, für den Coriolan wie für Rom, in seinem Glauben an die eigene Unersetzlichkeit."* (886)

At the end of the dialogue the four participants recite the lessons to be drawn, much as Azdak and Simon recite proverbs in *Der kaukasische Kreidekreis,* and R asks almost incredulously: "Meinen Sie, dass all dies und das Weitere aus dem Stück herausgelesen werden kann?" To which B replies: "Herausgelesen und hineingelesen."† (888) It is a succinct summary of Brecht's long, complex relationship to Shakespeare's works.

Die Plebejer proben den Aufstand by Günter Grass (b. 1927) is an offshoot of Brecht's dialogue and his adaptation, and thus a Shakespeare offshoot, once removed.[21] Having achieved success in fiction and drama, Grass was invited to speak in celebration of Shakespeare's four-hundredth anniversary; his title was "Vor- und Nachgeschichte der Tragödie des Coriolanus von Livius und Plutarch über Shake-

---

we agreed to begin only by discussing changes of interpretation so as to prove the usefulness of our analytical method even without adding new text. (259—my substitution of "change" for Willett's "amend.")

* It may be because he doesn't have a proper development. His switch from being the most Roman of the Romans to becoming their deadliest enemy is due precisely to the fact that he stays the same. . . . Our first examination made us feel the tragedy lay, both for *Coriolanus* and for Rome, in his belief that he was irreplaceable. (264)

† R: Do you think that all this and the rest of it can be read in the play?

B: Read in it and read into it. (264)

speare bis zu Brecht und mir." But more central to his speech than any of the writers in his title was the actual uprising of East German workers on June 17, 1953—an uprising crushed with Soviet tanks. On that date, Brecht cancelled rehearsals in order to write letters of protest to Ulbricht, Grotewohl, and the Russian Commissar Semionoff.[22] In the West, however, only Brecht's letter of adherence to the regime was published. Grass is no more faithful to historical fact than Brecht or Shakespeare.

In his speech, Grass summarizes aspects of his play: "Place: A theater in East Berlin. Someone who is addressed as 'Boss' by his assistants and the actors, is rehearsing *Coriolan*, Act I, Scene 1, the uprising of the Plebeians. . . . news of the uprising on Stalin-Allee filters into the theater where *Coriolan* is being rehearsed, conveyed first by stagehands, then by delegations from the construction workers, who disturb the Boss and the rehearsal."[23] Toward the end of the speech, Grass pronounces a harsh judgment on the Boss: "While the workers in the play appraise the tanks as a fate which cannot be resisted or at the most with stones, the theater Boss delivers an impromptu speech on the subject of whether and how tanks can be used on the stage: as usual, everything turns to theater in his hands; slogans, speaking choruses, whether to march in columns of ten or twelve, everything becomes for him an aesthetic question: a man of the theater, serene and untroubled."[24] Grass implicitly accuses of ivory-towerism the very playwright who declaimed most militantly against ivory towers. That accusation, easily delivered in West Berlin, is scarcely fair to Brecht in East Berlin. Moreover, it is not an accurate description of the play Grass wrote.

In Grass's drama, a rehearsal of *Coriolanus* is interrupted by news of a workers' uprising; their representatives seek a supportive letter from the Boss. He refuses to take them seriously, and Volumnia, the Weigel-figure, taunts him: "Sag, bist du eins mit Coriolan?" (30) She blends Shakespearean lines into her plea for the workers. But the Boss stands his ground, leaving the theater with the remark: "Wo ich hinblick: Teigkneter, die aus mir einen rasselnden Helden backen wollen."* (32) By Act II strikers and theater workers (playing Plebeians) nearly come to blows. When the Boss arrives, he blends the strikers into his rehearsal scene: "So komisch diese Prozession ist, so wertvoll kann sie uns sein."† (50) A Party poet wants the Boss to take an anti-strike stand, and all workers join to carry the official out of the theater.

In Act III more workers arrive at the theater with news of the spreading revolt. The Boss dictates an ironic supporting letter, which angers the strikers so that they tie nooses around the necks of him and his assistant (the Engel-figure). However, the latter calms them with the parable of the belly; as Shakespeare modified Plutarch's parable, and Brecht modified Shakespeare's, Grass modifies Brecht, introducing metaphors of excrement. Improbably, this persuades the strikers to loosen the nooses. But the peaceful moment is interrupted by the arrival of wounded workers; there are tanks in the streets, and there is real blood in the theater. Urged by a young hairdresser who has thrilled to dumb Kattrin in *Mutter Courage*, the Boss is momentarily seduced by the revolt, but Volumnia informs him that martial law has been declared. Gradually, the stage clears, and in a verse soliloquy the Boss blames himself: "Ich, wissend, listig, kühl, allein, / war ein Gedicht lang fast dabei. . . . / Es atmete der heilge Geist. / Ich hielt's für Zugluft, / rief: wer stört!"‡ (91-92)

In Grass's last act, the revolt has been quelled, order is

* Wherever I look: doughkneaders who want to bake a shining hero out of me. (32)

† But silly as their procession may be, we can get something out of it. (49)

‡ I, knowing, wily, cool-headed and alone, / Was almost with them for the time it takes / To breathe a poem. . . . / The Holy Spirit breathed, and I mistook / It for a draft, and cried: / Who's come here to molest me? (94-95)

restored, and the Boss's colleagues wish him to seek the good graces of the Party poet, which means signing a statement of adherence to the regime. The Boss refuses. As his colleagues watch fearfully, he declares that "wir, zum Beispiel, den Shakespeare nicht ändern können, solange wir uns nicht ändern." And adds: "Und wir wollten ihn abtragen, den Koloss Coriolan! Wir, selber kolossal und des Abbruchs würdig."* (100)

However, he does dictate an ambiguous letter, declaring solidarity with the regime in the first two paragraphs, and sympathy with the strikers in the last. His co-workers predict what the East German government actually did—publication only of his support. All the theater-workers feel guilt, and the Boss calls off the rehearsal. He will go to the country and try to write. At the end of the play, he is alone onstage. He looks at the tape-recorder and closes the "German tragedy" with a short soliloquy addressed to his several selves: "Fortan dahinleben mit Stimmen im Ohr: Du. Du. Ich sag dir, du. Weisst du, was du bist? Du bist, du, du bist . . . Unwissende. Ihr Unwissenden! Schuldbewusst klag ich euch an."† (107)

What Grass called "a German tragedy" was denounced in East Germany and received with mixed reactions in West Germany. Closely read, the play shows some sympathy for the Boss's failure to act—the Hamletic German tragedy—but onstage he appears as a coward and esthete. In basing an ambivalent protagonist on Brecht's simplest protagonist, who in turn is based on Shakespeare's simplest tragic protagonist, Grass revels in Brechtian wit, rhythms, and jargon. He caricatures the faithful Communist as Brecht had caricatured faithful Fascists—with inflated blank verse.

* . . . for instance, that we can't change Shakespeare unless we change ourselves.

And to think we wanted to demolish him, the colossus Coriolanus. We ourselves are colossal and deserve to be demolished. (103)

† Condemned to live forever with voices in my ears. You. You. I'll tell you. Do you know what you are? You, you, you're a . . . You poor babes in the woods! Bowed down with guilt, I accuse you! (111)

But Grass is unable to sustain his provocative situation through four acts, and the two nooses are *Grand Guignol* rather than convincing menace. A *pièce à clef,* Grass's play has faded with its *clef.* Grass is only slightly fairer to Brecht than Brecht was to the Shakespearean hero in *Die Rundköpfe, Ui,* and *Coriolan.*

Brecht was sometimes an astute Shakespeare commentator and always an appreciator of his dramaturgy. And yet the Bard sparked Brecht's shallowest plays. His rehearsal scenes are too simple-minded to be meaningful. The *Measure for Measure* transformations are at once confusing and simplistic. *Arturo Ui* abounds in charm and humor which contradict the theme. And *Coriolan,* for all its spectacular staging by the Berliner Ensemble, converts Shakespeare's tragedy to melodrama with its reductive good-evil ethos. None of Brecht's Shakespeare offshoots can compare with his major works. Change Shakespeare though he did, Brecht did not prove that he *could* change Shakespeare.

Chapter 9

Shakespearean Embers in Beckett

Differently from Shaw or Brecht, Beckett can be traced to Shakespeare. Shaw's Shakespeare offshoots are ephemeral or subliminal. Brecht's are pondered and partisan. But Beckett echoes Shakespearean phrases which come to serve as a tuning-fork for his own plays.

Beckett's early criticism and fiction often draw humor from learned Shakespeare references:

> We say farewell to M. de Charlus . . . now a humble and convulsive Lear, crowned by the silver torrent of his hair. (*Proust*)

> This meal that he was at such pains to make ready, he would devour it with a sense of rapture and victory, it would be like smiting the sledded Polacks on the ice. ("Dante and the Lobster")

> The tower began well; that was the funeral meats. But from the door up it was all relief and no honour; that was the marriage tables. ("Fingal")

> Ding-Dong ("Ding-Dong" [from the dirge in *The Tempest*])

> Belacqua tendered his right hand, innocent of any more mercantile commodity than that "gentle peace" recommended by the immortal Shakespeare, having first wiped it clean on his sleeve. This member, the Dogberry, after a brief converse with his incorruptible heart, was kind enough to invest with the office of a cuspidor. ("A Wet Night")

> Miranda ("Yellow")

> The Smeraldina was through with the death-chamber, not that she was callous, quite the reverse, but the livery of death, leaving aside its pale flag altogether, was too much for her. ("Yellow")

> "Then you thought again," said Ruby.
> "O yes," said Belacqua, "the usual pale cast." ("Love and Lethe")

> suck is not such that alters ("Sanies II")

> The economy of care was better served . . . when they knit up the sleave by day. (*Murphy*)

> His eyes coil into my very soul, said Mr. Fitzwein. His very what? said Mr. O'Meldon. (*Watt*)

> Mr. Nackybal [anagram of Caliban] (*Watt*)

In drama, however, Beckett's debt to Shakespeare underwent a sea change. In an unpublished scene, a phrase from *Hamlet* sets the tone for subsequent Beckett drama:

> *Mrs. D.* There are many, Madam, more sorely disappointed, willing to forget the frailties of a life long since transported to that undiscovered country from whose—
> *Mrs. W.* None of your Shakespeare to me, Madam.

In Beckett's best-known play, *Waiting for Godot*, the Shakespearean residue is small. Blind Pozzo led by dumb (perhaps mad?) Lucky of Act II recalls the line from *King Lear*, "'Tis the time's plague when madmen lead the blind." Lucky refers to "the divine Miranda," the *Tempest* name that Beckett earlier assigned to Belacqua's nurse in his story "Yellow." In the original French of *Godot* Miranda's name is preceded by a rather literary preposition: "à l'instar de la divine Miranda," but Beckett's English translation is more prosaic: "like the divine Miranda." In both languages it is God who is like the divine Miranda, suffering with those in torment—"Oh, I have suffered / With those that I saw suffer!" Before the end of Lucky's monologue, however, doubt accumulates about God's capacity to suffer, and perhaps such doubt reflects back on the divine Miranda, to whom He is compared.

A more oblique reminiscence of *The Tempest* occurs near the end of the play. Just before the second arrival of the Boy, Didi looks at a sleeping Gogo and ruminates: "At me too someone is looking, of me too someone is saying, He is sleeping, he knows nothing, let him sleep on."[1] (58b) Perhaps the source of this image is the famous "We are such stuff as dreams are made on / And our little life is rounded by a sleep."

But *Godot* is barely Shakespearean. Didi abridges Hamlet's "Words, words, words" to "Words, words." He twice varies Hamlet's most famous line to "That is not the question" and "What are we doing here, that is the question." One can visualize a graveyard Hamlet in the background of Didi's "Astride of a grave and a difficult birth. Down in the hole, lingeringly, the grave-digger puts on the forceps." (58a) And in certain lights, one can detect a resemblance between Edmund's "An admirable evasion of whoremaster man, to lay his goatish disposition to the charge of a star!" and Didi's "There's man all over for you, blaming on his boots the faults of his feet." (8a)

One can strain *Godot* for other Shakespearean parallels, as does Jan Kott when he quotes more liberally from that play than from *Endgame* in his challenging "*King Lear* or *Endgame*." One may view Didi and Gogo as two fools as well as two thieves, though Didi admonishes Gogo: "Don't be a fool," when the latter mistakes sunset for sunrise. On the other hand, Gogo declares: "We are all born mad. Some remain so." (51b) In Act II of *Godot*, the four fallen characters—madmen or fools?—recall *Lear*'s four huddling characters—madmen or fools?—in the hovel during the storm. Didi's line, before he falls down, seems apt enough for the landscape of *Lear*'s heath: "In an instant all will vanish and we'll be alone once more, in the midst of nothingness!" (52a) In Beckett's tragicomedy Godot is evoked as insistently as are the gods in *Lear,* only to remain as invisible. And yet these Shakespearean parallels are peripheral to *Godot,* a modern tragicomedy rather than heroic tragedy or romantic comedy. *Godot* draws tragic resonance from popular forms that are post-Shakespearean—music-hall and silent movies.

The Shakespeare filiation is more pronounced in Beckett's other two major plays, *Endgame* and *Happy Days. Endgame,* written as *Fin de partie* between 1954 and 1956, is Shakespearean in the metaphysics of its theatrical imagery, whereas *Happy Days,* written in English in 1961, is Shakespearean through explicit verbal quotation. More elusive is a reverberation of *King Lear* in the 1959 radio play, *Embers.*

Shakespeare lurks behind the total conception of *Endgame,* as Roy Walker first pointed out in a pastiche from *Richard II*: "The scene resembles the hollow crown of a head inside which Death keeps his court within a King, an antic who sits scoffing his state and grinning at his pomp. This is also a dream-peopled dungeon in which the royal prisoner is vexed to think how the word of Scripture has been set against the word."[2] In the original production of *Fin de partie* a gray curved backdrop vaguely suggested the interior of a skull, with eye-windows, but Beckett's own 1967 Berlin production called for a relentlessly rectangular set within which Clov wheels Hamm "right round the world." Curved or right-angled, ark and hell and candid stage, the set of Beckett's *Endgame* condenses the unlocalized playing areas of Shakespeare's Globe. Even the two windows, facing land and sea respectively, condense Shakespeare's rich references to *his* lands and seas, as the picture turned to the wall condenses and comments upon Shakespeare's many references to art. Only the Shakespearean mirror is missing, for *Endgame* itself "is to hold as 'twere the mirror up to Nature," and the very word Nature resonates through *Endgame*:

> *Hamm*: Nature has forgotten us.
> *Clov*: There's no more nature.
> *Hamm*: No more nature! You exaggerate.

But the rest of the play justifies Clov's exaggeration. As the storm on the heath—one aspect of nature in *King Lear*—parallels the human storm in the king, the gray "Zero" nature of *Endgame* parallels the near zero of its paralyzed king. Hamm has a fantasy of Flora and Pomona, but Clov sees only gray. In *Endgame* as in *King Lear*, nature reflects culture—within the theater. And in *Endgame*, as occasionally in *King Lear*, the protagonist wishes to annihilate nature and culture. During the storm Lear cries out: "Crack nature's moulds, all germens spill at once / That makes ingrateful man!" Beckett's Hamm has tried to depopulate the earth.

Roger Blin, first director of *Fin de partie* and first actor of Hamm, based his interpretation on Lear: "Quand j'ai eu entre les mains *Fin de partie*, j'y ai vu le thème de la mort des rois. J'ai tiré, peut-être indûment, mais volontairement, le personnage de Hamm vers le roi Lear. A Jacques Noël, qui faisait le décor, j'ai demandé un fauteuil qui évoquait une cathèdre gothique, une robe de chambre en velours cramoisi, avec des lambeaux de fourrure, et la gaffe dont Hamm se servait pour avancer devenait un sceptre. Ce qu'il y avait de royal dans le texte, d'impérieux dans le personnage, a été reçu comme 'shakespearien.' Beckett n'était pas contre."[3]* Most moving was the way Blin's royal hands seemed literally to smell of mortality.

* When I had *Endgame* in my hands, I saw in it the theme of the death of kings. Perhaps unduly but nevertheless deliberately, I slanted Hamm toward King Lear. From set designer Jacques Noël I asked an

Like Shakespeare's Lear, Beckett's Hamm is king on an unlocalized board, and Clov is fool—"What a fool I am!" As Shakespeare's Lear is madly aware that he has been a fool, so Hamm is intermittently aware that he is fool as well as king. Hamm's distortion of a line from Shakespeare implies a blend of king and fool: "My kingdom for a nightman!" Richard III offers his crumbling kingdom for a horse on which to wage heroic battle, but Hamm offers his depopulated and perhaps nonexistent kingdom for a garbageman to chuck his parents—"this muck"—into the sea. "Nightman" is at once a comic and imaginary garbageman, and tragic and inevitable death.

Nagg and Nell in their respective ashbins are the residue of Shakespeare's romantic lovers of the comedies, but Hamm and Clov derive from tragedy as king and fool, king and rebel, king and retainer. Clov's identity shifts with the dialogue, but it always rests on that of Hamm, who is "bang in the center."

No Shakespearean hero sits as still as Beckett's paralyzed Hamm, who nevertheless displays his Shakespearean ancestry. Armchair, toque, and gaff mirror throne, crown, and sceptre—as Blin indicated. Hamm's boasts recall Lear in power: "But for me, no father. But for Hamm, no home." (38) Hamm's rage echoes a murderous Macbeth, and both are haunted by ghosts. Hamm's contrition inverts a pardoning Prospero: "Forgive me. I said, Forgive me." (7, 12)

Hamm's name is Hamlet, cut to modern cloth. He too fears bad dreams, and he too delays: "And yet I hesitate, I hesitate to . . . to end." (3) Wittenberg may not be his alma mater, but he too is well educated—Bible, classics, science, music, painting, theater. He is absorbed in practice as well

armchair evoking a Gothic cathedra, a bathrobe of crimson velvet with strips of fur, and a sceptrelike gaff for Hamm. Whatever was royal in the text, imperious in the character, was taken as "Shakespearean." Beckett was not opposed to it.

as theory of theater. In spite of his name, Hamm's acting is rarely more hammy than the Prince's, and, as Hamlet directs the actors, Hamm directs himself with his thrice-uttered: "Me—to play." The tramps of *Godot* invent abortive games, but Hamm plays through a whole play; his sudarium is the curtain to be removed before the night's assumption of his several roles. Hamm is God and worshipper, father and son, fabulous voyager and fixed center.

Somewhat past the middle of Beckett's play, Hamm says (in the original French): "Finie la rigolade," which Beckett translates with Prospero's famous line from *The Tempest*: "Our revels now are ended." That line punctuates Nagg's extended curse of his son, and his failure to elicit a response when he knocks at Nell's bin-lid. She may be dead. The subsequent dialogue of *Endgame* has a dying fall, as though Hamm recalled Hamlet's "The readiness is all." Hamm is still not quite ready for nothingness, but his invention flags. He tries to talk about his story, he makes another journey around his room, he meditates associationally, he orders Clov to take a last look at the earth. When Clov reports sighting a small boy, *Endgame* subsides asymptotically toward its end.

By quotation of Prospero's line, Beckett specifically recalls *The Tempest*. But the biblical flood is the tempest behind *Endgame*, and Shakespeare's magical merciful storm seems irrelevant, in spite of the Prospero line. Prospero's tempest was his own creation, after which he intends to mete out justice to the Europeans in his power. The preplay catastrophe of *Endgame* is of uncertain origin, but Hamm is at once relieved and disbelieving that it has depopulated the earth. Powerful Prospero assents to a new human order through the marriage of his daughter Miranda to Prince Ferdinand; the "brave new world" may be possible after all. Powerless Hamm, in contrast, assents to eschatological disorder through entropy: "You're on earth. There's no cure for that!" (53, 68) *Endgame* offers no recollection of a divine Miranda, suffering with those who suffer. Instead, the play's only woman, whose name puns on knell, declares: "Nothing is funnier than unhappiness." (18)

Before the revels end in *Endgame,* Clov serves as Ariel and Caliban to Prospero. Resembling Caliban in clumsiness and surliness, Clov performs trivial but necessary tasks. Raising a tempest is beyond his wildest dreams, but he speaks of building a raft to cross the seas. Clov cannot prepare a banquet, but he can get a dog-biscuit from the cupboard. Clov cannot arouse alarm in a Harpy disguise, but he can set an alarm-clock to ring. Clov cannot summon hunting-hounds, but he can make a three-legged, sexless, ribbonless toy dog. Clov lends himself to Hamm's fantasies, as Ariel does to Prospero's, and he attends to Hamm's material needs, as Caliban does to Prospero's.

In his opening speech Beckett's Clov declares: "I can't be punished any more." And yet *Endgame* theatricalizes his life as punishment. Prospero subjugates Caliban with primitive physical punishments, but Clov's pains seem to be his own, and Hamm uses more subtle suasion. For both Caliban and Clov, however, language is a form of punishment. Caliban accuses Prospero: "You taught me language; and my profit on't / Is I know how to curse. The red plague rid you / For learning me language." Clov, who has not yet learned to curse, accuses Hamm: "I use the words you taught me. If they don't mean anything any more, teach me others. Or let me be silent." (44) For the last few minutes of playing time Clov *is* silent while Hamm dominates the stage in the last soliloquy of a dying hero. With the alarm-clock wound up, Hamm tries to unwind himself into nothingness. Prospero deliberately breaks his magic staff and throws away his book. Blind bookless Hamm throws away his useless gaff, his useless dog, his useless whistle. Prospero reintegrates himself into the social order whereas Hamm retreats behind his handkerchief-curtain: "Old stancher! You . . . remain." (84)

Endgame staunches nothing. What remains after the curtain falls or the book is closed is the vision of a heroic figure saying "No" to the Nothingness that tempts him because he has suffered with those who suffered. Lear asks his dead Cordelia: "Why should a dog, a horse, a rat, have life / And thou no breath at all?" Hamm knows there is no answer, but he also knows the pain that prompts the question.

Hamm has been called a toppled Prospero, and he has been compared to mad Lear. He also absorbs Timon-Misanthrope: "For these my present friends, as they are to me nothing, so in nothing bless them, and to nothing are they welcome." "My long sickness / Of health and living now begins to mend, / And nothing brings me all things."

But most consistently and insistently, Hamm recalls a doubting, denying, weary Hamlet: "Ah the old questions, the old answers, there's nothing like them!" (38) The phrase "No more" tolls through both plays. Behind Hamm's spare phrases one can hear Hamlet's luxuriant meditations: "Oh, that this too too sullied [or solid] flesh would melt. . . ." "How weary, stale, flat, and unprofitable / Seem to me all the uses of this world!" "O, what a rogue and peasant slave am I!" "The play's the thing / Wherein I'll catch the conscience of the king." "To be or not to be—that is the question." "How all occasions do inform against me." "That skull had a tongue in it, and could sing once." "How long will a man lie i' the earth ere he rot?" "The rest is silence." And there is finally stillness on the stage of *Endgame*.

Not so in *Embers*. The protagonist of a radio play, which exists through sound alone, Henry hears and makes us hear the continuous sucking sound of the sea—"so unlike the sound of the sea, that if you didn't see what it was you wouldn't know what it was." (96) To drown that sound, Henry summons voices to his mind, and he has fantasies of hard sounds that "mark time," assert life in time against the infinite impersonal sea.

Very early in *Embers* Henry evokes his father, "An old man, blind and foolish," (95) but the old man offers no words. Henry is more successful with the sound of hooves, and his imagination extrapolates to "A ten ton mammoth back from the dead, shoe it with steel and have it tramp the world down!" (96) This may be a distant echo of Lear's fantasy: "It were a delicate stratagem to shoe / A troop of horse with felt. I'll put't in proof, / And when have stol'n upon these son-in-laws, / Then kill, kill, kill, kill, kill, kill!" Henry too wants to kill, or at least to deny life, drawn as he is to the sea that has killed his father and that "is silent as the grave" beneath its sucking surface. At the same time, Henry wants to hear the hard sounds of life, and the radio play contains these two competing sounds—sucking and thudding—that are seductive to him. On the life-side, he utters a line—"Every syllable is a second gained." (117) —that recalls the time-speech metaphor of Macbeth's "to the last syllable of recorded time."

In a play within the play of *Embers*, a structure as dear to Beckett as to Shakespeare, two old men look at each other in a room where embers are dying, while outside is a white world. The setting differs, and yet the two *old* men, Bolton holding a candle before the tear-filled eyes of Holloway, recapitulate the final meeting of Lear and Gloucester (with perhaps an assist from Macbeth's "Out, out, brief candle"). Lear says to blind Gloucester: "I remember thine eyes well enough." And Gloucester says of Lear: "The king is mad. . . . Better I were distract." It is the beginning of the end of the tragedy. Henry tries to end his life in oblivion: "All day all night nothing. (*Pause*) Not a sound." (121) But on the radio we hear the sucking sound of the sea. The white world of the play within Beckett's play dissolves into the sea that sucks all that lives. No one is left to realize: "We that are young / Shall never see so much, nor live so long."

While we witness *Endgame*, it offers the only shelter against encroaching nothingness. While we listen to *Embers*, it offers the only firm sounds against the sucking sea. *Happy Days* offers a new setting for life's little persistences. Hamlet asked: "What should such fellows as I do crawling between heaven and earth?" But crawling Willie asks no questions, and Winnie is no longer able to crawl, fixed as she is between heaven and earth. Shakespeare's plays contain no comparable picture of a woman being burned to dust by the sun's heat. But as Winnie chirps cheerily through her "happy day," she explicitly quotes, or misquotes, Shakespeare.

Her stage life consists largely of speech, and her main subjects are her husband Willie, her props, her two stories, and her fourteen verse quotations. Of the last, six are from Shakespeare—two from *Hamlet,* two from *Romeo and Juliet,* one from *Cymbeline,* and one from *Twelfth Night.* Though the quotations are brief, they open out ironically into the pathos of her condition.

Winnie begins her first stage day by praying and brushing her teeth, but her mind soon turns to her sleeping husband, Willie. She then tries to read the print on her toothbrush handle, but she can see no further than "genuine . . . pure." Rue about her weakening sight leads to her first quotation: "what are those wonderful lines . . . (*wipes one eye*) . . . woe woe is me . . . (*wipes the other*) . . . to see what I see . . . (*looks for spectacles*)." (10) Ophelia, believing that Hamlet is mad, concludes *her* rueful soliloquy: "O, woe is me / T' have seen what I have seen, see what I see!" Winnie transposes Ophelia's exclamation into the present tense, coloring all she surveys with a woe that belies her declarations of happiness.

When Winnie later looks at Willie, she exclaims: "Oh this is going to be another happy day!" Then she puts on lipstick with the help of a mirror and murmurs: "Ensign crimson." Laying the mirror aside, she turns toward her bag and says: "Pale flag." (15) When Romeo looks at Juliet whom he believes dead, he addresses her passionately: "Thou art not conquered. Beauty's ensign yet / Is crimson in thy lips and in thy cheeks, / And death's pale flag is not advancèd there." As with Ophelia's words about Hamlet, Winnie refocuses Romeo's words upon herself. Winnie has applied lipstick in an effort to raise the crimson ensign of life, though she is half buried. As she turns to her bag for sustenance through time, she acknowledges the pale enemy, death.

Busy with Willie and her props, Winnie does not again resort to quotation till midway through her first happy day. Under the relentless sun she calls out to Willie: "Fear no more the heat o' the sun." (26) She urges Willie to repeat the line, and twice he snaps back: "Fear no more." In *Cymbeline,* when Imogen's brothers think her dead, they sing an elegiac duet. Like Romeo, the princes of *Cymbeline* address a living woman who looks like a corpse, and Winnie turns their words to herself—a living woman who is half in her grave. Winnie's situation is aptly summarized by Imogen when she awakens from her drugged sleep: " 'Twas but a bolt of nothing, shot at nothing, / Which the brain makes of fumes." But Winnie seems not to know these lines of Imogen, nor the closing couplet of her brothers' song: "Golden lads and girls all must, / As chimney sweepers, come to dust." In Beckett's world, death alone enables one to "fear no more"—a meaningless trisyllable for Winnie and Willie, who are determinedly alive.

Winnie has not yet come to dust, and she refuses to admit fear. Occasionally, Willie bolsters her courage. When she plays her "Merry Widow" music-box, he hums along. She claps for an encore, but receives silence. She understands that one cannot sing on order, for "song must come from the heart, that is what I always say, pour out from the inmost, like a thrush." "No, like the thrush, or the bird of dawning, with no thought of benefit, to oneself or anyone else." (40) In the opening scene of *Hamlet,* after the appearance of the Ghost, Marcellus speaks of Christmas Eve: "The bird of dawning singeth all night long, / And then, they say, no spirit dare stir abroad." So, in *Happy Days,* spontaneous song might momentarily banish spirits, but there is no more spontaneous song.

By Act II, Winnie's second happy day, she is buried to her throat. Her voice is weaker and her phrases shorter.

She can no longer rely on Willie or her props, but she still manages a few quotations. Her final words from Shakespeare are barely recognizable. Attempting an inventory of the features of her face, Winnie tries to see her cheeks: "(*eyes left*) . . . cheek . . . no . . . (*eyes right*) . . . no . . . (*distends cheeks*) . . . even if I puff them out . . . (*eyes left, distends cheeks again*) . . . no . . . no damask." (52-53) In *Twelfth Night* Viola-Cesario tells Duke Orsino about a fictitious sister: "She never told her love, / But let concealment, like a worm i' the bud / Feed on her damask cheek. She pined in thought, / And with a green and yellow melancholy / She sat like Patience on a monument, / Smiling at grief." Earlier, Winnie has deliberately turned Shakespeare's imagery upon herself, but in Act II of *Happy Days* she salvages a single striking word, without appreciating the relevance to herself of the whole passage. Viola invents a fiction to delineate her own condition, as Winnie invents a fiction to render *her* condition. But Viola's fiction—both the fragile blossom carrying the worm of death, and the statue's smile through grief—describes Winnie, who hides her grief in thirty-one smiles that are noted meticulously in Beckett's scenic directions.

Beckett's slighter plays contain only one explicit Shakespearean reminiscence. *Come and Go* is an exquisitely balanced "dramaticule" in which three ageless women speak nine short speeches each. The first full line of dialogue—Vi's "When did we three last meet?"—echoes the witches of *Macbeth*, evoking a feeling of fate. Beckett's three weird women are at once agents and victims of coming and going, strutting and fretting their hour upon the stage, which signifies nothing. None of the hundred-odd words of *Come and Go* is "nothing," and yet the dramaticule is bounded in, threatened by the infinite dark spaces of nothingness. After the Jack-in-the-box moon of *Godot*, the pervasive gray of *Endgame*, and the blinding brightness of *Happy Days*, the stage of *Come and Go* is merely alive with light. At first, silence and darkness threaten, but soon they beckon. And

Beckett's last few plays are brief breaths of light. So, Shakespeare's last romances may be interpreted as breaths of rosy light after the tragedies that edged nothingness.

Beckett's dramatic progress is not paced after Shakespeare, but both are possessed by nothing. In Beckett's work, as in Shakespeare's *King Lear,* the quest for self proceeds through a reduction toward nothing: a hundred knights to zero, castle to hovel to cliff that is not, court grandeur to a bare forked animal, studied rhetoric to garbled fragments—"Thou hast pared thy wit o' both sides and left nothing i' the middle." Beckett's fiction and drama pare away narrative, character, and wit in the quest to give expression to a being that quivers toward nothing.

Paul Jorgensen has analyzed the chameleon qualities that Shakespeare gives to *nothing,* word and concept, among which is a pun on *noting.*[4] Beckett's works too are Notes on Nothing. As in Shakespeare, all the world's a stage of fools, and all the men and women merely players. As in Shakespeare, Beckett garbs his characters to make one "think a man a worm." As in Shakespeare, "the first time we smell the air, we wawl and cry." And as in Shakespeare, the last scene is oblivion, sans teeth, sans eyes, sans taste, sans everything. But also as in Shakespeare, Beckett's scene may be a hair's breadth away from nothing, and yet that breadth is quick with life.

Afterword

In mid-twentieth-century Eric Bentley wrote: "All roads lead to Shakespeare, or perhaps it might be more correct to say that Shakespeare leads to all roads."[1] I have tried to chart some of the roads.

I began by simply piling up modern Shakespeare offshoots, but when patterns manifested themselves, I followed their form. It would have been tidier to separate English offshoots from French and German, not to mention American. The resulting book would have been neater, imposing order on what is largely a chance conglomeration. Unlike Shakespeare offshoots of the eighteenth or nineteenth centuries, those of the twentieth century rarely build upon one another, even within a particular country. As has been true of Shakespeare's plays proper, some of the most fascinating offshoots have jumped wide of the Channel—from a Paris *Ubu* at the beginning of the modern period to Herbert Blau's *Hamlet* rehearsing in Baltimore in late 1975. My regret, therefore, is not that I have crossed national lines, but that my linguistic inadequacies allowed me to cross so few.

In describing this conglomeration of offshoots, I have relished the interdisciplinary eclecticism. Tracing Shakespeare avatars, I have had to learn about individual biographies of writers and theatermen, different stage traditions, various philosophies, cultural backgrounds, and political movements from the French Revolution to today. From Tolstoy's inflexible Christianity to Césaire's dedicated Negritude, there has been a strong moral purpose behind the most provocative Shakespeare offshoots. From Sterne's Parson Yorick to Katsuhiro Oida's Noh Ariel, there has been an intense artistic awareness behind the most provocative Shakespeare offshoots. These stage vehicles have traversed many metaphoric distances, and my regret is not that I sometimes boarded other vehicles—fiction, essays—but that my lack of expertise prevented me from branching further, into dance, film, music, painting.

Behind these many Shakespeare offshoots is a desire to modernize the Bard. For dramatic offshoots, the most frequent aspect of modernization is political (if we define "political" broadly as pertaining to public affairs); from Renan's 1877 *Caliban* to the *Macbeth*s of Ionesco and Müller nearly a century later; from the largely Shakespearean text of *The Wars of the Roses* to the romantic fantasy of *Romanoff and Juliet*; from Dürrenmatt's cynical comedy about *Titus* to Bond's attempt at a modern tragedy of *Lear*; and including the two *Timon*s and several versions of *Coriolanus*. All these offshoots contain political attitudes which differ from Shakespeare. One might expect politics to be the motive force behind avatars of Shakespeare's Histories or Roman plays (newly appreciated in the twentieth century), but the same impetus lies behind several *Macbeth*s and *Tempest*s. Only *Hamlet*s refrain from politics.

Though the main *thematic* drive of modern offshoots is political, the *esthetic* drives are various—from shopworn Romanticism to the anti-establishment Alternative Theater. Unlike nineteenth-century Romantic plays, which were often political, modern throwbacks lack such suggestion—Bottomley, Hauptmann, MacKaye, or, more cynically, Cabell. Their common premise is that Shakespeare's characters are heroic creatures living in exotic worlds and rhapsodizing about their own emotions. Such leisurely verbalization was already burlesqued in Shakespeare's day (and even in his play *A Midsummer Night's Dream*), and burlesque continues in minor modern plays of which The Ridiculous Theater's *Stage Blood* is a recent example. Serious offshoots are sometimes lightened by burlesque elements—one-man armies, broomstick-forests, ad-spouting or bikini-clad Witches, ubiquitous puns and rhymes.

Not so prevalent as Romantic and burlesque offshoots are those of realism. Adhering to Alan Downer's three-pronged definition of realism as physical, psychological, and sociological, these offshoots assume that Shakespeare's characters are like you and me, with comparable problems. Thus, antisemitism and adultery usurp the focus of Ervine's *Lady of Belmont*; an Oedipal Hamlet poses in Rice's California livingroom, and an ESP Hamlet in Duke's English drawing-room; Bentley's H. Denmark is grounded in realistic modern psychology; Holz's "Papa Hamlet" depends on minutely observed details of poverty; a basically realistic veneer covers such trivialities as Maugham's *Mister Lear* and Kops' *Hamlet of Stepney Green*.

Most Shakespeare offshoots are non-realistic. Expressionism and Surrealism arose within the same decade in reaction against realism, and these movements are represented by works as dissimilar as Cummings's *him*, Tzara's *Mouchoir de Nuages*, Jahnn's *Richard III*, and the Britting *Hamlet* novel. Other departures from realism occur in plays of the absurd—Stoppard's *Rosencrantz and Guildenstern Are Dead*, Ionesco's *Macbett*—as well as in the rites of the Alternative Theater—Rumbelow, Galli, Schechner. But such labels as Expressionism, Surrealism, Absurdism, Alternative Theater are a help to the critic rather than a concern of the artist. Differently non-realistic are Welles' *Macbeth*, Sarment's *Hamlet*, Marowitz' *A Macbeth*, Brook's *Tempest*, and Césaire's *Une Tempête*, but they cannot be grouped into a single esthetic category. Similarly, the several fictional *Hamlet*s are non-realistic, but they are more difficult to pigeonhole than the drama.

Critical classification is a way of relating a jumble of works, and though I am dependent on critical classification, I have related the Shakespeare offshoots mainly through their springboard plays. What stands above all patterns are a few works of deep intensity. I think that I have been lyrical about Jarry's *Ubu*, Cummings' *him*, Sterne's *Tristram Shandy*, Goethe's *Wilhelm Meister*, Laforgue's "Hamlet,"

Holz' "Papa Hamlet," Joyce's *Ulysses,* Tzara's *Mouchoir de Nuages,* Rühm's *Ophelia und die Wörter,* Bond's *Lear,* Auden's "Sea and the Mirror," Césaire's *Une Tempête,* but I don't seem able to summon a coda that will embrace them all. Though I can cite no work of Shaw or Brecht as a Shakespeare offshoot of comparable quality, these modern playwrights might not have written their major works without the Shakespeare confrontation. And Beckett is a playwright apart.

It might seem appropriate to close the book with a ritual incantation—that Shakespeare towers above subject and style of adapters; that when realism and non-realism, when burlesque and politics and experiment have had their day, Shakespeare will rise like a pristine phoenix. In the meantime he is tramping among us here on earth, engaging creative artists in dialogue.

It might be argued that the most spirited dialogue has rarely been heard in the theater, and it might further be argued that the greatest actors of our time (with the exception of Berliner Ensemble Ekkehard Schall and a still young Jean-Louis Barrault) have played not in Shakespeare offshoots but in more or less faithful Shakespeare texts. I have no rebuttal to either of these arguments, but I would like to conclude with a defense of theater, which has in the past played a vital role in human culture. (And perhaps that *is* past.)

Despite the orderly sequence of many histories of theater, its artists have rarely had the opportunity to build on their accomplishments. I am not going to say that Shakespeare is the exception that proves the rule, because there is no rule. Usually, however, playwrights fall from notice within a decade of their first success. Most actors portray a dozen trivial characters for every role of substance. Many theatermen have shuttled from acting to directing to writing, without contributing anything memorable in any area. To underline the obvious, theater is the most ephemeral of arts. In spite of books, photographs, and video-tapes, theater lives in the unique occasion and the fragile memory.

It is on my own fragile memory that I close. The first professional play I can recall is Welles' Voodoo *Macbeth*. But when I write "recall," I am treating my memory with charity. Envying those whose sharp images can cut through the years, I remember a blur of brilliance and movement. Even the narrative, which I must have known, dissolves into that large and lively blur. At fourteen, I had never heard of textual violations, empathy, or catharsis. I didn't know that the Voodoo *Macbeth* was the first all-Black dramatic production on Broadway (I saw it at the Adelphi Theatre). I didn't know the names of any of the actors, and it wasn't until the following year's anti-fascist *Julius Caesar* that I learned the name of Orson Welles. I can no longer be sure that the Voodoo rhythms in my mind's ear, the high battlements in my mind's eye are not reconstructions from descriptions I later read. I am very sure, however, of my *excitement* at the intense and vibrant drama played—it seemed to me lived—against its spectacular background. And I have tried to convey some sense—some small sense—of such excitement when I write about theater, the most perishable of goods.

Notes

Chapter 1

[1] Rouben Mamoulian, ed., *Hamlet* (New York, 1965) is a printed example of reduction/emendation. Mamoulian writes "that what *Hamlet* needed was a good English translation," and he apparently thinks he provided it by eliminating some five hundred lines of Shakespeare's text and by modernizing words he finds incomprehensible. He reduces the number of acts to four, and he adds scenic directions. His only substantive change, for which he argues lengthily, is reduction of Hamlet's age from thirty to twenty.

[2] Christopher Spencer, ed., *Five Restoration Adaptations of Shakespeare* (Urbana, 1965), 7.

[3] John Barton and Peter Hall, *The Wars of the Roses* (London, 1970).

[4] Barbara Hodgdon, "The Wars of the Roses: Scholarship Speaks on the Stage," *Deutsche Shakespeare-Gesellschaft West Jahrbuch*, 1972, 175.

[5] I know of no complete history of translations in either language. M. Horn-Monval, *Les Traductions françaises de Shakespeare* (Paris, 1963) lists over two thousand translations. Brief, informative accounts are found in Henri Peyre, "Shakespeare and Modern French Criticism" and Herman J. Weigand, "Shakespeare in German Criticism" in Herbert Schueller, ed., *The Persistence of Shakespeare Idolatry* (Detroit, 1964). Older explorations are: Friedrich Gundolf, *Shakespeare und der Deutsche Geist* (Leipzig, 1911); C. M. Haines, *Shakespeare in France* (London, 1925); J. J. Jusserand, *Shakespeare en France sous l'Ancien Régime* (Paris, 1898). Helpful to me were Constance Beresford-Howe, *The French Translations of Hamlet* (unpublished doctoral dissertation, Brown University, 1950); Peter Gebhardt, *A. W. Schlegels Shakespeare-Übersetzung* (Göttingen, 1970); Michel Poirier, ed., *Shakespeare en France* (Paris, 1960); Robert Speaight, *Shakespeare on the Stage* (London, 1973).

[6] François Marie Arouet de Voltaire, *Oeuvres Complètes* (Paris, 1877), vol. xxx, 369-370.

[7] Victor Hugo, *William Shakespeare* (Paris, 1865), xiv.

[8] These piquant details come from Speaight, *loc. cit.*, 87-90. I have read only *Hamlet*, about which Ducis wrote the English actor, Garrick: "I looked on myself as a religious painter working on an altarpiece."

[9] One of the most astute modern critics, Kenneth Burke, guessed wrong about the timeliness of *Coriolanus*:

> An ironic turn of history has endowed this play with a new kind of "timely topic," owing to the vagaries of current dictatorships. But I would incline to contend that this "new immediacy" is more apparent than real. In the first place, Coriolanus isn't a good fit for the contemporary pattern because the frankness of his dislike for the common people would make him wholly incompetent as a rabble-rouser. A modern demagogue might secretly share Coriolanus's prejudices—but he certainly would not advertise the fact as Coriolanus did. His public heart would bleed for the poor, even while he was secretly shipping state funds to a Swiss bank, against the day when his empire would collapse, and he would flee the country, hoping to spend his last years in luxurious retirement on the Riviera. Presumably our nation is always in danger of pouring considerable funds down such ratholes. Thus, I feel that the attempt to present *Coriolanus* in the light of modern conditions can never quite succeed, since these conditions tend rather to conceal than to point up the cultural trends underlying its purgative use of the tension between upper and lower classes.

Language as Symbolic Action (Berkeley, 1960), 89. "Succeed" is a problematical word in the theater, and Burke neglects *Coriolanus* offshoots.

[10] T. S. Eliot, "Coriolan" in *The Complete Poems and Plays* (New York, 1950).

[11] Much of this information has been gleaned from Edouard Champion, *La Comédie Française, 1933-1934* (Paris, 1935), though I have sometimes read between the lines, since Champion uncritically champions the Comédie. My French friend, Denise Helmer, has indefatigably sketched the political background for me, also supplying relevant contemporary accounts.

[12] *Ibid.*, 164.

[13] René-Louis Piachaud, *Coriolan, Tragédie traduite et adaptée* (Geneva, 1947). This is a reprint of the Calmann-Lévy edition of 1934, omitting Piachaud's "Examen," which praises Shakespeare the aristocrat: "Tout comme Aristophane, Shakespeare est trop aristocrate pour mépriser le peuple." (p. 233) (Like Aristophanes,

Shakespeare is too much the aristocrat to despise the people.) The play's text also appears in *La Petite Illustration* (February 10, 1934). I also refer to the prompt-book of the Comédie Française, photocopied through the cooperation of Sylvie Chevalley, Librarian of the Comédie Française.

[14] Calmann-Lévy edition, 222.

[15] Champion, 177.

[16] All quotations from Shakespeare are from the *Complete Pelican Shakespeare* (Baltimore, 1969).

[17] Bertolt Brecht, *Coriolan* in *Gesammelte Werke* VI, 2395 ff. (Frankfurt, 1967). As is customary in Brecht research, any reference to Brecht's plays will be to this edition, by volume and page number.

[18] Ralph Mannheim and John Willett, tr., *Brecht: Collected Plays*, vol. 9 (New York, 1973), 396.

[19] Quoted by Manfred Wekwerth, *Notate über die Arbeit des Berliner Ensembles 1956 bis 1966* (Frankfurt, 1967), 130. See also Peter Gebhardt, "Brechts Coriolan-Bearbeitung" in *Deutsche Shakespeare-Gesellschaft West Jahrbuch*, 1972, 113-135.

[20] Their text is published as "Shakespeares *Coriolan* in der Bearbeitung von Bertolt Brecht" in *Spectaculum* VIII (Frankfurt, 1965).

[21] Wekwerth, *loc. cit.*, 119.

[22] Kenneth Tynan, "Brecht on Shakespeare" *The Observer* (October 4, 1964).

[23] See brief articles in *The Times* (London) for May 5, 6, and 7, 1971.

[24] The prompt-copy was sent me through the kindness of John Russell Brown, Literary Adviser of the National Theatre.

[25] John Osborne, *A Place Calling Itself Rome* (London, 1973).

[26] Well-summarized by Bernhard Kytzler, Shakespeare *Coriolan* (Frankfurt, 1965).

[27] Émile Fabre, *Timon d'Athènes* in *L'Illustration théâtrale*, vol. 5, #60 (n.d.).

[28] Ferdinand Bruckner, *Timon, Tragödie* (Berlin, 1932).

[29] Friedrich Dürrenmatt, *König Johann nach Shakespeare* (Zurich, 1968).

[30] Friedrich Dürrenmatt, *Titus Andronicus nach Shakespeare* (Zurich, 1970).

[31] Harmut Lange, *König Johann* in *Theaterstücke 1960-72* (Hamburg, 1973).

[32] Rudolf Stamm, "King John-König Johann," *Deutsche Shakespeare-Gesellschaft West Jahrbuch*, 1970, 30-48.

[33] Urs Mehlin, "Claus Bremer, Renate Voss, *Die jämmerliche Tragödie von Titus Andronicus*—Friedrich Dürrenmatt, *Titus Andronicus*—Hans Hollman, *Titus Titus*—Ein Vergleich," *Deutsche Shakespeare-Gesellschaft West Jahrbuch*, 1972, 73-98.

[34] Jan Kott, *Shakespeare Our Contemporary* (Garden City, 1966), 132.

[35] Both text and commentary are found in the Theater Bremen Program, 1967/68, #5, no page numbers.

[36] André Obey, *Théâtre I* (Villeneuve-Saint Georges, 1948).

[37] St. John Ervine, *The Lady of Belmont* (New York, 1924). For other plays on Shylock see Dolores K. Gros Louis, *Shakespeare by Many Other Names: Modern Dramatic Adaptations* (unpublished doctoral dissertation, University of Wisconsin, 1968).

[38] James Branch Cabell, *The Line of Love: Dizain des Mariages* (New York, 1926).

[39] George Jean Nathan, *The Avon Flows* (New York, 1937).

[40] Peter Ustinov, *Romanoff and Juliet* (London, 1972).

[41] Hans Henny Jahnn, *Die Krönung Richards III* in Paul Pörtner, ed., *Deutsches Theater des Expressionismus* (Stuttgart, n.d.). The play is omitted from the Suhrkamp edition of Jahnn's complete works.

[42] This account relies heavily on Henri Béhar, *Jarry* (Paris, 1973), though I had already read several of his sources, particularly P. Lié, "Comment Jarry et Lugné-Poe glorifièrent Ubu à l'Oeuvre," *Cahiers du Collège 'Pataphysique*, vol. 3-4, 37-51.

[43] Quoted in Charles Chassé, *Dans les Coulisses de la Gloire* (Paris, 1947), 105.

[44] All quotations from *Ubu* are from the admirable edition of Maurice Saillet, *Tout Ubu* (Paris, 1962).

[45] *Le Journal*, December 11, 1896. I quote from Louis Perche, *Jarry* (Paris, 1965), 34-35.

Suggestive details are found also in Béhar and in Roger Shattuck, *The Banquet Years* (New York, 1968); Jacques Robichez, *Le Symbolisme au théâtre* (Paris, 1957).

[46] Shattuck, 178.

[47] These examples are cited by Paul Jacopin, *L'Originalité du langage théâtrale dans Ubu Roi* (Institut d'Études théâtrales typescript, 1966-1967).

[48] See, for example, the penetrating article, K. S. Beaumont, "The Making of *Ubu*," *Theatre Research*, 1972, 139-154.

[49] Chassé, 56.

[50] Roland Barthes, "Ubu au TNP," *Théâtre Populaire* (May, 1958), 80.

Chapter 2

[1] Oliver Lawson Dick, ed., *Aubrey's Brief Lives* (London, 1950), 85.

[2] Christopher Spencer, ed., *Five Restoration Adaptations of Shakespeare* (Urbana, 1965), to which page numbers in the text refer. I have omitted Spencer's brackets but have faithfully copied his eighteenth-century printing.

[3] George C. Odell, *Shakespeare from Betterton to Irving* (New York, 1966), 340.

[4] W. B. Yeats, *Autobiographies* (New York, 1956), 348-349.

[5] Gordon Bottomley, *Gruach and Britain's Daughter* (London, 1921).

[6] First published in *La Revue Blanche* (January 1, 1897), the passage is quoted from *Tout Ubu*, 155.

[7] E. E. Cummings, *Three Plays and a Ballet* (New York, 1967).

[8] Robert E. Maurer, "E. E. Cummings' *him*," *The Bucknell Review* (May, 1956), 4.

[9] Eric Bentley, ed., *From the Modern Repertoire, Series 2* (Bloomington, 1952), 487.

[10] Walter Sokel, ed., *An Anthology of German Expressionist Drama* (New York, 1963), xii.

[11] Most of this information comes from Joseph McBride, *Orson Welles* (New York, 1972).

[12] John Houseman, *Run-Through* (New York, 1972), 168.

[13] *Ibid.*, 185.

[14] "Macbeth The Moor," *New York Times* (April 5, 1936), 1, 2.

[15] Houseman, 194.

[16] Quotations are taken from the New York Public Library copy of the "Complete Working Script of *Macbeth* by William Shakespeare, Negro Version, Conceived, Arranged, Staged by Orson Welles." For a detailed description of the production, see Richard France, "The 'Voodoo' *Macbeth* of Orson Welles," *Yale/theatre* (1974).

[17] "Harlem MacBeth Divine?" *New York Times* (June 21, 1936), 1.

[18] Charles Higham, *The Films of Orson Welles* (Berkeley, 1970).

[19] Houseman, 209.

[20] Erich Schumacher, *Macbeth auf der deutschen Bühne* (Emsdetten, 1938), 254.

[21] Rodney T. K. Symington, *Brecht und Shakespeare* (Bonn, 1970), 86-96.

[22] Schumacher, 255.

[23] Barbara Garson, *MacBird!* (New York, 1967).

[24] Richard Gilman, "*MacBird!* and Its Audience" in *New American Review, #1* (New York, 1967).

[25] Charles Marowitz, *'A Macbeth' Freely Adapted from Shakespeare's Tragedy* (London, 1971).

[26] Robert Brustein, *The Third Theatre* (New York, 1970), 10.

[27] Eugène Ionesco, *Macbett* (Paris, 1972).

[28] Serge Doubrovsky, "Ionesco and the Comic of Absurdity," *Yale French Studies #3*. Reprinted in Rosette Lamont, ed., *Ionesco* (Englewood Cliffs, 1973). See also Rosette Lamont, "From Macbeth to Macbett," *Modern Drama* (December, 1972) for a detailed comparison of the two plays.

[29] Lamont, p. 17.

[30] John L. Hess, "Ionesco Talks of his Latest 'Macbett,'" *New York Times* (January 18, 1972), 22.

[31] Heinar Müller, *Macbeth* in *Theater Heute* (June, 1972).

[32] Information about Müller comes from *Theater Heute* and Benjamin Heinrich, "Die zum Lächeln nicht Zwingbaren," *Die Zeit* (May 24, 1974). Quotations are from the latter.

[33] Franco Tonelli, *L'Esthétique de la Cruauté* (Paris, 1972).

[34] Most of the information on Artaud comes from Alain Virmaux, *Antonin Artaud et le Théâtre* (Paris, 1970).

[35] Quotations are taken from The Performance Group script, graciously lent me by Richard Schechner.

[36] Richard Schechner, *Environmental Theater* (New York, 1973), to which page numbers in the text refer.

[37] Richard Schechner, "Actuals," *Theatre Quarterly* (April-June, 1971), 63.

[38] Information is combined from my interview with Galli on September 7, 1973, from Ted Shank's notes, and from printed matter as indicated.

[39] Gérard Pont interview with Galli in *Paris Théâtre* (March 10-25, 1970), 22.

[40] *Ibid.*

[41] Edward Gordon Craig, *On the Art of the Theatre* (London, 1912), 264.

[42] Some of these remarks were suggested by Roy Walker, *The Time Is Free* (London, 1949) and Tom F. Driver, *The Sense of History in Greek and Shakespearean Drama* (New York, 1960).

[43] Driver, 145.

Chapter 3

A. Fiction

[1] Laurence Sterne, *Tristram Shandy* (New York, 1940).

[2] Laurence Sterne, *A Sentimental Journey* (Berkeley, 1967).

[3] On Sterne and Shakespeare: Richard A. Lanham, *Tristram Shandy: The Games of Pleasure* (Berkeley, 1973); Henri Fluchère, *Laurence Sterne* (Paris, 1961); Janice Hokenson, "Sterne's Shandean Self-Portrait" in *The Narrator as Artist* (unpublished doctoral dissertation at University of California, Santa Cruz, 1974). I am especially indebted to the last of these.

[4] The bibliography on Goethe compares with that on Shakespeare in quantity and lack of quality. Arthur Böhtlingk, *Shakespeare und unser Klassiker* (Leipzig, 1909) contains an impressionistic account of Goethe's presumed lifetime of devotion to Shakespeare. A modern study is sorely needed. Indispensable are the Goethe-Schiller letters and the comments on *Wilhelm Meister* of Friedrich Schlegel. See also Raymond Immerwahr, "Friedrich Schlegel's Essay *On Goethe's Meister,*" *Monatshefte* (1957); James Boyd, *Goethe's Knowledge of English Literature* (Oxford, 1932); Friedrich Gundolf, *Shakespeare und der deutsche Geist* (Leipzig, 1911); Heinrich Huesmann, *Shakespeare-Inszenierungen unter Goethe in Weimar* (Vienna, 1968); Hans Jürg Lüthi, *Der deutsche Hamletbild seit Goethe* (Bern, 1951).

[5] J. P. Eckermann, *Gespräche mit Goethe* (Jena, 1908).

[6] Johann Wolfgang Goethe, *Wilhelm Meisters Theatralische Sendung* (Bonn, 1949).

[7] Johann Wolfgang Goethe, *Wilhelm Meisters Lehrjahre* (Hamburg, 1950). Translations are by Thomas Carlyle.

[8] Dennis M. Mueller, "Wieland's *Hamlet* Translation and Wilhelm Meister," *Deutsche Shakespeare-Gesellschaft West Jahrbuch*, 1969.

[9] Arthur Eastman, *A Short History of Shakespearean Criticism* (New York, 1968), 80.

[10] Friedrich Schlegel, "Über Goethe's Meister" in Oscar Fambach, ed., *Goethe und seine Kritiker* (Düsseldorf, 1953), 55.

[11] Friedrich Gundolf, *Shakespeare und der deutsche Geist* (Leipzig, 1911), 317.

[12] Mueller, *loc. cit.*

[13] U. Henry Gerlach, "Wilhelm Meister's Observations about Hamlet," *University of Dayton Review*, VII, 3 (1971).

[14] J. P. Eckermann, *loc. cit.*, 147.

[15] Quoted in Boyd, 183.

[16] Gerhart Hauptmann, *Hamlet in Wittenberg* (Berlin, 1935).

[17] Most of this material is available in Felix A. Voigt and Walter A. Reichart, *Hauptmann und Shakespeare* (Goslar, 1947), which sins in indiscriminate eulogy of Hauptmann.

[18] Gerhart Hauptmann, *Im Wirbel der Berufung* (Berlin, 1936).

[19] Ilse Reis, *Gerhart Hauptmanns Hamlet-Interpretation in der Nachfolge Goethes* (Bonn, 1969).

[20] Quoted by Reis, 189.

[21] Eckermann, 205.

[22] H. H. Furness, ed., *Variorum Hamlet* (London, 1877).

[23] Jules Laforgue, "A Propos de Hamlet," *Le Symboliste* (October 22, 1886).

[24] Jules Laforgue, *Moralités légendaires* (Paris, 1964). Laforgue's relationship to Hamlet still needs study, despite the work of Helen Bailey, *Hamlet in France from Voltaire to Laforgue* (Geneva, 1964); Danielle Bajomée, "Hamlet, Moralité oubliée de J. Laforgue," *Revue des Langues Vivantes* 1967/68, 386-405; Warren Ramsey, ed., *Jules Laforgue: Essays on a Poet's Life and Work* (Carbondale, 1969); François Ruchon, *Jules Laforgue: Sa Vie. Son Oeuvre* (Geneva, 1924); Albert Sonnenfeld, "Hamlet the German and Jules Laforgue," *Yale French Studies, #33*, 92-100 (the whole issue of this journal contains revealing insights into French attitudes toward Hamlet); René Taupin, "The Myth of Hamlet in France in Mallarmé's Generation," *Modern Language Quarterly* (December, 1953).

[25] Pierre Reboul, *Laforgue* (Paris, 1960), 132.

[26] Jean-Louis Barrault, *Souvenirs pour demain* (Paris, 1972), 124.

[27] Arno Holz and Johannes Schlaf, *Papa Hamlet* (Stuttgart, n.d.). Also contains "Ein Dachstubenidyll."

[28] Quoted in Fritz Martini, *Das Wagnis der Sprache* (Stuttgart, 1954), 106.

[29] Dorrit Cohn, "Narrated Monologue: Definition of a Fictional Style," *Comparative Literature* (Spring, 1966), 97-112.

[30] James Joyce, *Ulysses* (New York, 1961).

[31] Richard Ellmann, *James Joyce* (New York, 1959), 161.

[32] *Portrait of the Artist as a Young Man* (New York, 1964), 215.

[33] The indispensable basis of any Joyce-Shakespeare research is William Schutte, *Joyce and Shakespeare* (New Haven, 1957). Also helpful are Richard Ellmann, *Ulysses on the Liffey* (New York, 1972); Edmund L. Epstein, *The Ordeal of Stephen Dedalus* (Carbondale, 1971); Stuart Gilbert, *James Joyce's Ulysses: A Study* (New York, 1952); Clive Hart and David Hayman, eds., *James Joyce's Ulysses* (Berkeley, 1974); Richard Kain, *Fabulous Voyager*

(Chicago, 1947); Hugh Kenner, *Dublin's Joyce* (Bloomington, 1956); Stanley Sultan, *The Argument of Ulysses* (Columbus, 1964); and Weldon Thornton, *Allusions in Ulysses* (Chapel Hill, 1968).

[34] Bernard Benstock, "Telemachus" in Hart and Hayman, 13.

[35] Schutte, 172-173.

[36] Gilbert, 221.

[37] Calvin A. Edwards, "The Hamlet Motif in Joyce's Ulysses," *Western Review* 15 (1950), 7.

[38] Schutte, 186.

[39] Sultan, 333.

[40] Richard Ellman, *James Joyce, passim.*

[41] Hart and Hayman, 152.

[42] M.J.C. Hodgart, "Shakespeare and Finnegans Wake," *Cambridge Journal* (September, 1953).

[43] Georg Britting, *Lebenslauf eines dicken Mannes der Hamlet Hiess* (Munich, 1957).

[44] James Branch Cabell, *Hamlet Had an Uncle* (London, 1940).

[45] Rayner Heppenstall and Michael Innes, *Three Tales of Hamlet* (London, 1950).

[46] Alethea Hayter, *Horatio's Version* (London, 1972).

Chapter 3

B. Drama

[1] George Odell, *Shakespeare from Betterton to Irving* (New York, 1966; original edition 1920), vol. 1, 386.

[2] Percy MacKaye, *The Mystery of Hamlet, King of Denmark* (New York, 1950).

[3] Voigt and Reichart, *passim.*

[4] *Hamlet in Wittenberg* (Berlin, 1935).

[5] Bernard Kops, *The Hamlet of Stepney Green* in *New English Dramatists* (London, 1959).

[6] Jean Sarment, *Le Mariage d'Hamlet* in *La Petite Illustration* (December 30, 1922).

[7] Alan Downer, *American Drama* (New York, 1960), 6-7.

[8] Ashley Dukes, *Return to Danes Hill* (London, 1958).

[9] Elmer Rice, *Cue for Passion* (New York, 1959).

[10] Elmer Rice, *Minority Report* (New York, 1963), 454.

[11] Graciously lent me by Eric Bentley. Unpublished.

[12] Eric Bentley, *Theatre of War* (New York, 1972), 33.

[13] Tristan Tzara, *Mouchoir de Nuages* (Paris, 1925), no pagination.

[14] Quoted in Henri Béhar, *Étude sur le théâtre dada et surréaliste* (Paris, 1967), 163.

[15] Louis Aragon, *Les Collages* (Paris, 1965), 144.

[16] *Ibid.*, 112.

[17] Rodney Symington, 97-98.

[18] Toby Cole, ed., *Playwrights on Playwriting* (New York, 1960), 100-101.

[19] Tom Stoppard, *Rosencrantz and Guilderstern Are Dead* (New York, 1967); for commentary see Anthony Callen, "Stoppard's Godot," *New Theatre* (Winter, 1969); C. J. Gianakaris, "Absurdism Altered," *Drama Survey* (Winter, 1968-1969).

[20] *New York Times* (October 23, 1967).

[21] Charles Marowitz, *The Marowitz Hamlet* (London, 1968).

[22] John Russell Brown, *Theatre Language* (London, 1972), 249.

[23] *Time Out* (April 21-27, 1972).

[24] Joseph Papp, *William Shakespeare's "Naked" Hamlet* (New York, 1969).

[25] Paul Baker, *Hamlet ESP* (New York, 1971).

[26] Gerhard Rühm, *Ophelia und die Wörter* (Darmstadt, 1972).

[27] *Im Wirbel der Berufung*, 278.

Chapter 4

[1] Kenneth Mur, *Shakespeare's Tragic Sequence* (London, 1952), 118.

[2] Walter W. Greg, "The Date of *King Lear* and Shakespeare's Use of Earlier Versions of the Lear Story," *The Library* (1940). See also Wilfrid Perrett, *The Story of King Lear from Geoffrey of Monmouth to Shakespeare* (Berlin, 1904); Robert Adger Law, "*King Leir* and *King Lear*: An Examination of the Two Plays," in *Studies in Honor of T. W. Baldwin* (Urbana, 1958).

[3] E. B. Everett, ed., *Six Early Plays, Anglistica,* XIV (Copenhagen, 1965).

[4] A. C. Bradley, *Shakespearean Tragedy* (London, 1971), 235 ff.

[5] Quoted in the Variorum *King Lear*, 444.

[6] Christopher Spencer, ed., *Five Restoration Adaptations of Shakespeare* (Urbana, 1965), 203.

[7] Quoted in the Variorum *King Lear*, 419.

[8] *Ibid.*, 450-451.

[9] Charles Lamb, "The Tragedies of Shakespeare," in *Shakespeare Criticism 1623-1840* (London, 1954), 206.

[10] F. O. Matthiessen, *American Renaissance* (New York, 1941). See also Richard B. Sewall, "Ahab's Quenchless Feud," *Comparative Drama* (Fall, 1967), 207-218.

[11] Leo Tolstoy, "Shakespeare and the Drama," *Fortnightly Review* (December, 1906). Reprinted in V. Tchertkoff, tr., *Tolstoy on Shakespeare* (New York, 1906).

[12] Quoted in Edwin Wilson, ed., *Shaw On Shakespeare* (New York, 1961), 117.

[13] Wilson, 66.

[14] G. Wilson Knight, *The Wheel of Fire* (New York, 1962). Originally published in 1930.

[15] George Orwell, "Lear, Tolstoy and the Fool," in *Shooting an Elephant and Other Essays* (New York, 1950).

[16] George Woodcock, *The Crystal Spirit* (Boston, 1966), 308-309.

[17] Sigmund Freud, "Das Motiv der Kästenwahl," *Gesammelte Werke* (London, 1946), vol. x, 24-37.

[18] Marshall McLuhan, *The Gutenberg Galaxy* (New York, 1969).

[19] Cf. Edwin Muir, *Essays on Literature and Society* (London, 1949), p. 42. "The sisters are harpies, but as rulers they act in the approved contemporary Machiavellian convention."

[20] Marvin Rosenberg, *The Masques of King Lear* (Berkeley, 1973), 274.

[21] Bradley, 235.

[22] Kott, 158.

[23] Gordon Bottomley, *King Lear's Wife* (London, 1920).

[24] Robin Maugham, *Mister Lear* (London, 1963).

[25] Information on the GSR *Lear* comes from Ted Shank, authority on the New Theater.

[26] "Drama and the Dialectics of Violence," *Theatre Quarterly* (Jan.-March, 1972), 5-6.

[27] *Ibid.*, 6.

[28] Edward Bond, *Lear* (New York, 1972).

[29] "Interview with Edward Bond," *Gambit* #17, 24.

[30] *Theatre Quarterly*, 8.

[31] *Ibid.*

[32] *Ibid.*, 9.

Chapter 5

[1] Frank Kermode, ed., "*The Tempest* on the Jacobean Stage" in *The Tempest*, Arden Edition (London, 1961).

[2] Ashley H. Thorndike, "Introduction" to Rudyard Kipling, *How Shakespere came to write "The Tempest"* (New York, 1916).

[3] Robert Browning, "Caliban Upon Setebos" in *Poetical Works 1833-1864*, Ian Jack, ed. (London, 1970), 836-844.

[4] These quotations are conveniently found in D. J. Palmer, ed., *Shakespeare: The Tempest* (London, 1968), to which page numbers in the text refer.

[5] E. K. Brown, "The First Person in 'Caliban upon Setebos,'" *Modern Language Notes* (1951).

[6] Ernest Renan, *Caliban, suite de la Tempête*, and *L'Eau de Jouvence* in *Oeuvres*, vol. III (Paris, 1947). I am grateful to Professor Colin Smith for sending me his exceptionally informative edition of *Caliban* (Manchester, 1954).

[7] Of Renan's four philosophical dramas, only *L'Abbesse de Jouarre* has been performed—by Duse in Italian in 1886. In 1887 Antoine thought of the same play for Bernhardt, but the plan never came to production.

[8] Smith, 39.

[9] Quoted in Henri Gouhier, *Renan auteur dramatique* (Paris, 1972), 125.

[10] Smith, 33.

[11] Percy MacKaye, *Caliban by the Yellow Sands* (New York, 1916).

[12] D. Heyward Brock and James M. Welsh, "Percy MacKaye: Community Drama and the Masque Tradition," *Comparative Drama* (Spring, 1972), 75. See also Jane P. Franck, "*Caliban* at Lewisohn Stadium, 1916" in Anne Paolucci, ed., *1594-1964: Shakespeare Encomium* (New York, 1964).

[13] W. H. Auden, "The Sea and the Mirror" in *The Collected Poetry* (New York, 1945).

[14] Monroe K. Spears, *The Poetry of W. H. Auden* (New York, 1963), 218.

[15] *Ibid.*, 247.

[16] Palmer, 89.

[17] Irving Wardle, "Tempest with a footnote," *The Times* (May 8, 1968), 9a.

[18] Quoted from *The Tempest* program by Margaret Croyden, *Lunatics, Lovers, and Poets* (New York, 1974). All other information about Brooks's *Tempest*, which I did not see, comes from a film of it and from Croyden's book, to which page numbers in the text refer.

[19] Aimé Césaire, *Une Tempête* (Paris, 1969).

[20] Herbert Marshall and Mildred Stock, *Ira Aldridge: The Negro Tragedian* (London, 1958).

[21] Kermode, xxiv. Information about the name Caliban is on xxxviii.

[22] Palmer, 144.

[23] J. C. Trewin, *Shakespeare on the English Stage: 1900-1964* (London, 1964), 32.

[24] Aimé Césaire, *Cahier d'un retour au pays natal* (Paris, 1971).

[25] Lilyan Kesteloot, *Aimé Césaire* (Paris, 1962).

26 Michel Benamou, "Entretien avec Aimé Césaire," *Cahiers Césairiens* (Spring, 1974), 4.

27 Judith G. Miller, "Césaire and Serreau, une sorte de symbiose," *Cahiers Césairiens* (Spring, 1974), 20-25.

28 L. S. Belhassen, "Un Poète politique: Aimé Césaire," *Le Magazine littéraire* No. 34 (November, 1969). English translation in Lee Baxandall, ed., *Radical Perspectives in the Arts* (Baltimore, 1972), 172.

29 I am indebted to Barry Barankin for this scene breakdown.

30 The Césaire scholar Tom Hale informs me that Césaire probably worked from Shakespeare's English and Cluny's French translation of *The Tempest*, but *Une Tempête* is distinctively Césairian.

31 On the significance of the god Eshu, Thomas A. Hale, "Sur *Une Tempête* d'Aimé Césaire," *Études Littéraires*, vol. 6, No. 1 (April, 1973), 30, fn. 16. The entire article illuminates Césaire's play, as do Thomas A. Hale, "Aimé Césaire: A Bio-Bibliography," *Africana Journal*, v, 1 (1974), Gérard Durozoi, "De Shakespeare à Aimé Césaire," *Afrique littéraire et artistique* (April, 1970) and Lucien Attoun, "Aimé Cesaire et le Théâtre Nègre," *Le Theatre* 1970-71.

32 Peter Rohrsen, "Ein antikolonialistischer Sturm," *Deutsche Shakespeare-Gesellschaft West Jahrbuch*, 1972, 156.

33 I confess to some selection for an Everyman-Caliban, since I chose not to discuss the Company Theater *Caliban*. It is too late in the book to introduce trivia.

Chapter 6

1 Margaret Croyden, *Lunatics, Lovers, and Poets: The Contemporary Experimental Theatre* (New York, 1974), 95.

2 All quotations from Triple Action Theatre scripts are from copies generously supplied me by its director, Steve Rumbelow. Information about the company comes from Rumbelow.

Chapter 7

1 Archibald Henderson, *George Bernard Shaw: Man of the Century* (New York, 1956), 715-716.

2 Many of these comments are reprinted in Edwin Wilson, ed., *Shaw on Shakespeare* (New York, 1961), to which page numbers in my text refer.

3 The Shaw-Shakespeare issue of *The Shaw Review* (May, 1971) provides bibliographical data.

4 *Our Theatres in the Nineties* (New York, 1931).

[5] Henderson, 30.

[6] *Ibid.*, 1.

[7] *Ibid.*, 30.

[8] E. J. West, ed., *Shaw on Theatre* (New York, 1958), 273.

[9] *The Shaw Review* (May, 1971), 60.

[10] *Ibid.*, 67.

[11] *The Quintessence of Ibsenism* in Dan Laurence, ed., *Selected Non-Dramatic Writings of Bernard Shaw* (Boston, 1965), 236.

[12] Henderson, 709.

[13] Archibald Henderson, *Bernard Shaw, Playboy and Prophet* (New York, 1932), 334.

[14] Bernard Shaw, *Complete Plays with Prefaces* (New York, 1963), vol. III, 509.

[15] Tchertkoff, 166.

[16] Cf. Gordon W. Couchman, "The First Playbill of 'Caesar': Shaw's List of Authorities," *Shaw Review* (May, 1970).

[17] Gale K. Larson, "Caesar and Cleopatra: The Making of a History Play," *Shaw Review* (May, 1971).

[18] *Complete Plays and Prefaces*, vol. II, 621.

[19] *Ibid.*, 643.

[20] Bernard Dukore, "Macbeth Skit," *Educational Theatre Journal* (October, 1967).

[21] "Arnold Bennett thinks Playwriting easier than Novel Writing" in *Pen Portraits and Reviews* (London, 1932). Quotations from 51, 52.

[22] West, 132-133.

[23] Cf. Max Reinhardt on his fairy-tale movie of *A Midsummer Night's Dream*: "I have set the condition that this work should represent Shakespeare and nothing but Shakespeare"; and Laurence Olivier on his Oedipal movie *Hamlet*: "My whole aim and purpose has been to make a film of *Hamlet* as Shakespeare himself, were he living now, might make it." Quoted in James Clay and Daniel Krempel, *The Theatrical Image* (New York, 1967), 14.

[24] Stanley Weintraub takes this literally in "Heartbreak House: Shaw's *Lear*," *Modern Drama* (December, 1972).

[25] Martin Meisel, *Shaw and the Nineteenth-Century Theater* (Princeton, 1963).

[26] *Complete Plays and Prefaces*, vol. III, xxi.

Chapter 8

[1] Information on Brecht's attitude toward Shakespeare collated from Reinhold Grimm, *Bertolt Brecht* (Stuttgart, 1971);

Rodney T. K. Symington, *Brecht und Shakespeare* (Bonn, 1970); Klaus Volker, *Brecht-Chronik* (Munich, 1971).

[2] Volker, 94.

[3] Helge Hultberg, "Bert Brecht und Shakespeare," *Orbis Litterarum* (1959); Symington, *loc. cit.*

[4] Bernard Dort, *Théâtre Public* (Paris, 1967), 87.

[5] John Fuegi, *The Essential Brecht* (Los Angeles, 1972).

[6] Werner Mittenzwei, *Bertolt Brecht* (Berlin, 1962).

[7] *Ibid.*, 162.

[8] Cf. Ulrich Weisstein, "Two Measures for One," *Germanic Review* (1968).

[9] Mittenzwei, 161.

[10] Symington, 127.

[11] Mittenzwei, 384.

[12] *Versuche*, vol. 8, 362.

[13] *Ibid.*, 363.

[14] Mittenzwei, 176.

[15] Ralph Mannheim and John Willett, x.

[16] I saw Andy Doe's Alternative Theater production in July, 1974, in the versatile space of an Oakland yard. Having once before directed the play at Pomona College, Doe thinks that the Oakland production may have been the third one ever done.

[17] *Versuche über Brecht* (Frankfurt, 1966), 135.

[18] Walter H. Sokel, "Brecht's Concept of Character," *Comparative Drama* (Fall, 1971), 190.

[19] *Brecht: A Choice of Evils* (London, 1959), 97-98.

[20] Mannheim and Willett, 395. Translations from *Coriolanus* are by Ralph Mannheim. Translations from the Coriolanus dialogue are by John Willett; page numbers refer to his *Brecht on Theatre* (New York, 1964).

[21] Günter Grass, *Die Plebejer proben den Aufstand* (Berlin, 1966); translation is by Ralph Mannheim (New York, 1966) who also translated Grass' Shakespeare speech, which was published in German in *Akzente* 3 (1964).

[22] Klaus Völker, *Brecht-Chronik* (Munich, 1971), 146-147.

[23] Mannheim, xxxiv.

[24] *Ibid.*, xxxvi.

Chapter 9

[1] All references to Beckett's works are to the Grove Press editions, to which page numbers in my text refer.

[2] Roy Walker, "Love, Chess, and Death," *The Twentieth Cen-*

tury (December, 1958), 541. The whole article is full of suggestive Shakespeare analogies.

[3] *Texte Programme* of *Macbeth* for Roger Blin's production, Théâtre National de Strasbourg, 1972, 163-164.

[4] Paul Jorgensen, "Much Ado About *Nothing*," *Shakespeare Quarterly* v (1954).

Afterword

[1] Eric Bentley, *What Is Theatre?* (New York, 1952), 107.

Appendix A

Published Offshoots in Dramatic Form*

Auden, W. H., *The Sea and the Mirror,* 1944
Baker, Paul, *Hamlet ESP,* 1970
Barton, John and Hall, Peter, *The Wars of the Roses,* 1966
Bond, Edward, *Lear,* 1972
Bottomley, Gordon, *King Lear's Wife,* 1915
Gruach, 1922
Brecht, Bertolt, *Die Rundköpfe und die Spitzköpfe,* 1936
Rehearsal Scenes for *Hamlet, Macbeth, Romeo and Juliet,* 1939
Der aufhaltsame Aufstieg des Arturo Ui, 1941
Coriolan, 1952
Bruckner, Ferdinand, *Timon, Tragödie,* 1932
Césaire, Aimé, *Une Tempête,* 1969
Cummings, E. E., *him,* 1927
Dukes, Ashley, *Return to Danes Hill,* 1958
Dürrenmatt, Friedrich, *König Johann,* 1968
Titus Andronicus, 1970
Ervine, St. John, *The Lady of Belmont,* 1924
Fabre, Émile, *Timon d'Athènes,* 1908
Garson, Barbara, *MacBird!,* 1965
Ionesco, Eugène, *Macbett,* 1972
Jahnn, Hans Henny, *Die Krönung Richards III,* 1921
Jarry, Alfred, *Ubu Roi,* 1896
Kops, Bernard, *The Hamlet of Stepney Green,* 1956
Lange, Harmut, *König Johann,* 1965

* Dates are those of completion, insofar as these could be ascertained.

MacKaye, Percy, *Caliban by the Yellow Sands*, 1916
The Mystery of Hamlet, King of Denmark, 1947
Marowitz, Charles, *The Marowitz Hamlet*, 1966
A Macbeth, 1969
Maugham, Robin, *Mister Lear*, 1963
Müller, Heinar, *Macbeth*, 1972
Nathan, George Jean, *The Avon Flows*, 1937
Obey, André, *Le Viol de Lucrèce*, 1931
Vénus et Adonis, 1931
Osborne, John, *A Place Calling Itself Rome*, 1973
Papp, Joseph, *William Shakespeare's "Naked" Hamlet*, 1967
Piachaud, René-Louis, *Coriolan*, 1934
Renan, Ernest, *Caliban*, 1877
L'Eau de Jouvence, 1879
Rice, Elmer, *Cue for Passion*, 1958
Rühm, Gerhard, *Ophelia und die Wörter*, 1972
Sarment, Jean, *Le Mariage de Hamlet*, 1922
Shaw, George Bernard, *Caesar and Cleopatra*, 1898
Macbeth Skit, 1916
Cymbeline Refinished, 1937
Shakes versus Shav, 1949
Stoppard, Tom, *Rosencrantz and Guildenstern Are Dead*, 1966
Ustinov, Peter, *Romanoff and Juliet*, 1958
Wekwerth, Manfred and Tenschert, Joachim, *Coriolan*, 1965

Appendix B

Offshoots Discussed in the Book*

1. English Language

MACBETH

George Bernard Shaw, *Macbeth Skit*, 1916
Arnold Bennett thinks Playwriting easier than Novel Writing, 1916
Gordon Bottomley, *Gruach*, 1921
E. E. Cummings, *him*, 1927
Orson Welles, *"Voodoo" Macbeth*, 1936
Barbara Garson, *MacBird!*, 1965
Charles Marowitz, *A Macbeth*, 1969
The Performance Group *Makbeth*, 1969
Triple Action Theatre *Macbeth*, 1969

HAMLET

a. Fiction

Laurence Sterne, *Tristram Shandy*, 1760
A Sentimental Journey, 1767
James, Joyce, *Ulysses*, 1922
Finnegans Wake, 1941
James Branch Cabell, *Hamlet Had an Uncle*, 1940
Rayner Heppenstall and Michael Innes, *Three Tales of Hamlet*, 1950
Alethea Hayter, *Horatio's Version*, 1972

b. Drama

Percy MacKaye, *The Mystery of Hamlet, King of Denmark*, 1948

* Page numbers given in the text of the book refer to the editions listed here.

Bernard Kops, *The Hamlet of Stepney Green*, 1956
Eric Bentley, *H for Hamlet*, 1956
Ashley Dukes, *Return to Danes Hill*, 1958
Elmer Rice, *Cue for Passion*, 1958
Tom Stoppard, *Rosencrantz and Guildenstern Are Dead*, 1966
Charles Marowitz, *The Marowitz Hamlet*, 1966
Joseph Papp, *William Shakespeare's "Naked" Hamlet*, 1967
Paul Baker, *Hamlet ESP*, 1971
Triple Action Theatre *Hamlet*, 1972

KING LEAR

Gordon Bottomley, *King Lear's Wife*, 1915
Robin Maugham, *Mister Lear*, 1963
Edward Bond, *Lear*, 1972
Triple Action Theatre *Leir Blindi*, 1973

THE TEMPEST

Robert Browning, *Caliban Upon Setebos*, 1864
Percy MacKaye, *Caliban by the Yellow Sands*, 1916
W. H. Auden, *The Sea and the Mirror*, 1944
Triple Action Theatre *Tempest*, 1972

HISTORY PLAYS

John Barton and Peter Hall, *The Wars of the Roses*, 1964
Triple Action Theatre *Richard II, Richard III*, 1973

ROMAN PLAYS

George Bernard Shaw, *Caesar and Cleopatra*, 1898
Triple Action Theatre *Julius Caesar*, 1971
John Osborne, *A Place Calling Itself Rome*, 1973

MISCELLANEOUS

James Branch Cabell, "The Episode Called Love—Letters of Falstaff" in *The Line of Love*, 1905
St. John Ervine, *The Lady of Belmont*, 1924

George Jean Nathan, *The Avon Flows*, 1937
Peter Ustinov, *Romanoff and Juliet*, 1958

2. French Language

MACBETH

Emilio Galli, *Autopsie de Macbeth*, 1970
Eugène Ionesco, *Macbett*, 1972

HAMLET

Jules Laforgue, *A Propos de Hamlet*, 1886
Hamlet ou les suites de la piété filiale, 1887
Jean Sarment, *Le Mariage de Hamlet*, 1922
Tristan Tzara, *Mouchoir de Nuages*, 1924
Emilio Galli, *Hamlet*, 1972

THE TEMPEST

Ernest Renan, *Caliban*, 1877
L'Eau de Jouvence, 1879
Aimé Césaire, *Une Tempête*, 1969

ROMAN PLAYS

André Obey, *Le Viol de Lucrèce*, 1931
Vénus et Adonis, 1931
René-Louis Piachaud, *Coriolan*, 1934

MISCELLANEOUS

Alfred Jarry, *Ubu Roi*, 1896
Émile Fabre, *Timon d'Athènes*, 1907

3. German Language

MACBETH

Bertolt Brecht, *Radio Macbeth*, 1927

Bertolt Brecht, *Der Mord im Pförtnetrhaus,* 1939
Heinar Müller, *Macbeth,* 1972

HAMLET

Johann Wolfgang Goethe, *Wilhelm Meisters Theatralische Sendung,* 1783
Wilhelm Meisters Lehrjahre, 1796
Arno Holz and Johannes Schlaf, *Papa Hamlet,* 1888
Gerhart Hauptmann, *Ur-Hamlet,* 1927
Hamlet in Wittenberg, 1935
Im Wirbel der Berufung, 1936
Bertolt Brecht, Radio *Hamlet,* 1931
Die Fähre, 1939
Georg Britting, *Lebenslauf eines dicken Mannes der Hamlet Hiess,* 1952
Gerhard Rühm, *Ophelia und die Wörter,* 1972

HISTORY PLAYS

Hans Henny Jahnn, *Die Krönung Richards III,* 1921
Harmut Lange, *König Johann,* 1965
Friedrich Dürrenmatt, *König Johann,* 1968

ROMAN PLAYS

Bertolt Brecht, *Der aufhaltsame Aufstieg des Arturo Ui,* 1941
Coriolan, 1952
Manfred Wekwerth and Joachim Tenschert, *Coriolan,* 1965
Günter Grass, *Die Plebejer Proben den Aufstand,* 1966
Friedrich Dürrenmatt, *Titus Andronicus,* 1970

MISCELLANEOUS

Ferdinand Bruckner, *Timon, Tragödie,* 1932

Bertolt Brecht, *Die Spitzköpfe und die Rundköpfe,* 1933
Die Rundköpfe und die Spitzköpfe, 1936
Romeo und Julia, 1939

Index

Library of Congress Cataloging in Publication Data

Cohn, Ruby.
Modern Shakespeare offshoots.
Includes bibliographical references and index.
1. Shakespeare, William, 1564-1616—Adaptations.
2. Shakespeare, William, 1564-1616—Influence.
3. Drama—20th century—History and criticism.
I. Title.
PR2880.A1C6 822.3'3 75-2984
ISBN 0-691-06289-7
ISBN 0-691-10034-9 pbk.